NON-LEAGUE FOOTBALL TABLES OF YORKSHIRE & LINCOLNSHIRE 1889-2021

EDITOR
Michael Robinson

FOREWORD

Following the success of our 'Non-League Football Tables' series of books, the first of which was published in 2002, we long considered introducing a number of regionalised titles about various football leagues both past and present.

The first book in the series, 'Non-League Football Tables of South West England 1892-2015' was duly published in 2015. Since then, books covering North West England (1889-2016), South East England (1894-2017), North East England (1889-2018), the West Midlands of England (1889-2019) and the East Midlands of England (1889-2020) have been published. These books are all available for purchase at the address below, each priced £11.99.

We initially envisioned just six books in the series but, such has been their popularity that Mick has continued his work and this seventh edition covers the Non-League Football Tables of Yorkshire and Lincolnshire. Thanks to the assistance of readers, this book also contains some updated information (including corrected and previously-missing tables), for the Notts Alliance which was covered in our East Midlands book published in 2020.

The Leagues which currently form the apex of the 'Non-League Pyramid', namely the National League (formerly the Football Conference) and its three feeder leagues (Northern Premier, Southern Premier & Isthmian) continue to be covered by our yearly National League and Non-League Football Tables books.

As always, we are indebted to Mick Blakeman for providing tables for the various Leagues included in this book.

British Library Cataloguing in Publication Data
A catalogue record for this book is available from the British Library

ISBN: 978-1-86223-473-4

Copyright © 2021   Soccer Books Limited, 72 St. Peters Avenue, Cleethorpes, DN35 8HU, United Kingdom   (01472 696226)

All rights are reserved. No part of this publication may be reproduced, stored into a retrieval system or transmitted, in any form or by any means, electronic, mechanical, photocopying, recording, or otherwise, without the prior written permission of Soccer Books Limited.

Printed in the UK by 4edge Ltd.

CONTENTS

Sheffield & District League 1889-1895 .... Pages 4-5

Wharncliffe Charity Cup 1894-1909 .... Pages 5-7

Sheffield & Hallamshire Challenge Cup 1893-1896 .... Pages 7-8

Sheffield Association League 1896-1939 .... Pages 8-16

West Yorkshire League 1894-1896 .... Page 17

Yorkshire League (I) 1897-1900 .... Pages 17-18

West Yorkshire League 1902-1910 .... Pages 19-21

Yorkshire Combination 1910-1914 .... Pages 21-22

Yorkshire League (II) 1920-1982 .... Pages 23-41

Midland Combination 1924-1928 .... Pages 42-43

Lincolnshire League (I) 1894-1921 .... Pages 44-46

Lincolnshire League (II) 1933-1938 .... Page 46

Lincolnshire League (III) 1948-2021 .... Pages 47-62

Northern Counties (East) League 1982-2021 .... Pages 63-82

Sheffield & Hallamshire County Senior League 1983-2021 .... Pages 82-99

Humber Premier League 2000-2021 .... Pages 100-106

Notts Alliance – Updated Information .... Pages 106-112

(See also the Non-League Football Tables of the East Midlands of England 1889-2020)

SHEFFIELD & DISTRICT LEAGUE 1889-1895

The Sheffield & District League was formed following a joint initiative by two of the city's clubs – Heeley and Walkley – who organised a meeting on Thursday 20th June 1889 at the Athol Hotel on Upper Charles Street. In addition to the two instigators of the idea, other attendees included representatives of Sheffield United, Clinton, Owlerton and Attercliffe while Doncaster Rovers and Rotherham Swifts regretted their inability to attend.

After further meetings, it was announced on 22nd August that the league was fully formed with 8 founder members: Attercliffe, Clinton, Ecclesfield, Eckington Works, Exchange (who had just changed their name from Park Grange), Kilnhurst, Owlerton and Walkley. However, the league received very little newspaper coverage in its first season and many games were left unplayed. The latest table found, shown below, was published in the South Yorkshire Times on 25th April 1890.

1889-90

Kilnhurst	13	9	0	4	39	21	18
Ecclesfield	14	6	6	2	33	20	18
Clinton	11	7	0	4	29	27	14
Walkley	14	5	1	8	21	36	11
Eckington Works	8	3	2	3	21	21	8
Owlerton	6	2	1	3	13	15	5
Exchange	5	1	0	4	7	17	2
Attercliffe	6	1	0	5	6	20	2

Exchange suspended their membership as they were unable to find a ground and Attercliffe left the league. Barnsley St. Peter's, Carbrook Church, Mexborough and Sheffield Montrose all joined. Heeley also put in an application to join that was accepted on 25th August. However, a week later, Heeley wrote to the league saying that they could not accept all the league's rules, asking for them to be relaxed in their favour. The league refused to do this and so Heeley's membership was terminated before the start of the season.

1890-91

Kilnhurst	14	8	4	2	68	19	20
Ecclesfield	14	8	3	3	40	27	19
Mexborough	14	6	5	3	33	24	17
Eckington Works	14	5	4	5	32	37	14
Carbrook Church	14	5	3	6	24	39	13
Barnsley St. Peters	14	3	4	7	22	38	10
Owlerton	14	2	6	6	20	44	10
Sheffield Montrose	14	2	5	7	31	42	9

Walkley resigned and disbanded at the end of October after losing their ground. Their record was deleted: 3 0 0 3 2 15 0
Clinton resigned and disbanded during the last week of March and their record at the time was deleted: 10 2 2 6 15 45 6
Sheffield Montrose suspended their membership as they were unable to find a ground. Chesterfield Town, Kiveton Park and Melville all joined.

1891-92

Chesterfield Town	18	14	2	2	63	34	30
Mexborough	18	12	2	4	97	23	26
Kilnhurst	18	10	4	4	51	35	24
Barnsley St. Peters	18	11	2	5	50	37	24
Kiveton Park	18	9	2	7	68	37	20
Ecclesfield	18	8	2	8	35	50	18
Eckington Works	18	7	2	9	33	51	16
Melville	18	4	4	10	34	65	12
Carbrook Church	18	2	2	14	27	67	6
Owlerton	18	2	0	16	21	80	4

Carbrook Church and Melville both moved to the newly formed Sheffield & District Alliance and Owlerton also left the league. Sheepbridge Works, Sheffield Wednesday Wanderers (Sheffield Wednesday Reserves), Rotherham United (Rotherham Town Reserves) and Wath all joined from the Hallamshire League, Penistone & Thurlstone Athletic joined as a newly formed club and Worksop Town and Attercliffe also joined.

1892-93

Sheffield Wednesday Wanderers	26	18	2	6	92	34	38
Mexborough	26	16	4	6	110	53	36
Attercliffe	26	17	2	7	67	36	36
Barnsley St. Peters	26	15	3	8	84	45	33
Chesterfield Town	26	14	4	8	59	34	32
Rotherham United	26	15	4	7	85	64	32
Eckington Works	26	14	4	8	63	60	32
Kilnhurst	26	13	2	11	60	51	28
Wath	26	12	4	10	68	68	28
Sheepbridge Works	26	9	2	15	62	84	20
Kiveton Park	26	9	2	15	54	85	20
Worksop Town	26	6	2	18	50	93	14
Ecclesfield	26	4	3	19	33	89	11
Penistone & Thurlstone Athletic	26	0	2	24	40	131	2

Rotherham United had 2 points deducted.
The Sheffield & Hallamshire F.A. had decided that their Challenge Cup competition, which had been played on a knock-out basis since it was first introduced in 1876, would in future be played as a league and would consist of 14 clubs. Of those 14 clubs, 11 were members of the Sheffield & District League, the 3 omitted being Penistone & Thurlstone Athletic, Ecclesfield and Kiveton Park. The tables of the Sheffield & Hallamshire Challenge Cup are shown below.

The Sheffield & District League continued to operate in 1893-94 but with a much truncated fixture list. Chesterfield Town, Sheepbridge Works and Eckington Works all left to join the newly formed East Derbyshire Championship instead. Kiveton Park and Ecclesfield also both left and moved to the Sheffield & Hallamshire Minor Cup (played on a league basis), Rotherham United played only in the new Sheffield & Hallamshire Challenge Cup and Penistone & Thurlstone Athletic disbanded.

Sheffield Club and Sheffield United Strollers (Sheffield United Reserves) both joined from the Midland Alliance and Ardsley joined from the Hallamshire League. These three clubs also joined the new Sheffield & Hallamshire Challenge Cup.

Sheffield & District League 1893-1895 + Wharncliffe Charity Cup

1893-94

The league was organised into two equal strength divisions with a play-off between the two divisional winners to decide the championship.

Division One

Sheffield Wednesday Wanderers	8	6	0	2	28	13	12
Sheffield United Strollers	8	4	2	2	16	11	10
Attercliffe	8	4	1	3	11	8	9
Worksop Town	8	2	2	4	10	19	6
Sheffield Club	8	1	1	6	12	26	3

Division Two

Mexborough	8	6	1	1	20	5	13
Barnsley St. Peters	8	4	3	1	19	8	11
Wath	8	3	1	4	12	17	7
Kilnhurst	8	3	0	5	11	19	6
Ardsley	8	1	1	6	4	17	3

Championship Play-Off

Mexborough vs Sheffield Wednesday Wanderers   1-0
(26th April 1894, played at Barnsley – Attendance: 2,000)

Sheffield Club left the league but continued playing in the Sheffield & Hallamshire Challenge Cup. Doncaster Rovers joined while continuing to play in the Midland League. Chesterfield Town, Eckington Works and Sheepbridge Works all rejoined from the East Derbyshire Championship while continuing to play in the Sheffield & Hallamshire Challenge Cup. Staveley Wanderers also joined from the East Derbyshire Championship (which then closed down for a season) and changed their name to Staveley. Kiveton Park joined from the Sheffield & Hallamshire Alliance Cup and Wombwell Town joined from the Sheffield & Hallamshire Minor Cup (both of which were played in a league format).

1894-95

The league was organised into three geographical divisions – Northern, Southern and Central with the Northern and Southern Division winners playing-off to decide the championship. The Central Section clubs competed for the Wharncliffe Charity Cup (see below) which had previously been played on a knock-out basis since its introduction in 1878.

Northern Division

Wath	8	6	1	1	25	14	13
Ardsley	8	4	0	4	19	15	8
Attercliffe	8	4	0	4	15	14	8
Kilnhurst	8	2	2	4	14	20	6
Wombwell Town	8	2	1	5	11	21	5

Southern Division

Eckington Works	6	5	0	1	24	8	10
Worksop Town	6	4	0	2	27	5	8
Sheepbridge Works	6	2	0	4	10	12	4
Staveley	6	1	0	5	1	37	2

Kiveton Park resigned during the season and their record was deleted.

Championship Play-off

Eckington Works vs Wath   2-2
(25th April 1895, played at the Attercliffe ground, Carbrook)

Championship Play-Off Replay

Eckington Works vs Wath   1-0
(29th April 1895, played at the Attercliffe ground, Carbrook)

The Sheffield & District League closed down at the end of the season. All of its clubs continued and played in the Sheffield & Hallamshire Challenge Cup except Kiveton Park who joined the Sheffield & Hallamshire Minor Cup (which was played on a league basis).

WHARNCLIFFE CHARITY CUP 1894-1909

The Earl of Wharncliffe, whose ancestral home was Wortley Hall between Sheffield and Barnsley, was patron of the Sheffield Football Association and in 1878, he presented a cup to be competed for by the Association's member clubs. It was decided that the new cup should be used as the prize for a knock-out competition, the profits from which would be donated to local medical charities.

The competition was thus known as the Wharncliffe Charity Cup and in its early years, it attracted great interest. However, once league football became the norm, the interest in regional cup competitions waned significantly and the Wharncliffe Charity Cup was no exception. In 1894, it was decided that instead of being the prize for a knock-out competition, the trophy would be awarded to the winners of the Central Division of the Sheffield & District League.

Winners of the Wharncliffe Charity Cup 1878-1894

1878-79	Sheffield Wednesday		1886-87	Staveley
1879-80	Heeley		1887-88	Sheffield Wednesday
1880-81	Competition abandoned		1888-89	Staveley
1881-82	Sheffield Wednesday		1889-90	Staveley
1882-83	Sheffield Wednesday		1890-91	Final not played
1883-84	Lockwood Brothers		1891-92	Final not played
1884-85	Heeley		1892-93	Final drawn, no replay
1885-86	Sheffield Wednesday		1893-94	Sheffield United

Wharncliffe Charity Cup 1894-1907

1894-95

Sheffield & District League – Central Division

Mexborough	10	6	3	1	27	14	15
Chesterfield Town	10	5	0	5	14	15	10
Doncaster Rovers	10	3	3	4	16	15	9
Barnsley St. Peters	10	4	1	5	19	21	9
Sheffield Wednesday Reserves	10	4	1	5	17	31	9
Sheffield United Reserves	10	3	2	5	24	21	8

Although the Sheffield & District League closed down at the end of the 1894-95 season, its former Central Division continued as the Wharncliffe Charity Cup. Doncaster Rovers left and were replaced by Wath.

1895-96

Barnsley St. Peters	10	7	0	3	25	12	14
Sheffield United Reserves	10	7	0	3	27	13	14
Sheffield Wednesday Reserves	10	4	2	4	15	16	10
Mexborough	10	4	1	5	18	23	9
Chesterfield Town	10	3	2	5	18	25	8
Wath	10	2	1	7	16	30	5

Barnsley St. Peters, Chesterfield Town and Mexborough all left the competition. Attercliffe, Birdwell, Kilnhurst, Sheepbridge Works, Staveley and Wombwell all joined whilst also playing in the new Sheffield Association League.

1896-97

Sheffield United Reserves	16	12	1	3	61	16	25
Sheffield Wednesday Reserves	16	12	0	4	51	20	24
Staveley	16	9	0	7	27	42	18
Wath	14	8	1	5	29	14	17
Sheepbridge Works	16	8	0	8	30	38	16
Wombwell Town	16	5	2	9	34	33	12
Attercliffe	15	4	2	9	15	40	10
Birdwell	15	3	3	9	21	39	9
Kilnhurst	16	3	3	10	21	47	9

The two outstanding games were probably not played.

1897-99

The Wharncliffe Charity Cup was not competed for either as a league or as a knock-out competition in 1897-98 or 1898-99. It was revived for the 1899-1900 season as a league that provided extra fixtures for 10 of South Yorkshire's leading non-League clubs.

1899-1900

Sheffield Wednesday Reserves	16	12	4	0	68	11	28
Sheffield United Reserves	16	11	4	1	50	15	26
Worksop	17	7	3	7	35	26	17
Doncaster Rovers	14	6	2	6	29	23	14
Wath	11	5	1	5	19	26	11
Attercliffe	11	3	3	5	8	13	9
Sheffield Club	12	3	2	7	11	31	8
Mexborough	15	3	2	10	20	45	8
Wombwell	10	1	1	8	9	44	3

It appears that one of Worksop's games was incorrectly described as being played in the Wharncliffe Charity Cup.
The remaining outstanding games were probably not played.

1900-01

The competition was played as a knock-out format this season.
The only known result is that Monk Bretton beat Roundel 2-1 in the Final.

1901-02

Sheffield United Reserves	12	10	1	1	38	8	21
Sheffield Wednesday Reserves	12	8	1	3	33	11	17
Rotherham	12	5	1	6	21	28	11
Worksop Town	12	4	2	6	31	27	10
Thornhill United	12	4	2	6	10	21	10
Monk Bretton	12	4	2	6	23	34	10
Sheffield Club	12	1	2	9	12	50	4

1902-03

Sheffield Wednesday Reserves	14	12	1	1	51	10	25
Sheffield United Reserves	14	8	2	4	44	21	18
Barnsley Reserves	14	7	2	5	48	19	16
Thornhill United	14	7	2	5	25	23	16
Rotherham	14	6	2	6	25	29	14
Roundel	14	6	1	7	22	35	13
Sheffield Club	14	3	2	9	22	58	8
Attercliffe	14	1	0	13	10	52	2

1903-04

Sheffield United Reserves	12	10	2	0	49	13	22
Barnsley Reserves	12	7	2	3	31	23	16
Sheffield Wednesday Reserves	12	6	3	3	32	15	15
Thornhill United	12	4	3	5	19	24	11
Rotherham	12	5	0	7	23	19	10
Sheffield Club	12	2	3	7	12	31	7
Attercliffe	12	0	2	10	10	47	2

1904-05

Sheffield Wednesday Reserves	14	10	1	3	42	11	21
Denaby United	14	10	1	3	36	17	21
Rotherham	14	8	1	5	19	15	17
Mexborough Town	14	7	2	5	29	22	16
Sheffield United Reserves	14	6	2	6	28	20	14
Barnsley Reserves	14	6	0	8	23	33	12
Thornhill United	14	3	3	8	18	27	9
Sheffield Club	14	0	2	12	16	66	2

1905-06

Sheffield Wednesday Reserves	14	12	0	2	39	5	24
Sheffield United Reserves	14	9	2	3	24	13	20
Mexborough Town	14	7	3	4	25	24	17
Barnsley Reserves	14	7	1	6	25	29	15
Rotherham County	14	5	2	7	23	21	12
Rotherham Town	14	6	0	8	24	22	12
Denaby United	14	5	0	9	13	25	10
Rawmarsh Albion	14	0	2	12	8	42	2

1906-07

Sheffield United Reserves	14	8	2	4	27	16	18
Rotherham County	14	6	4	4	23	21	16
South Kirkby Colliery	14	6	3	5	20	15	15
Rotherham Town	14	6	2	6	16	19	14
Mexborough Town	14	6	2	6	20	24	14
Rawmarsh Albion	14	4	5	5	18	14	13
Sheffield Wednesday Reserves	14	4	3	7	24	23	11
Barnsley Reserves	14	3	3	8	14	26	9

1907-08

The competition was played as a knock-out format this season.

Sheffield Wednesday Reserves beat Rotherham County 3-2 in the Final.

1908-09

Sheffield Wednesday Reserves	8	4	3	1	16	8	11
Sheffield United Reserves	8	4	2	2	19	13	10
Rotherham County	8	3	3	2	12	10	9
South Kirkby Colliery	8	3	2	3	11	13	8
Wath Athletic	8	0	2	6	8	22	2

After 1909, the competition reverted to a knock-out format, apart from during the 1915-16 season when it was used as an emergency wartime league.

SHEFFIELD & HALLAMSHIRE CHALLENGE CUP 1893-1896

The Sheffield Football Association was formed in 1867 and established its own Challenge Cup competition in 1876. It merged with the Hallamshire Football Association on 29th September 1886, thus becoming the Sheffield & Hallamshire Football Association, that title being applied to the Challenge Cup from 1887-88 onwards. The Challenge Cup continued as a knock-out competition until 1893, when it changed to a league format.

Winners of the Sheffield Challenge Cup 1876-1887

1876-77	Sheffield Wednesday
1877-78	Sheffield Wednesday
1878-79	Thursday Wanderers
1879-80	Staveley
1880-81	Sheffield Wednesday
1881-82	Heeley
1882-83	Sheffield Wednesday
1883-84	Lockwood Brothers
1884-85	Lockwood Brothers
1885-86	Mexborough
1886-87	Sheffield

Winners of the Sheffield & Hallamshire Challenge Cup 1887-93

1887-88	Sheffield Wednesday
1888-89	Rotherham Town
1889-90	Rotherham Town
1890-91	Doncaster Rovers
1891-92	Sheffield United
1892-93	Sheffield United Reserves

The competition adopted a league format in 1893 with 14 founder members. 11 of these clubs were all members of the Sheffield & District League in 1892-93: Attercliffe, Barnsley St. Peters, Chesterfield Town, Eckington Works, Kilnhurst, Mexborough, Rotherham United (Rotherham Town Reserves), Sheffield Wednesday Wanderers (Reserves), Sheepbridge Works, Wath and Worksop Town.
The oter clubs were Sheffield Club and Sheffield United Strollers (Reserves) who both joined from the Midland Alliance and Ardsley who joined from the Hallamshire League.

1893-94

Mexborough	26	20	4	2	95	25	44
Sheffield United Strollers	26	20	2	4	85	23	42
Sheffield Wednesday Wanderers	26	17	6	3	78	31	40
Barnsley St. Peters	26	15	5	6	67	50	35
Worksop Town	26	11	5	10	59	63	27
Chesterfield Town	26	11	4	11	65	51	26
Wath	26	10	4	12	60	56	24
Sheepbridge Works	26	10	3	13	52	65	23
Eckington Works	26	10	3	13	39	60	23
Attercliffe	26	8	3	15	45	59	19
Rotherham United	26	8	3	15	45	81	19
Ardsley	26	9	0	17	42	68	18
Kilnhurst	26	7	2	17	38	77	16
Sheffield Club	26	4	0	22	35	96	8

Ecclesfield joined from the Sheffield & Hallamshire Minor Cup.
Rotherham United changed their name to Rotherham Town Reserves, Sheffield United Strollers changed their name to Sheffield United Reserves and Sheffield Wednesday Wanderers changed their name to Sheffield Wednesday Reserves.

1894-95

Sheffield Wednesday Reserves	28	23	1	4	106	26	47
Sheffield United Reserves	28	20	4	4	83	29	44
Chesterfield Town	28	17	3	8	68	44	37
Mexborough	28	15	5	8	80	42	35
Barnsley St. Peters	28	17	3	8	67	43	35
Wath	28	14	5	9	65	53	33
Eckington Works	28	15	2	11	78	67	32
Worksop Town	28	12	4	12	62	56	28
Ardsley	28	9	6	13	64	62	24
Sheepbridge Works	28	10	3	15	51	68	23
Rotherham Town Reserves	28	10	2	16	49	87	22
Kilnhurst	28	6	5	17	48	77	17
Ecclesfield	28	7	1	20	41	111	15
Attercliffe	28	5	4	19	35	84	14
Sheffield Club	28	5	2	21	44	92	12

Barnsley St. Peters had 2 points deducted.
Barnsley St. Peters moved to the Midland League and Ecclesfield moved to the Sheffield & Hallamshire Minor Cup. Wombwell Town joined from the Sheffield & Hallamshire Minor Cup and Staveley joined as a newly formed professional club.

1895-96

Mexborough	28	24	4	0	124	28	52
Sheffield United Reserves	28	20	4	4	82	24	44
Sheffield Wednesday Reserves	28	19	2	7	129	47	40
Sheepbridge Works	28	16	4	8	80	66	36
Chesterfield Town	28	16	3	9	71	37	35
Kilnhurst	28	14	5	9	41	47	33
Worksop Town	28	13	6	9	53	35	32
Wath	28	12	5	11	54	65	29
Wombwell Town	28	12	1	15	55	64	25
Sheffield Club	28	8	5	15	45	67	21
Attercliffe	28	8	5	15	43	67	21
Staveley	28	8	2	18	51	71	18
Eckington Works	28	5	4	19	38	124	14
Ardsley	28	4	5	19	31	102	13
Rotherham Town Reserves	28	2	3	23	23	75	7

Rotherham Town Reserves failed to fulfil their last 6 fixtures and their opponents were each awarded a win.

For the 1896-97 season, the Sheffield & Hallamshire Challenge Cup reverted to a knock-out format and so the Sheffield Association League was formed to replaced the Challenge Cup league.

Nine of the 15 Challenge Cup league members – Attercliffe, Kilnhurst, Sheepbridge Works, Sheffield Club, Sheffield United Reserves, Sheffield Wednesday Reserves, Staveley, Wath and Wombwell Town – joined the new league. Chesterfield Town, Mexborough and Worksop Town all moved to the Midland League, Eckington Works moved to the East Derbyshire Championship, Rotherham Town disbanded and Ardsley also left.

SHEFFIELD ASSOCIATION LEAGUE 1896-1939

The Sheffield Association League was formed in 1896 as a replacement for the Sheffield & Hallamshire Challenge Cup which had reverted to a knock-out format. Of the Association League's 10 founder members, Birdwell joined from the Sheffield & Hallamshire Minor Cup while the other 9 all joined from the Sheffield & Hallamshire Challenge Cup.

1896-97

Sheffield United Reserves	18	14	3	1	53	10	31
Sheffield Wednesday Reserves	18	11	3	4	54	13	25
Wath	18	11	3	4	51	24	25
Sheffield Club	18	10	2	6	43	23	22
Sheepbridge Works	18	10	2	6	47	28	22
Kilnhurst	18	6	1	11	23	31	13
Birdwell	18	5	3	10	34	44	13
Staveley	18	5	1	12	17	52	11
Attercliffe	18	4	2	12	21	64	10
Wombwell Town	18	4	0	14	20	64	8

Sheffield United Reserves and Sheffield Wednesday Reserves both left to join the newly formed Yorkshire League. They also both joined the United Counties League as did Sheffield Club and Sheepbridge Works. Birdwell moved to the Barnsley Challenge Cup League and Staveley moved to the East Derbyshire Championship. Channing Rovers, Hoyland Town, Owlerton Swifts, Parkgate United, Rotherham Church Institute, Swinton Town and Thornhill United all joined from the Sheffield Alliance and Worksop Town joined from the Midland League.

1897-98

Parkgate United	22	15	2	5	52	26	32
Wombwell Town	22	14	4	4	49	38	32
Worksop Town	22	13	5	4	66	21	31
Kilnhurst	22	10	7	5	53	33	27
Owlerton Swifts	22	11	3	8	54	37	25
Thornhill United	22	9	5	8	41	43	23
Wath	22	7	5	10	40	47	19
Attercliffe	22	6	4	12	29	46	16
Swinton Town	22	5	6	11	30	53	16
Hoyland Town	22	6	3	13	28	53	15
Channing Rovers	22	5	5	12	30	55	15
Rotherham Church Institute	22	5	3	14	26	47	13

Kilnhurst disbanded and Rotherham Church Institute also left the league. Birdwell and Royston United both joined from the Barnsley Challenge Cup League and Kimberworth and Pyebank both joined from the Sheffield Alliance.

1898-99

Worksop Town	26	20	3	3	100	31	43
Parkgate United	26	19	4	3	81	22	42
Wath	26	17	5	4	63	31	39
Wombwell Town	26	18	1	7	92	30	37
Royston United	26	14	4	8	68	44	32
Pyebank	26	11	1	14	43	53	23
Attercliffe	26	9	5	12	38	54	23
Birdwell	25	9	4	12	32	49	22
Hoyland Town	26	8	6	12	35	78	22
Thornhill United	26	8	5	13	41	42	21
Swinton Town	26	7	1	18	47	83	15
Channing Rovers	26	5	5	16	42	82	15
Owlerton Swifts	25	5	4	16	39	46	14
Kimberworth	26	4	6	16	31	73	14

Birdwell vs Overton Swifts not played.
league had introduced a new rule that the championship would be decided by a play-off between the top two clubs even if the top club had a clear advantage in points. Thus Worksop Town and Parkgate United met at Attercliffe's Carbrook ground on 22nd April to decide the title. The game was drawn 2-2 and the two clubs were declared joint champions.

Channing Rovers and Kimberworth both moved to the Hatchard Cup League and Owlerton Swifts disbanded. Wath moved ground to the new Athletic Ground in the town and changed their name to Wath Athletic.

The league was split into two divisions. The top 7 clubs from the 1898-99 season were placed in the new Division One and the remaining 4 clubs in Division Two.

Division One expanded to 10 clubs as Mexborough, Sheffield Club and Sheffield Wednesday Reserves all joined from the Yorkshire League.

Division Two expanded to 9 clubs as Barnsley Reserves and Montrose Works both joined from the Hatchard Cup League, Doncaster Rovers Reserves joined from the South Yorkshire League, Gainsborough Trinity Reserves joined from the Lincolnshire League and Rotherham joined as a club newly formed by a merger of two minor clubs in the town, Rotherham Casuals and Rotherham Grammar School.

Sheffield Association League 1899-1905

1899-1900

Division One

Sheffield Wednesday Reserves	16	14	1	1	54	9	29
Worksop Town	16	12	2	2	65	16	26
Royston United	16	8	1	7	34	33	17
Attercliffe	16	8	1	7	34	36	17
Mexborough	16	6	5	5	26	33	17
Wath Athletic	15	6	3	6	31	41	15
Sheffield Club	16	5	3	8	18	36	13
Wombwell Town	15	5	0	10	24	46	10
Pyebank	16	2	0	14	17	56	4

Parkgate United resigned and disbanded during the season and their record at the time was deleted: 5 1 2 2 9 12 4

Worksop Town moved to the Midland League while Mexborough and Pyebank both disbanded.

Division Two

Rotherham	16	10	5	1	47	23	25
Thornhill United	16	10	3	3	54	22	23
Gainsborough Trinity Reserves	16	10	2	4	44	22	22
Montrose Works	16	6	5	5	32	28	17
Barnsley Reserves	16	6	5	5	42	29	17
Doncaster Rovers Reserves	16	6	3	7	36	36	15
Swinton Town	16	6	3	7	36	38	15
Hoyland Town	16	3	2	11	19	61	8
Birdwell	16	2	0	14	12	60	4

Birdwell and Hoyland Town both moved to the Barnsley Challenge Cup, Doncaster Rovers Reserves moved to both the South Yorkshire League and the Hatchard Cup and Barnsley disbanded their reserve team. The league reverted to a single division. Denaby United joined from the South Yorkshire League, Hunslet joined from the Yorkshire League, Monk Bretton joined from the Barnsley Charity Cup League and Sheffield United Reserves joined from the Wharncliffe Charity Cup.

1900-01

Sheffield Wednesday Reserves	28	23	3	2	110	25	49
Sheffield United Reserves	28	22	2	4	115	34	46
Thornhill United	28	20	2	6	96	48	42
Monk Bretton	28	16	4	8	69	51	36
Royston United	28	14	5	9	53	48	33
Rotherham	28	11	7	10	64	46	29
Hunslet	28	11	4	13	50	69	26
Denaby United	28	9	8	11	44	56	26
Wombwell Town	28	9	6	13	39	45	24
Montrose Works	27	8	5	14	36	59	21
Sheffield Club	28	8	6	14	36	71	22
Swinton Town	27	7	5	15	32	66	19
Gainsborough Trinity Reserves	28	9	2	17	54	73	20
Attercliffe	28	5	7	16	27	56	17
Wath Athletic	28	3	4	21	24	99	10

Montrose Works and Swinton Town both disbanded. Sheffield Wednesday Reserves moved to the Midland League and Sheffield United Reserves also left the league. Doncaster Rovers Reserves joined from the Hatchard Cup and the South Yorkshire League, Roundel joined from the Hatchard Cup and Barnsley Reserves joined after a season's inactivity.

1901-02

Barnsley Reserves	24	16	5	3	80	31	37
Denaby United	23	14	4	5	52	30	32
Royston United	24	12	7	5	47	29	31
Thornhill United	24	13	1	10	48	44	27
Rotherham	24	11	4	9	53	33	26
Gainsborough Trinity Reserves	23	11	2	10	39	28	24
Monk Bretton	24	10	4	10	44	48	24
Roundel	24	10	4	10	54	46	24
Attercliffe	24	10	4	10	61	44	24
Hunslet	23	7	5	11	30	64	19
Doncaster Rovers Reserves	24	7	4	13	43	58	18
Sheffield Club	24	5	1	18	38	72	11
Wath Athletic	23	3	3	17	26	88	9

Wombwell Town resigned and disbanded at the end of February and their record at the time was deleted: 13 3 1 9 11 45 7

Denaby United, Doncaster Rovers Reserves and Gainsborough Trinity Reserves all moved to the Midland League, Hunslet moved to the West Yorkshire League, Monk Bretton disbanded and Barnsley Reserves also left the league. Hemsworth joined from the Barnsley Minor Cup and Denaby United Reserves joined.

1902-03

Rotherham	16	12	3	1	44	12	27
Thornhill United	15	11	1	3	41	13	23
Wath Athletic	16	10	2	4	36	24	22
Roundel	16	8	3	5	39	31	19
Attercliffe	16	4	4	8	21	30	12
Sheffield Club	16	4	3	9	25	39	11
Royston United	16	3	4	9	21	34	10
Denaby United Reserves	16	2	6	8	19	41	10
Hemsworth	15	4	2	9	13	33	10

Rotherham and Thornhill United both moved to the Midland League and Hemsworth moved to the Barnsley Minor Cup. Holmes, Mexborough West End, Rawmarsh Albion, Rotherham Reserves, Thorpe Hesley and Worksop Town Reserves all joined from the Hatchard Cup, South Kirkby Colliery joined from the Barnsley Minor Cup, Thornhill United Reserves joined from the Sheffield Minor Cup, Doncaster Rovers Reserves joined from the Midland League and Mexborough Town joined as a newly formed club.

1903-04

Mexborough Town	26	21	4	1	105	21	46
Thornhill United Reserves	26	16	6	4	65	37	38
Rotherham Reserves	26	15	6	5	49	31	36
Doncaster Rovers Reserves	25	16	3	6	58	32	35
Mexborough West End	26	12	5	9	65	44	29
Worksop Town Reserves	26	11	3	12	46	67	25
Thorpe Hesley	26	11	2	13	48	50	24
Sheffield Club	26	10	3	13	55	59	23
Attercliffe	26	10	2	14	44	48	22
Denaby United Reserves	25	7	6	12	26	53	20
Rawmarsh Albion	26	7	3	16	38	55	17
South Kirkby Colliery	26	7	3	16	34	75	17
Wath Athletic	26	5	6	15	32	54	16
Holmes	26	5	4	17	38	77	14

Roundel resigned and disbanded in mid-September because their ground had been taken over for building. Their record at the time was deleted when it stood as: 4 2 1 1 9 6 5

Royston United resigned and disbanded in mid-February and their record at the time was deleted: 13 7 1 5 29 21 15

Thorpe Hesley and Worksop Town Reserves both moved to the Hatchard Cup, Sheffield Club moved to the newly formed Sheffield Amateur League and Doncaster Rovers Reserves moved to the Midland League. Attercliffe, Holmes, Mexborough West End and Wath Athletic all disbanded and Denaby United disbanded their reserve side. Highthorn and Kilnhurst Town both joined from the South Yorkshire League.

1904-05

Thornhill United Reserves	12	8	2	2	30	18	18
Mexborough Town	12	8	0	4	28	17	16
South Kirkby Colliery	12	4	3	5	20	18	11
Highthorn	12	4	3	5	24	27	11
Rotherham Reserves	12	3	4	5	18	17	10
Rawmarsh Albion	12	4	1	7	18	28	9
Kilnhurst Town	12	4	1	7	19	32	9

Mexborough Town moved to the Midland League and were replaced by their reserves. Catcliffe, Doncaster St. James, Hallam and Rotherham Main all joined from the Hatchard Cup, Wycliffe and Sheffield Club both joined from the Sheffield Amateur League and Denaby United's re-formed reserve side also joined. Thornhill United Reserves changed their name to Rotherham County Reserves and Rotherham Reserves changed their name to Rotherham Town Reserves.

Sheffield Association League 1905-1911

1905-06

Team	P	W	D	L	F	A	Pts
South Kirkby Colliery	24	18	3	3	60	28	39
Denaby United Reserves	24	16	5	3	57	29	37
Rawmarsh Albion	24	11	9	4	45	33	31
Rotherham Town Reserves	23	12	4	7	65	29	28
Rotherham Main	24	10	6	8	52	40	26
Rotherham County Reserves	24	10	6	8	50	42	26
Mexborough Town Reserves	24	10	5	9	53	49	25
Catcliffe	24	9	4	11	59	46	22
Hallam	24	9	3	12	48	47	21
Kilnhurst Town	24	6	9	9	53	64	21
Wycliffe	24	5	5	14	27	48	15
Sheffield Club	23	4	6	13	35	75	14
Doncaster St. James	24	3	3	18	32	77	9
Highthorn resigned and disbanded in early March and their record at the time was deleted:	16	2	2	12	12	46	6

Hallam and Doncaster St. James both moved to the Hatchard Cup while Wycliffe also left the league. Parkgate & Rawmarsh United joined from the Sheffield Thursday League, Tinsley Club joined from the Hatchard Cup and Doncaster Rovers Reserves joined after a season's inactivity.

1906-07

Team	P	W	D	L	F	A	Pts
South Kirkby Colliery	24	18	4	2	84	21	40
Rotherham Town Reserves	24	17	2	5	56	27	36
Rawmarsh Albion	23	12	5	6	54	29	29
Kilnhurst Town	23	13	1	9	61	41	27
Tinsley Club	24	12	3	9	46	42	27
Rotherham County Reserves	24	11	4	9	53	54	26
Rotherham Main	24	12	1	11	46	41	25
Catcliffe	22	11	2	9	50	35	24
Parkgate & Rawmarsh United	24	9	3	12	42	54	21
Denaby United Reserves	24	6	5	13	36	62	17
Doncaster Rovers Reserves	24	6	3	15	33	60	15
Sheffield Club	24	5	2	17	36	84	12
Mexborough Town Reserves	24	4	1	19	38	77	9

Catcliffe disbanded. Grimethorpe joined from the Barnsley Minor Cup having changed their name to Grimethorpe ILP, Wath Athletic joined as a newly re-formed club while Hickleton Main and Rother Vale also both joined.

1907-08

Team	P	W	D	L	F	A	Pts
Wath Athletic	30	24	3	3	97	18	51
South Kirkby Colliery	29	21	2	6	98	24	44
Denaby United Reserves	30	17	7	6	73	34	41
Rawmarsh Albion	30	15	9	6	67	45	39
Rotherham Town Reserves	29	14	10	5	84	45	38
Rotherham County Reserves	29	15	4	10	69	49	34
Doncaster Rovers Reserves	29	13	4	12	51	59	30
Parkgate & Rawmarsh United	30	11	4	15	73	56	26
Grimethorpe ILP	30	9	6	15	65	101	24
Hickleton Main	28	10	4	14	51	97	24
Mexborough Town Reserves	30	9	5	16	49	66	23
Rother Vale	29	9	5	15	41	98	23
Kilnhurst Town	29	10	1	18	55	90	21
Tinsley Club	30	7	5	18	33	50	19
Rotherham Main	30	6	7	17	39	85	19
Sheffield Club	30	7	3	20	51	85	17

Sheffield Club moved to the Sheffield Amateur League and Tinsley Club disbanded. Silverwood Colliery and Worksop Town Reserves both joined from the Hatchard Cup and Monckton Athletic joined from the Barnsley Minor League.

1908-09

Team	P	W	D	L	F	A	Pts
Denaby United Reserves	28	19	6	3	83	40	44
South Kirkby Colliery	28	19	2	7	68	36	40
Monckton Athletic	28	18	2	8	82	38	38
Wath Athletic	28	17	4	7	67	40	38
Rotherham County Reserves	28	17	3	8	60	46	37
Rawmarsh Albion	28	14	3	11	51	37	31
Mexborough Town Reserves	28	12	5	11	58	59	29
Rotherham Town Reserves	28	11	5	12	60	53	27
Worksop Town Reserves	28	11	4	13	64	76	26
Doncaster Rovers Reserves	28	8	7	13	53	54	23
Hickleton Main	28	9	3	16	42	68	21
Silverwood Colliery	28	7	6	15	32	65	20
Parkgate & Rawmarsh United	28	8	3	17	45	64	19
Rotherham Main	27	4	4	19	38	68	12
Kilnhurst Town	27	4	4	19	35	93	12

Rother Vale were expelled on 22nd April for failure to fulfil several fixtures. Their record was deleted: 25 5 2 18 29 96 12
Grimethorpe ILP resigned from the league in early November and their record at the time was deleted 4 1 1 2 4 9 3
Rotherham Main disbanded and Rotherham County disbanded their reserve side. Darfield United joined from the Barnsley Minor League.

1909-10

Team	P	W	D	L	F	A	Pts
Monckton Athletic	26	19	2	5	83	30	40
Wath Athletic	26	18	4	4	64	25	40
Parkgate & Rawmarsh United	26	18	1	7	78	44	37
South Kirkby Colliery	26	15	3	8	55	39	33
Rotherham Town Reserves	26	12	7	7	49	35	31
Doncaster Rovers Reserves	26	13	4	9	53	59	30
Denaby United Reserves	26	12	2	12	51	39	26
Mexborough Town Reserves	26	11	3	12	47	48	25
Hickleton Main	26	10	5	11	56	63	25
Darfield United	26	10	4	12	47	51	24
Rawmarsh Albion	26	5	5	16	36	61	15
Silverwood Colliery	26	5	4	17	36	74	14
Worksop Town Reserves	26	5	3	18	35	83	13
Kilnhurst Town	26	3	6	17	32	70	12

Worksop Town Reserves moved to the Portland Minor League, Denaby United and Rotherham Town both disbanded their reserve sides and Rawmarsh Albion disbanded. Frickley Colliery Athletic joined from the South Yorkshire League, Conisbrough St. Peter's joined from the Sheffield Minor League, Rotherham Amateurs joined from the Sheffield Amateur League, Rotherham County Reserves joined after a season's inactivity and Brodsworth Main Colliery also joined.

1910-11

Team	P	W	D	L	F	A	Pts
Wath Athletic	26	21	2	3	99	28	44
Rotherham County Reserves	26	17	3	6	75	30	37
Darfield United	25	13	6	6	58	38	32
Doncaster Rovers Reserves	26	12	7	7	60	39	31
Silverwood Colliery	26	14	3	9	50	38	31
Frickley Colliery Athletic	25	13	4	8	71	46	30
Hickleton Main	25	11	5	9	51	36	27
South Kirkby Colliery	26	12	1	13	61	53	25
Conisbrough St. Peter's	25	10	4	11	50	58	24
Kilnhurst Town	26	8	7	11	45	61	23
Rotherham Amateurs	26	8	5	13	46	66	21
Parkgate & Rawmarsh United	26	6	4	16	47	75	16
Mexborough Town Reserves	26	4	3	19	36	99	11
Brodsworth Main Colliery	26	3	2	21	29	109	8

Monckton Athletic were suspended in mid-March for non-payment of referees' fees and their record was deleted. The club's record at the time stood as follows: 16 8 2 6 41 19 18
Two games were not played.
Darfield United moved to the Barnsley Association League and Rotherham Amateurs moved to the Sheffield Amateur League. Bentley Colliery joined from the Doncaster Junior League, Rotherham Town Reserves and Denaby United Reserves both joined after a season's inactivity and Rawmarsh Town joined as a newly formed club.

Sheffield Association League 1911-1920

1911-12

Wath Athletic	30	24	1	5	82	21	49
Frickley Colliery Athletic	30	24	1	5	96	31	49
South Kirkby Colliery	30	22	3	5	114	28	47
Hickleton Main	30	19	7	4	96	47	45
Silverwood Colliery	30	13	5	12	53	55	31
Doncaster Rovers Reserves	30	14	2	14	49	47	30
Rotherham County Reserves	30	13	4	13	57	56	30
Rawmarsh Town	30	12	3	15	85	86	27
Rotherham Town Reserves	30	10	5	15	41	59	25
Bentley Colliery	30	10	5	15	44	72	25
Mexborough Town Reserves	30	10	4	16	48	65	24
Kilnhurst Town	30	11	2	17	47	74	24
Conisbrough St. Peter's	30	9	5	16	53	81	23
Parkgate & Rawmarsh United	30	9	3	18	55	104	21
Brodsworth Main Colliery	30	8	3	19	32	71	19
Denaby United Reserves	30	7	3	20	42	87	17

Rotherham County and Rotherham Town both disbanded their reserve sides and Parkgate & Rawmarsh United also disbanded. Gainsborough Trinity Reserves joined from the Midland League and Rotherham Amateurs joined from the Sheffield Amateur League.

1912-13

Wath Athletic	28	20	4	4	90	32	44
South Kirkby Colliery	28	18	6	4	88	40	42
Gainsborough Trinity Reserves	28	19	3	6	86	43	41
Kilnhurst Town	28	17	5	6	65	41	39
Silverwood Colliery	28	16	5	7	80	43	37
Hickleton Main	28	16	5	7	69	44	37
Bentley Colliery	27	14	4	9	74	40	32
Rotherham Amateurs	28	11	6	11	46	54	28
Rawmarsh Town	28	9	4	15	43	83	22
Conisbrough St. Peter's	28	9	3	16	47	78	21
Frickley Colliery Athletic	28	8	4	16	43	59	20
Doncaster Rovers Reserves	28	9	1	18	52	62	19
Brodsworth Main Colliery	27	8	3	16	45	67	19
Denaby United Reserves	28	5	5	18	40	109	15
Mexborough Town Reserves	28	2	2	24	19	94	6

The game between Bentley Colliery and Brodsworth Main Colliery ended before full time and the result was declared void.
Doncaster Rovers Reserves moved to the Doncaster & District League and Mexborough Town disbanded their reserve side. Denaby United joined from the Midland League, replacing their reserve side which was also disbanded. Darfield United joined from the Barnsley Junior League, Rotherham Town Reserves joined after a season's inactivity and Bolton Athletic also joined.

1913-14

South Kirkby Colliery	29	21	7	1	124	36	49
Gainsborough Trinity Reserves	30	19	2	9	104	47	40
Bentley Colliery	28	15	8	5	81	38	38
Denaby United	29	15	5	9	59	52	35
Brodsworth Main Colliery	30	12	8	10	47	45	32
Rawmarsh Town	28	10	12	6	52	60	32
Hickleton Main	30	12	7	11	52	44	31
Silverwood Colliery	30	14	1	15	88	65	29
Rotherham Town Reserves	30	12	4	14	63	78	28
Wath Athletic	29	10	7	12	49	34	27
Rotherham Amateurs	27	10	4	13	57	61	24
Darfield United	28	10	4	14	45	48	24
Bolton Athletic	30	8	7	15	49	77	23
Kilnhurst Town	28	8	5	15	40	80	21
Conisbrough St. Peter's	30	8	4	18	56	113	20
Frickley Colliery Athletic	30	4	3	23	31	102	11

Rotherham Town disbanded their reserve side and were replaced by Rotherham County's reformed reserve side.

1914-15

Rotherham County Reserves	24	15	6	3	91	34	36
Bentley Colliery	23	15	2	6	78	38	32
Wath Athletic	24	15	2	7	51	36	32
South Kirkby Colliery	24	15	1	8	61	38	31
Denaby United	23	14	0	9	42	34	28
Kilnhurst Town	23	11	2	10	45	56	24
Hickleton Main	22	10	2	10	50	43	22
Silverwood Colliery	24	9	2	13	50	52	20
Frickley Colliery Athletic	23	9	2	12	40	54	20
Brodsworth Main Colliery	24	8	4	12	38	54	20
Darfield United	24	8	2	14	40	69	18
Gainsborough Trinity Reserves	23	6	2	15	30	70	14
Rotherham Amateurs	23	2	3	18	29	74	7

Conisbrough St. Peter's resigned from the league in late November and their record was deleted: 8 0 0 8 2 42 0
Bolton Athletic resigned from the league in early January and their record at the time was deleted: 10 0 2 8 8 38 2
Rawmarsh Town were unable to complete their fixtures and their record was deleted in March: 14 5 4 5 28 42 14
Bentley Colliery, Brodsworth Main Colliery, Denaby United, Wath Athletic, Frickley Colliery Athletic, Gainsborough Trinity Reserves and Rotherham Amateurs all left the league. Hoyland Town, Mexborough Town and Parkgate C.C. all joined the league.

1915-16

Hoyland Town	10	7	1	2	17	8	15
Rotherham County Reserves	10	5	1	4	14	10	11
Parkgate C.C.	10	5	0	5	25	11	10
Mexborough Town	9	4	1	4	17	15	9
Kilnhurst Town	10	3	3	4	11	15	9
South Kirkby Colliery	9	2	0	7	4	29	4

Hickleton Main, Silverwood Colliery and Darfield United all resigned during the season and their records were deleted.
Only 4 clubs signified that they would be able to play in the 1916-17 season and so the competition was therefore abandoned until 1919 when it was re-formed with 14 clubs.

1919-20

No final table has been found for this season.

The member clubs are listed below:

Bentley Colliery (Champions), Bolton Hall Rovers, Brodsworth Main, Denaby United, Frickley Colliery Athletic, Maltby Main Colliery, Parkgate Works Sports, Rossington Main, Rotherham Amateurs, Silverwood Colliery, Simplex Sports, South Kirkby Colliery, Thurnscoe Park Avenue, Wath Athletic (14 clubs).

Denaby United moved to the Midland League and were replaced by their reserves and Wath Athletic moved to the Yorkshire League and were replaced by their reserves. Bolton Hall Rovers, Brodsworth Main, Parkgate Works Sports, Rossington Main and Simplex Sports also left the league. Dinnington Main, Doncaster Rovers Reserves, Eckington Works, Gainsborough Town, Mexborough Reserves, Rotherham Town Reserves, Tinsley W.M.C., Wombwell Reserves and Worksop Town Reserves all joined.

1920-21

No final table has been found for this season.

The member clubs are listed below:

Frickley Colliery Athletic (Champions), Bentley Colliery, Denaby United Reserves, Dinnington Main, Doncaster Rovers Reserves, Eckington Works, Gainsborough Town (Trinity Reserves), Maltby Main Colliery, Mexborough Reserves, Rotherham Amateurs, Rotherham Town Reserves, Silverwood Colliery, South Kirkby Colliery, Thurnscoe Park Avenue, Tinsley W.M.C., Wath Athletic Reserves. Wombwell Reserves, Worksop Town Reserves.

Doncaster Rovers Reserves, Wath Athletic Reserves and Wombwell Reserves all moved to the Yorkshire League. Goldthorpe Comrades, Houghton Main Reserves, Scunthorpe & Lindsey United Reserves and Sheffield Wednesday "A" joined.

1921-22

No final table has been found for this season.

Worksop Town Reserves finished top of the table but there was a play-off between the four clubs who finished highest to decide the champions. 15 other clubs were members of the league: Bentley Colliery, Denaby United Reserves, Dinnington Main, Goldthorpe Comrades, Houghton Main Reserves, Maltby Main Colliery, Mexborough Reserves, Rotherham Amateurs, Rotherham Town Reserves, Scunthorpe & Lindsey United Reserves, Sheffield Wednesday "A", Silverwood Colliery, South Kirkby Colliery, Thurnscoe Park Avenue, Tinsley W.M.C..

Championship Play-offs – Semi-finals

Worksop Town Reserves vs Frickley Colliery Athletic   2-0
(Played in Doncaster on 27th April 1922)

Eckington Works vs Gainsborough Trinity Reserves   1-1
(Played in Beighton 1st May 1922)

Replay

Eckington Works vs Gainsborough Trinity Reserves   1-2
(Played in Rotherham on 4th May 1922)

Final

Gainsborough Trinity Reserves vs Worksop Town Res.   1-0
(Played in Doncaster on 6th May 1922)

Bentley Colliery and Frickley Colliery both moved to the Yorkshire League and were replaced by their reserves. Mexborough Reserves, Houghton Main Reserves, Gainsborough Trinity Reserves, Thurnscoe Park Avenue, Rotherham Town Reserves and Sheffield Wednesday "A" all left the league. Wath Athletic Reserves joined from the Yorkshire League while Bullcroft Colliery and Rossington Main also both joined.

1922-23

No final table has been found for this season.

Worksop Town Reserves (champions), Bentley Colliery Reserves, Bullcroft Colliery, Denaby United Reserves, Dinnington Main, Eckington Works, Frickley Colliery Athletic Reserves, Goldthorpe Comrades, Maltby Main Colliery, Rossington Main, Rotherham Amateurs, Scunthorpe & Lindsey United Reserves, Silverwood Colliery, South Kirkby Colliery, Tinsley W.M.C., Wath Athletic Reserves (16 clubs).

Bentley Colliery Reserves and Scunthorpe & Lindsey United Reserves both left the league. Beighton Recreation and Treeton Reading Room both joined from the Wragg League, New Stubbin Colliery joined from the Sheffield Minor League and Attercliffe joined as a newly formed club. Goldthorpe Comrades changed their name to Goldthorpe United.

1923-24

Eckington Works	34	21	10	3	99	42	52
Maltby Main Colliery	34	20	6	8	82	46	46
Beighton Recreation	34	18	10	6	70	43	46
Treeton R.R.	34	19	8	7	82	50	46
Frickley Colliery Reserves	34	20	6	8	77	49	46
Attercliffe	34	19	7	8	69	51	45
Worksop Town Reserves	34	18	4	12	79	66	40
Rotherham Amateurs	34	14	7	13	76	56	35
Dinnington Main	34	13	8	13	72	67	34
Goldthorpe United	34	11	9	14	47	64	31
Wath Athletic Reserves	34	11	10	13	65	75	32
Bullcroft Colliery	34	10	9	15	45	60	29
Denaby United Reserves	34	9	10	15	63	66	28
New Stubbin Colliery	34	6	12	16	50	74	24
Tinsley W.M.C.	34	6	11	17	52	81	23
Rossington Main	34	8	6	20	39	71	22
South Kirkby Colliery	34	5	8	21	44	92	18
Silverwood Colliery	34	5	5	24	39	105	15

Bullcroft Colliery moved to the Yorkshire League and were replaced by their reserves. Frickley Colliery Reserves also moved to the Yorkshire League. Worksop Town Reserves moved to the Derbyshire Senior League and both Wath Athletic Reserves and Tinsley W.M.C. also left. Brodsworth Main Reserves joined the league. Beighton Recreation changed their name to Beighton Miners Welfare.

1924-25

Attercliffe	28	21	5	2	91	32	47
Beighton Miners Welfare	28	18	4	6	87	40	40
Denaby United Reserves	28	17	5	6	74	34	39
South Kirkby Colliery	28	14	9	5	59	33	37
Maltby Main Colliery	27	14	6	7	58	47	34
Rotherham Amateurs	28	15	4	9	51	48	34
Bullcroft Colliery Reserves	28	14	4	10	68	51	32
Eckington Works	27	12	2	13	49	69	26
Treeton Reading Room	28	10	2	16	50	58	22
Brodsworth Main	28	10	1	17	42	67	21
Rossington Main	28	6	7	15	34	52	19
Goldthorpe United	28	7	5	16	42	61	19
Dinnington Main	28	7	4	17	44	60	18
New Stubbin Colliery	28	7	3	18	37	78	17
Silverwood Colliery	28	6	1	21	53	108	13

One game was not played.

1925-26

No final table has been found for this season.

Maltby Main Colliery (champions), Anston Athletic, Attercliffe, Beighton Miners Welfare, Dinnington Main, Kiveton Park Colliery, New Stubbin Colliery, Norton Woodseats, Rotherham Amateurs, Rotherham United Reserves, Sheffield Club, Treeton Reading Room, Worksop Town Reserves (13 clubs).

Beighton Miners Welfare, Rotherham Amateurs and Sheffield Club all left. Ecclesfield United, Manton Colliery and Retford Comrades all joined.

Sheffield Association League 1926-1930

1926-27

Note: The league adopted a system whereby a cut-off date was chosen and the top 4 teams in the table at that date qualified to play-off for the championship. The date chosen was around 4 weeks before the end of the season and the remaining league fixtures would still be played. The top 4 were chosen regardless of how many league games they had played by the cut-off date and so they could get overtaken after the cut-off date by other teams and would not necessarily finish in the top 4 in the final table.

Worksop Town Reserves	24	20	1	3	77	39	41
Maltby Main Colliery (champions)	24	15	4	5	91	43	34
Norton Woodseats	24	15	3	6	86	43	33
Anston Athletic	24	12	4	8	79	52	28
Dinnington Main	24	11	4	9	58	60	26
New Stubbin Colliery	24	10	5	9	53	59	25
Manton Colliery	24	8	7	9	57	53	23
Ecclesfield United	24	10	3	11	66	76	23
Retford Comrades	24	10	0	14	61	86	20
Rotherham United Reserves	24	7	2	15	55	74	16
Kiveton Park Colliery	24	6	4	14	48	96	16
Treeton Reading Room	24	6	3	15	45	70	15
Attercliffe	24	5	2	17	47	72	12

Championship Play-offs – Semi-finals

Worksop Town Reserves vs Maltby Main	1-1

(Played in Dinnington on 16th April 1927)

Norton Woodseats vs Anston Athletic	3-4

(Played in Worksop on 19th April 1927)

Replay

Worksop Town Reserves vs Maltby Main	1-3

(Played in Worksop on 23rd April 1927)

Final

Maltby Main vs Anston Athletic	1-1

(Played in Dinnington on 2nd May 1927)

Final Replay

Maltby Main vs Anston Athletic	5-2

(Played in Dinnington on 5th May 1927)

Retford Comrades left the league. Hallam joined from the Sheffield Amateur League and Rotherham Amateurs also joined.

1927-28

No final table has been found for this season.

Hallam (finished 1st in the table), Anston Athletic, Attercliffe, Dinnington Main, Ecclesfield United, Kiveton Park Colliery, Maltby Main Colliery, Manton Colliery, New Stubbin Colliery, Norton Woodseats, Rotherham Amateurs, Rotherham United Reserves, Treeton Reading Room, Worksop Town Reserves. (14 clubs)

Championship Play-offs – Semi-finals

Ecclesfield United vs Hallam	4-3

(Played at Cammell Sports Ground, Shiregreen on 24th April)

Norton Woodseats vs Maltby Main Colliery	4-0

(Played at Cammell Sports Ground, Shiregreen on 28th April)

Final

Norton Woodseats vs Ecclesfield United	3-1

(Played at Hillsborough on 1st May 1928)

Anston Athletic, Attercliffe, Manton Colliery and New Stubbin Colliery all left the league. Denaby United Reserves, Firbeck Main, Handsworth United, Rawmarsh Athletic and Silverwood Colliery all joined.
Rotherham United Reserves were replaced by Rotherham United "A".

1928-29

Ecclesfield United	28	19	3	6	87	51	41
Denaby United Reserves	28	16	6	6	78	52	38
Rawmarsh Athletic	28	15	7	6	84	43	37
Norton Woodseats	28	17	3	8	87	47	37
Worksop Town Reserves	28	17	3	8	83	47	37
Firbeck Main	28	16	3	9	69	47	35
Kiveton Park Colliery	28	14	4	10	67	61	32
Hallam	28	13	3	12	76	77	29
Dinnington Main	28	12	2	14	60	64	26
Rotherham United "A"	28	11	3	14	58	80	25
Silverwood Colliery	28	10	5	13	79	81	25
Treeton Reading Room	28	7	6	15	50	71	20
Handsworth United	28	6	5	17	45	81	17
Maltby Main Colliery	28	6	2	20	39	77	14
Rotherham Amateurs	28	3	1	24	36	116	7

Championship Play-offs – Test matches

Norton Woodseats vs Worksop Town Reserves	2-3

(Played in Dinnington on 13th April 1929)
Rawmarsh Athletic received a bye

Semi-finals

Denaby United Reserves vs Rawmarsh Athletic	2-1

(Played at Hampden Road, Mexborough on 22nd April 1929)

Worksop Town Reserves vs Ecclesfield United	4-0

(Played at Cammell Sports Ground, Shiregreen on 23rd April)

Final

Worksop Town Reserves vs Denaby United Reserves	2-2

(Played in Worksop on 29th April 1929)

Final Replay

Denaby United Reserves vs Worksop Town Reserves	2-3

(Played in Denaby on 4th May 1929)

Kiveton Park, Maltby Main Colliery, Rotherham Amateurs and Treeton Reading Room all left the league. Woodhouse Brunswick joined as a newly formed club while Eastwood W.M.C., New Stubbin Colliery and South Kirkby Colliery also joined.

1929-30

Dinnington Main	27	20	2	5	82	42	42
Rawmarsh Athletic	28	15	9	4	66	36	39
South Kirkby Colliery	27	16	4	7	86	36	36
Hallam	28	14	8	6	90	64	36
Norton Woodseats	28	13	8	7	84	54	34
Denaby United Reserves	27	12	8	7	83	67	32
Worksop Town Reserves	28	12	3	13	62	69	27
Ecclesfield United	28	11	3	14	71	81	25
Firbeck Main	28	12	1	15	62	72	25
Silverwood Colliery	28	10	3	15	57	87	23
Woodhouse Brunswick	28	9	4	15	78	91	22
Handsworth United	28	8	6	14	51	60	22
Eastwood W.M.C.	27	11	0	16	71	87	22
New Stubbin Colliery	28	6	4	18	44	94	16
Rotherham United "A"	28	5	5	18	58	102	15

The results of the 2 outstanding games have not been found.

Championship Play-offs – Test match

Hallam vs Norton Woodseats 4-3
(Played at Woodhouse Brunswick on 12th April 1930)

Semi-finals

South Kirkby Colliery vs Dinnington Main 2-0
(Played in Worksop on 12th April 1930)

Rawmarsh Athletic vs Hallam 2-1
(Played at Cammell Sports Ground, Shiregreen on 19th April)

Final

South Kirkby Colliery vs Rawmarsh Athletic 1-0
(Played in Mexborough on 26th April 1930)

Worksop Town disbanded while Denaby United Reserves and Rotherham United "A" also left the league. Wath Athletic joined from the Midland League while Ardsley Athletic, Goldthorpe United and Wombwell Reserves also joined. Dinnington Main changed their name to Dinnington Athletic.

1930-31

South Kirkby Colliery	30	25	3	2	110	27	53
Dinnington Athletic	30	19	5	6	105	51	43
Goldthorpe United	30	17	7	6	60	42	41
Silverwood Colliery	30	13	11	6	81	47	37
Ardsley Athletic	30	15	4	11	77	70	34
Norton Woodseats	30	14	5	11	74	55	33
Woodhouse Brunswick	30	12	8	10	80	72	32
Wath Athletic	30	13	5	12	69	65	31
Firbeck Main	30	13	4	13	83	72	30
New Stubbin Colliery	30	10	6	14	62	78	26
Handsworth United	30	10	5	15	57	67	25
Wombwell Reserves	30	11	3	16	65	99	25
Rawmarsh Welfare	30	8	6	16	66	93	22
Eastwood W.M.C.	30	8	2	20	55	96	18
Hallam	30	6	5	19	68	105	17
Ecclesfield United	30	5	3	22	44	117	13

Championship Play-offs – Semi-finals

South Kirkby Colliery vs Dinnington Athletic 2-1
(Played in Grimethorpe on 18th April 1931)

Goldthorpe United vs Silverwood Colliery 2-0
(Played in Wath on 18th April 1931)

Final

South Kirkby Colliery vs Goldthorpe United 1-1
(Played in Wath on 25th April 1931)

Replay

South Kirkby Colliery vs Goldthorpe United 3-0
(Played in Grimethorpe on 2nd May 1931)

Eastwood W.M.C. and Ecclesfield United both left the league. Goole Town Reserves, Owston Park Rangers and Rossington Main all joined from the Doncaster Senior League, Worksop Town joined as a newly re-formed club and Cudworth Village, Grimethorpe Colliery Institute, Highgate Halfway, Monckton Athletic, Sheffield United "A", Thurcroft Main and Thurnscoe Victoria also joined.

The league was split into two equal divisions of equal status.

1931-32

Division One

South Kirkby Colliery	24	16	4	4	65	28	36
Wath Athletic	24	12	11	1	50	23	35
Ardsley Athletic	24	13	5	6	68	52	31
Rawmarsh Welfare	24	14	3	7	63	56	31
Thurnscoe Victoria	24	12	5	7	43	41	29
Wombwell Reserves	24	10	4	10	62	59	24
Goldthorpe United	24	9	5	10	44	36	23
Monckton Athletic	24	8	5	11	59	47	21
Grimethorpe Colliery Institute	24	8	4	12	54	58	20
Silverwood Colliery	24	7	5	12	51	53	19
New Stubbin Colliery	24	8	2	14	43	61	18
Highgate Halfway	24	4	7	13	43	69	15
Cudworth Village	24	3	4	17	33	93	10

New Stubbin Colliery and Highgate Halfway both left the league. Treeton Reading Room joined.

Division Two

No final table has been found for Division Two this season.

Dinnington Athletic (1st), Norton Woodseats (2nd), Firbeck Main, Goole Town Reserves, Hallam, Handsworth United, Owston Park Rangers, Rossington Main, Sheffield United "A", Thurcroft Main, Woodhouse Brunswick, Worksop Town.

Woodhouse Brunswick disbanded because the landlord of the Brunswick Hotel, who owned the ground, formed a new club called Woodhouse Alliance and that club replaced Woodhouse Brunswick in the league. Goole Town Reserves left the league and Pilkington Recreation joined.

Championship Play-offs – Semi-finals

South Kirkby Colliery vs Dinnington Athletic 3-1
(Played in Mexborough on 9th April 1932)

Wath Athletic vs Norton Woodseats 2-1
(Played in Mexborough on 16th April 1932)

Final

Wath Athletic vs South Kirkby Colliery 2-0
(Played in Grimethorpe on 23rd April 1932)

1932-33

Division One

Thurnscoe Victoria	22	15	3	4	90	37	33
South Kirkby Colliery	22	13	5	4	77	35	31
Silverwood Colliery	22	12	4	6	61	38	28
Goldthorpe United	22	13	2	7	56	33	28
Rawmarsh Welfare	22	10	5	7	67	45	25
Wath Athletic	22	9	6	7	50	36	24
Grimethorpe Colliery Institute	22	9	6	7	42	44	24
Monckton Athletic	22	9	5	8	57	52	23
Cudworth Village	22	5	5	12	53	68	15
Treeton Reading Room	22	3	7	12	35	62	13
Ardsley Athletic	22	3	5	14	33	100	11
Wombwell Reserves	22	3	3	16	24	102	9

South Kirkby Colliery moved to the Yorkshire League and were replaced by their reserves who joined from the Doncaster Senior League. Treeton Reading Room, Wath Athletic and Wombwell all disbanded while Ardsley Athletic and Cudworth Village also left the league.

Sheffield Association League 1933-1936

Division Two

Dinnington Athletic	22	16	2	4	84	37	34
Owston Park Rangers	22	14	4	4	80	34	32
Woodhouse Alliance	22	15	2	5	72	46	32
Worksop Town	22	15	1	6	76	40	31
Thurcroft Main	22	10	4	8	59	54	24
Pilkington Recreation	22	10	3	9	53	56	23
Sheffield United "A"	22	10	2	10	64	54	22
Firbeck Main	22	9	2	11	45	52	20
Rossington Main	22	7	2	13	60	84	16
Norton Woodseats	22	5	3	14	47	61	13
Handsworth United	22	2	5	15	41	101	9
Hallam	22	2	4	16	36	92	8

Worksop Town moved to the Central Combination, Norton Woodseats moved to the Sheffield Amateur League and Handsworth United disbanded. Firbeck Main and Hallam also left the league. Bentley Colliery and Thorne Town Recreation both joined.

Championship Play-offs – Test match

Silverwood Colliery vs Goldthorpe United   3-1
(Played in Mexborough on 1st April 1933)

Semi-finals

Thurnscoe Victoria vs Dinnington Athletic   2-1
(Played in Wath on 8th April 1933)

Silverwood Colliery vs Woodhouse Alliance   2-0
(Played in Dinnington on 15th April 1933)

Final

Silverwood Colliery vs Thurnscoe Victoria   2-0
(Played in Grimethorpe on 22nd April 1933)

1933-34

The league reverted to a single division.

Thurnscoe Victoria	30	21	3	6	89	49	45
Bentley Colliery	30	21	1	8	91	44	43
Rawmarsh Welfare	30	18	4	8	75	44	40
Sheffield United "A"	30	18	4	8	82	51	40
Woodhouse Alliance	30	16	3	11	65	49	35
Silverwood Colliery	30	16	3	11	83	58	35
Goldthorpe United	30	15	3	12	68	49	33
Dinnington Athletic	30	13	7	10	65	59	33
Moncton Athletic	30	13	5	12	73	62	31
Rossington Main	30	13	4	13	63	57	30
Pilkington Recreation	30	12	5	13	65	74	29
Owston Park Rangers	30	8	2	20	46	81	18
Thorne Town Recreation	30	7	4	19	56	120	18
Grimethorpe Colliery Institute	30	7	3	20	57	91	17
South Kirkby Colliery Reserves	30	8	1	21	54	87	17
Thurcroft Main	30	5	6	19	40	95	16

Championship Play-offs – Semi-finals

Thurnscoe Victoria vs Sheffield United "A"   2-1
(Played in Goldthorpe on 14th April 1934)

Rawmarsh Welfare vs Bentley Colliery   1-0
(Played in Mexborough on 21st April 1934)

Final

Thurnscoe Victoria vs Rawmarsh Welfare   2-0
(Played in Mexborough on 28th April 1934)

Sheffield United "A" moved to the Yorkshire League, Grimethorpe Colliery Institute disbanded and Goldthorpe United, Thorne Town Recreation, Thurcroft Main and Woodhouse Alliance also all left the league. Norton Woodseats joined from the Sheffield Amateur League and Firbeck Main also joined.

1934-35

Dinnington Athletic	22	15	2	5	72	28	32
Thurnscoe Victoria	22	13	4	5	66	36	30
Rossington Main	22	13	3	6	52	33	29
Rawmarsh Welfare	22	12	2	8	46	42	26
Bentley Colliery	22	11	2	9	57	52	24
Owston Park Rangers	22	11	2	9	39	51	24
South Kirkby Colliery Reserves	22	7	8	7	46	41	22
Norton Woodseats	22	8	4	10	46	51	20
Firbeck Main	22	7	3	12	47	69	17
Silverwood Colliery	22	7	2	13	54	60	16
Pilkington Recreation	22	6	3	13	33	59	15
Monckton Athletic	22	2	5	15	30	66	9

Championship Play-offs – Semi-finals

Thurnscoe Victoria vs Rawmarsh Welfare   2-1
(Played in Mexborough on 22nd April 1935)

Dinnington Athletic vs Rossington Main   1-1
(Played in Dinnington on 22nd April 1935)

Replay

Dinnington Athletic vs Rossington Main   2-0
(Played in Doncaster on 25th April 1935)

Final

Dinnington Athletic vs Thurnscoe Victoria   3-0
(Played in Wath on 27th April 1935)

Firbeck Main and Monckton Athletic both left the league. Armthorpe Welfare joined from the Doncaster Red Triangle League and Sheffield Club also joined.

1935-36

Rawmarsh Welfare	21	14	2	5	64	29	30
Norton Woodseats	22	13	4	5	55	24	30
Armthorpe Welfare	22	13	4	5	58	34	30
Dinnington Athletic	22	13	4	5	61	44	30
Pilkington Recreation	22	13	3	6	63	30	29
Rossington Main	21	8	5	8	54	42	21
Thurnscoe Victoria	22	8	4	10	43	71	20
South Kirkby Colliery Reserves	21	6	4	11	27	50	16
Bentley Colliery	21	5	6	10	30	58	16
Sheffield	20	6	2	12	52	57	14
Owston Park Rangers	22	4	4	14	35	67	12
Silverwood Colliery	22	4	2	16	37	73	10

The results of the 3 outstanding games have not been found.

Semi-finals

Dinnington Athletic vs Rawmarsh Welfare   1-3
(Played in Dinnington on 11th April 1936)

Armthorpe Welfare vs Norton Woodseats   0-2
(Played in Dinnington on 14th April 1936)

Final

Rawmarsh Welfare vs Norton Woodseats   2-1
(Played at Millmoor on 20th April 1936)

Dinnington Athletic moved to the Yorkshire League and were replaced by their reserves. Owston Park Rangers and Silverwood Colliery also left the league. Sheffield University joined from the Yorkshire League and The Hall Sports, Firbeck Main, Lopham Street Methodists and Fulwood also all joined.

1936-37

No final table has been found for this season.

The Hall Sports (1st), Pilkington Recreation, Norton Woodseats and Thurnscoe Victoria (all qualified for the championship play-offs). Armthorpe Welfare, Bentley Colliery, Dinnington Athletic Reserves, Firbeck Main, Fulwood, Lopham Street Methodists, Rawmarsh Welfare, Rossington Main, Sheffield Club, Sheffield University, South Kirkby Colliery Reserves.

Championship Play-offs – Semi-finals

Thurnscoe Victoria vs Pilkington Recreation	3-1
(Played in Mexborough on 17th April 1937)	
The Hall Sports vs Norton Woodseats	2-2
(Played at Hillsborough on 19th April 1937)	

Replay

The Hall Sports vs Norton Woodseats	3-1
(Played at Hillsborough on 23rd April 1937)	

Final

Thurnscoe Victoria vs The Hall Sports	5-1
(Played at Hillsborough on 26th April 1937)	

The Hall Sports and Firbeck Main both left the league.
Frickley Colliery Reserves joined as a newly formed side and Beighton Miners Welfare, R.A.F. Finningley and Worksop Town Reserves also joined.

1937-38

The system of the top 4 clubs playing off for the championship was abandoned.

Norton Woodseats	32	27	0	5	114	44	54
Rawmarsh Welfare	32	23	3	6	93	55	49
Beighton Miners Welfare	32	19	10	3	119	51	48
Pilkington Recreation	32	20	3	9	104	59	43
Thurnscoe Victoria	32	15	6	11	72	61	36
Lopham Street Methodists	31	15	5	11	84	75	35
Dinnington Athletic Reserves	32	15	4	13	75	63	34
Armthorpe Welfare	31	14	5	12	89	60	33
Fulwood	31	13	5	13	82	86	31
Sheffield Club	32	11	6	15	80	79	28
Worksop Town Reserves	32	12	4	16	85	97	28
Rossington Main	32	11	4	17	80	90	26
Frickley Colliery Reserves	32	12	2	18	59	88	26
Sheffield University	32	9	6	17	56	81	24
South Kirkby Colliery Reserves	32	9	4	19	55	93	22
Bentley Colliery	32	8	1	23	53	95	17
R.A.F. Finningley	31	1	4	26	35	148	6

Pilkington Recreation and R.A.F. Finningley both left the league.
Brodsworth Main, The Hall Sports and Thurcroft Main all joined.

1938-39

Rawmarsh Welfare	32	26	2	4	123	52	54
Brodsworth Main	32	22	3	7	126	61	47
Beighton Miners Welfare	32	20	6	6	118	71	46
Norton Woodseats	32	20	4	8	127	55	44
Sheffield Club	32	18	2	12	111	74	38
The Hall Sports	32	15	6	11	89	68	36
Thurcroft Main	31	13	7	11	78	78	33
Frickley Colliery Reserves	32	14	5	13	85	80	33
Worksop Town Reserves	32	13	5	14	87	88	31
Bentley Colliery	32	10	7	15	67	95	27
South Kirkby Colliery Reserves	32	11	4	17	61	99	26
Fulwood	32	9	6	17	66	88	24
Lopham Street Methodists	32	10	4	18	78	108	24
Sheffield University	32	10	4	18	76	118	24
Armthorpe Welfare	32	9	6	17	61	110	24
Dinnington Athletic Reserves	32	6	5	21	55	101	17
Rossington Main	31	5	6	20	49	125	16

One game was not played.
Thurnscoe Victoria resigned during the season and their record was deleted.
Dinnington Athletic Reserves, The Hall Sports and Rossington Main all left. Bolsover Colliery joined from the Yorkshire League while Grimethorpe Rovers, Maltby Main and Manvers Main also all joined.

1939-40

The league ceased to operate when war was declared on 3rd September 1939.

WEST YORKSHIRE LEAGUE 1894-1896

The West Yorkshire League was the first senior league in the Leeds area and was formed in 1894 with 12 founder members: Altofts, Castleford, Castleford Albion, Featherstone, Ferrybridge, Hunslet, Leeds, Normanton, Oulton, Pontefract, Pontefract Garrison and Rothwell.

1894-95

Leeds	20	18	1	1	95	20	37
Castleford	20	14	1	5	69	42	29
Altofts	20	10	3	7	64	49	23
Pontefract	17	9	4	4	41	22	22
Normanton	20	8	4	8	63	45	20
Hunslet	17	7	4	6	44	43	18
Featherstone	18	7	2	9	39	46	16
Pontefract Garrison	19	5	5	9	33	47	15
Oulton	19	5	3	11	25	49	13
Rothwell	19	5	1	13	24	45	11
Ferrybridge	19	2	0	17	25	99	4

The 6 outstanding games were not played.
Castleford Albion resigned and ceased playing in October and their record at the time was deleted: 6 0 0 6 2 54 0
Newly formed Halifax A.F.C. applied to replace them and although their application was rejected, they did join for the 1895-96 season.
Buckstone Park A.F.C. also applied to join and, after agreeing to being taken over by the Bradford Athletic, Cricket & Football (Rugby) club, they joined the league as Bradford. Pontefract left the league.

1895-96

Bradford	20	14	3	3	72	32	31
Hunslet	19	14	1	4	75	25	29
Altofts	20	12	4	4	48	33	28
Normanton	19	11	3	5	52	28	25
Leeds	19	11	1	7	45	24	23
Featherstone	18	8	6	4	45	29	22
Pontefract Garrison	19	7	3	9	26	43	17
Halifax	18	8	0	10	39	45	16
Castleford	19	2	2	15	21	55	6
Oulton	19	2	2	15	19	71	6
Rothwell	18	2	1	15	9	71	5

Ferrybridge resigned from the league in March 1896 and their record at the time was deleted: 11 0 0 11 4 55 0

Championship decider

Hunslet vs Bradford 2-2
(Played at the Clarence Cricket Ground, Star & Garter Inn, Kirkstall on 30th April 1896 – Attendance: 1,000)

Hunslet claimed the championship due to a better goal average but the league management committee said there was nothing in the rules to allow this and the matter appears to have been left undecided.

The league closed down at the end of the season.

With no appropriate senior league in which they could compete, its member clubs reverted to playing friendlies and cup-ties in 1896-97.

YORKSHIRE LEAGUE (I) 1897-1900

The initiative concerning the formation of a league for the whole of Yorkshire came from the Sheffield & Hallamshire F.A. in 1897 and after being agreed by the West Yorkshire F.A., 10 clubs became founder members – Barnsley, Bradford, Doncaster Rovers, Halifax, Huddersfield, Hunslet, Leeds, Mexborough, Sheffield United Reserves and Sheffield Wednesday Reserves. The first meetings of the league were held at the Maunche Hotel, which was part of the Corn Exchange buildings in Exchange Street, Sheffield but venues for meetings soon alternated between Sheffield and Leeds.

Barnsley (who had changed their name from Barnsley St. Peter's on 1st May 1897), Doncaster Rovers and Mexborough all fielded their first teams while also continuing to play in the Midland League. Bradford, Halifax, Hunslet and Leeds had all played in the West Yorkshire League in 1895-96 but did not play in a league in 1896-97. Sheffield United Reserves and Sheffield Wednesday Reserves both joined from the Sheffield Association League while Huddersfield had not previously played in any league. Mexborough, Sheffield United Reserves and Sheffield Wednesday Reserves had all also played in the Sheffield & North Derbyshire League in 1896-97. For the 1897-98 season, Sheffield United Reserves and Sheffield Wednesday Reserves both also joined the re-formed United Counties League.

1897-98

Sheffield United Reserves	18	11	5	2	55	15	27
Mexborough	18	12	2	4	51	22	26
Barnsley	18	11	3	4	62	27	25
Doncaster Rovers	18	11	2	5	61	26	24
Sheffield Wednesday Reserves	18	11	1	6	56	26	23
Hunslet	18	7	5	6	32	38	19
Leeds	18	5	1	12	26	52	11
Halifax	18	4	3	11	26	54	11
Bradford	18	3	3	12	26	72	9
Huddersfield	18	2	1	15	14	77	5

Barnsley moved to the Football League while both Leeds and Halifax disbanded. Dewsbury joined from the West Yorkshire League, Sheffield Club joined from the United Counties League and Wombwell Town joined while continuing to play in the Sheffield Association League.

1898-99

The games between the two Sheffield reserve teams and those when the Sheffield reserve teams played Doncaster Rovers and Mexborough also counted towards the Midland League, which the Sheffield reserve teams had just joined and so all four teams were also playing in that league.

Wombwell Town	18	13	4	1	48	11	30
Doncaster Rovers	18	13	1	4	78	20	27
Sheffield United Reserves	18	12	2	4	55	20	26
Sheffield Wednesday Reserves	18	12	1	5	58	27	25
Mexborough	18	11	2	5	40	28	24
Hunslet	18	7	3	8	38	27	17
Sheffield Club	18	4	1	13	36	65	9
Bradford	18	4	1	13	25	49	9
Huddersfield	18	4	1	13	15	73	9
Dewsbury	18	1	2	15	10	78	4

Six clubs moved to the Wharncliffe Charity Cup which had changed to a league format instead of a knock-out competition.

They were: Doncaster Rovers, Mexborough, Sheffield Club, Sheffield United Reserves, Sheffield Wednesday Reserves and Wombwell Town. Mexborough, Sheffield Wednesday Reserves and Sheffield Club all also joined the Sheffield Association League in which Wombwell Town continued while Doncaster Rovers also continued in the Midland League. Bradford disbanded. Ossett joined while continuing to play in the West Yorkshire League and Featherstone also joined. Featherstone are thought to have been a new club formed as a replacement for the disbanded Rugby Union club.

1899-1900

Hunslet	8	5	2	1	26	8	12
Huddersfield	8	5	2	1	14	7	12
Featherstone	8	3	2	3	23	22	8
Ossett	8	2	1	5	5	22	5
Dewsbury	8	1	1	6	13	21	3

Hunslet and Huddersfield were each awarded 2 points as Ossett did not fulfil their fixtures with them and later disbanded.
Hunslet moved to the Sheffield Association League.
Dewsbury and Huddersfield played only cup-ties and friendlies in 1900-01 and Featherstone are thought to have disbanded after just one season.

WEST YORKSHIRE LEAGUE 1902-1910

A "new" West Yorkshire League was formed at a meeting of the West Yorkshire Football Association held in the Green Dragon Hotel, Leeds on 14th May 1902. The Green Dragon was situated on what was then Guildford Street and is now The Headrow and after a period as the Guildford Hotel, the pub is now known as 115, the Headrow.

The 12 intended founder members were: Airedale, Altofts, Beeston Hill Parish Church, Dewsbury Celtic, Girlington, Huddersfield, Hunslet, Mirfield United, Oulton, Rawdon, Rothwell White Rose and Sowerby Bridge. However, Girlington disbanded in mid-July and were replaced by Morley.

Altofts, Beeston Hill Parish Church, Oulton and Rothwell White Rose all joined from the Leeds & District League; Dewsbury Celtic, Mirfield United and Morley all joined from the Heavy Woollen District League; Airedale and Rawdon both joined from the Bradford & District League; Hunslet joined from the Sheffield Association League; Sowerby Bridge joined from the Halifax & District League and Huddersfield also joined.

1902-03

The final table which has been found showed points only.

Altofts	18	30
Morley	18	25
Mirfield United	18	23
Huddersfield	18	18
Oulton	18	18
Beeston Hill Parish Church	18	15
Airedale	17	14
Sowerby Bridge	18	13
Rawdon	17	11
Rothwell White Rose	18	11

Rawdon vs Airedale was not played.

Airedale left the league but continued to play in the Bradford & District League. Bradford City Reserves and Heckmondwike both joined as newly formed clubs while Lindley joined from the Huddersfield & District League, Upper Armley Christ Church joined from the Leeds & District League and Dewsbury & Savile also joined. However, Lindley resigned and disbanded shortly before the start of the 1903-04 season and Sowerby Bridge were removed from the league at the same time because they also had disbanded.

1903-04 (+ Points)

	P	W	D	L	+Pt	Pts
Mirfield United	22	17	4	1	0	38
Bradford City Reserves	22	14	4	4	1	32
Oulton	22	13	3	6	1	29
Huddersfield	22	10	2	10	2	22
Rothwell White Rose	22	9	3	10	1	21
Altofts	22	8	4	10	0	20
Morley	22	8	4	10	2	20
Upper Armley Christ Church	22	8	3	11	2	19
Heckmondwike	22	8	2	12	2	18
Dewsbury & Savile	22	8	1	13	1	17
Rawdon	22	7	2	13	7	16
Beeston Hill Parish Church	22	5	2	15	1	12

+ Points. 10 games were not played and clubs' wins, draws and losses were adjusted depending on whether or not they were deemed to have defaulted in the unplayed games, producing the table shown above.

The total number of points added as a result of these adjustments is shown in the column headed "+ Points". The Goals For and Goals Against record was not published.

Rawdon left the league. Starbeck joined from the Harrogate & District League and Elland Ramsdenians joined from the Halifax & District League. A newly formed club also joined, initially as Hunslet, but it became Leeds City before the start of the season.

1904-05

Bradford City Reserves	26	19	5	2	90	29	43
Heckmondwike	26	17	4	5	69	31	38
Huddersfield	24	12	1	11	52	43	25
Dewsbury & Savile	23	10	5	8	40	33	25
Altofts	25	11	3	11	39	37	25
Morley	26	10	5	11	25	38	25
Mirfield United	24	10	3	11	44	43	23
Rothwell White Rose	24	8	7	9	38	45	23
Elland Ramsdenians	26	10	4	12	44	54	22
Oulton	25	9	3	13	41	53	21
Leeds City	24	7	7	10	33	49	21
Upper Armley Christ Church	24	8	4	12	33	34	20
Beeston Hill Parish Church	26	7	6	13	33	72	20
Starbeck	23	3	8	12	30	48	14

Elland Ramsdenians had 2 points deducted.
9 games were not played.
Leeds City moved to the Football League, Huddersfield disbanded and Dewsbury & Savile also left the league. Altofts Parish Church and Hunslet Woodville both joined.

A second division was formed with 9 clubs.

1905-06

Promoted clubs are shown in **bold** type.

Division One

Bradford City Reserves	23	20	2	1	42	
Heckmondwike	24	16	4	4	36	
Altofts Parish Church	21	10	7	4	27	
Morley	22	10	6	6	26	
Altofts	21	11	2	8	24	
Rothwell White Rose	23	7	8	8	22	
Upper Armley Christ Church	21	9	3	9	21	
Mirfield United	20	7	5	8	19	
Oulton	23	8	3	12	19	
Starbeck	20	8	1	11	17	
Hunslet Woodville	24	4	6	14	14	
Beeston Hill Parish Church	19	2	2	15	6	
Elland Ramsdenians	16	2	1	13	5	

Elland Ramsdenians resigned and disbanded in February.

Note: No final table has been found. The above was arrived at by taking a table published in the Bradford Weekly Telegraph on 13th April 1906 (that excluded For and Against goal records) and adding all subsequent published results. However, the results of 17 games were not found. It is known that Bradford City Reserves drew their one outstanding game but it is not known who their opponents were.

Beeston Hill Parish Church, Hunslet Woodville, Oulton and Rothwell White Rose all moved to the Leeds & District League, Bradford City Reserves moved to the Midland League and Upper Armley Christ Church disbanded. Cleckheaton, Goole Town and Selby Mizpah all joined.

Division Two

No table has been found.

The 9 members of the division were: Guiseley Celtic (1st), Bingley (2nd), Burley-in-Wharfedale, Menston, Otley, Ravensthorpe Clarence, Rawdon, Swaine Hill United and Thornhill Lees Albion.

Thornhill Lees Albion moved to the Heavy Woollen League. Bradford Rovers, Bradford St. Cuthbert's and White Abbey Wesleyans all joined from the Bradford & District League, Skipton Town joined from the Craven Amateur League having changed their name from Skipton, Bowling Old Lane joined as a newly formed club and Airedale joined.

1906-07

Division One

Heckmondwike	18	13	2	3	49	16	28
Guiseley Celtic	18	12	4	2	47	25	28
Goole Town	18	12	2	4	27	23	26
Mirfield United	18	8	4	6	37	26	20
Bingley	18	6	4	8	26	37	16
Altofts	18	4	6	8	20	23	14
Morley	18	5	4	9	32	39	14
Selby Mizpah	18	5	4	9	35	43	14
Starbeck	18	5	2	11	34	50	12
Cleckheaton	18	2	4	12	24	60	8

Altofts Parish Church resigned and disbanded in October and their record at the time was deleted: 3 2 0 1 4 13 2

Championship Play-off

Heckmondwike vs Guiseley Celtic   3-3
(Played at Bowling Old Lane on 13th April 1907)

Replay

Heckmondwike vs Guiseley Celtic   1-0
(Played at Valley Parade on 27th April 1907)

Bingley and Cleckheaton both disbanded. Castleford Town and Kippax Parish Church both joined from the Leeds & District League while Bradford Park Avenue Reserves and Wakefield City both joined as newly formed clubs.

Division Two

Swaine Hill United	20	16	0	4	69	36	32
Bradford St. Cuthbert's	20	15	2	3	69	23	32
Bowling Old Lane	20	13	1	6	46	34	27
Otley	20	11	1	8	60	28	23
Ravensthorpe Clarence	20	10	2	8	45	33	22
Burley-in-Wharfedale	20	8	3	9	39	57	19
Airedale	20	8	2	10	43	45	18
Skipton Town	20	6	1	13	30	60	13
White Abbey Wesleyans	20	5	3	12	29	66	13
Bradford Rovers	20	5	1	14	37	69	11
Menston	20	4	2	14	25	41	10

Rawdon either withdrew before the start of the season or after very few games had been played.

Championship Play-off

Swaine Hill United vs Bradford St. Cuthbert's   3-2
(Played at Bingley on 30th April 1907)

Airedale, Bradford St. Cuthbert's and White Abbey Wesleyans all left the league. Keighley Celtic and Shipley Celtic both joined from the Keighley & District League while Calverley, Dewsbury & Savile, Fairweather Green, Farsley, Girlington and Horsforth also all joined.

1907-08

Division One

Heckmondwike	22	17	3	2	37
Castleford Town	21	15	0	6	30
Selby Mizpah	22	11	3	8	25
Goole Town	22	10	5	7	25
Morley	22	10	4	8	24
Guiseley Celtic	20	11	2	7	24
Bradford Park Avenue Reserves	22	13	0	9	24
Mirfield United	21	10	3	8	23
Kippax Parish Church	22	6	5	11	17
Starbeck	22	5	4	13	14
Bowling Old Lane	22	3	2	17	8
Swaine Hill United	22	2	3	17	7

Note: The table above is the latest found. No goal record was published. Bradford Park Avenue Reserves had 2 points deducted.
Altofts and Wakefield City both resigned during the season and their records were deleted.
Bowling Old Lane, Bradford Park Avenue Reserves and Guiseley Celtic all left the legue. Barnoldswick United, Knaresborough, Rothwell White Rose and Skipton Town all joined.

Division Two

Burley-in-Wharfedale	25	20	2	3	81	21	42
Skipton Town	23	17	2	4	59	30	36
Otley	24	17	0	7	64	23	34
Shipley Celtic	23	13	2	8	42	28	28
Girlington	25	12	4	9	48	40	28
Calverley	25	13	1	11	73	55	27
Bradford Rovers	25	11	2	12	46	53	24
Dewsbury & Savile	23	9	4	10	58	58	22
Keighley Celtic	25	10	1	14	48	52	21
Horsforth	25	10	1	14	38	50	21
Fairweather Green	24	6	8	10	45	54	20
Farsley	25	7	2	16	31	59	16
Ravensthorpe Clarence	23	7	1	15	37	75	15
Menston	25	3	0	22	17	83	6

The table above is the latest found, taken from the Wharfedale & Airedale Observer on 1st May 1908.

Division Two closed down at the end of the season.

West Yorkshire League 1908-1910 + Yorkshire Combination 1910-1912

1908-09

Castleford Town	22	18	3	1	91	17	39
Goole Town	22	16	5	1	61	29	37
Morley	22	10	5	7	52	28	25
Mirfield United	22	10	4	8	53	51	24
Knaresborough	22	11	3	8	43	32	25
Starbeck	22	8	4	10	28	49	20
Kippax Parish Church	19	8	1	10	28	30	17
Heckmondwike	19	5	5	9	33	38	15
Barnoldswick United	20	7	1	12	31	42	15
Selby Mizpah	22	6	2	14	39	60	14
Rothwell White Rose	22	6	1	15	21	70	13
Skipton Town	20	5	0	15	26	60	10

Swaine Hill United resigned during the season. Their record was deleted.
Note: Different newspapers published different final tables, each of which contained at least one error. The table above has been compiled using the different versions and is thought to be most accurate available.

1909-10

Goole Town	12	8	1	3	25	9	17
Mirfield United	12	6	3	3	28	23	15
Huddersfield Town Reserves	7	6	0	1	15	4	12
Knaresborough	10	5	0	5	19	15	10
Heckmondwike	11	4	2	5	16	25	10
Starbeck	12	3	2	7	13	26	8
Selby Mizpah	12	1	2	9	15	31	4

The West Yorkshire League closed down at the end of the season.

YORKSHIRE COMBINATION 1910-1914

The idea of a league to cover the whole of Yorkshire had been discussed over several years and it finally came to fruition at the annual meeting of the West Yorkshire Football Association in early June 1910 when it was decided that the West Yorkshire League should be reconstructed as a county-wide competition.

A further meeting was held at the Hotel Metropole, King Street, Leeds on 16th June when 10 clubs became founder members of the new league, which was to be called the Yorkshire Combination. Five of the founder members had played in the West Yorkshire League in 1909-10 – Goole Town, Heckmondwike, Knaresborough, Mirfield United and Starbeck. Knaresborough were also members of the Northern League and continued to play in it in 1910-11, fielding their first team in both the Northern League and Yorkshire Combination, but Scarborough and York City both left the Northern League to join the Yorkshire Combination.

Bradford (Park Avenue) and Bradford City both moved their reserve sides from the Midland League to the new league and the 10th founder member were Morley who were playing in the West Yorkshire League in 1908-09 but did not play in any league in 1909-10.

1910-11

Bradford City Reserves	18	15	3	0	66	8	33
Scarborough	18	12	1	5	53	36	25
Mirfield United	18	11	3	4	41	31	25
Bradford Park Avenue Reserves	18	10	4	4	54	19	24
Goole Town	18	7	1	10	30	46	15
Morley	18	4	6	8	16	34	14
Heckmondwike	18	4	5	9	20	28	13
York City	18	5	3	10	17	38	13
Knaresborough	18	2	7	9	22	38	11
Starbeck	18	1	5	12	13	54	7

Starbeck moved to the Harrogate & District League. West Vale Ramblers joined from the Bradford & District League, Thornhill Lees Albion joined from the Heavy Woollen District League, Stourton United joined from the Leeds League, Halifax Town and Leeds United both joined as newly formed clubs and Fryston Colliery also joined. Knaresborough Town left the Northern League to concentrate on the Yorkshire Combination. Stanningley & Pudsey United Rugby Union club had been suspended *sine die* by the Rugby Football Union for including ex-Northern Union (now known as Rugby League) players in their teams and so decided to switch to instead play Association Football as Pudsey & Stanningley United, joining the Yorkshire Combination. They also formed a Northern Union club called Stanningley & Pudsey United shortly afterwards.

1911-12

Bradford City Reserves	26	20	3	3	98	25	43
Bradford Park Avenue Reserves	26	18	4	4	102	31	40
Goole Town	26	16	4	6	76	36	36
Scarborough	26	16	4	6	69	46	36
Morley	26	16	4	6	58	39	36
Mirfield United	26	14	6	6	55	32	34
Halifax Town	26	14	2	10	66	40	30
York City	26	8	4	14	37	70	20
Fryston Colliery	26	9	1	16	50	61	19
Knaresborough	26	6	6	14	48	66	18
West Vale Ramblers	26	7	2	17	36	91	16
Thornhill Lees Albion	26	6	3	17	35	81	15
Stourton United	26	4	4	18	32	77	12
Heckmondwike	26	2	5	19	23	90	9

Leeds United and Pudsey & Stanningley United both resigned and disbanded during the season and their records were deleted. Bradford City Reserves moved to the Central League and Stourton United also left the league. Stourton appear to have then been inactive until they joined the Leeds & District Junior League in 1914. Goole Town, Halifax Town and York City all moved to the Midland League and replaced their first teams with their reserves in the Yorkshire Combination. This was the first league that Halifax Town Reserves had joined.

Huddersfield Town Reserves joined from the Midland League and Hebden Bridge joined from the Bradford & District League.

1912-13

Huddersfield Town Reserves	24	19	1	4	110	27	39
Bradford Park Avenue Reserves	24	16	4	4	83	24	36
Mirfield United	24	15	6	3	63	25	36
Fryston Colliery	24	15	2	7	63	63	32
Goole Town Reserves	24	11	3	10	48	33	25
Scarborough	24	10	4	10	57	51	24
Morley	24	8	7	9	40	48	23
Hebden Bridge	24	10	2	12	48	65	22
Heckmondwike	23	8	3	12	48	64	19
York City Reserves	24	8	2	14	44	64	18
Knaresborough	24	6	5	13	28	83	17
Thornhill Lees Albion	24	4	2	18	25	72	10
Halifax Town Reserves	23	4	1	18	32	70	9

One game was not played.
West Vale Ramblers resigned from the league in November 1912 and their record was deleted. They joined the Bradford & District League in 1913. Huddersfield Town Reserves moved to the Central League, Knaresborough moved to the York & District League and Morley disbanded. Halifax Town Reserves also left and did not play in a league in 1913-14.
Marsden United joined the league.

1913-14

Bradford Park Avenue Reserves	18	14	0	4	65	24	28
Mirfield United	18	11	3	4	48	21	25
Goole Town Reserves	18	9	3	6	34	33	21
Fryston Colliery	17	7	3	7	31	22	17
Scarborough	18	8	1	9	41	42	17
Marsden United	17	7	1	9	35	35	15
York City Reserves	18	6	3	9	29	36	15
Heckmondwike	17	5	4	8	27	38	14
Thornhill Lees Albion	17	6	0	11	19	38	12
Hebden Bridge	18	6	0	12	24	64	12

The results of the two outstanding games have not been found.

Bradford Park Avenue Reserves and Heckmondwike both moved to the Midland League, Scarborough moved to the Northern League, Hebden Bridge moved to the Lancashire Combination, Goole Town Reserves moved to the Doncaster & District League, Marsden United moved to the Huddersfield League and Fryston Colliery and Thornhill Lees Albion both moved to the Leeds Senior League. Mirfield United also moved to the Leeds Senior League but disbanded in October 1914.

The Yorkshire Combination then closed down.

Fryston Colliery were reported as having played two Yorkshire Combination games in September 1914, beating Calverley 1-0 on 5th September and Mirfield United 8-1 on 12th September but it seems likely that these were misreported as Yorkshire Combination games and were probably Leeds Senior League games.

Note: Thanks are due to Rob Grillo who very kindly sent us information from his own personal records on the development of football in the West Riding of Yorkshire before 1915. Much of that information has been included in the tables above and more detail on the history of West Riding football in those early years is included in Rob's book "A Noble Winter's Game". Visit www.robgrillo.co.uk for further information.

YORKSHIRE LEAGUE (II) 1920-1982

The idea of a league to cover the whole of Yorkshire and act as a stepping stone between local football and League football was promoted by the West Riding Football Association who called a meeting held at the Griffin Hotel Leeds on 27th April 1920. The meeting was attended by delegates from Bradford (Park Avenue), Goole Shipyards, Harrogate, Hebden Bridge, Horsforth, Leeds University, Leeds Y.M.C.A., Rowntrees (York), Scarborough, Wakefield City and Yorkshire Amateurs.

Following further meetings and discussions, the new league was formally launched at another meeting in Leeds, on 26th May. There were 10 clubs who became members immediately with others able to join before a set cut-off date. The 10 clubs were Acomb, Bradford (Park Avenue) Reserves, Dewsbury & Savile, Goole Shipyards, Harrogate, Rowntrees (York), Selby Town, Wakefield City, York Y.M.C.A. and Yorkshire Amateurs. Fryston Colliery Welfare, Wath Athletic and Wombwell also joined before the deadline, making up a 13-team league.

Acomb, Selby Town and Rowntrees (York) all joined from the York & District League, Goole Shipyards joined from the Goole & District League, Harrogate joined from the West Riding League, Fryston Colliery Welfare joined from the Castleford & District League and Wath Athletic joined from the Sheffield Association League. Wakefield City, Wombwell and York Y.M.C.A. were all newly-formed clubs and Bradford (Park Avenue) Reserves was a newly-formed team. No league has been found in 1919-20 in which Dewsbury & Savile or Yorkshire Amateurs were playing.

1920-21

Bradford (Park Avenue) Reserves	24	18	3	3	85	28	39
Wombwell	24	16	4	4	67	18	36
Wath Athletic	24	15	4	5	56	29	34
Harrogate	24	15	3	6	66	41	33
Selby Town	24	11	5	8	55	47	27
Wakefield City	24	10	6	8	41	33	26
Goole Shipyards	24	10	4	10	52	48	24
Rowntrees (York)	24	9	2	13	42	45	20
Acomb	24	8	3	13	43	66	19
Fryston Colliery Welfare	24	7	5	12	35	59	19
Dewsbury & Savile	24	7	2	15	35	63	16
Yorkshire Amateurs	24	6	3	15	42	66	15
York Y.M.C.A.	24	2	0	22	18	95	4

Harrogate, Wakefield City, Wath Athletic and Wombwell all moved to the Midland League, placing their reserves in the Yorkshire League, Wath Athletic Reserves and Wombwell Reserves both having joined from the Sheffield Association League. Goole Shipyards moved to the Goole & District League and Dewsbury & Savile also left the league. Brodsworth Main and Hook Shipyards (Goole) both joined from the Doncaster & District League, Houghton Main joined from the Barnsley Association League, Doncaster Rovers Reserves joined from the Sheffield Association League while both Castleford Town Reserves and Halifax Town Reserves joined as newly-formed teams.

1921-22

Houghton Main	32	24	4	4	86	25	52
Bradford (Park Avenue) Reserves	32	23	4	5	119	36	50
Brodsworth Main	32	20	7	5	81	34	47
Wombwell Reserves	32	21	4	7	86	45	46
Halifax Town Reserves	32	18	5	9	87	40	41
Doncaster Rovers Reserves	32	17	4	11	84	40	38
Selby Town	32	15	7	10	94	51	37
Rowntrees (York)	32	14	9	9	60	44	37
Acomb	32	18	1	13	61	86	37
Wath Athletic Reserves	32	14	5	13	80	59	33
Fryston Colliery Welfare	32	13	2	17	76	65	28
Harrogate Reserves	32	10	5	17	62	74	25
Yorkshire Amateurs	32	9	4	19	69	72	22
Castleford Town Reserves	32	7	6	19	49	86	20
Hook Shipyards (Goole)	32	7	4	21	40	51	18
Wakefield City Reserves	32	3	4	25	33	140	10
York Y.M.C.A.	32	1	1	30	23	239	3

Wath Athletic Reserves moved to the Sheffield Association League, Rowntrees (York) and York Y.M.C.A. both moved to the York & District League and Castleford Town disbanded their reserve side. Hook Shipyards (Goole) also left the league. Bentley Colliery and Frickley Colliery both joined from the Sheffield Association League while Castleford & Allerton United and Rothwell Athletic both joined from the West Riding League. Harrogate and Wakefield City rejoined from the Midland League replacing their reserves with their first teams. Harrogate Reserves moved to the Harrogate & District League.

1922-23

Bradford (Park Avenue) Reserves	30	24	2	4	119	43	50
Halifax Town Reserves	30	22	3	5	90	37	47
Frickley Colliery	30	18	3	9	58	35	39
Castleford & Allerton United	30	17	4	9	58	40	38
Doncaster Rovers Reserves	30	14	8	8	52	38	36
Wakefield City	30	11	11	8	53	39	33
Selby Town	30	14	5	11	56	52	33
Wombwell Reserves	30	11	9	10	55	44	31
Brodsworth Main	30	11	9	10	51	56	31
Bentley Colliery	30	12	5	13	57	52	29
Fryston Colliery Welfare	30	9	6	15	45	48	24
Yorkshire Amateurs	30	8	7	15	49	78	23
Harrogate	30	8	6	16	30	50	22
Rothwell Athletic	30	6	5	19	27	81	17
Houghton Main	30	5	5	20	36	76	15
Acomb	30	4	4	22	42	108	12

Doncaster Rovers Reserves moved to the Midland League and Houghton Main moved to the Barnsley Association League, changing their name to Darfield. Acomb also left the league. Methley Perseverance and Altofts West Riding Colliery both joined from the West Riding League, Leeds Harehills joined from the West Yorkshire Amateur League, Monckton Athletic joined from the Barnsley Association League and York City's newly formed reserve team also joined.

1923-24

Methley Perseverance	34	24	6	4	84	24	54
Frickley Colliery	34	22	8	4	96	41	52
Bradford (Park Avenue) Reserves	34	22	5	7	96	38	49
Monckton Athletic	34	17	8	9	71	41	42
Altofts West Riding Colliery	34	17	5	12	67	47	39
Halifax Town Reserves	34	16	6	12	66	56	38
Brodsworth Main	34	15	7	12	62	65	37
Leeds Harehills	34	14	7	13	51	54	35
Wakefield City	34	15	5	14	51	54	35
Castleford & Allerton United	34	13	7	14	51	52	33
Harrogate	34	14	3	17	69	73	31
York City Reserves	34	10	9	15	36	58	29
Bentley Colliery	34	10	8	16	46	56	28
Wombwell Reserves	34	10	6	18	46	77	26
Fryston Colliery Welfare	34	10	5	19	46	60	25
Selby Town	34	10	4	20	65	81	24
Yorkshire Amateurs	34	8	4	22	50	99	20
Rothwell Athletic	34	6	3	25	28	106	15

Bradford (Park Avenue) Reserves and Halifax Town Reserves both moved to the Midland Combination and Frickley Colliery moved to the Midland League but were replaced by their reserves who joined from the Sheffield Association League. Wombwell Reserves moved to the Barnsley Association League, Leeds Harehills moved to the Leeds Senior Amateur League, Rothwell Athletic moved to the West Yorkshire Amateur League and Yorkshire Amateurs moved to the Leeds Alliance. Bridlington Town joined from the East Riding County League, Bullcroft Colliery joined from the Sheffield Association League while Goole Town and Leeds City also both joined as newly re-formed clubs.

1924-25

Brodsworth Main	30	21	4	5	73	28	46
Selby Town	30	17	6	7	77	57	40
Castleford & Allerton United	30	16	6	8	66	37	38
Fryston Colliery Welfare	30	17	3	10	58	41	37
Goole Town	30	15	6	9	49	46	36
Leeds City	30	13	7	10	59	44	33
Harrogate	30	12	7	11	46	49	31
Methley Perseverance	30	10	8	12	59	64	28
Bridlington Town	30	11	6	13	55	67	28
Altofts West Riding Colliery	30	9	8	13	30	44	26
Frickley Colliery Reserves	30	11	3	16	45	48	25
Bullcroft Colliery	30	11	3	16	49	66	25
Bentley Colliery	30	9	7	14	40	61	25
Wakefield City	30	7	9	14	38	48	23
York City Reserves	30	7	6	17	48	65	20
Monckton Athletic	30	8	3	19	40	59	19

Bentley Colliery, Bullcroft Colliery and Frickley Colliery Reserves all moved to the newly formed Doncaster & District Senior League. Scarborough Penguins joined from the Scarborough & District League, Selby Olympia joined from the York & District League and Brighouse joined as a newly formed club.

1925-26

Methley Perseverance	28	20	4	4	99	36	44
Selby Town	28	20	4	4	73	46	44
Altofts West Riding Colliery	28	17	3	8	76	54	37
Leeds City	28	15	4	9	84	55	34
Harrogate	28	14	5	9	62	52	33
Brodsworth Main	28	13	5	10	81	66	31
Monckton Athletic	28	11	7	10	84	82	29
Scarborough Penguins	28	12	3	13	56	68	27
Castleford & Allerton United	28	11	2	15	62	61	24
Bridlington Town	28	9	6	13	55	69	24
Goole Town	28	9	6	13	49	72	24
Selby Olympia	28	8	5	15	66	75	21
York City Reserves	28	7	4	17	53	76	18
Wakefield City	28	6	4	18	35	71	16
Fryston Colliery Welfare	28	4	6	18	39	77	14

Brighouse were expelled on 23rd February 1926 for non-fulfilment of fixtures. Their record was deleted: 10 3 0 7 18 40 6
Castleford Town joined from the Midland League and Scarborough joined from the Northern League. Fryston Colliery Welfare left the league and are thought not to have played in a league in 1926-27 before moving to the Leeds Amateur Senior League for the 1927-28 season. Selby Olympia became known as O.C.O. Selby, a shortened form of the Olympia Oil & Cake Company (Selby).

1926-27

Harrogate	30	21	6	3	102	51	48
Castleford Town	30	20	5	5	87	37	45
Selby Town	30	19	5	6	94	48	43
Goole Town	30	17	3	10	92	71	37
Scarborough Penguins	30	17	1	12	72	63	35
O.C.O. Selby	30	15	4	11	67	46	34
Castleford & Allerton United	30	14	6	10	66	56	34
York City Reserves	30	10	8	12	73	54	28
Brodsworth Main	30	12	4	14	63	77	28
Scarborough	30	10	7	13	74	69	27
Leeds City	30	11	4	15	69	59	26
Monckton Athletic	30	11	2	17	58	94	24
Methley Perseverance	30	10	3	17	69	111	23
Altofts West Riding Colliery	30	10	3	17	42	74	23
Bridlington Town	30	9	3	18	52	70	21
Wakefield City	30	0	4	26	24	123	4

Scarborough moved to the Midland League, Monckton Athletic moved to the Barnsley Association League and Leeds City disbanded.

Yorkshire League (II) 1927-1932

1927-28

Goole Town	24	17	3	4	88	47	37
Selby Town	24	16	4	4	88	35	36
Altofts West Riding Colliery	24	16	4	4	73	31	36
Castleford Town	24	17	2	5	89	47	36
Harrogate	24	15	3	6	85	46	33
Bridlington Town	23	14	2	7	74	55	30
Brodsworth Main	24	9	4	11	57	59	22
O.C.O. Selby	24	9	2	13	49	60	20
York City Reserves	22	8	2	12	38	63	18
Castleford & Allerton United	24	6	4	14	62	83	16
Scarborough Penguins	23	5	2	16	56	82	12
Methley Perseverance	20	2	2	16	24	67	6
Wakefield City	24	1	0	23	31	134	2

Methley Perseverance were unable to complete their fixtures because of extended runs in local cup competitions.
Castleford & Allerton United moved into junior football after losing their Lock Lane ground and Wakefield City disbanded. Bradford (Park Avenue) Reserves and Halifax Town Reserves both joined from the Midland Combination, Bradford City Reserves joined from the Central League, Pontefract Borough joined from the Castleford & District League and Hull City's newly formed "A" side also joined.

1928-29

Bradford (Park Avenue) Reserves	30	28	2	0	191	23	58
Selby Town	30	18	5	7	73	74	41
Bradford City Reserves	30	18	2	10	108	52	38
Halifax Town Reserves	30	15	7	8	87	47	37
Goole Town	30	15	3	12	81	82	33
Methley Perseverance	30	14	3	13	76	88	31
York City Reserves	30	13	5	12	61	85	31
Bridlington Town	30	13	2	15	93	71	28
Altofts West Riding Colliery	30	11	5	14	95	98	27
O.C.O. Selby	30	9	7	14	77	96	25
Scarborough Reserves	30	11	3	16	60	81	25
Hull City "A"	30	11	2	17	73	85	24
Castleford Town	30	8	7	15	77	100	23
Harrogate	30	9	5	16	56	90	23
Brodsworth Main	30	9	2	19	63	114	20
Pontefract Borough	30	7	2	21	76	148	16

Scarborough Penguins merged with Scarborough on 26th October 1928 at which point Scarborough Penguins became Scarborough Reserves. Bradford (Park Avenue) Reserves moved to the Midland League and Castleford Town disbanded. Leeds United "A" joined as a newly formed team.

1929-30

Bradford City Reserves	26	19	4	3	100	44	42
Leeds United "A"	26	17	6	3	86	29	40
Harrogate	26	15	4	7	73	49	34
Scarborough Reserves	26	15	4	7	52	35	34
Goole Town	26	12	5	9	60	45	29
Selby Town	26	13	1	12	76	69	27
Bridlington Town	26	11	4	11	54	56	26
Halifax Town Reserves	25	9	5	11	53	53	23
York City Reserves	26	9	4	13	69	72	22
Huddersfield Town "A"	26	5	9	12	39	57	19
Brodsworth Main	26	7	5	14	35	57	19
Hull City "A"	25	8	2	15	58	93	18
O.C.O. Selby	26	5	5	16	41	70	15
Altofts West Riding Colliery	26	6	2	18	42	103	14

Halifax Town Reserves vs Hull City "A" was not played.
Methley Perseverance were taken over by Huddersfield Town and changed their name to Huddersfield Town "A" on 20th December 1929.
Pontefract Borough resigned and disbanded in February 1930 and their record at the time was deleted: 18 1 2 15 17 138 4

Bradford City Reserves moved to the Midland League, Altofts West Riding Colliery moved to the West Riding County Amateur League, Hull City disbanded their "A" team and Scarborough disbanded their reserve team. East Riding Amateurs joined as a newly formed club and Yorkshire Amateurs joined having played only friendlies and cup-ties in 1929-30.

1930-31

As there were only 12 clubs in membership of the league, it was decided to run a subsidiary competition.

Leeds United "A"	22	19	1	2	103	29	39
York City Reserves	22	18	0	4	87	40	36
Selby Town	22	13	5	4	81	50	31
Goole Town	22	13	3	6	68	40	29
Yorkshire Amateurs	22	10	2	10	52	51	22
Huddersfield Town "A"	22	10	1	11	59	51	21
Halifax Town Reserves	22	7	3	12	49	77	17
Harrogate	22	8	0	14	71	87	16
Bridlington Town	22	6	4	12	48	72	16
O.C.O. Selby	22	7	1	14	51	75	15
Brodsworth Main	22	7	1	14	44	83	15
East Riding Amateurs	22	3	1	18	37	95	7

York City Reserves moved to the Midland League, Harrogate moved to the Northern League, Brodsworth Main moved to the Doncaster & District Senior League, O.C.O. Selby moved to the York & District League and East Riding Amateurs moved to the East Riding County League.

Subsidiary Competition – Section A

York City Reserves	10	9	0	1	46	17	18
Selby Town	10	5	1	4	28	27	11
Bridlington Town	9	4	1	4	27	25	9
Goole Town	9	4	0	5	22	22	8
East Riding Amateurs	10	2	3	5	23	39	7
O.C.O. Selby	10	2	1	7	15	31	5

One game was not played.

Subsidiary Competition – Section B

Leeds United "A"	10	9	1	0	47	14	19
Yorkshire Amateurs	10	6	3	1	28	16	15
Huddersfield Town "A"	10	5	1	4	22	23	11
Halifax Town Reserves	10	2	2	6	25	35	6
Harrogate	10	2	1	7	15	41	5
Brodsworth Main	10	2	0	8	20	28	4

Subsidiary Competition – Final

Leeds United "A" vs York City Reserves   5-4
(Played at Goole on 2nd May 1931)

1931-32

As there were only 7 clubs in membership of the league, it was decided to run two separate league competitions with the two clubs finishing top of each table playing-off to decide the league championship.

First Competition

Huddersfield Town "A"	12	7	1	4	28	18	15
Selby Town	12	6	3	3	30	23	15
Leeds United "A"	12	6	2	4	28	18	14
Halifax Town Reserves	12	6	0	6	29	26	12
Yorkshire Amateurs	12	6	0	6	35	35	12
Goole Town	12	4	2	6	18	37	10
Bridlington Town	12	2	2	8	24	35	6

Second Competition

Yorkshire Amateurs	12	6	4	2	26	18	16
Halifax Town Reserves	12	7	0	5	31	25	14
Selby Town	12	5	4	3	25	21	14
Leeds United "A"	12	4	4	4	33	20	12
Huddersfield Town "A"	12	3	5	4	22	29	11
Goole Town	12	3	4	5	19	18	10
Bridlington Town	12	3	1	8	23	48	7

Brodsworth Main and Thorne Colliery both joined from the Doncaster & District Senior League and Sheffield University also joined.

Championship Decider

Huddersfield Town "A" vs Yorkshire Amateurs 1-0

(Played at South Kirkby Colliery on 4th May 1933)

1932-33

There were 10 clubs in membership of the league and so it was again decided to run two separate league competitions. The first competition would decide the championship and there would also be a Subsidiary Competition.

Yorkshire League

Selby Town	18	13	3	2	58	20	29
Leeds United "A"	18	12	3	3	45	25	27
Huddersfield Town "A"	18	10	5	3	55	31	25
Goole Town	18	11	2	5	41	24	24
Yorkshire Amateurs	18	9	5	4	46	26	23
Halifax Town Reserves	18	7	2	9	41	46	16
Brodsworth Main	18	5	5	8	36	46	15
Thorne Colliery	18	3	2	13	28	60	8
Bridlington Town	18	3	2	13	31	65	8
Sheffield University	18	2	1	15	28	66	5

Brodsworth Main, Sheffield University and Yorkshire Amateurs did not take part in the Second Competition in order to avoid fixture congestion.

Subsidiary Competition

Huddersfield Town "A"	12	8	1	3	38	13	17
Goole Town	12	7	1	4	31	21	15
Leeds United "A"	12	6	2	4	32	25	14
Selby Town	12	6	1	5	23	19	13
Bridlington Town	12	5	1	6	25	37	11
Halifax Town Reserves	12	4	2	6	21	29	10
Thorne Colliery	12	1	2	9	11	37	4

Upton Colliery joined from the Doncaster & District Senior League, Bradford City "A" joined as a newly-formed team and South Kirkby Colliery joined having been playing in both the Sheffield Association League and the Doncaster & District Senior League.

1933-34

Huddersfield Town "A"	24	16	3	5	62	25	35
South Kirkby Colliery	24	14	6	4	42	24	34
Selby Town	24	15	3	6	71	36	33
Upton Colliery	24	11	6	7	63	54	28
Leeds United "A"	24	12	3	9	57	45	27
Bridlington Town	24	11	4	9	42	33	26
Halifax Town Reserves	24	10	5	9	45	41	25
Yorkshire Amateurs	24	10	4	10	42	43	24
Goole Town	24	11	1	12	68	55	23
Bradford City "A"	24	9	5	10	55	64	23
Thorne Colliery	24	7	5	12	53	58	19
Sheffield University	24	2	4	18	30	87	8
Brodsworth Main	24	3	1	20	26	91	7

York City Reserves joined from the Midland League, Altofts West Riding Colliery joined from the West Riding County Amateur League, Sheffield United "A" joined from the Sheffield Association League, Castleford Town joined as a newly-formed club and Sheffield Wednesday "A" joined as a newly-formed team.

1934-35

Selby Town	34	25	2	7	127	58	52
Upton Colliery	34	24	4	6	88	46	52
Sheffield Wednesday "A"	34	23	4	7	125	60	50
Leeds United "A"	34	19	8	7	90	59	46
Yorkshire Amateurs	34	19	5	10	85	66	43
Huddersfield Town "A"	34	17	8	9	79	53	42
Halifax Town Reserves	34	18	4	12	110	66	40
South Kirkby Colliery	34	13	9	12	83	66	35
York City Reserves	34	16	2	16	82	79	34
Bradford City "A"	34	11	10	13	73	74	32
Sheffield United "A"	34	12	4	18	87	104	28
Thorne Colliery	34	11	5	18	79	92	27
Castleford Town	34	11	3	20	74	114	25
Bridlington Town	34	10	4	20	77	108	24
Altofts West Riding Colliery	34	9	6	19	69	111	24
Goole Town	34	9	6	19	69	119	24
Brodsworth Main	34	7	5	22	52	115	19
Sheffield University	34	5	5	24	49	108	15

Brodsworth Main disbanded. Barnoldswick Town joined from the West Lancashire League, Worksop Town joined from the Central Combination and Bradford (Park Avenue) "A" joined as a newly-formed team.

1935-36

Selby Town	38	25	5	8	144	67	55
Sheffield Wednesday "A"	38	26	3	9	124	62	55
Worksop Town	38	23	7	8	116	60	53
Thorne Colliery	38	24	5	9	113	65	53
Bradford City "A"	38	21	8	9	111	66	50
Leeds United "A"	38	20	6	12	112	70	46
Huddersfield Town "A"	38	19	6	13	88	59	44
Upton Colliery	38	19	5	14	78	75	43
South Kirkby Colliery	38	16	10	12	102	83	42
Goole Town	38	17	8	13	88	76	42
Halifax Town Reserves	38	17	6	15	91	70	40
York City Reserves	38	14	6	18	99	103	34
Bridlington Town	38	13	6	19	76	104	32
Yorkshire Amateurs	38	13	6	19	75	102	32
Altofts West Riding Colliery	38	14	4	20	101	123	32
Barnoldswick Town	38	11	8	19	83	125	30
Bradford (Park Avenue) "A"	38	10	9	19	83	119	29
Sheffield United "A"	38	12	5	21	95	91	29
Castleford Town	38	4	5	29	61	157	13
Sheffield University	38	2	2	34	30	193	6

Sheffield University moved to the Sheffield Association League and Dinnington Athletic joined from the Sheffield Association League.

1936-37

Goole Town	36	23	8	5	101	49	54
York City Reserves	36	23	3	10	99	59	49
Upton Colliery	36	20	9	7	108	69	49
South Kirkby Colliery	36	19	8	9	109	74	46
Worksop Town	36	17	12	7	86	60	46
Huddersfield Town "A"	36	18	7	11	75	55	43
Sheffield Wednesday "A"	36	17	6	13	94	73	40
Leeds United "A"	36	17	5	14	114	75	39
Dinnington Athletic	36	15	7	14	90	79	37
Selby Town	36	14	6	16	92	87	34
Bridlington Town	36	14	5	17	76	81	33
Halifax Town Reserves	36	14	5	17	77	84	33
Bradford City "A"	36	13	4	19	83	92	30
Sheffield United "A"	36	12	5	19	93	104	29
Thorne Colliery	36	11	6	19	73	103	28
Bradford (Park Avenue) "A"	36	9	10	17	72	112	28
Yorkshire Amateurs	36	10	6	20	61	89	26
Altofts West Riding Colliery	36	6	8	22	70	145	20
Ollerton Colliery	36	9	2	25	65	148	20

Castleford Town disbanded in December 1936 and their fixtures and record were taken over by Ollerton Colliery who also continued playing in the Central Combination:

	16	0	0	16	17	91	0

Yorkshire League (II) 1937-1945

Barnoldswick Town resigned from the league on 2nd February 1937 and their record was deleted: 19   2   1   16   28   95   5
They joined the Nelson, Colne & District Amateur League in 1937-38. Bradford City disbanded their "A" team. Bolsover Colliery joined from the Central Combination and Barnsley "A" joined as a newly-formed team. Ollerton Colliery left the Central Combination which closed down.

1937-38

York City Reserves	38	26	7	5	118	60	59
Ollerton Colliery	38	23	5	10	101	53	51
Selby Town	38	23	4	11	114	62	50
Dinnington Athletic	38	21	7	10	91	72	49
Worksop Town	38	19	5	14	82	59	43
Bridlington Town	38	17	9	12	74	61	43
Leeds United "A"	38	18	6	14	83	54	42
Huddersfield Town "A"	38	15	10	13	74	66	40
Sheffield Wednesday "A"	38	17	4	17	100	91	38
Halifax Town Reserves	38	17	4	17	84	85	38
Goole Town	38	17	4	17	61	83	38
Bolsover Colliery	38	15	6	17	78	84	36
Thorne Colliery	38	15	5	18	75	76	35
Yorkshire Amateurs	38	13	8	17	65	82	34
Barnsley "A"	38	15	3	20	72	81	33
Sheffield United "A"	38	12	7	19	76	85	31
South Kirkby Colliery	38	11	7	20	61	82	29
Upton Colliery	38	11	5	22	59	91	27
Bradford (Park Avenue) "A"	38	11	5	22	63	108	27
Altofts West Riding Colliery	38	7	3	28	39	135	17

Bradford (Park Avenue) "A" left the league.
Chesterfield "A" joined from the Derbyshire Senior League.

1938-39

Sheffield Wednesday "A"	38	31	3	4	138	44	65
Leeds United "A"	38	30	1	7	125	47	61
York City Reserves	38	24	8	6	121	44	56
Ollerton Colliery	38	21	5	12	83	64	47
Huddersfield Town "A"	38	19	8	11	91	71	46
Bridlington Town	38	17	11	10	99	71	45
Worksop Town	38	18	8	12	92	64	44
Chesterfield "A"	38	15	9	14	77	69	39
Upton Colliery	38	16	6	16	78	76	38
Dinnington Athletic	38	14	8	16	85	78	36
Sheffield United "A"	38	13	9	16	103	85	35
Barnsley "A"	38	12	11	15	87	87	35
Thorne Colliery	38	15	5	18	80	90	35
South Kirkby Colliery	38	13	8	17	90	94	34
Goole Town	38	14	4	20	74	91	32
Halifax Town Reserves	38	11	8	19	81	112	30
Bolsover Colliery	38	11	8	19	82	125	30
Yorkshire Amateurs	38	10	6	22	58	103	26
Selby Town	38	9	6	23	84	118	24
Altofts West Riding Colliery	38	0	2	36	30	225	2

Bolsover Colliery moved to the Sheffield Association League while both Dinnington Athletic and Altofts West Riding Colliery ceased activity during the 1939-40 season. Gainsborough Trinity Reserves and Scunthorpe & Lindsey United Reserves both joined from the North Lindsey League and Ransome & Marles (Newark) joined from the Notts Alliance.

1939-40

15 games had been played before war was declared on 3rd September and the league immediately closed down. The table produced by those 15 games is shown below:

Leeds United "A"	2	2	0	0	4	2	4
Bridlington Town	1	1	0	0	2	0	2
Goole Town	1	1	0	0	4	0	2
Sheffield Wednesday "A"	1	1	0	0	7	1	2
Barnsley "A"	1	1	0	0	4	1	2
Scunthorpe & Lindsey United Res.	1	1	0	0	4	1	2
Chesterfield "A"	1	1	0	0	3	1	2
Huddersfield Town "A"	2	1	0	1	6	5	2
Ollerton Colliery	2	1	0	1	1	1	2
Sheffield United "A"	2	1	0	1	5	5	2
Halifax Town Reserves	2	1	0	1	4	5	2
Yorkshire Amateurs	3	1	0	2	6	8	2
York City Reserves	2	1	0	1	2	4	2
Gainsborough Trinity Reserves	2	0	1	1	3	4	1
Thorne Colliery	2	0	1	1	1	2	1
South Kirkby Colliery	1	0	0	1	2	5	0
Upton Colliery	1	0	0	1	1	7	0
Worksop Town	1	0	0	1	0	2	0
Selby Town	1	0	0	1	0	1	0
Ransome & Marles (Newark)	1	0	0	1	0	4	0

The league attempted to form a war-time competition but only Ransome & Marles (Newark), South Kirkby Colliery, Thorne Colliery and Upton Colliery were able to continue, the remaining sides either being unable to raise a team or finding travel too difficult.

1940-45

A fresh attempt to revive the league was made for the 1940-41 season but only 5 clubs were in a position to play and so the league then decided to cease all activity until the war had ended.

The league finally got back underway in 1945. Pre-war members Goole Town, Halifax Town Reserves, Huddersfield Town "A" Scunthorpe & Lindsey United Reserves, Selby Town, South Kirkby Colliery, Thorne Colliery, York City Reserves and Yorkshire Amateurs all rejoined but Barnsley "A", Bridlington Town, Gainsborough Trinity Reserves, Leeds United "A", Sheffield United "A" and Sheffield Wednesday "A" were not ready to resume playing.

Of the other 5 pre-war members who did not rejoin, Ollerton Colliery and Ransome & Marles (Newark) both moved to the Midland League, Chesterfield "A" moved to the Sheffield Association League while Worksop Town had disbanded. Upton Colliery had intended to rejoin the league but an underground fire that started on 29th April 1945 in the colliery was unable to be brought under control for several days and the colliery had to be closed for many months until it could be made safe again.

There were 6 new clubs who joined the league:
Bradford City Reserves had been pre-war members of the Midland League, Firbeck Main Colliery had been pre-war members of the Worksop Senior League, Ossett Town had been pre-war members of the Leeds League which changed its name to the West Yorkshire League in June 1939 while Hull Amateurs and Wombwell Athletic both joined as newly-formed clubs. Bradford United also joined and was attached to East Bierley of the West Riding Amateur League but identified itself as a separate club so that it could field professionals.

Yorkshire League (II) 1945-1950

1945-46

Wombwell Athletic	28	24	0	4	103	36	48
Thorne Colliery	28	17	5	6	67	50	39
Huddersfield Town "A"	28	16	6	6	82	58	38
Goole Town	28	11	7	10	81	54	29
Bradford United	28	12	5	11	72	60	29
Yorkshire Amateurs	28	13	3	12	72	61	29
Scunthorpe & Lindsey United Res.	28	11	6	11	57	71	28
Firbeck Main Colliery	28	11	5	12	78	74	27
Bradford City Reserves	28	11	5	12	71	71	27
Selby Town	28	9	8	11	65	76	26
York City Reserves	28	8	10	10	48	57	26
Halifax Town Reserves	28	8	7	13	52	83	23
Ossett Town	28	8	4	16	52	77	20
South Kirkby Colliery	28	5	6	17	51	74	16
Hull Amateurs	28	6	3	19	51	100	15

Bradford City Reserves moved to the Midland League and Firbeck Main Colliery also left the league. Chesterfield "A" joined from the Sheffield Association League, Keighley Town joined from the Bradford Amateur League while Sheffield Wednesday "A", Leeds United "A" and Gainsborough Trinity Reserves all rejoined after being inactive in 1945-46. Harworth Colliery joined, having played in the Doncaster & District Senior League in 1939-40 and Upton Colliery rejoined as the colliery itself had now reopened.

1946-47

Thorne Colliery	38	25	6	7	117	56	56
Bradford United	38	25	5	8	151	68	55
Huddersfield Town "A"	38	21	7	10	125	64	49
York City Reserves	38	22	5	11	115	74	49
Ossett Town	38	20	9	9	96	87	49
Selby Town	38	20	6	12	106	75	46
Halifax Town Reserves	38	18	9	11	109	77	45
Wombwell Athletic	38	20	4	14	114	95	44
Scunthorpe & Lindsey United Res.	38	20	3	15	105	74	43
Chesterfield "A"	38	15	9	14	101	83	39
Goole Town	38	16	5	17	88	87	37
Harworth Colliery	38	14	8	16	82	76	36
Sheffield Wednesday "A"	38	14	7	17	69	88	35
South Kirkby Colliery	38	13	8	17	79	85	34
Leeds United "A"	38	15	4	19	83	99	34
Yorkshire Amateurs	38	16	2	20	94	130	34
Gainsborough Trinity Reserves	38	9	9	20	63	107	27
Keighley Town	38	9	5	24	63	87	23
Hull Amateurs	38	6	6	26	49	155	18
Upton Colliery	38	2	3	33	46	188	7

York City Reserves moved to the Midland League, Upton Colliery moved to the Sheffield Association League and Hull Amateurs also left the league. Brodsworth Main, Barnsley "A" and Sheffield United "A" all joined.

1947-48

Goole Town	38	29	5	4	118	48	63
Gainsborough Trinity Reserves	38	24	3	11	99	53	51
Selby Town	38	20	10	8	92	73	50
Harworth Colliery	38	22	4	12	92	70	48
Bradford United	38	20	6	12	104	56	46
Ossett Town	38	17	11	10	91	95	45
Barnsley "A"	38	18	8	12	68	59	44
Thorne Colliery	38	19	2	17	90	83	40
Scunthorpe & Lindsey United Res.	38	15	9	14	83	90	39
Wombwell Athletic	38	17	4	17	85	92	38
Chesterfield "A"	38	15	5	18	82	70	35
Halifax Town Reserves	38	13	9	16	77	72	35
Sheffield Wednesday "A"	38	15	5	18	81	83	35
South Kirkby Colliery	38	14	6	18	82	92	34
Yorkshire Amateurs	38	15	2	21	89	97	32
Leeds United "A"	38	12	8	18	78	93	32
Sheffield United "A"	38	11	7	20	61	105	29
Brodsworth Main	38	11	5	22	80	98	27
Huddersfield Town "A"	38	6	7	25	53	118	19
Keighley Town	38	6	6	26	53	111	18

Bradford United moved to the West Yorkshire League and Keighley Town disbanded. Rotherham United "A" and Bradford (Park Avenue) "A" joined. Goole Town moved to the Midland League and replaced their first team with their reserves in the Yorkshire League.

1948-49

Sheffield United "A"	38	26	4	8	98	49	56
Goole Town Reserves	38	26	3	9	114	55	55
Gainsborough Trinity Reserves	38	22	6	10	99	60	50
Selby Town	38	20	4	14	93	69	44
Ossett Town	38	19	6	13	94	73	44
Rotherham United "A"	38	17	9	12	79	62	43
Halifax Town Reserves	38	18	7	13	86	82	43
Huddersfield Town "A"	38	15	9	14	65	72	39
Leeds United "A"	38	17	5	16	85	93	39
Wombwell Athletic	38	15	8	15	74	81	38
Chesterfield "A"	38	14	9	15	68	92	37
Scunthorpe & Lindsey United Res.	38	12	12	14	83	82	36
Barnsley "A"	38	13	9	16	79	86	35
Sheffield Wednesday "A"	38	13	8	17	70	78	34
Harworth Colliery	38	10	13	15	90	98	33
Yorkshire Amateurs	38	11	9	18	62	74	31
Thorne Colliery	38	12	5	21	68	91	29
Brodsworth Main	38	9	8	21	65	106	26
South Kirkby Colliery	**38**	**11**	**3**	**24**	**85**	**107**	**25**
Bradford (Park Avenue) "A"	**38**	**10**	**3**	**25**	**65**	**112**	**23**

Halifax Town Reserves moved to the Midland League and were replaced by Halifax Town "A". South Kirkby Colliery and Bradford (Park Avenue) "A" were relegated to the new Division Two which also included 16 new members. Beighton Miners Welfare, Bentley Colliery, Dinnington Athletic, Kiveton Park, Maltby Main, Norton Woodseats, Sheffield, Stocksbridge Works and Worksop Town Reserves all joined from the Sheffield Association League, Farsley Celtic joined from the West Riding County Amateur League, Retford Town Reserves joined as a newly-formed club while Doncaster Rovers "A", Frickley Colliery Reserves, Hull City "A", Scarborough Reserves and York City "A" all also joined.

1949-50

Promoted clubs are shown in **bold**, relegated clubs are shown in ***bold italics***

Division One

Goole Town Reserves	34	27	3	4	91	37	57
Wombwell Athletic	34	22	6	6	73	29	50
Ossett Town	34	22	4	8	120	61	48
Scunthorpe & Lindsey United Res.	34	17	11	6	75	44	45
Yorkshire Amateurs	34	19	5	10	85	55	43
Gainsborough Trinity Reserves	34	15	10	9	79	57	40
Rotherham United "A"	34	15	7	12	64	54	37
Selby Town	34	15	6	13	82	63	36
Sheffield United "A"	34	15	4	15	75	52	34
Barnsley "A"	34	13	7	14	53	49	33
Sheffield Wednesday "A"	34	12	7	15	52	55	31
Huddersfield Town "A"	34	12	6	16	58	65	30
Brodsworth Main	34	11	8	15	53	68	30
Leeds United "A"	34	11	7	16	62	67	29
Halifax Town "A"	34	11	4	19	52	71	26
Chesterfield "A"	**34**	**6**	**7**	**21**	**48**	**90**	**19**
Thorne Colliery	**34**	**7**	**5**	**22**	**62**	**124**	**19**
Harworth Colliery	34	2	1	31	31	174	5

Scunthorpe & Lindsey United Reserves moved to the Midland League and Harworth Colliery moved to the Retford League.

Yorkshire League (II) 1950-1953

Division Two

Team	P	W	D	L	F	A	Pts
Retford Town Reserves	34	23	5	6	91	55	51
Beighton Miners Welfare	34	21	7	6	103	60	49
Scarborough Reserves	34	20	8	6	95	47	48
Dinnington Athletic	34	21	6	7	82	53	48
Norton Woodseats	34	20	4	10	86	49	44
Bentley Colliery	34	19	6	9	96	69	44
Stocksbridge Works	34	20	3	11	78	68	43
Farsley Celtic	34	16	5	13	100	76	37
Bradford (Park Avenue) "A"	34	15	6	13	71	65	36
Sheffield	34	14	4	16	89	79	32
Hull City "A"	34	14	4	16	99	89	32
Worksop Town Reserves	34	12	6	16	78	86	30
Doncaster Rovers "A"	34	11	8	15	60	78	30
South Kirkby Colliery	34	9	6	19	61	86	24
Frickley Colliery Reserves	34	8	7	19	71	109	23
Maltby Main	34	4	8	22	48	117	16
York City "A"	34	4	7	23	54	94	15
Kiveton Park	34	3	4	27	47	129	10

Bradford United joined from the West Yorkshire League.

1950-51

Division One

Team	P	W	D	L	F	A	Pts
Sheffield Wednesday "A"	34	24	4	6	101	47	52
Selby Town	34	22	2	10	103	68	46
Beighton Miners Welfare	34	21	3	10	95	58	45
Scarborough Reserves	34	20	4	10	86	57	44
Goole Town Reserves	34	19	4	11	77	51	42
Ossett Town	34	20	2	12	93	65	42
Gainsborough Trinity Reserves	34	13	10	11	87	86	36
Retford Town Reserves	34	15	5	14	60	44	35
Yorkshire Amateurs	34	15	4	15	67	68	34
Barnsley "A"	34	13	7	14	56	44	33
Wombwell Athletic	34	12	8	14	71	82	32
Rotherham United "A"	34	13	5	16	72	61	31
Sheffield United "A"	34	10	10	14	61	64	30
Leeds United "A"	34	12	2	20	68	104	26
Huddersfield Town "A"	**34**	**11**	**3**	**20**	**61**	**87**	**25**
Dinnington Athletic	34	7	9	18	55	107	23
Brodsworth Main	**34**	**6**	**8**	**20**	**52**	**96**	**20**
Halifax Town "A"	**34**	**6**	**4**	**24**	**44**	**120**	**16**

Dinnington Athletic left the league.

Division Two

Team	P	W	D	L	F	A	Pts
Stocksbridge Works	**32**	**23**	**5**	**4**	**106**	**30**	**51**
Worksop Town Reserves	**32**	**22**	**5**	**5**	**94**	**51**	**49**
Hull City "A"	**32**	**20**	**5**	**7**	**77**	**50**	**45**
Norton Woodseats	**32**	**19**	**5**	**8**	**75**	**33**	**43**
Bentley Colliery	32	20	3	9	105	63	43
Chesterfield "A"	32	17	7	8	102	51	41
Sheffield	32	16	5	11	85	55	37
Farsley Celtic	32	16	4	12	77	67	36
Bradford United	32	15	3	14	78	58	33
Doncaster Rovers "A"	32	13	7	12	66	58	33
Thorne Colliery	32	15	3	14	74	89	33
Frickley Colliery Reserves	32	10	8	14	50	60	28
Bradford (Park Avenue) "A"	32	8	2	22	39	99	18
South Kirkby Colliery	32	7	3	22	49	84	17
Kiveton Park	32	5	3	24	48	109	13
York City "A"	32	5	3	24	43	125	13
Maltby Main	32	3	5	24	32	118	11

Bradford United disbanded and York City disbanded their "A" team.
Kiveton Park moved to the Worksop & District League.

1951-52

Division One

Team	P	W	D	L	F	A	Pts
Stocksbridge Works	34	22	9	3	94	36	53
Retford Town Reserves	34	23	7	4	99	39	53
Beighton Miners Welfare	34	19	9	6	92	48	47
Goole Town Reserves	34	20	7	7	75	50	47
Selby Town	34	19	8	7	99	57	46
Hull City "A"	34	19	7	8	90	54	45
Sheffield Wednesday "A"	34	17	4	13	84	64	38
Leeds United "A"	34	14	6	14	77	77	34
Norton Woodseats	34	12	7	15	64	60	31
Rotherham United "A"	34	13	5	16	73	82	31
Ossett Town	34	13	5	16	61	71	31
Barnsley "A"	34	12	3	19	55	76	27
Sheffield United "A"	34	10	5	19	59	91	25
Wombwell Athletic	34	9	6	19	64	86	24
Gainsborough Trinity Reserves	34	8	5	21	61	102	21
Yorkshire Amateurs	**34**	**7**	**7**	**20**	**46**	**99**	**21**
Scarborough Reserves	**34**	**8**	**4**	**22**	**56**	**120**	**20**
Worksop Town Reserves	**34**	**6**	**6**	**22**	**39**	**76**	**18**

Gainsborough Trinity Reserves moved to the Lincolnshire League.

Division Two

Team	P	W	D	L	F	A	Pts
Farsley Celtic	**24**	**17**	**1**	**6**	**78**	**37**	**35**
Bentley Colliery	**24**	**14**	**5**	**5**	**54**	**43**	**33**
Sheffield	**24**	**13**	**5**	**6**	**85**	**41**	**31**
Doncaster Rovers "A"	**24**	**14**	**3**	**7**	**73**	**43**	**31**
Chesterfield "A"	24	14	3	7	58	39	31
Huddersfield Town "A"	24	11	3	10	61	43	25
Bradford (Park Avenue) "A"	24	11	2	11	48	49	24
South Kirkby Colliery	24	11	2	11	55	61	24
Thorne Colliery	24	10	4	10	47	56	24
Brodsworth Main	24	8	2	14	52	54	18
Frickley Colliery Reserves	24	7	4	13	46	61	18
Halifax Town "A"	24	3	3	18	35	91	9
Maltby Main	24	3	3	18	26	100	9

Halifax Town disbanded their "A" team. Hallam joined from the Sheffield Association League, Briggs Sports Club joined from the Doncaster & District Senior League and Hampton Sports Club also joined.

1952-53

Division One

Team	P	W	D	L	F	A	Pts
Selby Town	34	26	2	6	106	54	54
Beighton Miners Welfare	34	21	6	7	93	52	48
Stocksbridge Works	34	19	4	11	104	54	42
Retford Town Reserves	34	17	8	9	106	69	42
Hull City "A"	34	16	4	14	74	55	36
Bentley Colliery	34	13	10	11	79	74	36
Ossett Town	34	14	8	12	85	85	36
Sheffield	34	15	6	13	72	76	36
Rotherham United "A"	34	14	7	13	79	69	35
Barnsley "A"	34	13	8	13	54	66	34
Norton Woodseats	34	15	3	16	53	63	33
Sheffield Wednesday "A"	34	11	10	13	59	69	32
Goole Town Reserves	34	10	10	14	77	95	30
Farsley Celtic	34	12	5	17	77	84	29
Leeds United "A"	**34**	**12**	**5**	**17**	**65**	**80**	**29**
Wombwell Athletic	**34**	**10**	**3**	**21**	**53**	**102**	**23**
Doncaster Rovers "A"	**34**	**8**	**3**	**23**	**45**	**91**	**19**
Sheffield United "A"	**34**	**6**	**6**	**22**	**50**	**93**	**18**

Retford Town joined from the Central Alliance, replacing their reserves who moved to the Sheffield Association League.

Division Two

Huddersfield Town "A"	26	22	1	3	106	27	45
Yorkshire Amateurs	26	15	3	8	64	33	33
Scarborough Reserves	26	15	1	10	72	50	31
South Kirkby Colliery	26	13	4	9	76	64	30
Worksop Town Reserves	26	13	2	11	62	56	28
Bradford (Park Avenue) "A"	26	9	10	7	56	62	28
Frickley Colliery Reserves	26	9	7	10	60	67	25
Thorne Colliery	26	10	3	13	54	59	23
Chesterfield "A"	26	10	3	13	50	69	23
Briggs Sports Club	26	10	3	13	57	83	23
Hallam	26	9	4	13	59	57	22
Brodsworth Main	26	8	4	14	45	77	20
Hampton Sports Club	26	6	7	13	49	62	19
Maltby Main	26	4	6	16	38	82	14

Rawmarsh Welfare joined from the Sheffield Association League and Dunscroft Welfare also joined.

1953-54

Division One

Selby Town	34	23	6	5	99	50	52
Huddersfield Town "A"	34	22	4	8	88	57	48
Rotherham United "A"	34	16	9	9	90	70	41
Norton Woodseats	34	17	6	11	85	55	40
Stocksbridge Works	34	12	15	7	76	50	39
Bentley Colliery	34	17	5	12	83	82	39
Barnsley "A"	34	15	7	12	94	68	37
Retford Town	34	15	6	13	78	74	36
Sheffield Wednesday "A"	34	11	10	13	67	65	32
Scarborough Reserves	34	15	2	17	79	105	32
Beighton Miners Welfare	34	13	5	16	82	92	31
Farsley Celtic	34	10	10	14	75	72	30
Ossett Town	34	10	10	14	61	81	30
Yorkshire Amateurs	34	9	11	14	56	64	29
Sheffield	*34*	*12*	*5*	*17*	*73*	*88*	*29*
Goole Town Reserves	34	11	5	18	62	93	27
Hull City "A"	*34*	*7*	*12*	*15*	*54*	*68*	*26*
South Kirkby Colliery	*34*	*4*	*6*	*24*	*59*	*127*	*14*

Goole Town Reserves left the league.

Division Two

Rawmarsh Welfare	**30**	**23**	**3**	**4**	**76**	**35**	**49**
Sheffield United "A"	**30**	**20**	**7**	**3**	**103**	**35**	**47**
Chesterfield "A"	**30**	**18**	**9**	**3**	**86**	**44**	**45**
Thorne Colliery	**30**	**19**	**5**	**6**	**77**	**34**	**43**
Leeds United "A"	30	19	3	8	97	40	41
Wombwell Athletic	30	13	8	9	62	53	34
Doncaster Rovers "A"	30	11	8	11	56	50	30
Hallam	30	12	5	13	68	62	29
Briggs Sports Club	30	11	7	12	61	66	29
Hampton Sports Club	30	11	4	15	60	81	26
Frickley Colliery Reserves	30	8	8	14	52	69	24
Worksop Town Reserves	30	8	5	17	49	66	21
Bradford (Park Avenue) "A"	30	6	8	16	53	85	20
Maltby Main	30	6	4	20	40	111	16
Brodsworth Main	30	4	5	21	46	95	13
Dunscroft Welfare	30	6	1	23	49	109	13

Halifax Town Reserves joined from the Midland League.

1954-55

Division One

Stocksbridge Works	34	22	4	8	78	46	48
Norton Woodseats	34	19	9	6	72	50	47
Sheffield United "A"	34	17	9	8	77	53	43
Barnsley "A"	34	16	9	9	97	59	41
Bentley Colliery	34	18	5	11	90	69	41
Selby Town	34	15	8	11	82	67	38
Beighton Miners Welfare	34	13	11	10	75	76	37
Huddersfield Town "A"	34	16	3	15	87	65	35
Sheffield Wednesday "A"	34	15	5	14	56	64	35
Chesterfield "A"	34	13	8	13	64	72	34
Ossett Town	34	13	6	15	70	90	32
Retford Town	34	11	8	15	66	73	30
Farsley Celtic	34	10	9	15	68	68	29
Yorkshire Amateurs	34	10	9	15	58	71	29
Rotherham United "A"	34	9	9	16	66	73	27
Scarborough Reserves	*34*	*10*	*6*	*18*	*58*	*88*	*26*
Thorne Colliery	*34*	*9*	*3*	*22*	*50*	*90*	*21*
Rawmarsh Welfare	*34*	*6*	*7*	*21*	*53*	*93*	*19*

Chesterfield "A" left the league.

Division Two

Hull City "A"	**30**	**22**	**4**	**4**	**113**	**28**	**48**
Halifax Town Reserves	**30**	**23**	**0**	**7**	**110**	**50**	**46**
Sheffield	**30**	**19**	**6**	**5**	**96**	**38**	**44**
Leeds United "A"	**30**	**20**	**3**	**7**	**86**	**38**	**43**
South Kirkby Colliery	30	19	4	7	93	51	42
Worksop Town Reserves	30	16	4	10	69	52	36
Hampton Sports Club	30	13	10	7	69	53	36
Wombwell Athletic	30	17	1	12	65	60	35
Frickley Colliery Reserves	30	9	7	14	55	84	25
Hallam	30	9	5	16	51	60	23
Doncaster Rovers "A"	30	8	5	17	53	80	21
Briggs Sports Club	30	8	3	19	57	94	19
Brodsworth Main	30	8	2	20	70	99	18
Bradford (Park Avenue) "A"	30	8	2	20	55	102	18
Dunscroft Welfare	30	6	2	22	50	126	14
Maltby Main	30	4	4	22	37	114	12

Maltby Main moved to the Rotherham Association League and Doncaster Rovers "A" also left the league. Salts (Saltaire) joined from the West Riding County Amateur League, Harrogate Railway Athletic joined from the West Yorkshire League and York City "A" also joined. Dunscroft Welfare changed their name to Hatfield Main.

1955-56

Division One

Stocksbridge Works	34	18	10	6	85	58	46
Selby Town	34	19	4	11	78	54	42
Sheffield Wednesday "A"	34	16	8	10	86	57	40
Halifax Town Reserves	34	18	4	12	71	57	40
Farsley Celtic	34	18	4	12	60	58	40
Sheffield	34	18	4	12	84	85	40
Huddersfield Town "A"	34	18	3	13	75	58	39
Hull City "A"	34	16	7	11	69	58	39
Beighton Miners Welfare	34	18	3	13	80	70	39
Sheffield United "A"	34	14	10	10	81	71	38
Ossett Town	34	14	4	16	64	80	32
Barnsley "A"	34	10	9	15	56	68	29
Norton Woodseats	34	12	4	18	80	83	28
Rotherham United "A"	34	13	2	19	71	75	28
Yorkshire Amateurs	*34*	*12*	*3*	*19*	*68*	*96*	*27*
Retford Town	*34*	*10*	*4*	*20*	*76*	*95*	*24*
Leeds United "A"	*34*	*9*	*6*	*19*	*52*	*77*	*24*
Bentley Colliery	*34*	*7*	*3*	*24*	*60*	*96*	*17*

Yorkshire League (II) 1956-1959

Division Two

	P	W	D	L	F	A	Pts
Rawmarsh Welfare	30	21	3	6	87	52	45
Thorne Colliery	30	20	2	8	95	53	42
York City "A"	30	17	7	6	91	48	41
Salts (Saltaire)	30	18	4	8	93	46	40
Hallam	30	18	4	8	70	47	40
Scarborough Reserves	30	16	3	11	88	60	35
Worksop Town Reserves	30	12	10	8	63	52	34
Harrogate Railway Athletic	30	12	5	13	78	87	29
South Kirkby Colliery	30	12	5	13	70	80	29
Bradford (Park Avenue) "A"	30	9	7	14	70	77	25
Hampton Sports Club	30	9	6	15	66	84	24
Brodsworth Main	30	10	3	17	68	92	23
Frickley Colliery Reserves	30	10	2	18	66	82	22
Wombwell Athletic	30	7	8	15	55	81	22
Hatfield Main	30	8	3	19	46	88	19
Briggs Sports Club	30	4	2	24	38	115	10

Worksop Town Reserves were awarded a win after their game with Briggs Sports Club was not played.
Goole Town Reserves joined the league.
Wombwell Athletic changed their name to Wombwell & Darfield.

1956-57

Division One

	P	W	D	L	F	A	Pts
Stocksbridge Works	34	20	8	6	100	55	48
Sheffield Wednesday "A"	34	18	8	8	86	42	44
Selby Town	34	19	5	10	99	57	43
Farsley Celtic	34	17	7	10	68	43	41
Halifax Town Reserves	34	17	6	11	70	46	40
Sheffield United "A"	34	17	6	11	90	65	40
Norton Woodseats	34	17	6	11	66	54	40
Huddersfield Town "A"	34	18	4	12	79	76	40
Beighton Miners Welfare	34	16	7	11	74	73	39
Sheffield	34	18	1	15	81	67	37
Barnsley "A"	34	16	4	14	74	70	36
Ossett Town	34	13	5	16	73	83	31
Salts (Saltaire)	34	12	7	15	68	86	31
Rawmarsh Welfare	34	9	6	19	48	83	24
Rotherham United "A"	34	7	8	19	67	96	22
Thorne Colliery	34	9	3	22	68	107	21
York City "A"	**34**	**8**	**2**	**24**	**49**	**93**	**18**
Hull City "A"	34	5	7	22	43	107	17

Barnsley "A", Hull City "A" and Rotherham United "A" all moved to the North Midland Combination.

Division Two

	P	W	D	L	F	A	Pts
Retford Town	32	20	7	5	113	55	47
Hallam	32	21	5	6	87	43	47
Bentley Colliery	32	22	3	7	91	45	45
Frickley Colliery Reserves	**32**	**20**	**3**	**9**	**97**	**54**	**43**
South Kirkby Colliery	32	19	5	8	75	64	43
Worksop Town Reserves	32	17	6	9	88	53	40
Leeds United "A"	32	16	5	11	86	49	37
Goole Town Reserves	32	17	2	13	71	66	36
Hampton Sports Club	32	16	1	15	68	68	33
Yorkshire Amateurs	32	14	5	13	68	72	33
Harrogate Railway Athletic	32	13	4	15	82	75	30
Brodsworth Main	32	9	7	16	60	80	25
Scarborough Reserves	32	8	5	19	55	85	21
Bradford (Park Avenue) "A"	32	9	2	21	57	94	20
Hatfield Main	32	7	3	22	41	103	17
Briggs Sports Club	32	5	3	24	44	104	13
Wombwell & Darfield	32	4	4	24	52	125	12

Bentley Colliery had two points deducted for fielding an ineligible player.
Brodsworth Main and Briggs Sports Club both moved to the Doncaster & District Senior League and Bradford (Park Avenue) "A" moved to the North Midland Combination. Harrogate Town, Ossett Albion and East End Park W.M.C. all joined from the West Yorkshire League.

1957-58

Division One

	P	W	D	L	F	A	Pts
Stocksbridge Works	34	23	5	6	98	45	51
Farsley Celtic	34	19	6	9	85	42	44
Sheffield Wednesday "A"	34	17	9	8	97	49	43
Selby Town	34	19	5	10	86	53	43
Halifax Town Reserves	34	18	5	11	93	66	41
Norton Woodseats	34	17	7	10	75	58	41
Bentley Colliery	34	16	7	11	73	68	39
Beighton Miners Welfare	34	16	7	11	77	73	39
Sheffield United "A"	34	16	6	12	90	68	38
Sheffield	34	15	6	13	58	63	36
Frickley Colliery Reserves	34	15	5	14	65	71	35
Ossett Town	34	14	6	14	86	86	34
Retford Town	34	11	8	15	75	76	30
Hallam	34	11	6	17	50	76	28
Salts (Saltaire)	34	12	2	20	70	93	26
Rawmarsh Welfare	**34**	**10**	**6**	**18**	**58**	**79**	**26**
Huddersfield Town "A"	34	6	3	25	54	83	15
Thorne Colliery	**34**	**1**	**1**	**32**	**34**	**175**	**3**

Huddersfield Town "A" moved to the North Midland Combination and Halifax Town Reserves moved to the North Regional League.

Division Two

	P	W	D	L	F	A	Pts
East End Park W.M.C.	26	20	2	4	76	28	42
Scarborough Reserves	26	17	4	5	65	32	38
Harrogate Railway Athletic	26	15	6	5	71	41	36
Worksop Town Reserves	26	11	8	7	65	53	30
Yorkshire Amateurs	26	14	1	11	58	45	29
South Kirkby Colliery	26	12	4	10	81	69	28
Ossett Albion	26	11	4	11	50	50	26
Goole Town Reserves	26	10	7	9	58	58	25
York City "A"	26	9	5	12	42	54	23
Leeds United "A"	26	8	5	13	42	60	21
Hatfield Main	26	7	6	13	46	89	20
Hampton Sports Club	26	5	8	13	37	55	18
Harrogate Town	26	4	7	15	43	62	15
Wombwell & Darfield	26	4	3	19	42	80	11

Goole Town Reserves had 2 points deducted for fielding an ineligible player. Leeds United "A" moved to the North Midland Combination. Dodworth Miners Welfare joined from the Barnsley Association League and Retford British Ropes joined from the Central Alliance.
Wombwell & Darfield changed their name to Wombwell.

1958-59

Division One

	P	W	D	L	F	A	Pts
Retford Town	34	24	1	9	94	52	49
Farsley Celtic	34	19	9	6	74	39	47
East End Park W.M.C.	34	19	6	9	73	53	44
Sheffield Wednesday "A"	34	18	7	9	62	35	43
Stocksbridge Works	34	17	5	12	79	58	39
Scarborough Reserves	34	15	8	11	79	58	38
Beighton Miners Welfare	34	17	4	13	90	76	38
Sheffield United "A"	34	15	6	13	62	56	36
Frickley Colliery Reserves	34	17	2	15	83	85	36
Bentley Colliery	34	14	7	13	77	75	35
Norton Woodseats	34	15	3	16	72	74	33
Sheffield	34	11	8	15	70	78	30
Selby Town	34	11	7	16	69	75	29
Hallam	34	11	4	19	57	78	26
Worksop Town Reserves	34	9	8	17	45	78	26
Ossett Town	**34**	**10**	**5**	**19**	**79**	**81**	**25**
Harrogate Railway Athletic	**34**	**6**	**7**	**21**	**48**	**84**	**19**
Salts (Saltaire)	**34**	**7**	**5**	**22**	**45**	**123**	**19**

Worksop Town Reserves left the league.

1959-60

Division Two

Yorkshire Amateurs	24	19	4	1	79	23	42
Ossett Albion	24	16	2	6	77	37	34
Goole Town Reserves	24	14	6	4	79	39	34
Rawmarsh Welfare	24	14	3	7	60	48	31
South Kirkby Colliery	24	13	2	9	72	52	28
Harrogate Town	24	12	4	8	74	61	28
Dodworth Miners Welfare	24	9	6	9	62	44	24
York City "A"	24	10	4	10	41	47	24
Thorne Colliery	24	9	3	12	69	79	21
Hampton Sports Club	24	7	1	16	34	57	15
Retford British Ropes	24	5	5	14	36	87	15
Wombwell	24	3	3	18	41	75	9
Hatfield Main	24	2	3	19	44	119	7

Grimethorpe Miners Welfare joined from the Sheffield Association League, Bridlington Town joined from the East Riding Amateur League and Doncaster United joined as a newly formed club.

1960-61

Division One

Sheffield Wednesday "A"	34	27	4	3	90	32	58
Stocksbridge Works	34	25	4	5	89	39	54
Farsley Celtic	34	24	4	6	68	30	52
Retford Town	34	17	11	6	90	51	45
Grimethorpe Miners Welfare	34	15	10	9	85	64	40
Frickley Colliery Reserves	34	15	9	10	62	47	39
Ossett Albion	34	17	5	12	61	61	39
Scarborough Reserves	34	17	3	14	67	53	37
Selby Town	34	16	5	13	69	60	37
Bridlington Town	34	16	5	13	57	51	37
Sheffield United "A"	34	16	4	14	68	49	36
Norton Woodseats	34	14	5	15	69	71	33
Yorkshire Amateurs	34	10	6	18	50	76	26
East End Park W.M.C.	34	10	5	19	49	66	25
Ossett Town	34	7	5	22	63	113	19
Doncaster United	*34*	*4*	*6*	*24*	*37*	*86*	*14*
Sheffield	*34*	*4*	*5*	*25*	*40*	*94*	*13*
Bentley Colliery	34	1	6	27	23	94	8

Retford Town moved to the Midland League while Bentley Colliery left senior football and joined Division Three of the Bentley & District League. Sheffield Wednesday "A" and Sheffield United "A" also left the league.

1959-60

Division One

Farsley Celtic	34	21	10	3	77	30	52
Ossett Albion	34	19	7	8	76	47	45
Sheffield United "A"	34	18	8	8	86	51	44
Sheffield Wednesday "A"	34	18	6	10	77	53	42
Retford Town	34	16	7	11	85	66	39
Norton Woodseats	34	14	10	10	70	62	38
Scarborough Reserves	34	14	10	10	69	70	38
Yorkshire Amateurs	34	13	11	10	67	53	37
Frickley Colliery Reserves	34	13	10	11	65	53	36
East End Park W.M.C.	34	13	9	12	54	53	35
Selby Town	34	16	3	15	62	68	35
Stocksbridge Works	34	13	6	15	58	50	32
Bentley Colliery	34	9	11	14	59	69	29
Sheffield	34	11	6	17	59	80	28
Beighton Miners Welfare	*34*	*8*	*8*	*18*	*57*	*83*	*24*
Goole Town Reserves	*34*	*9*	*6*	*19*	*68*	*101*	*24*
Hallam	*34*	*5*	*7*	*22*	*51*	*96*	*17*
Rawmarsh Welfare	*34*	*4*	*9*	*21*	*42*	*97*	*17*

Division Two

Grimethorpe Miners Welfare	28	22	1	5	109	37	45
Bridlington Town	28	21	3	4	86	37	45
Ossett Town	28	18	3	7	112	53	39
Doncaster United	28	15	9	4	76	44	39
Harrogate Town	28	15	6	7	62	34	36
South Kirkby Colliery	28	13	5	10	76	69	31
Hampton Sports Club	28	12	5	11	59	42	29
York City "A"	28	10	7	11	59	59	27
Salts (Saltaire)	28	9	7	12	54	60	25
Thorne Colliery	28	10	4	14	67	77	24
Harrogate Railway Athletic	28	10	2	16	68	91	22
Hatfield Main	28	9	1	18	59	102	17
Wombwell	28	7	1	20	49	106	15
Dodworth Miners Welfare	28	4	6	18	33	84	14
Retford British Ropes	28	3	4	21	35	109	10

Hatfield Main had 2 points deducted for fielding an ineligible player. Swillington Miners Welfare joined from the West Yorkshire League, Gainsborough Trinity Reserves joined from the Lincolnshire League, Swallownest Miners Welfare joined from the Sheffield Association League and Bridlington Trinity joined from the East Riding Amateur League.

Division Two

Hallam	**36**	**26**	**8**	**2**	**132**	**42**	**60**
Swillington Miners Welfare	**36**	**26**	**3**	**7**	**132**	**55**	**55**
Harrogate Town	**36**	**24**	**6**	**6**	**96**	**42**	**54**
Goole Town Reserves	**36**	**23**	**7**	**6**	**126**	**66**	**53**
Bridlington Trinity	36	18	10	8	80	53	46
Thorne Colliery	36	17	10	9	107	77	44
South Kirkby Colliery	36	16	4	16	68	78	36
Hatfield Main	36	16	3	17	81	78	35
Harrogate Railway Athletic	36	14	7	15	82	81	35
Gainsborough Trinity Reserves	36	16	3	17	78	83	35
Hampton Sports Club	36	16	3	17	80	87	35
Rawmarsh Welfare	36	13	8	15	88	89	34
Salts (Saltaire)	36	13	8	15	79	81	34
Swallownest Miners Welfare	36	11	6	19	60	77	28
Dodworth Miners Welfare	36	9	7	20	66	110	25
York City "A"	36	10	5	21	50	87	25
Beighton Miners Welfare	36	10	3	23	61	111	23
Wombwell	36	4	6	26	52	130	14
Retford British Ropes	36	3	7	26	37	128	13

Gainsborough Trinity Reserves moved to the Lincolnshire League, Retford British Ropes moved to the Doncaster & District Senior League while Hampton Sports Club, Beighton Miners Welfare and Dodworth Miners Welfare also left. Wombwell changed their name to Wombwell Sporting Association. Hull Brunswick joined from the East Riding Amateur League and Brodsworth Main also joined.

A new Division Three was formed with 9 new members – the reserves of Farsley Celtic, Harrogate Town and Salts (Saltaire) who all joined from the West Riding County Amateur League, plus Leeds United "A" and the reserves of East End Park W.M.C., Harrogate Railway Athletic, Ossett Albion, Ossett Town and Yorkshire Amateurs. No club was ever promoted or relegated between Division Two and Division Three.

Yorkshire League (II) 1961-1964

1961-62

Division One

Stocksbridge Works	30	22	4	4	90	28	48
Ossett Albion	30	21	5	4	84	40	47
Bridlington Town	30	19	7	4	61	25	45
Farsley Celtic	30	15	5	10	40	35	35
Yorkshire Amateurs	30	14	5	11	69	58	33
Harrogate Town	30	13	6	11	56	45	32
Norton Woodseats	30	14	3	13	59	59	31
Hallam	30	12	5	13	65	59	29
Selby Town	30	12	5	13	51	53	29
East End Park W.M.C.	30	9	9	12	45	55	27
Scarborough Reserves	30	12	2	16	66	76	26
Goole Town Reserves	30	10	5	15	55	66	25
Grimethorpe Miners Welfare	30	9	6	15	60	86	24
Swillington Miners Welfare	**30**	**7**	**7**	**16**	**59**	**85**	**21**
Frickley Colliery Reserves	**30**	**5**	**8**	**17**	**35**	**65**	**18**
Ossett Town	**30**	**4**	**2**	**24**	**39**	**99**	**10**

East End Park W.M.C. moved to the West Yorkshire League.

Division Two

Bridlington Trinity	**26**	**19**	**4**	**3**	**73**	**23**	**42**
Doncaster United	**26**	**17**	**4**	**5**	**75**	**37**	**38**
Swallownest Miners Welfare	**26**	**18**	**2**	**6**	**81**	**42**	**38**
Hatfield Main	**26**	**17**	**2**	**7**	**86**	**47**	**36**
Wombwell Sporting Association	26	14	2	10	70	51	30
Rawmarsh Welfare	26	12	5	9	69	52	29
Sheffield	26	11	5	10	61	48	27
Harrogate Railway Athletic	26	11	3	12	63	74	25
Hull Brunswick	26	10	4	12	59	52	24
Thorne Colliery	26	6	8	12	52	60	20
Brodsworth Main	26	8	3	15	49	71	19
Salts (Saltaire)	26	9	1	16	47	72	19
York City "A"	26	6	2	18	27	64	14
South Kirkby Colliery	26	0	3	23	24	145	3

Mexborough Town joined as a newly-formed club and Dodworth Miners Welfare also joined.

Division Three

Farsley Celtic Reserves	16	13	1	2	68	10	27
Ossett Albion Reserves	16	7	3	6	44	43	17
Leeds United "A"	16	8	0	8	39	35	16
Yorkshire Amateurs Reserves	16	6	3	7	32	37	15
Salts (Saltaire) Reserves	16	7	1	8	33	40	15
Harrogate Town Reserves	16	5	4	7	21	36	14
Ossett Town Reserves	16	7	0	9	41	56	14
East End Park W.M.C. Reserves	16	5	3	8	43	39	13
Harrogate Railway Athletic Res.	16	5	3	8	25	50	13

Leeds United "A" and East End Park W.M.C. Reserves both left the league.

1962-63

Division One

Stocksbridge Works	30	19	7	4	83	28	45
Harrogate Town	30	18	4	8	70	34	40
Farsley Celtic	30	15	6	9	60	37	36
Ossett Albion	30	13	9	8	63	49	35
Bridlington Town	30	14	7	9	47	44	35
Bridlington Trinity	30	12	7	11	69	70	31
Norton Woodseats	30	11	8	11	52	51	30
Swallownest Miners Welfare	30	12	4	14	56	55	28
Scarborough Reserves	30	10	8	12	50	55	28
Selby Town	30	12	4	14	45	58	28
Doncaster United	30	9	10	11	35	49	28
Hallam	30	11	5	14	60	60	27
Hatfield Main	**30**	**10**	**5**	**15**	**55**	**69**	**25**
Goole Town Reserves	**30**	**9**	**6**	**15**	**49**	**61**	**24**
Yorkshire Amateurs	**30**	**8**	**6**	**16**	**44**	**70**	**22**
Grimethorpe Miners Welfare	**30**	**6**	**6**	**18**	**40**	**89**	**18**

Division Two

Wombwell Sporting Association	28	21	4	3	67	20	46
Mexborough Town	28	15	11	2	64	28	41
Swillington Miners Welfare	28	16	7	5	82	40	39
Hull Brunswick	28	17	4	7	85	48	38
Sheffield	28	18	0	10	78	44	36
Ossett Town	28	13	7	8	82	54	33
Salts (Saltaire)	28	13	4	11	58	38	30
Harrogate Railway Athletic	28	12	6	10	62	45	30
Rawmarsh Welfare	28	13	4	11	67	61	30
Frickley Colliery Reserves	28	10	5	13	60	60	25
Brodsworth Main	28	10	4	14	53	53	24
Thorne Colliery	28	6	2	20	59	84	14
York City "A"	28	5	4	19	45	83	14
South Kirkby Colliery	28	4	3	21	38	134	11
Dodworth Miners Welfare	28	4	1	23	33	141	9

Kiveton Park joined from the East Derbyshire League.
York City "A" left the league.
Brodsworth Main changed their name to Brodsworth Miners Welfare.

Division Three

Farsley Celtic Reserves	12	10	1	1	37	13	21
Ossett Albion Reserves	12	7	1	4	32	19	15
Yorkshire Amateurs Reserves	12	6	1	5	26	23	13
Salts (Saltaire) Reserves	12	5	2	5	24	29	12
Harrogate Railway Athletic Res.	12	5	1	6	25	32	11
Harrogate Town Reserves	12	3	2	7	19	31	8
Ossett Town Reserves	12	2	0	10	20	36	4

Keighley Central joined from the West Yorkshire League and Slazengers also joined.

1963-64

Division One

Bridlington Trinity	30	18	6	6	76	42	42
Mexborough Town	30	19	2	9	79	53	40
Harrogate Town	30	15	6	9	53	29	36
Bridlington Town	30	14	6	10	50	37	34
Ossett Albion	30	12	10	8	47	37	34
Scarborough Reserves	30	16	2	12	70	64	34
Farsley Celtic	30	13	7	10	51	35	33
Wombwell Sporting Association	30	13	5	12	40	35	31
Hull Brunswick	30	9	9	12	47	62	27
Hallam	30	12	3	15	40	61	27
Selby Town	30	10	6	14	55	71	26
Swillington Miners Welfare	30	10	6	14	45	64	26
Swallownest Miners Welfare	**30**	**9**	**6**	**15**	**50**	**57**	**24**
Stocksbridge Works	**30**	**7**	**8**	**15**	**38**	**48**	**22**
Norton Woodseats	**30**	**9**	**4**	**17**	**44**	**67**	**22**
Doncaster United	**30**	**8**	**6**	**16**	**37**	**60**	**22**

Division Two

Rawmarsh Welfare	**28**	**19**	**2**	**7**	**88**	**51**	**40**
Hatfield Main	**28**	**19**	**1**	**8**	**71**	**35**	**39**
Harrogate Railway Athletic	**28**	**18**	**3**	**7**	**69**	**39**	**39**
Brodsworth Miners Welfare	**28**	**17**	**4**	**7**	**86**	**49**	**38**
Yorkshire Amateurs	28	16	4	8	66	48	36
Sheffield	28	15	6	7	65	48	36
Goole Town Reserves	28	15	4	9	57	48	34
Kiveton Park	28	13	3	12	69	43	29
Salts (Saltaire)	28	10	8	10	45	40	28
Grimethorpe Miners Welfare	28	13	2	13	61	64	28
Ossett Town	28	8	6	14	55	62	22
Frickley Colliery Reserves	28	7	6	15	47	67	20
Thorne Colliery	28	5	6	17	53	78	16
Dodworth Miners Welfare	28	5	3	20	40	106	11
South Kirkby Colliery	28	2	0	26	36	136	4

South Kirkby Colliery moved to the Doncaster & District Senior League and Dodworth Miners Welfare also left the league. Barton Town joined from the Lincolnshire League and Retford Town Reserves also joined.

Yorkshire League (II) 1964-1967

Division Three

Keighley Central	16	12	3	1	47	13	27
Farsley Celtic Reserves	16	10	4	2	38	16	24
Harrogate Town Reserves	16	8	5	3	26	24	21
Ossett Albion Reserves	16	8	1	7	29	26	17
Yorkshire Amateurs Reserves	16	6	2	8	34	32	14
Harrogate Railway Athletic Res.	16	5	4	7	24	34	14
Salts (Saltaire) Reserves	16	4	3	9	21	33	11
Ossett Town Reserves	16	4	2	10	28	55	10
Slazengers	16	2	2	12	25	39	6

Division Three closed down and all 9 members left the league.
Keighley Central returned to the West Yorkshire League.

1964-65   Division One

Wombwell Sporting Association	30	18	8	4	82	28	44
Swillington Miners Welfare	30	20	3	7	89	51	43
Ossett Albion	30	17	6	7	68	29	40
Hatfield Main	30	16	6	8	68	50	38
Bridlington Town	30	14	9	7	69	41	37
Bridlington Trinity	30	16	5	9	70	62	37
Farsley Celtic	30	14	8	8	60	44	36
Scarborough Reserves	30	14	5	11	71	57	33
Mexborough Town	30	11	8	11	58	57	30
Rawmarsh Welfare	30	13	4	13	64	74	30
Hallam	30	11	4	15	55	56	26
Harrogate Town	30	9	7	14	46	55	25
Selby Town	30	7	6	17	50	85	20
Harrogate Railway Athletic	*30*	*6*	*5*	*19*	*44*	*70*	*17*
Hull Brunswick	*30*	*7*	*2*	*21*	*42*	*92*	*16*
Brodsworth Miners Welfare	*30*	*3*	*2*	*25*	*44*	*129*	*8*

Swillington Miners Welfare left the league.

Division Two

Stocksbridge Works	*28*	*20*	*4*	*4*	*85*	*29*	*44*
Barton Town	*28*	*18*	*4*	*6*	*88*	*35*	*40*
Frickley Colliery Reserves	*28*	*17*	*4*	*7*	*56*	*37*	*38*
Goole Town Reserves	*28*	*15*	*5*	*8*	*65*	*37*	*35*
Kiveton Park	28	14	5	9	51	32	33
Retford Town Reserves	28	11	8	9	54	41	30
Yorkshire Amateurs	28	13	3	12	54	61	29
Sheffield	28	12	4	12	47	41	28
Doncaster United	28	9	8	11	41	46	26
Swallownest Miners Welfare	28	10	5	13	47	55	25
Grimethorpe Miners Welfare	28	10	3	15	45	60	23
Norton Woodseats	28	9	5	14	45	62	23
Thorne Colliery	28	7	7	14	43	72	21
Salts (Saltaire)	28	6	4	18	30	75	16
Ossett Town	28	4	2	22	26	94	10

Salts (Saltaire) moved to the West Yorkshire League and Grimethorpe Miners Welfare also left the league. Denaby United joined from the Midland League while Heeley Amateurs and Leeds Ashley Road also joined.

1965-66   Division One

Wombwell Sporting Association	30	18	7	5	62	37	43
Hatfield Main	30	19	2	9	100	54	40
Selby Town	30	15	10	5	67	37	40
Ossett Albion	30	19	2	9	64	40	40
Bridlington Town	30	16	6	8	62	44	38
Bridlington Trinity	30	16	2	12	85	60	34
Farsley Celtic	30	15	4	11	49	36	34
Barton Town	30	15	4	11	83	68	34
Mexborough Town	30	14	4	12	66	51	32
Goole Town Reserves	30	13	4	13	50	52	30
Scarborough Reserves	30	11	5	14	51	52	27
Hallam	30	11	4	15	50	59	26
Frickley Colliery Reserves	30	7	7	16	41	77	21
Harrogate Town	30	8	3	19	49	65	19
Rawmarsh Welfare	*30*	*4*	*5*	*21*	*34*	*98*	*13*
Stocksbridge Works	*30*	*2*	*5*	*23*	*41*	*124*	*9*

Goole Town Reserves left the league.

Division Two

Norton Woodseats	**28**	**18**	**5**	**5**	**85**	**35**	**41**
Thorne Colliery	**28**	**17**	**5**	**6**	**90**	**49**	**39**
Sheffield	**28**	**15**	**5**	**8**	**61**	**33**	**35**
Kiveton Park	**28**	**15**	**4**	**9**	**73**	**57**	**34**
Denaby United	28	14	5	9	84	40	33
Hull Brunswick	28	15	3	10	70	60	33
Heeley Amateurs	28	13	6	9	56	62	32
Retford Town Reserves	28	11	8	9	66	48	30
Harrogate Railway Athletic	28	12	2	14	64	51	26
Swallownest Miners Welfare	28	11	4	13	55	70	26
Yorkshire Amateurs	28	8	7	13	46	57	23
Doncaster United	28	10	3	15	54	68	23
Ossett Town	28	8	4	16	44	104	20
Leeds Ashley Road	28	7	4	17	47	61	18
Brodsworth Miners Welfare	28	2	3	23	32	129	7

Micklefield Welfare joined from the West Yorkshire League, York City Reserves and Bradford City Reserves both joined from the North Regional League and Hampton Sports also joined.

1966-67
Division One

Bridlington Trinity	32	22	3	7	101	43	47
Bridlington Town	32	21	5	6	83	43	47
Wombwell Sporting Association	32	15	12	5	57	35	42
Thorne Colliery	32	16	9	7	68	53	41
Hatfield Main	32	17	4	11	70	46	38
Barton Town	32	16	2	14	69	69	34
Farsley Celtic	32	14	6	12	44	44	34
Mexborough Town	32	15	4	13	61	65	34
Kiveton Park	32	15	4	13	53	60	34
Hallam	32	13	6	13	50	50	32
Selby Town	32	13	5	14	60	60	31
Norton Woodseats	32	13	5	14	53	55	31
Ossett Albion	32	11	9	12	52	54	31
Frickley Colliery Reserves	32	10	2	20	56	73	22
Scarborough Reserves	*32*	*9*	*4*	*19*	*51*	*78*	*22*
Sheffield	*32*	*7*	*2*	*23*	*49*	*76*	*16*
Harrogate Town	*32*	*1*	*6*	*25*	*34*	*110*	*8*

Frickley Colliery Reserves left the league.

Division Two

Hull Brunswick	**32**	**25**	**3**	**4**	**105**	**40**	**53**
Denaby United	**32**	**23**	**2**	**7**	**91**	**40**	**48**
York City Reserves	**32**	**21**	**3**	**8**	**96**	**42**	**45**
Stocksbridge Works	**32**	**17**	**7**	**8**	**79**	**53**	**41**
Bradford City Reserves	32	18	4	10	72	41	40
Doncaster United	32	17	6	9	55	38	40
Retford Town Reserves	32	17	4	11	66	54	38
Hampton Sports	32	12	7	13	53	54	31
Harrogate Railway Athletic	32	14	3	15	54	58	31
Leeds Ashley Road	32	13	4	15	53	67	30
Micklefield Welfare	32	12	4	16	37	57	28
Rawmarsh Welfare	32	10	7	15	60	69	27
Yorkshire Amateurs	32	9	4	19	39	60	22
Ossett Town	32	8	6	18	51	79	22
Heeley Amateurs	32	7	6	19	53	97	20
Swallownest Miners Welfare	32	5	6	21	38	82	16
Brodsworth Miners Welfare	32	4	4	24	30	111	12

Bradford City Reserves left the league. Lincoln United joined from the Lincolnshire League and Thackley joined from the West Yorkshire League.

Yorkshire League (II) 1967-1970

1967-68

Division One

Bridlington Trinity	32	24	4	4	90	42	52
Denaby United	32	18	10	4	67	29	46
Bridlington Town	32	20	6	6	74	47	46
Hatfield Main	32	18	7	7	69	39	43
Kiveton Park	32	15	9	8	54	40	39
Farsley Celtic	32	15	7	10	48	34	37
Hull Brunswick	32	14	9	9	60	45	37
Wombwell Sporting Association	32	14	8	10	56	40	36
Selby Town	32	14	8	10	65	61	36
Barton Town	32	13	5	14	67	65	31
Ossett Albion	32	9	10	13	40	58	28
York City Reserves	32	11	3	18	71	46	25
Mexborough Town	32	8	8	16	54	74	24
Norton Woodseats	32	6	10	16	51	71	22
Hallam	32	5	8	19	48	86	18
Thorne Colliery	32	6	4	22	49	94	16
Stocksbridge Works	***32***	***2***	***4***	***26***	***28***	***99***	***8***

Barton Town moved to the Midland League.
York City Reserves left the league.

Division Two

Lincoln United	**32**	**23**	**5**	**4**	**96**	**23**	**51**
Hampton Sports	32	20	6	6	79	35	46
Retford Town Reserves	32	19	8	5	75	38	46
Thackley	32	17	9	6	54	28	43
Heeley Amateurs	32	20	3	9	62	49	43
Leeds Ashley Road	32	16	5	11	55	51	37
Micklefield Welfare	32	15	6	11	58	47	36
Sheffield	32	14	7	11	56	44	35
Harrogate Railway Athletic	32	12	9	11	44	62	33
Scarborough Reserves	32	12	7	13	62	66	31
Yorkshire Amateurs	32	9	7	16	37	62	25
Swallownest Miners Welfare	32	7	10	15	45	60	24
Doncaster United	32	8	5	19	40	51	21
Rawmarsh Welfare	32	7	7	18	54	70	21
Brodsworth Miners Welfare	32	6	8	18	38	71	20
Ossett Town	32	6	6	20	36	86	18
Harrogate Town	32	5	4	23	31	83	14

Guiseley joined from the West Yorkshire League, Hall Road Rangers joined from the East Riding County League and Frecheville Community Association joined from the Sheffield & Hallamshire County Senior League.

1968-69

Division One

Farsley Celtic	34	21	9	4	60	21	51
Mexborough Town	34	24	2	8	69	29	50
Kiveton Park	34	23	4	7	69	35	50
Selby Town	34	18	12	4	78	44	48
Bridlington Trinity	34	19	7	8	68	41	45
Bridlington Town	34	19	6	9	63	42	44
Wombwell Sporting Association	34	18	6	10	72	39	42
Denaby United	34	15	3	16	63	49	33
Thackley	34	12	9	13	41	46	33
Lincoln United	34	12	8	14	59	55	32
Hatfield Main	34	12	8	14	53	51	32
Ossett Albion	34	10	6	18	58	80	26
Hallam	34	10	6	18	53	84	26
Retford Town Reserves	34	9	5	20	56	74	23
Norton Woodseats	34	8	5	21	43	98	21
Hull Brunswick	***34***	***6***	***7***	***21***	***51***	***78***	***19***
Thorne Colliery	***34***	***7***	***5***	***22***	***51***	***100***	***19***
Hampton Sports	***34***	***8***	***2***	***24***	***54***	***97***	***18***

Retford Town Reserves left the league.

Division Two

Rawmarsh Welfare	32	23	5	4	110	35	51
Heeley Amateurs	32	21	5	6	81	25	47
Swallownest Miners Welfare	32	21	5	6	101	43	47
Frecheville Community Assoc.	32	21	4	7	83	27	46
Scarborough Reserves	32	18	4	10	84	54	40
Yorkshire Amateurs	32	16	3	13	64	68	35
Guiseley	32	15	4	13	79	74	34
Harrogate Railway Athletic	32	15	4	13	54	64	34
Sheffield	32	13	7	12	62	61	33
Leeds Ashley Road	32	11	10	11	55	65	32
Brodsworth Miners Welfare	32	11	6	15	68	68	28
Ossett Town	32	10	7	15	53	72	27
Stocksbridge Works	32	9	6	17	78	106	24
Hall Road Rangers	32	7	8	17	68	107	22
Doncaster United	32	7	2	23	50	96	16
Harrogate Town	32	7	2	23	42	85	16
Micklefield Welfare	32	4	4	24	39	128	12

Mickleheld Welfare moved to the West Yorkshire League and Doncaster United disbanded. Emley joined from the Huddersfield League, North Ferriby United joined from the East Riding Amateur League, Firth Vickers joined from the Sheffield & Hallamshire County Senior League and Dinnington Athletic also joined.

1969-70

Division One

Rawmarsh Welfare	34	26	2	6	90	39	54
Bridlington Trinity	34	20	8	6	70	44	48
Mexborough Town	34	20	6	8	66	41	46
Farsley Celtic	34	17	10	7	55	28	44
Selby Town	34	18	8	8	69	47	44
Wombwell Sporting Association	34	16	9	9	69	50	41
Denaby United	34	15	8	11	58	40	38
Bridlington Town	34	14	9	11	68	50	37
Lincoln United	34	16	5	13	58	47	37
Hallam	34	13	6	15	72	76	32
Ossett Albion	34	12	7	15	44	46	31
Frecheville Community Association	34	12	4	18	52	54	28
Thackley	***34***	***11***	***5***	***18***	***37***	***43***	***27***
Swallownest Miners Welfare	***34***	***10***	***5***	***19***	***46***	***70***	***25***
Norton Woodseats	***34***	***8***	***9***	***17***	***46***	***87***	***25***
Hatfield Main	***34***	***7***	***6***	***21***	***41***	***73***	***20***
Kiveton Park	***34***	***6***	***6***	***22***	***39***	***100***	***18***
Heeley Amateurs	***34***	***5***	***7***	***22***	***45***	***90***	***17***

Barton Town joined from the Midland League and Winterton Rangers joined from the Lincolnshire League.

Division Two

Dinnington Athletic	34	24	7	3	91	37	55
Emley	34	23	4	7	79	29	50
North Ferriby United	34	20	9	5	95	46	49
Hull Brunswick	34	20	6	8	103	52	46
Scarborough Reserves	34	17	7	10	76	47	41
Yorkshire Amateurs	34	14	9	11	57	54	37
Brodsworth Miners Welfare	34	15	5	14	60	59	35
Thorne Colliery	34	15	5	14	76	84	35
Stocksbridge Works	***34***	***14***	***6***	***14***	***67***	***66***	***34***
Harrogate Town	***34***	***12***	***10***	***12***	***40***	***54***	***34***
Sheffield	***34***	***9***	***12***	***13***	***41***	***51***	***30***
Guiseley	***34***	***10***	***8***	***16***	***68***	***83***	***28***
Hampton Sports	34	11	5	18	60	82	27
Harrogate Railway Athletic	***34***	***10***	***7***	***17***	***39***	***55***	***27***
Firth Vickers	***34***	***11***	***4***	***19***	***54***	***83***	***26***
Leeds Ashley Road	***34***	***9***	***5***	***20***	***47***	***84***	***23***
Hall Road Rangers	***34***	***8***	***6***	***20***	***45***	***79***	***22***
Ossett Town	***34***	***3***	***7***	***24***	***29***	***74***	***13***

Hampton Sports left the league.

A new Division Three was formed of 15 clubs. The 9 clubs in bold italics above were relegated to the new division and 6 new clubs joined. Sheffield Water Works joined from the Sheffield & Hallamshire County Senior League, Bradford Park Avenue Reserves joined from the Northern Intermediate League, Brook Sports joined from the West Riding County Amateur League and International Harvesters joined from the Doncaster & District Senior League. Leeds & Carnegie College joined as a newly-formed club and St. John College (York) also joined.

1970-71

Division One

Lincoln United	26	16	7	3	56	26	39
Farsley Celtic	26	13	9	4	41	25	35
Rawmarsh Welfare	26	13	8	5	49	30	34
Mexborough Town	26	12	7	7	56	40	31
Hallam	26	13	5	8	49	42	31
Bridlington Town	26	10	7	9	43	35	27
Denaby United	26	11	4	11	44	37	26
Ossett Albion	26	8	8	10	30	36	24
Bridlington Trinity	26	9	4	13	43	50	22
Winterton Rangers	26	8	6	12	40	48	22
Frecheville Community Association	26	8	6	12	41	51	22
Selby Town	26	7	5	14	42	54	19
Barton Town	*26*	*5*	*9*	*12*	*41*	*65*	*19*
Wombwell Sporting Association	*26*	*3*	*7*	*16*	*20*	*56*	*13*

Division Two

North Ferriby United	**26**	**17**	**6**	**3**	**69**	**19**	**40**
Thackley	**26**	**16**	**6**	**4**	**55**	**21**	**38**
Scarborough Reserves	**26**	**16**	**3**	**7**	**67**	**38**	**35**
Emley	**26**	**14**	**7**	**5**	**51**	**29**	**35**
Hull Brunswick	26	13	7	6	46	36	33
Hatfield Main	26	14	4	8	46	36	32
Dinnington Athletic	26	11	3	12	42	37	25
Norton Woodseats	26	9	3	14	45	51	21
Kiveton Park	26	9	3	14	41	62	21
Yorkshire Amateurs	26	7	4	15	42	51	18
Heeley Amateurs	26	6	6	14	33	64	18
Thorne Colliery	26	5	6	15	35	69	16
Brodsworth Miners Welfare	26	7	2	17	24	55	16
Swallownest Miners Welfare	26	6	4	16	31	71	16

Swallownest Miners Welfare left the league.

Division Three

Stocksbridge Works	**28**	**19**	**5**	**4**	**74**	**38**	**43**
Brook Sports	**28**	**16**	**8**	**4**	**60**	**46**	**40**
Leeds & Carnegie College	**28**	**15**	**5**	**8**	**69**	**32**	**35**
Guiseley	**28**	**14**	**5**	**9**	**68**	**52**	**33**
Harrogate Railway Athletic	28	13	5	10	42	40	31
Sheffield	28	12	6	10	61	52	30
St. John College (York)	28	9	10	9	45	37	28
Ossett Town	28	10	8	10	48	44	28
Leeds Ashley Road	28	10	7	11	48	41	27
Hall Road Rangers	28	11	4	13	49	66	26
International Harvesters	28	9	7	12	50	52	25
Harrogate Town	28	8	8	6	14	34	45	22
Bradford (Park Avenue) Reserves	28	8	5	15	39	53	21
Firth Vickers	28	8	3	17	43	72	19
Sheffield Water Works	28	3	6	19	23	81	12

Firth Vickers moved to the Sheffield & Hallamshire County Senior League. Woolley Miners Welfare and Worsbrough Bridge Miners Welfare both joined from the Sheffield & Hallamshire County Senior League while Blackburn Welfare and Retford Town Reserves also joined.

1971-72

Division One

Winterton Rangers	30	20	5	5	60	30	45
Farsley Celtic	30	16	7	7	43	28	39
Bridlington Town	30	12	9	9	35	28	33
Mexborough Town	30	14	5	11	49	43	33
Denaby United	30	12	9	9	52	47	33
North Ferriby United	30	14	5	11	53	49	33
Selby Town	30	12	6	12	41	45	30
Emley	30	12	5	13	38	40	29
Hallam	30	12	4	14	48	68	28
Lincoln United	30	10	6	14	39	41	26
Frecheville Community Association	30	10	6	14	36	46	26
Rawmarsh Welfare	30	9	7	14	42	43	25
Thackley	*30*	*6*	*13*	*11*	*35*	*38*	*25*
Scarborough Reserves	*30*	*10*	*5*	*15*	*44*	*49*	*25*
Ossett Albion	*30*	*9*	*7*	*14*	*34*	*44*	*25*
Bridlington Trinity	30	9	7	14	33	43	25

Bridlington Trinity moved to the Midland League.

Division Two

Barton Town	**28**	**20**	**5**	**3**	**89**	**28**	**45**
Yorkshire Amateurs	**28**	**17**	**8**	**3**	**60**	**28**	**42**
Kiveton Park	**28**	**16**	**10**	**2**	**70**	**34**	**42**
Brook Sports	**28**	**13**	**7**	**8**	**53**	**47**	**33**
Leeds & Carnegie College	28	12	7	9	46	35	31
Hull Brunswick	28	11	7	10	48	32	29
Hatfield Main	28	12	5	11	42	36	29
Guiseley	28	10	6	12	45	43	26
Stocksbridge Works	28	9	8	11	35	40	26
Wombwell Sporting Association	28	8	8	12	37	41	24
Thorne Colliery	28	8	6	14	46	79	22
Dinnington Athletic	28	7	7	14	34	67	21
Norton Woodseats	28	6	7	15	33	56	19
Heeley	*28*	*7*	*5*	*16*	*32*	*66*	*19*
Brodsworth Miners Welfare	*28*	*4*	*4*	*20*	*26*	*64*	*12*

Division Three

Leeds Ashley Road	**26**	**16**	**7**	**3**	**58**	**21**	**39**
Harrogate Town	**26**	**15**	**6**	**5**	**54**	**27**	**36**
Worsbrough Bridge M.W.	**26**	**17**	**1**	**8**	**75**	**38**	**35**
Woolley Miners Welfare	**26**	**15**	**5**	**6**	**63**	**42**	**35**
St. John College (York)	26	16	2	8	49	49	34
Ossett Town	26	12	4	10	44	35	28
Sheffield	26	12	4	10	39	39	28
Bradford (Park Avenue) Reserves	26	11	4	11	44	36	26
International Harvesters	26	8	7	11	46	42	23
Hall Road Rangers	26	8	6	12	40	41	22
Harrogate Railway Athletic	26	8	5	13	29	40	21
Retford Town Reserves	26	5	4	17	36	65	14
Blackburn Welfare	26	5	4	17	35	64	14
Sheffield Water Works	26	4	1	21	26	99	9

Liversedge joined from the West Riding County Amateur League, Pickering Town joined from the York & District League and Sheffield Polytechnic and Worksop Town Reserves also joined.

Yorkshire League (II) 1972-1974

1972-73

Division One

Team	P	W	D	L	F	A	Pts
Mexborough Town	30	17	10	3	65	32	44
Emley	30	14	11	5	52	29	39
Barton Town	30	18	2	10	54	33	38
Denaby United	30	16	5	9	56	37	37
Farsley Celtic	30	15	7	8	53	37	37
Lincoln United	30	13	7	10	39	37	33
Winterton Rangers	30	10	11	9	59	57	31
Yorkshire Amateurs	30	11	8	11	30	33	30
Frecheville Community Association	30	9	10	11	37	37	28
Hallam	30	11	6	13	60	67	28
Kiveton Park	30	11	6	13	50	71	28
Rawmarsh Welfare	30	10	7	13	51	53	27
North Ferriby United	**30**	**9**	**6**	**15**	**52**	**46**	**24**
Brook Sports	**30**	**7**	**7**	**16**	**51**	**82**	**21**
Selby Town	**30**	**7**	**6**	**17**	**33**	**63**	**20**
Bridlington Town	**30**	**4**	**7**	**19**	**45**	**73**	**15**

Division Two

Team	P	W	D	L	F	A	Pts
Leeds & Carnegie College	**30**	**21**	**1**	**8**	**73**	**30**	**43**
Woolley Miners Welfare	**30**	**19**	**4**	**7**	**85**	**57**	**42**
Worsbrough Bridge M.W.	**30**	**18**	**5**	**7**	**74**	**39**	**41**
Hatfield Main	**30**	**18**	**2**	**10**	**66**	**37**	**38**
Leeds Ashley Road	30	15	5	10	57	37	35
Harrogate Town	30	16	3	11	55	44	35
Ossett Albion	30	14	3	13	55	49	31
Scarborough Reserves	30	14	2	14	64	52	30
Hull Brunswick	30	12	6	12	33	43	30
Thackley	30	9	9	12	35	37	27
Wombwell Sporting Association	30	9	9	12	41	55	27
Guiseley	30	10	7	13	43	62	27
Norton Woodseats	30	11	3	16	54	75	25
Dinnington Athletic	30	7	9	14	41	48	23
Stocksbridge Works	**30**	**8**	**5**	**17**	**36**	**54**	**21**
Thorne Colliery	**30**	**1**	**3**	**26**	**30**	**123**	**5**

Hull Brunswick disbanded.

Division Three

Team	P	W	D	L	F	A	Pts
Hall Road Rangers	**30**	**15**	**11**	**4**	**56**	**37**	**41**
Liversedge	**30**	**18**	**4**	**8**	**63**	**35**	**40**
Ossett Town	**30**	**16**	**6**	**8**	**49**	**35**	**38**
Bradford (Park Avenue) Reserves	30	16	5	9	68	43	37
Pickering Town	30	15	7	8	61	45	37
Worksop Town Reserves	30	15	6	9	55	42	36
Blackburn Welfare	30	13	9	8	62	48	35
Sheffield	30	13	9	8	55	45	35
Harrogate Railway Athletic	30	11	11	8	36	30	33
International Harvesters	30	11	7	12	55	48	29
Sheffield Water Works	30	8	7	15	43	63	23
St. John College (York)	30	8	5	17	39	70	21
Retford Town Reserves	30	9	2	19	44	66	20
Brodsworth Miners Welfare	30	5	9	16	32	50	19
Heeley	30	8	2	20	44	77	18
Sheffield Polytechnic	30	6	6	18	32	60	18

Harrogate Railway Athletic moved to the Harrogate & District League and Bradford (Park Avenue) Reserves and Retford Town Reserves also left. Maltby Miners Welfare joined from the Sheffield & Hallamshire County Senior League, Bentley Victoria joined from the Doncaster & District Senior League, Redfearn National Glass joined from the Barnsley Association League and Tadcaster Albion also joined.

1973-74

Division One

Team	P	W	D	L	F	A	Pts
Lincoln United	30	19	4	7	61	33	42
Emley	30	19	4	7	54	35	42
Farsley Celtic	30	16	7	7	60	37	39
Mexborough Town	30	14	9	7	72	44	37
Hallam	30	13	8	9	66	64	34
Denaby United	30	13	7	10	44	42	33
Hatfield Main	30	11	8	11	62	56	30
Worsbrough Bridge M.W.	30	12	6	12	53	58	30
Winterton Rangers	30	11	6	13	51	53	28
Frecheville Community Association	30	10	8	12	34	39	28
Leeds & Carnegie College	30	11	6	13	49	66	28
Yorkshire Amateurs	30	11	5	14	44	45	27
Kiveton Park	**30**	**9**	**5**	**16**	**43**	**53**	**23**
Barton Town	**30**	**9**	**3**	**18**	**38**	**57**	**21**
Rawmarsh Welfare	**30**	**7**	**6**	**17**	**37**	**54**	**20**
Woolley Miners Welfare	**30**	**8**	**2**	**20**	**44**	**76**	**18**

Mexborough Town moved to the Midland League and were replaced by their reserves.

Division Two

Team	P	W	D	L	F	A	Pts
Thackley	**30**	**21**	**5**	**4**	**58**	**19**	**47**
Ossett Albion	**30**	**19**	**9**	**2**	**66**	**27**	**47**
North Ferriby United	**30**	**17**	**8**	**5**	**61**	**34**	**42**
Guiseley	**30**	**16**	**7**	**7**	**52**	**33**	**39**
Liversedge	30	15	7	8	45	33	37
Scarborough Reserves	30	13	5	12	43	41	31
Leeds Ashley Road	30	12	6	12	41	47	30
Hall Road Rangers	30	8	11	11	40	45	27
Harrogate Town	30	9	9	12	37	43	27
Bridlington Town	30	10	6	14	46	53	26
Dinnington Athletic	30	10	5	15	37	53	25
Ossett Town	30	9	6	15	47	53	24
Selby Town	30	7	10	13	33	48	24
Brook Sports	**30**	**8**	**6**	**16**	**37**	**44**	**22**
Wombwell Sporting Association	**30**	**7**	**3**	**20**	**24**	**61**	**17**
Norton Woodseats	**30**	**5**	**5**	**20**	**30**	**63**	**15**

Dinnington Athletic moved to the Rotherham Association League.

Division Three

Team	P	W	D	L	F	A	Pts
Pickering Town	**30**	**22**	**4**	**4**	**96**	**34**	**48**
Maltby Miners Welfare	**30**	**17**	**10**	**3**	**60**	**27**	**44**
Bentley Victoria	**30**	**19**	**6**	**5**	**76**	**39**	**44**
Redfearn National Glass	**30**	**17**	**8**	**5**	**73**	**40**	**42**
Heeley	30	16	4	10	75	45	36
St. John College (York)	30	16	4	10	64	51	36
International Harvesters	30	13	7	10	56	42	33
Stocksbridge Works	30	13	4	13	73	49	30
Sheffield Water Works	30	11	7	12	47	57	29
Sheffield	30	12	4	14	62	52	28
Tadcaster Albion	30	13	2	15	54	54	28
Worksop Town Reserves	30	11	3	16	46	63	25
Brodsworth Miners Welfare	30	5	8	17	33	66	18
Sheffield Polytechnic	30	3	10	17	33	67	16
Blackburn Welfare	30	4	4	22	33	108	12
Thorne Colliery	30	3	5	22	41	128	11

Worksop Town Reserves and Sheffield Polytechnic both left the league. B.S.C. Parkgate joined from the Sheffield & Hallamshire County Senior League and York Railway Institute joined from the York & District League. Bentley Victoria changed their name to Bentley Victoria Welfare.

Yorkshire League (II) 1974-1976

1974-75

Division One

Ossett Albion	30	19	5	6	59	34	43
Frecheville Community Association	30	18	6	6	50	29	42
Thackley	30	13	13	4	35	21	39
Farsley Celtic	30	14	9	7	32	31	37
Emley	30	11	11	8	55	39	33
Lincoln United	30	12	7	11	45	33	31
Hallam	30	12	7	11	50	45	31
Winterton Rangers	30	10	9	11	49	60	29
Leeds & Carnegie College	30	10	8	12	52	57	28
North Ferriby United	30	10	7	13	48	48	27
Hatfield Main	30	9	8	13	53	53	26
Worsbrough Bridge M.W.	30	8	9	13	41	58	25
Guiseley	*30*	*8*	*9*	*13*	*35*	*54*	*25*
Mexborough Town Reserves	30	6	12	12	41	51	24
Denaby United	*30*	*4*	*14*	*12*	*44*	*55*	*22*
Yorkshire Amateurs	*30*	*5*	*8*	*17*	*29*	*50*	*18*

Mexborough Town Reserves left the league.

Division Two

Bridlington Town	**28**	**15**	**9**	**4**	**43**	**26**	**39**
Pickering Town	**28**	**14**	**9**	**5**	**55**	**32**	**37**
Redfearn National Glass	**28**	**14**	**7**	**7**	**43**	**31**	**35**
Maltby Miners Welfare	**28**	**15**	**4**	**9**	**43**	**32**	**34**
Liversedge	28	14	5	9	56	32	33
Barton Town	28	11	6	11	41	41	28
Kiveton Park	28	9	9	10	37	37	27
Bentley Victoria Welfare	28	9	8	11	38	44	26
Hall Road Rangers	28	7	11	10	33	45	25
Harrogate Town	28	8	8	12	41	37	24
Woolley Miners Welfare	28	6	12	10	34	47	24
Leeds Ashley Road	28	9	5	14	32	37	23
Scarborough Reserves	*28*	*7*	*9*	*12*	*29*	*44*	*23*
Rawmarsh Welfare	*28*	*6*	*9*	*13*	*37*	*55*	*21*
Ossett Town	*28*	*6*	*9*	*13*	*27*	*49*	*19*

Ossett Town had 2 points deducted.

Division Three

Stocksbridge Works	**30**	**25**	**2**	**3**	**91**	**28**	**52**
Selby Town	**30**	**20**	**6**	**4**	**77**	**31**	**46**
Tadcaster Albion	**30**	**20**	**6**	**4**	**70**	**37**	**46**
Norton Woodseats	**30**	**19**	**6**	**5**	**82**	**38**	**44**
Sheffield	30	15	5	10	58	45	35
Thorne Colliery	30	13	7	10	59	47	33
St. John College (York)	30	13	6	11	62	47	32
Wombwell Sporting Association	30	13	4	13	44	61	30
B.S.C. Parkgate	30	10	9	11	58	49	29
Heeley	30	8	7	15	47	65	23
Brook Sports	30	9	4	17	41	59	22
International Harvesters	30	6	9	15	29	48	21
Sheffield Water Works	30	7	7	16	27	62	21
York Railway Institute	30	7	4	19	42	78	18
Brodsworth Miners Welfare	30	7	1	22	45	82	15
Blackburn Welfare	30	5	3	22	31	86	13

International Harvesters moved to the Doncaster & District Senior League and Blackburn Welfare also left the league. Rossington Miners Welfare joined from the Doncaster & District Senior League and Collingham and Dodworth Miners Welfare also joined.

1975-76

Division One

Emley	30	21	7	2	68	25	49
North Ferriby United	30	21	4	5	70	25	46
Hallam	30	15	4	11	58	44	34
Bridlington Town	30	14	6	10	41	38	34
Leeds & Carnegie College	30	14	5	11	52	40	33
Thackley	30	10	13	7	28	26	33
Hatfield Main	30	11	10	9	48	45	32
Redfearn National Glass	30	11	10	9	45	47	32
Ossett Albion	30	12	6	12	46	43	30
Winterton Rangers	30	10	8	12	44	44	28
Lincoln United	30	10	7	13	41	50	27
Pickering Town	30	9	8	13	36	49	26
Farsley Celtic	*30*	*7*	*9*	*14*	*28*	*46*	*23*
Maltby Miners Welfare	*30*	*9*	*3*	*18*	*45*	*70*	*21*
Worsbrough Bridge M.W.	*30*	*8*	*1*	*21*	*41*	*60*	*17*
Frecheville Community Assoc.	*30*	*6*	*3*	*21*	*44*	*83*	*15*

Leeds & Carnegie College changed their name to Leeds & Carnegie Polytechnic.

Division Two

Guiseley	**28**	**19**	**7**	**2**	**69**	**26**	**45**
Leeds Ashley Road	**28**	**18**	**7**	**3**	**58**	**23**	**43**
Liversedge	**28**	**14**	**10**	**4**	**47**	**25**	**38**
Denaby United	**28**	**16**	**3**	**9**	**44**	**32**	**35**
Kiveton Park	28	15	4	9	50	28	34
Woolley Miners Welfare	28	13	6	9	54	49	32
Tadcaster Albion	28	13	5	10	55	55	31
Barton Town	28	9	12	7	40	32	30
Selby Town	28	9	8	11	28	34	26
Norton Woodseats	28	11	3	14	47	48	25
Yorkshire Amateurs	28	4	11	13	29	56	19
Harrogate Town	28	5	8	15	30	51	18
Bentley Victoria Welfare	*28*	*4*	*10*	*14*	*29*	*50*	*18*
Hall Road Rangers	*28*	*5*	*5*	*18*	*29*	*62*	*15*
Stocksbridge Works	*28*	*3*	*5*	*20*	*31*	*69*	*11*

Division Three

Rawmarsh Welfare	**30**	**20**	**5**	**5**	**62**	**21**	**45**
Scarborough Reserves	**30**	**20**	**5**	**5**	**74**	**40**	**45**
Ossett Town	**30**	**20**	**5**	**5**	**60**	**34**	**45**
Sheffield	**30**	**14**	**9**	**7**	**50**	**29**	**37**
B.S.C. Parkgate	30	13	9	8	53	52	35
Thorne Colliery	30	13	6	11	55	42	32
Brook Sports	30	14	2	14	51	38	30
Wombwell Sporting Association	30	12	6	12	43	42	30
Collingham	30	11	8	11	46	45	30
Dodworth Miners Welfare	30	9	11	10	46	44	29
Sheffield Water Works	30	11	6	13	44	51	28
St. John College (York)	30	7	10	13	49	54	24
Heeley	30	10	4	16	43	63	24
Rossington Miners Welfare	30	6	9	15	24	42	21
York Railway Institute	30	5	5	20	40	73	15
Brodsworth Miners Welfare	30	4	2	24	26	96	10

Brodsworth Miners Welfare left the league. Fryston Colliery Welfare joined from the West Yorkshire League and Pilkington Recreation joined from the Sheffield & Hallamshire County Senior League.

Yorkshire League (II) 1976-1978

1976-77

Division One

	P	W	D	L	F	A	Pts
Winterton Rangers	30	17	10	3	77	31	44
Emley	30	18	8	4	66	38	44
Ossett Albion	30	17	5	8	51	28	39
Guiseley	30	18	3	9	55	37	39
Leeds Ashley Road	30	16	6	8	48	35	38
Thackley	30	14	9	7	44	26	37
Hallam	30	14	9	7	47	33	37
North Ferriby United	30	14	8	8	62	38	36
Bridlington Town	30	9	10	11	45	43	28
Leeds & Carnegie Polytechnic	30	11	3	16	45	42	25
Lincoln United	30	8	9	13	45	51	25
Denaby United	30	8	7	15	40	60	23
Redfearn National Glass	30	7	9	14	40	64	23
Liversedge	*30*	*7*	*6*	*17*	*37*	*57*	*20*
Hatfield Main	*30*	*3*	*7*	*20*	*30*	*87*	*13*
Pickering Town	*30*	*4*	*1*	*25*	*23*	*85*	*9*

Redfearn National Glass moved to the Barnsley Association League.

Division Two

	P	W	D	L	F	A	Pts
Sheffield	**30**	**15**	**10**	**5**	**42**	**26**	**40**
Tadcaster Albion	**30**	**15**	**7**	**8**	**53**	**33**	**37**
Frecheville Community Assoc.	**30**	**14**	**9**	**7**	**50**	**33**	**37**
Farsley Celtic	**30**	**16**	**4**	**10**	**42**	**24**	**36**
Ossett Town	30	14	8	8	48	31	36
Barton Town	30	10	14	6	48	38	34
Kiveton Park	30	11	10	9	45	45	32
Norton Woodseats	30	11	9	10	48	41	31
Worsbrough Bridge M.W.	30	11	9	10	49	45	31
Harrogate Town	30	9	12	9	45	50	30
Maltby Miners Welfare	30	9	11	10	47	55	29
Scarborough Reserves	30	10	8	12	43	48	28
Yorkshire Amateurs	*30*	*6*	*15*	*9*	*34*	*39*	*27*
Rawmarsh Welfare	*30*	*5*	*10*	*15*	*32*	*49*	*20*
Woolley Miners Welfare	*30*	*7*	*4*	*19*	*42*	*71*	*18*
Selby Town	*30*	*3*	*8*	*19*	*26*	*66*	*14*

Division Three

	P	W	D	L	F	A	Pts
Bentley Victoria Welfare	30	19	6	5	70	38	44
Fryston Colliery Welfare	30	16	6	8	64	39	38
Brook Sports	30	15	6	9	54	33	36
Collingham	30	13	10	7	51	34	36
Hall Road Rangers	30	14	7	9	50	35	35
Thorne Colliery	30	13	7	10	47	38	33
York Railway Institute	30	12	8	10	68	64	32
Dodworth Miners Welfare	30	11	9	10	50	57	31
Wombwell Sporting Association	30	11	9	10	36	44	31
Sheffield Water Works	30	10	8	12	41	41	28
St. John College (York)	30	11	6	13	58	61	28
Rossington Miners Welfare	30	9	6	15	46	55	24
Stocksbridge Works	30	10	4	16	40	60	24
B.S.C. Parkgate	30	8	5	17	41	59	21
Heeley	30	7	9	14	38	63	19
Pilkington Recreation	30	4	8	18	30	63	16

Heeley had 4 points deducted.
Heeley left the league. Harworth Colliery Institute joined from the Sheffield & Hallamshire County Senior League.

1977-78

Division One

	P	W	D	L	F	A	Pts
Emley	30	20	7	3	63	33	47
Winterton Rangers	30	15	12	3	62	35	42
Thackley	30	13	11	6	41	27	37
North Ferriby United	30	12	11	7	50	40	35
Guiseley	30	13	8	9	59	41	34
Hallam	30	14	6	10	47	42	34
Sheffield	30	12	9	9	42	35	33
Frecheville Community Association	30	10	9	11	41	41	29
Tadcaster Albion	30	9	10	11	42	51	28
Bridlington Town	30	11	5	14	41	49	27
Lincoln United	30	8	9	13	42	61	25
Leeds Ashley Road	30	9	6	15	35	45	24
Ossett Albion	*30*	*6*	*10*	*14*	*49*	*58*	*22*
Leeds & Carnegie Polytechnic	*30*	*9*	*3*	*18*	*38*	*46*	*21*
Farsley Celtic	*30*	*5*	*11*	*14*	*41*	*63*	*21*
Denaby United	*30*	*8*	*5*	*17*	*39*	*65*	*21*

Division Two

	P	W	D	L	F	A	Pts
Kiveton Park	**28**	**17**	**3**	**8**	**52**	**27**	**37**
Ossett Town	**28**	**14**	**7**	**7**	**43**	**27**	**35**
Bentley Victoria Welfare	**28**	**13**	**8**	**7**	**53**	**34**	**34**
Scarborough Reserves	**28**	**15**	**4**	**9**	**43**	**28**	**34**
Liversedge	28	12	10	6	41	34	34
Norton Woodseats	28	13	6	9	45	33	32
Maltby Miners Welfare	28	11	9	8	47	33	31
Barton Town	28	13	3	12	43	36	29
Worsbrough Bridge M.W.	28	10	9	9	45	47	29
Brook Sports	28	11	6	11	46	48	28
Hatfield Main	28	11	4	13	43	47	26
Fryston Colliery Welfare	28	7	8	13	29	45	22
Harrogate Town	*28*	*7*	*6*	*15*	*38*	*55*	*20*
Pickering Town	*28*	*8*	*3*	*17*	*38*	*73*	*19*
Collingham	*28*	*2*	*6*	*20*	*22*	*61*	*10*

Division Three

	P	W	D	L	F	A	Pts
Yorkshire Amateurs	**30**	**18**	**7**	**5**	**59**	**23**	**43**
Wombwell Sporting Association	**30**	**17**	**7**	**6**	**45**	**28**	**41**
Rawmarsh Welfare	**30**	**16**	**8**	**6**	**66**	**40**	**40**
Thorne Colliery	**30**	**15**	**9**	**6**	**60**	**40**	**39**
Sheffield Water Works	30	15	8	7	52	25	38
Dodworth Miners Welfare	30	13	12	5	71	43	38
York Railway Institute	30	15	7	8	71	41	37
Hall Road Rangers	30	10	11	9	52	47	31
Pilkington Recreation	30	12	6	12	54	47	30
Harworth Colliery Institute	30	12	5	13	53	61	29
Stocksbridge Works	30	13	2	15	42	50	28
B.S.C. Parkgate	30	10	4	16	40	59	24
Selby Town	30	7	8	15	47	60	22
Woolley Miners Welfare	30	7	7	16	45	68	21
St. John College (York)	30	3	7	20	40	86	13
Rossington Miners Welfare	30	1	4	25	22	101	6

St. John College (York) moved to the York & District League.
Garforth Miners joined from the West Yorkshire League.

Yorkshire League (II) 1978-1980

1978-79

Division One

Winterton Rangers	30	19	5	6	54	21	43
Emley	30	18	5	7	58	31	41
North Ferriby United	30	16	9	5	55	31	41
Guiseley	30	11	9	10	35	32	31
Thackley	30	13	5	12	41	39	31
Ossett Town	30	14	2	14	42	37	30
Scarborough Reserves	30	10	10	10	34	36	30
Sheffield	30	9	11	10	26	28	29
Leeds Ashley Road	30	10	8	12	34	37	28
Hallam	30	12	4	14	33	42	28
Bridlington Town	30	11	6	13	36	48	28
Frecheville Community Association	30	7	13	10	33	42	27
Tadcaster Albion	*30*	*9*	*8*	*13*	*33*	*39*	*26*
Bentley Victoria Welfare	*30*	*9*	*7*	*14*	*34*	*38*	*25*
Kiveton Park	*30*	*8*	*7*	*15*	*44*	*54*	*23*
Lincoln United	*30*	*5*	*9*	*16*	*28*	*65*	*19*

Division Two

Ossett Albion	30	17	9	4	37	18	43
Fryston Colliery Welfare	30	15	6	9	56	36	36
Thorne Colliery	30	12	12	6	45	34	36
Liversedge	30	13	9	8	39	33	35
Brook Sports	30	12	8	10	45	48	32
Farsley Celtic	30	10	11	9	49	38	31
Hatfield Main	30	11	9	10	39	36	31
Maltby Miners Welfare	30	8	12	10	37	38	28
Denaby United	30	10	7	13	47	51	27
Norton Woodseats	30	10	7	13	38	47	27
Yorkshire Amateurs	30	9	9	12	34	46	27
Barton Town	30	10	6	14	43	47	26
Rawmarsh Welfare	*30*	*8*	*10*	*12*	*45*	*51*	*26*
Worsbrough Bridge M.W.	*30*	*11*	*4*	*15*	*39*	*48*	*26*
Leeds & Carnegie Polytechnic	30	11	3	16	55	58	25
Wombwell Sporting Association	*30*	*9*	*6*	*15*	*33*	*52*	*24*

Leeds & Carnegie Polytechnic moved to the Northern Universities League.

Division Three

York Railway Institute	28	17	5	6	70	41	39
Stocksbridge Works	28	16	6	6	46	31	38
Harworth Colliery Institute	28	17	5	6	49	23	37
B.S.C. Parkgate	28	15	6	7	57	42	36
Hall Road Rangers	28	15	4	9	62	42	33
Pickering Town	28	13	7	8	67	47	33
Selby Town	28	14	4	10	37	30	32
Dodworth Miners Welfare	28	12	6	10	54	47	28
Woolley Miners Welfare	28	10	3	15	45	52	23
Collingham	28	8	7	13	42	51	23
Pilkington Recreation	28	9	5	14	36	45	23
Sheffield Water Works	28	8	7	13	32	45	23
Harrogate Town	28	7	6	15	27	55	20
Garforth Miners	28	5	7	16	30	62	17
Rossington Miners Welfare	28	3	4	21	29	70	10

Harworth Colliery Institute and Dodworth Miners Welfare each had 2 points deducted.
Hall Road Rangers had 1 point deducted.
Dodworth Miners Welfare left the league.
Pontefract Collieries joined from the West Yorkshire League.

1979-80

Division One

Emley	30	22	6	2	62	21	50
Guiseley	30	20	7	3	62	23	47
Thackley	30	13	9	8	43	35	35
Scarborough Reserves	30	14	6	10	43	37	34
Sheffield	30	11	11	8	34	24	33
Winterton Rangers	30	15	2	13	49	39	32
Hallam	30	13	5	12	42	46	31
North Ferriby United	30	9	12	9	32	30	30
Liversedge	30	10	9	11	34	33	29
Leeds Ashley Road	30	10	8	12	39	36	28
Frecheville Community Association	30	10	7	13	30	37	27
Bridlington Town	30	9	7	14	42	50	25
Thorne Colliery	*30*	*8*	*7*	*15*	*35*	*52*	*23*
Ossett Town	*30*	*7*	*8*	*15*	*31*	*47*	*22*
Fryston Colliery Welfare	*30*	*7*	*6*	*17*	*22*	*49*	*20*
Ossett Albion	*30*	*4*	*6*	*20*	*26*	*67*	*14*

Division Two

Barton Town	30	22	4	4	62	20	48
Bentley Victoria Welfare	30	19	6	5	70	38	44
Kiveton Park	30	17	8	5	61	38	42
Maltby Miners Welfare	30	15	9	6	50	30	39
Hatfield Main	30	14	8	8	54	29	36
B.S.C. Parkgate	30	15	4	11	44	37	34
York Railway Institute	30	12	9	9	47	49	33
Farsley Celtic	30	13	6	11	49	43	32
Norton Woodseats	30	11	10	9	43	39	32
Lincoln United	30	10	7	13	46	64	27
Harworth Colliery Institute	30	8	10	12	32	40	26
Yorkshire Amateurs	30	6	9	15	31	48	21
Brook Sports	*30*	*6*	*9*	*15*	*32*	*55*	*21*
Denaby United	*30*	*6*	*5*	*19*	*29*	*51*	*17*
Tadcaster Albion	*30*	*4*	*9*	*17*	*23*	*49*	*17*
Stocksbridge Works	*30*	*1*	*9*	*20*	*25*	*68*	*11*

Division Three

Hall Road Rangers	26	15	6	5	62	29	36
Garforth Miners	26	14	6	6	40	25	34
Rawmarsh Welfare	26	14	6	6	43	33	34
Pilkington Recreation	26	13	7	6	41	28	33
Pontefract Collieries	26	11	8	7	39	29	30
Harrogate Town	26	11	6	9	44	36	28
Worsbrough Bridge M.W.	26	9	7	10	31	31	25
Woolley Miners Welfare	26	7	11	8	35	36	25
Selby Town	26	8	9	9	32	41	25
Pickering Town	26	11	2	13	44	34	24
Collingham	26	9	6	11	26	36	24
Sheffield Water Works	26	9	5	12	41	44	23
Rossington Miners Welfare	26	4	4	18	25	70	12
Wombwell Sporting Association	26	3	5	18	25	56	11

Rossington Miners Welfare moved to the Doncaster & District Senior League. Bradley Rangers joined from the West Yorkshire League, Harrogate Railway Athletic joined from the Harrogate & District League and Grimethorpe Miners Welfare joined from the Doncaster & District Senior League. Sheffield Waterworks changed their name to Y.W.A. (Southern).

Yorkshire League (II) 1980-1982

1980-81 Division One

Leeds Ashley Road	30	18	8	4	58	25	44
Emley	30	17	8	5	61	36	42
North Ferriby United	30	16	8	6	40	23	40
Thackley	30	14	7	9	48	39	35
Guiseley	30	10	12	8	48	41	32
Winterton Rangers	30	12	8	10	35	31	32
Scarborough Reserves	30	13	5	12	55	49	31
Frecheville Community Association	30	10	11	9	41	38	31
Hallam	30	11	7	12	42	39	29
Liversedge	30	11	7	12	35	49	29
Barton Town	30	8	10	12	39	41	26
Sheffield	30	9	8	13	24	41	26
Bentley Victoria Welfare	30	9	7	14	47	47	25
Maltby Miners Welfare	**30**	**9**	**7**	**14**	**37**	**41**	**25**
Kiveton Park	**30**	**9**	**7**	**14**	**40**	**50**	**25**
Bridlington Town	**30**	**1**	**6**	**23**	**12**	**72**	**8**

Barton Town moved to the Lincolnshire League.

Division Two

Ossett Albion	**30**	**15**	**8**	**7**	**46**	**30**	**38**
York Railway Institute	**30**	**13**	**10**	**7**	**52**	**46**	**36**
Lincoln United	**30**	**10**	**14**	**6**	**48**	**40**	**34**
Farsley Celtic	**30**	**12**	**10**	**8**	**36**	**28**	**34**
Garforth Miners	30	12	9	9	49	42	33
Pilkington Recreation	30	12	9	9	48	42	33
B.S.C. Parkgate	30	11	9	10	31	35	31
Harworth Colliery Institute	30	10	10	10	46	40	30
Norton Woodseats	30	11	7	12	34	31	29
Yorkshire Amateurs	30	8	13	9	36	40	29
Hall Road Rangers	30	7	14	9	37	44	28
Ossett Town	30	11	5	14	37	41	27
Fryston Colliery Welfare	30	11	5	14	34	40	27
Hatfield Main	30	8	11	11	36	43	27
Thorne Colliery	**30**	**9**	**5**	**16**	**44**	**53**	**23**
Rawmarsh Welfare	**30**	**4**	**13**	**13**	**27**	**46**	**21**

Division Three

Bradley Rangers	**30**	**20**	**4**	**6**	**68**	**33**	**44**
Harrogate Town	**30**	**20**	**4**	**6**	**64**	**31**	**44**
Y.W.A. (Southern)	30	18	5	7	59	29	41
Grimethorpe Miners Welfare	**30**	**14**	**9**	**7**	**54**	**29**	**37**
Stocksbridge Works	30	16	5	9	56	44	37
Denaby United	30	14	8	8	55	36	36
Worsbrough Bridge M.W.	30	14	8	8	57	49	36
Pickering Town	30	12	10	8	43	34	34
Pontefract Collieries	30	13	8	9	48	41	34
Harrogate Railway Athletic	30	10	5	15	30	38	25
Tadcaster Albion	30	9	6	15	46	52	24
Wombwell Sporting Association	30	7	10	13	33	49	24
Brook Sports	30	6	9	15	30	51	21
Woolley Miners Welfare	30	6	5	19	34	61	17
Collingham	30	4	6	20	21	56	14
Selby Town	30	4	4	22	26	91	12

Y.W.A. (Southern) left the league.
Phoenix Park joined from the West Riding County Amateur League.

At the end of the 1981-82 season, the Yorkshire League merged with the Midland League to form the Northern Counties (East) League and all clubs, with the exception of Rawmarsh Welfare, moved into one of the divisions of the NCEL, as follows.

From Division One:
• Bentley Victoria Welfare, Emley, Guiseley, Thackley and Winterton Rangers all moved to the NCEL – Premier Division.
• Farsley Celtic, Leeds Ashley Road, Liversedge, North Ferriby United, Ossett Albion, Scarborough Reserves and York Railway Institute all moved to the NCEL – Division One (North).
• Frecheville Community Association, Hallam, Lincoln United and Sheffield all moved to the NCEL – Division One (South).

From Division Two:
• Bradley Rangers, Bridlington Town, Garforth Miners, Hall Road Rangers, Harrogate Town, Hatfield Main and Ossett Town all moved to the NCEL – Division One (North).

1981-82

Division One

Emley	30	16	9	5	57	27	41
Guiseley	30	17	5	8	52	33	39
Leeds Ashley Road	30	15	9	6	44	30	39
Scarborough Reserves	30	15	7	8	51	38	37
Bentley Victoria Welfare	30	13	9	8	46	37	35
Lincoln United	30	13	8	9	47	35	34
Winterton Rangers	30	13	8	9	37	30	34
Thackley	30	13	7	10	51	35	33
Ossett Albion	30	10	11	9	28	26	31
North Ferriby United	30	10	7	13	46	46	27
Sheffield	30	10	7	13	33	46	27
Hallam	30	10	6	14	46	53	26
Frecheville Community Association	30	11	3	16	39	48	25
Farsley Celtic	30	10	2	18	38	54	22
Liversedge	30	6	5	19	24	52	17
York Railway Institute	30	5	3	22	28	77	13

Division Two

Harrogate Town	30	16	8	6	56	29	40
Ossett Town	30	17	6	7	51	29	40
Garforth Miners	30	14	11	5	44	27	39
Bradley Rangers	30	14	10	6	42	31	38
Maltby Miners Welfare	30	13	8	9	48	39	34
B.S.C. Parkgate	30	13	8	9	43	40	34
Norton Woodseats	30	14	5	11	35	28	33
Hatfield Main	30	10	10	10	42	41	30
Hall Road Rangers	30	11	8	11	32	37	30
Harworth Colliery Institute	30	11	7	12	40	37	29
Bridlington Town	30	9	6	15	35	55	24
Grimethorpe Miners Welfare	30	7	9	14	39	42	23
Pilkington Recreation	30	5	12	13	29	41	22
Yorkshire Amateurs	30	9	4	17	27	53	22
Kiveton Park	30	7	7	16	37	52	21
Fryston Colliery Welfare	30	5	11	14	37	56	21

Division Three

Pontefract Collieries	28	24	2	2	62	23	50
Denaby United	28	16	5	7	44	29	37
Woolley Miners Welfare	28	16	4	8	51	28	36
Worsbrough Bridge M.W.	28	13	9	6	54	35	35
Tadcaster Albion	28	13	7	8	52	37	33
Stocksbridge Works	28	11	8	9	51	35	30
Phoenix Park	28	12	5	11	37	37	29
Wombwell Sporting Association	28	10	9	9	29	31	29
Pickering Town	28	11	4	13	38	41	26
Selby Town	28	9	6	13	34	39	24
Brook Sports	28	10	4	14	33	41	24
Collingham	28	8	7	13	27	36	23
Harrogate Railway Athletic	28	6	6	16	24	53	18
Rawmarsh Welfare	28	4	7	17	22	64	15
Thorne Colliery	28	4	3	21	39	68	11

• B.S.C. Parkgate, Harworth Colliery Institute, Maltby Miners Welfare and Norton Woodseats all moved to the NCEL – Division One (South).
• Fryston Colliery Welfare, Grimethorpe Miners Welfare, Pilkington Recreation and Yorkshire Amateurs moved to the NCEL – Division Two (N).
• Kiveton Park moved to Division Two (South).

From Division Three:
• Denaby United moved to the NCEL – Division One (South).
• Brook Sports, Collingham, Harrogate Railway Athletic, Phoenix Park, Pickering Town, Pontefract Collieries, Selby Town, Tadcaster Albion and Thorne Colliery all moved to the NCEL – Division Two (North).
• Stocksbridge Works, Wombwell Sporting Association, Woolley Miners Welfare and Worsbrough Bridge Miners Welfare all moved to the NCEL – Division Two (South).
• Rawmarsh Welfare disbanded but did raise a team to fulfil a tie in the Sheffield & Hallamshire Cup.

MIDLAND COMBINATION 1924-1928

The first meeting concerning the formation of a new league for reserve teams of Football League clubs was held at the Grand Hotel, Manchester on 21st March 1924 with Alderman H. Cropper of Chesterfield in the chair. It was thought that the proposed new league would improve the standard of reserve team matches for clubs in Yorkshire and the East Midlands and it was announced that 12 clubs had agreed in principle with the idea.

A second meeting was held at the Griffin Hotel, Leeds on 28th March when representatives of Barnsley, Bradford Park Avenue, Chesterfield, Coventry City, Doncaster Rovers, Grimsby Town, Halifax Town, Hull City, Leicester City, New Brighton, Nottingham Forest, Notts County, Rotherham County and Stockport County attended. The Central League was also represented as it was envisaged that the new league would become the Second Division of that league while the Midland League's representative was concerned that it faced the potential loss of 8 of its member clubs, largely because those clubs believed that Midland League football was causing too many injuries due to its over-physical nature.

Coventry City and Leicester City dropped out of the new competition which became a league in its own right rather than a second division of the Central League and in June, it adopted the title of the Midland Combination. The Midland League strongly opposed the formation of the new league and at a meeting in Scarborough at the start of July, the F.A.'s League Sanctions Committee recommended that the new league should not be allowed to go ahead. However, the F.A. Council overruled the decision of its Committee and so the Midland Combination started operations in 1924 with 12 founder members, all of which were Football League clubs' reserve sides.

Barnsley, Chesterfield, Doncaster Rovers, Grimsby Town, Hull City, Nottingham Forest, Notts County and Rotherham County all joined from the Midland League. Bradford Park Avenue and Halifax Town both joined from the Yorkshire League, New Brighton joined from the Liverpool County Combination and Stockport County joined from the Cheshire League.

As there would be only 22 matches in the league, it was decided also to run a subsidiary competition, known as the Midland Combination Cup, which was split into North and South geographical sections with the two section winners meeting in a play-off final to decide the champions.

1924-25

(All reserve sides)

Chesterfield	22	15	0	7	43	23	30
Barnsley	22	12	1	9	38	34	25
Bradford Park Avenue	22	10	4	8	44	34	24
Halifax Town	22	8	7	7	43	32	23
Notts County	22	8	7	7	33	29	23
Hull City	22	9	5	8	44	45	23
Grimsby Town	22	8	6	8	37	31	22
Stockport County	22	8	5	9	38	34	21
Doncaster Rovers	22	8	5	9	34	39	21
New Brighton	22	8	3	11	39	44	19
Nottingham Forest	22	6	6	10	31	33	18
Rotherham County	22	7	1	14	21	67	15

Rotherham County merged with Rotherham Town to form Rotherham United whose reserves replaced Rotherham County Reserves.
Rochdale Reserves joined from the Lancashire Combination.

Midland Combination 1925-1928

Midland Combination Cup – South

Grimsby Town	10	6	2	2	28	10	14
Doncaster Rovers	10	6	2	2	22	9	14
Nottingham Forest	10	4	2	4	17	15	10
Notts County	10	2	4	4	10	12	8
Rotherham County	10	3	1	6	13	25	7
Chesterfield	10	2	3	5	8	27	7

Midland Combination Cup – North

Barnsley	10	7	1	2	24	14	15
Stockport County	10	4	3	3	18	12	11
Bradford Park Avenue	10	5	0	5	16	11	10
New Brighton	10	3	3	4	13	22	9
Halifax Town	10	3	2	5	13	20	8
Hull City	10	2	3	5	14	19	7

Midland Combination Cup – Final

Grimsby Town vs Barnsley   3-3
(Played at Grimsby on 10th September 1925)

Replay

Barnsley vs Grimsby Town   0-1
(Played at Barnsley, 24th September 1925)

1925-26

(All reserve sides)

Grimsby Town	24	14	5	5	72	26	33
Barnsley	24	15	3	6	76	39	33
Bradford Park Avenue	24	14	2	8	62	49	30
Hull City	24	12	5	7	70	50	29
Doncaster Rovers	24	12	3	9	58	60	27
Notts County	24	13	0	11	50	45	26
Stockport County	24	13	0	11	54	58	26
New Brighton	24	9	6	9	43	40	24
Nottingham Forest	24	7	8	9	50	54	22
Rochdale	24	8	4	12	53	61	20
Chesterfield	24	8	2	14	36	64	18
Halifax Town	24	6	5	13	38	55	17
Rotherham United	24	3	1	20	37	98	7

New Brighton Reserves moved to the Liverpool County Combination and Mansfield Town (first team) joined from the Midland League.

Midland Combination Cup – South

Grimsby Town	12	9	2	1	40	15	20
Hull City	12	6	1	5	37	27	13
Nottingham Forest	12	6	1	5	24	18	13
Chesterfield	12	5	2	5	25	28	12
Notts County	12	5	2	5	23	27	12
Rotherham United	12	2	3	7	18	36	7
Doncaster Rovers	12	3	1	8	14	30	7

Midland Combination Cup – North

Rochdale	10	6	1	3	28	16	13
Halifax	10	4	4	2	21	14	12
New Brighton	10	4	4	2	16	13	12
Barnsley	10	4	2	4	22	20	10
Stockport	10	4	1	5	21	24	9
Bradford	10	1	2	7	11	32	4

Midland Combination Cup – Final

Grimsby Town vs Rochdale   3-0
(Played at Grimsby on 16th September 1926)

1926-27

(First teams are shown in bold type, the remainder are all reserve sides)

Hull City	24	20	3	1	77	29	43
Mansfield Town	**24**	**15**	**6**	**3**	**62**	**28**	**36**
Bradford Park Avenue	24	13	3	8	54	38	29
Halifax Town	24	13	3	8	52	43	29
Grimsby Town	24	13	1	10	48	43	27
Doncaster Rovers	24	10	5	9	41	36	25
Stockport County	24	9	5	10	56	61	23
Barnsley	24	10	2	12	50	48	22
Rochdale	24	8	3	13	48	63	19
Nottingham Forest	24	7	4	13	40	61	18
Chesterfield	24	6	5	13	50	57	17
Notts County	24	7	1	16	44	82	15
Rotherham United	24	3	3	18	40	73	9

Mansfield Town, Grimsby Town Reserves, Nottingham Forest Reserves and Notts County Reserves all moved to the Midland League and Stockport County Reserves moved to the Cheshire League.
Sutton Town (first team) joined from the Midland League while Kettering Town Reserves and Peterborough & Fletton United Reserves both joined from the East Midlands League.

Midland Combination Cup – South

Mansfield Town	12	7	4	1	35	13	18
Grimsby Town	12	7	4	1	29	12	18
Chesterfield	12	5	1	6	23	38	11
Nottingham Forest	12	3	4	5	21	25	10
Notts County	12	4	2	6	25	30	10
Doncaster Rovers	12	4	2	6	15	23	10
Rotherham United	12	2	3	7	22	29	7

Midland Combination Cup – North

Stockport County	10	5	3	2	29	20	13
Bradford Park Avenue	10	5	2	3	17	18	12
Halifax Town	10	5	1	4	24	23	11
Rochdale	10	5	1	4	19	20	11
Barnsley	10	2	4	4	20	20	8
Hull City	10	1	3	6	13	21	5

As the champions of both sections of the Midland Combination Cup left the league at the end of the season, no final was played.

1927-28

Clubs played each other 4 times to replace the Subsidiary competition.
(First teams are shown in bold type, the remainder are all reserve sides)

Bradford Park Avenue	40	25	6	9	119	50	56
Hull City	40	22	5	13	92	52	49
Halifax Town	40	22	5	13	94	69	49
Kettering Town	40	18	9	13	75	62	45
Barnsley	40	17	8	15	82	70	42
Peterborough & Fletton United	40	19	4	17	79	88	42
Doncaster Rovers	40	19	3	18	82	69	41
Chesterfield	40	14	7	19	78	88	35
Rotherham United	40	12	5	23	66	97	29
Rochdale	40	10	6	24	55	101	26
Sutton Town	**40**	**9**	**8**	**23**	**63**	**139**	**26**

At the end of the season, the Midland Combination closed down.

Five reserve sides moved to the Midland League – Barnsley, Chesterfield, Doncaster Rovers, Hull City and Rotherham United while Bradford Park Avenue and Halifax Town both moved to the Yorkshire League, Kettering Town and Peterborough & Fletton United both moved to the East Midlands League, Rochdale moved to the Manchester League and Sutton Town (first team) moved to the Derbyshire Senior League.

LINCOLNSHIRE LEAGUE (I) 1894-1921

The first attempt to form a Lincolnshire League took place on Saturday 29th April 1893 when representatives of Gainsborough Trinity, Grantham Rovers, Grimsby Town and Lincoln City met in the Queen's Hotel, Lincoln. However nothing came of this attempt as agreement could not be reached on how the league should be run. While Gainsborough, Grantham and Lincoln thought it should be run by a management committee consisting of a representative from each club, Grimsby considered such formality unnecessary.

The idea was raised again during the summer of 1894 and was pursued by Mr. J.H. Strawson, the secretary of Lincoln City. After much difficulty, it was announced on 18th August that it had been brought to a successful conclusion with 8 founder members: Boston Town, Gainsborough Athletic, Gainsborough Parish Church, Gainsborough Trinity Reserves, Grimsby All Saints, Horncastle, Lincoln Casuals and Lincoln City Swifts (Reserves). It was hoped to attract a team from Grantham but they judged that Grimsby was too far to travel. Shortly before the start of the season, Grimsby All Saints withdrew but it was the newly-formed Boston Town who replaced them.

1894-95

Gainsborough Trinity Reserves	11	11	0	0	47	11	22
Lincoln City Swifts	12	9	1	2	34	17	19
Boston Town	11	4	0	7	42	33	8
Lincoln Lindum	12	3	2	7	26	27	8
Lincoln Casuals	11	4	0	7	28	37	8
Gainsborough Parish Church	10	3	2	5	23	33	8
Horncastle	11	2	1	8	19	61	5

Gainsborough Athletic resigned and disbanded in mid-November and their record was deleted: 4 0 0 4 4 34 0
The 3 outstanding fixtures are believed not to have been played.

At the end of the season, Boston Town merged with Boston Victoria to form Boston F.C..

The Lincolnshire League had insufficient entrants to operate in the 1895-96 season but restarted in 1896-97 with 7 clubs: Cleethorpes, Gainsborough Trinity Reserves, Grimsby All Saints, Grimsby Town Reserves, Lincoln Adelaide, Lincoln City Swifts and Scunthorpe Town.

1896-97

Gainsborough Trinity Reserves	10	8	0	2	51	10	16
Grimsby Town Reserves	10	6	2	2	24	19	14
Lincoln City Reserves	9	5	3	1	26	15	13
Lincoln Adelaide	10	3	0	7	23	33	6
Scunthorpe Town	8	1	3	4	13	37	5
Grimsby All Saints	9	0	2	7	9	32	2

Cleethorpes resigned in October 1896 before playing any games. The 2 outstanding fixtures are believed not to have been played.

The league again had insufficient entrants to operate in the 1897-98 season but was revived for a second time in 1898-99 with 7 members: Boston Town, Boston Victoria, Gainsborough Trinity Reserves, Grantham Avenue, Grimsby All Saints, Horncastle Town and Lincoln City Reserves.

1898-99

Grimsby All Saints	11	9	2	0	65	12	20
Lincoln City Reserves	12	9	1	2	55	19	19
Gainsborough Trinity Reserves	12	6	1	5	34	21	13
Grantham Avenue	12	5	1	6	35	27	11
Boston Victoria	12	4	0	8	8	27	8
Horncastle Town	11	3	0	8	11	67	6
Boston Town	12	2	1	9	12	47	5

Grimsby All Saints failed to fulfil their fixture away to Horncastle Town. Grantham Avenue moved to the Notts & District League while Grimsby All Saints, Lincoln City Reserves and Horncastle Town also left the league. Lincoln Adelaide, Lincoln Blue Star and Lincoln St. Mary's all joined.

1899-1900

Lincoln Adelaide	8	5	2	1	24	15	12
Gainsborough Trinity Res.	6	5	0	1	23	9	10
Lincoln St. Mary's	7	3	1	3	13	14	7
Lincoln Blue Star	7	2	1	4	12	17	5
Boston Victoria	8	1	0	7	6	23	2

Boston Town were expelled in March 1900 for refusing to fulfil their fixtures with Boston Victoria. Gainsborough Trinity Reserves failed to fulfil their two remaining fixtures and Lincoln Adelaide were declared champions.

1900-01

Only 4 clubs – Boston Victoria, Gainsborough Working Men, Lincoln Adelaide and Lincoln Blue Star – entered the league for the 1900-01 season. Many others were invited to join but declined because of the high travelling costs. Boston Victoria then withdrew and the league was declared defunct on 15th September 1900.

Lincolnshire League (I) 1901-1920

1901-12

An attempt to re-form the league was made at a meeting in the Indian Queen, Dolphin Lane, Boston in March 1905 with Boston Town, Grantham Avenue, Grimsby Rangers, Lincoln City Reserves and Sleaford Town all expressing an interest while Horncastle, Louth Town and Gainsborough Trinity Reserves were also invited. However, once more the travelling costs proved too great an obstacle and the idea was dropped.

The league was eventually re-established in 1912 when it was decided to split it into two geographical divisions in order to overcome the issue of travelling costs. The North Division consisted of Cleethorpes Town, Gainsborough Parish Church, Grimsby Haycroft Rovers, Grimsby St. John, Immingham and Scunthorpe & Lindsey United Reserves. In the South Division were Boston Swifts, Boston Town, Caythorpe St. Vincent's, Grantham Avenue Reserves, Grantham Reserves and Spalding Town. The two divisional champions would meet in a play-off at the end of the season to decide the overall champions.

1912-13

Northern Division

Grimsby Haycroft Rovers (2)	8	5	2	1	28	13	14
Scunthorpe & Lindsey United Res.	10	5	1	4	29	18	11
Cleethorpes Town (2)	8	3	3	2	12	9	11
Gainsborough Parish Church (4)	6	2	1	3	15	14	9
Immingham (2)	8	3	1	4	11	15	9
Grimsby St. John	10	3	0	7	8	34	6

Five games were left unplayed and in each case, the club deemed to be the innocent party were awarded the points, totals shown in italics in brackets. Immingham and Grimsby St. John both left the league while Frodingham & Brumby United and Grimsby Rovers both joined.

Southern Division

Boston Swifts	10	10	0	0	40	9	20
Boston Town	9	6	1	2	35	17	13
Caythorpe St. Vincent's	10	3	1	6	15	19	7
Grantham Reserves	9	3	1	5	19	27	7
Grantham Avenue Reserves	10	2	2	6	16	28	6
Spalding Town	10	2	1	7	15	40	5

One match was not played.
Donington Town joined from the Sleaford & District League.

1912-13 Championship Play-off

Boston Swifts vs Grimsby Haycroft Rovers 1-1
(Played at the Boston Town ground in Shodfriars Lane on 19th April 1913)

Boston Swifts vs Grimsby Haycroft Rovers 1-1
(Played at Blundell Park, Grimsby on 24th April 1913)

Boston Swifts vs Grimsby Haycroft Rovers 2-3
(Played at the Boston Town ground in Shodfriars Lane on 13th September 1913)

1913-14

Northern Division

No published tables have been found for this division for 1913-14. The results of just 16 of the 28 games played are known so it has not been possible to compile a final table.

Two games were not played: Gainsborough Parish Church vs Grimsby Rovers and Cleethorpes Town vs Gainsborough Parish Church. In the first game only, Gainsborough Parish Church were awarded 2 points.

The finishing order was:
1. Grimsby Haycroft Rovers
2. Cleethorpes Town
3. Scunthorpe & Lindsey United Reserves
4. Gainsborough Parish Church
5. Grimsby Rovers
6. Frodingham & Brumby United

Southern Division

Boston Town	11	10	1	0	69	10	21
Boston Swifts	12	7	4	1	56	9	18
Caythorpe St. Vincent's	11	6	1	4	22	25	13
Spalding Town	12	4	2	6	20	51	10
Grantham Avenue Reserves	12	4	1	7	33	45	9
Donington Town	12	3	2	7	12	37	8
Grantham Reserves	12	0	3	9	12	47	3

Caythorpe St. Vincent's vs Boston Town was not played.

1913-14 Championship Play-off

Boston Town vs Grimsby Haycroft Rovers 1-1
(Played at Blundell Park, Grimsby on 23rd April 1914)

Boston Town vs Grimsby Haycroft Rovers 4-1
(Played at Shodfriars Lane, Boston on 29th April 1914)

1914-15

The league was reorganised into Divisions One and Two with 7 clubs in each division.

Division One consisted of Boston Town and Boston Swifts from the Southern Division together with all the former members of the Northern Division apart from Gainsborough Parish Church who left the league. Grimsby Town had completely taken over the Grimsby Rovers club, together with their ground and Rovers would operate as Grimsby Town's third or "A" team.

Division Two consisted of Spalding Town from the Southern Division plus Boston Amateurs, Boston Johnson's Limited, Boston Swifts Reserves, Boston Town Reserves, Skegness United and Spilsby United who all joined from the Boston & District League.

Caythorpe St. Vincent's, Donington Town, Grantham Reserves and Grantham Avenue Reserves all left the league.

However, shortly after the arrangements for the season had been made, the Great War started and Boston Amateurs, Boston Johnson's Limited, Boston Town Reserves and Spilsby United all resigned from the league because virtually all their players had joined the Army. The Second Division was cancelled.

The First Division did start the season but clubs found it increasingly difficult to field sides as players joined the Army and the league gradually faded away before disappearing completely in January 1915.

1920

The league was re-formed in July 1920 with 9 clubs: Boston Town, Boston West End, Grantham Reserves, Horncastle Athletic, Horncastle Town, Lincoln City Reserves, R.A.F. Cranwell Reserves, Spalding United and Spilsby United. Skegness United were also initially included but after consultation in the club committee, they withdrew because of the high travelling costs that would be involved. Digby R.A.F. joined shortly after the season began, increasing membership to 10. Although there were no clubs north of Lincoln, the league still took the title "Lincolnshire League."

1920-21

Lincoln City Reserves	14	10	2	2	48	11	22
Spalding United	14	10	1	3	39	14	21
Horncastle Town	13	7	2	4	32	22	16
Grantham Reserves	14	6	3	5	31	22	15
Horncastle Athletic	13	5	3	5	22	30	13
Boston West End	14	5	2	7	22	23	12
R.A.F. Cranwell Reserves	12	2	3	7	19	32	7
Spilsby United	14	0	2	12	13	72	2

Boston Town disbanded at the end of October and their record at the time was deleted: 4 0 1 3 6 23 1

Digby R.A.F. resigned from the league in January and their record at the time was deleted: 9 2 1 6 19 34 5

No results have been found for the 2 outstanding fixtures which may not have been played.

The Lincolnshire League disbanded at the end of the season while the Sleaford & District League changed their name to the Sleaford & South Lincolnshire League. Grantham Reserves and Spalding United both moved to that league while Horncastle Town moved to the Lincoln League.

LINCOLNSHIRE LEAGUE (II) 1933-1938

The title "Lincolnshire League" was revived in 1933 when the county's five Midland League clubs – Boston United, Gainsborough Trinity, Grimsby Town Reserves, Lincoln City Reserves and Scunthorpe & Lindsey United – decided that a competition consisting of a series of local derbies would provide an interesting set of additional fixtures. It was planned that the league's members would field their full Midland League sides but in practice, they often decided to use these games to try out new players and the competition was rarely able to attract supporters to games in the hoped for numbers.

1933-34

Lincoln City Reserves	8	7	0	1	23	13	14
Grimsby Town Reserves	8	6	0	2	25	12	12
Scunthorpe United	8	3	0	5	20	22	6
Gainsborough Trinity	8	2	1	5	20	19	5
Boston United	8	1	1	6	14	36	3

1934-35

The league received little press coverage with only a few results published and no tables at all have been found. It is believed that the same 5 clubs competed as in 1933-34 and it is likely that Gainsborough Trinity were champions.

1935-36

The table shown is the latest found.

Scunthorpe United	9	6	2	1	22	7	14
Boston United	10	6	1	3	23	12	13
Grantham	10	4	1	5	16	17	9
Gainsborough Trinity	8	3	2	3	15	15	8
Lincoln City Reserves	10	3	2	5	11	21	8
Grimsby Town Reserves	7	1	0	6	6	15	2

The three outstanding games may not have been played.

1936-37

Grimsby Town Reserves	8	4	3	1	20	13	11
Scunthorpe United	8	4	1	3	23	18	9
Boston United	8	3	2	3	17	26	8
Lincoln City Reserves	8	3	2	3	26	19	8
Gainsborough Trinity	8	2	0	6	19	29	4

1937-38

Scunthorpe United	6	4	2	0	16	5	10
Boston United	6	3	0	3	12	9	6
Gainsborough Trinity	6	2	1	3	13	18	5
Grimsby Town Reserves	6	1	1	4	6	15	3

At the end of the season, the Lincolnshire League closed down.

LINCOLNSHIRE LEAGUE (III) 1948-2021

The Lincolnshire League was re-formed at a meeting held in Brigg on 2nd February 1948. As the initiative for the league came from the north of the county, it was not surprising that the 14 founder members all came from that part of Lincolnshire.

Lincoln Amateurs, Lincoln City School Old Boys, Lincoln City "A", Lincoln Clayton's and Lincoln Rovers all joined from the Lincoln League, Appleby Frodingham Athletic, Brigg Town and Lysaght's Sports all joined from the Scunthorpe & District League, Alford United joined from the Boston & District League, and R.A.F. Manby joined from the East Lincolnshire Combination. Skegness Town had been playing in both the Boston & District League and the East Lincolnshire Combination while Louth United were a club newly-formed by a merger between Louth Nationals from the East Lincolnshire Combination and Louth Town. Grimsby Town "A" and Immingham Town also joined.

1948-49

Alford United	26	19	3	4	95	40	41
Grimsby Town "A"	26	19	2	5	103	34	40
Brigg Town	26	18	4	4	99	52	40
Appleby Frodingham Athletic	26	16	4	6	76	52	36
Louth United	26	13	5	8	63	52	31
Lincoln Rovers	26	14	2	10	85	57	30
Lysaght's Sports	26	11	1	14	62	87	23
Lincoln C.S.O.B.	26	9	4	13	59	54	22
Immingham Town	26	9	4	13	50	59	22
Lincoln Amateurs	26	8	4	14	53	78	20
Skegness Town	26	8	3	15	62	89	19
Lincoln Clayton's	26	8	2	16	64	70	18
Lincoln City "A"	26	7	4	15	52	84	18
R.A.F. Manby	26	1	2	23	31	146	4

Mablethorpe United joined from the Badley League and Barton Town joined from the Scunthorpe & District League.

1949-50

Brigg Town	30	25	2	3	115	36	52
Skegness Town	30	20	6	4	136	43	46
Immingham Town	30	18	5	7	69	43	41
Grimsby Town "A"	30	17	6	7	103	55	40
Barton Town	30	18	4	8	81	41	40
Alford United	30	17	5	8	94	60	39
Lincoln Rovers	30	15	5	10	74	56	35
Lincoln C.S.O.B.	30	13	8	9	77	66	34
Appleby Frodingham Athletic	30	12	6	12	74	83	30
Louth United	30	12	2	16	72	85	26
Lincoln City "A"	30	11	3	16	78	93	25
Lysaght's Sports	30	7	6	17	69	105	20
Mablethorpe United	30	9	0	21	88	116	18
Lincoln Amateurs	30	5	6	19	59	113	16
Lincoln Clayton's	30	3	6	21	45	129	12
R.A.F. Manby	30	1	4	25	41	151	6

Lincoln Amateurs moved to the Lincoln League and R.A.F. Manby moved to the Lincolnshire Services League.
Ashby Institute and Scunthorpe United "A" both joined from the Scunthorpe & District League.

1950-51

Alford United	30	23	4	3	123	29	50
Brigg Town	30	20	5	5	78	26	45
Barton Town	30	19	6	5	72	45	44
Mablethorpe United	30	15	7	8	64	55	37
Skegness Town	30	16	3	11	84	77	35
Grimsby Town "A"	30	14	6	10	68	40	34
Immingham Town	30	13	7	10	59	60	33
Ashby Institute	30	12	5	13	63	69	29
Lincoln City "A"	30	12	4	14	68	75	28
Appleby Frodingham Athletic	30	10	6	14	55	72	26
Lincoln Claytons	30	9	6	15	59	81	24
Scunthorpe United "A"	30	9	3	18	70	91	21
Lysaght's Sports	30	7	6	17	71	100	20
Louth United	30	6	7	17	42	89	19
Lincoln Rovers	30	7	4	19	51	80	18
Lincoln C.S.O.B.	30	7	3	20	45	83	17

1951-52

Skegness Town	28	21	4	3	106	46	46
Appleby Frodingham Athletic	28	20	4	4	76	34	44
Alford United	28	19	3	6	96	50	41
Grimsby Town "A"	28	16	7	5	84	40	39
Brigg Town	28	17	3	8	80	52	37
Barton Town	28	10	6	12	64	69	26
Lysaght's Sports	28	9	7	12	62	81	25
Lincoln C.S.O.B.	28	7	10	11	49	62	24
Lincoln Clayton's	28	11	2	15	65	83	24
Ashby Institute	28	9	4	15	59	82	22
Scunthorpe United "A"	28	8	6	14	53	77	22
Mablethorpe United	28	6	7	15	54	91	19
Louth United	28	5	8	15	44	74	18
Lincoln Rovers	28	6	5	17	63	90	17
Lincoln City "A"	28	5	6	17	54	78	16

Immingham Town failed to fulfil several fixtures, their secretary resigned and the club simply ceased operating. They were heavily fined and formally expelled from the league on 27th January 1952. Their record at the time was deleted: 13 5 1 7 21 30 11
At least eight of Lincoln Rovers' players were due to be called up for National Service and so the club disbanded. Gainsborough Trinity Reserves joined from the Yorkshire League while Grimsby Borough Police and Spalding United Reserves also both joined.

Lincolnshire League (III) 1952-1958

1952-53

Grimsby Town "A"	32	23	5	4	111	33	51
Ashby Institute	32	22	4	6	97	45	48
Skegness Town	32	22	1	9	131	51	45
Brigg Town	32	21	2	9	101	49	44
Grimsby Borough Police	32	18	5	9	71	56	41
Spalding United Reserves	32	18	3	11	108	73	39
Alford United	32	17	3	12	86	72	37
Gainsborough Trinity Reserves	32	16	4	12	80	64	36
Scunthorpe United "A"	32	14	4	14	78	79	32
Barton Town	32	12	6	14	72	79	30
Lincoln City "A"	32	12	5	15	73	71	29
Lincoln C.S.O.B.	32	10	4	18	51	87	24
Appleby Frodingham Athletic	32	8	8	16	55	95	24
Lysaght's Sports	32	8	5	19	46	106	21
Lincoln Clayton's	32	6	8	18	62	96	20
Mablethorpe United	32	6	4	22	46	75	16
Louth United	32	3	1	28	33	170	7

Long Sutton Town joined from the Peterborough & District League.
Mablethorpe United left the league.

1953-54

Brigg Town	32	26	2	4	116	48	54
Skegness Town	32	24	3	5	141	49	51
Gainsborough Trinity Reserves	32	22	6	4	108	49	50
Alford United	32	20	6	6	132	59	46
Grimsby Borough Police	32	19	4	9	92	54	42
Ashby Institute	32	19	3	10	92	51	41
Lincoln City "A"	32	18	2	12	78	55	38
Grimsby Town "A"	32	12	7	13	68	66	31
Spalding United Reserves	32	13	4	15	89	111	30
Louth United	32	9	6	17	58	82	24
Lincoln C.S.O.B.	32	7	10	15	57	81	24
Barton Town	32	10	3	19	61	92	23
Lincoln Clayton's	32	11	1	20	81	139	23
Scunthorpe United "A"	32	8	5	19	48	86	21
Lysaght's Sports	32	8	4	20	56	109	20
Appleby Frodingham Athletic	32	5	6	21	58	115	16
Long Sutton Town	32	4	2	26	58	147	10

Boston United Reserves joined from the United Counties League and Grimsby Borough Police left the league.

1954-55

Gainsborough Trinity Reserves	32	24	4	4	115	49	52
Ashby Institute	32	24	2	6	108	41	50
Brigg Town	32	23	2	7	111	61	48
Skegness Town	32	21	4	7	129	62	46
Alford United	32	19	5	8	124	68	43
Boston United Reserves	32	18	4	10	108	73	40
Grimsby Town "A"	32	17	3	12	91	64	37
Lincoln City "A"	32	14	6	12	90	72	34
Scunthorpe United "A"	32	14	3	15	85	63	31
Lincoln C.S.O.B.	32	12	7	13	67	75	31
Louth United	32	12	5	15	62	87	29
Lincoln Clayton's	32	12	2	18	66	106	26
Spalding United Reserves	32	9	6	17	61	78	24
Barton Town	32	9	1	22	68	114	19
Long Sutton Town	32	7	3	22	50	117	17
Appleby Frodingham Athletic	32	5	5	22	53	121	15
Lysaght's Sports	32	1	0	31	35	172	2

Appleby Frodingham Athletic moved to the Scunthorpe & District League.

1955-56

Skegness Town	30	25	1	4	122	30	51
Louth United	30	22	3	5	106	49	47
Brigg Town	30	19	5	6	76	32	43
Boston United Reserves	30	17	5	8	80	63	39
Gainsborough Trinity Reserves	30	17	4	9	88	50	38
Spalding United Reserves	30	17	4	9	90	58	38
Alford United	30	17	3	10	77	61	37
Ashby Institute	30	13	8	9	61	57	34
Scunthorpe United "A"	30	10	7	13	63	63	27
Lincoln City "A"	30	11	4	15	64	80	26
Lincoln C.S.O.B.	30	7	6	17	43	81	20
Grimsby Town "A"	30	8	3	19	54	71	19
Barton Town	30	7	4	19	62	101	18
Lysaght's Sports	30	7	3	20	53	107	17
Long Sutton Town	30	6	3	21	31	94	15
Lincoln Clayton's	30	4	3	23	51	124	11

Skegness Town moved to the Central Alliance and were replaced by their reserves who joined from the Boston & District League.
Appleby Frodingham Athletic joined from the Scunthorpe & District League and Grimsby Borough Police also joined.

1956-57

Ashby Institute	34	26	4	4	105	45	56
Boston United Reserves	34	25	4	5	150	55	54
Louth United	34	24	6	4	142	54	52
Gainsborough Trinity Reserves	34	21	6	7	94	53	48
Brigg Town	34	19	7	8	84	58	45
Alford United	34	20	3	11	110	59	43
Grimsby Town "A"	34	20	3	11	97	67	43
Skegness Town Reserves	34	15	7	12	95	70	37
Grimsby Borough Police	34	16	4	14	85	81	36
Scunthorpe United "A"	34	16	2	16	94	76	34
Lincoln City "A"	34	14	4	16	94	86	32
Spalding United Reserves	34	13	6	15	77	80	32
Lincoln C.S.O.B.	34	14	2	18	72	102	30
Appleby Frodingham Athletic	34	8	4	22	60	122	20
Long Sutton Town	34	7	0	27	61	139	14
Lysaght's Sports	34	4	5	25	41	98	13
Lincoln Clayton's	34	5	3	26	47	142	13
Barton Town	34	4	2	28	44	165	10

Scunthorpe United "A" left the league.
Holbeach United Reserves joined.

1957-58

Louth United	34	25	4	5	121	53	54
Grimsby Borough Police	34	23	7	4	102	37	53
Ashby Institute	34	23	4	7	87	37	50
Gainsborough Trinity Reserves	34	24	2	8	106	70	50
Brigg Town	34	20	6	8	97	53	46
Holbeach United Reserves	34	19	5	10	99	65	43
Boston United Reserves	34	17	4	13	97	77	38
Alford United	34	14	9	11	87	57	37
Grimsby Town "A"	34	14	6	14	80	83	34
Skegness Town Reserves	34	12	6	16	55	85	30
Lincoln City "A"	34	12	5	17	84	79	29
Barton Town	34	13	2	19	70	74	28
Spalding United Reserves	34	12	4	18	66	83	28
Appleby Frodingham Athletic	34	12	2	20	58	83	26
Lincoln C.S.O.B.	34	10	5	19	71	109	25
Long Sutton Town	34	7	5	22	52	111	19
Lysaght's Sports	34	5	4	25	41	118	14
Lincoln Clayton's	34	2	4	28	41	140	8

Long Sutton Town moved to the Peterborough & District League.

Lincolnshire League (III) 1958-1963

1958-59

Grimsby Borough Police	32	23	3	6	114	59	49
Gainsborough Trinity Reserves	32	21	4	7	107	50	46
Alford United	32	20	5	7	88	42	45
Brigg Town	32	19	5	8	84	48	43
Barton Town	32	19	3	10	82	57	41
Louth United	32	18	3	11	87	64	39
Boston United Reserves	32	17	5	10	70	57	39
Lincoln City "A"	32	16	6	10	90	59	38
Holbeach United Reserves	32	13	4	15	62	65	30
Grimsby Town "A"	32	13	1	18	72	76	27
Appleby Frodingham Athletic	32	13	3	16	72	89	29
Skegness Town Reserves	32	13	1	18	72	76	27
Ashby Institute	32	11	2	19	55	74	24
Lincoln Clayton's	32	9	3	20	62	119	21
Lincoln C.S.O.B.	32	6	5	21	51	95	17
Lysaght's Sports	32	6	2	24	35	101	14
Spalding United Reserves	32	5	3	24	51	124	13

1959-60

Grimsby Borough Police	32	21	8	3	84	39	50
Barton Town	32	22	3	7	108	47	47
Gainsborough Trinity Reserves	32	20	5	7	81	53	45
Boston United Reserves	32	17	6	9	85	43	40
Lincoln City "A"	32	15	8	9	59	48	38
Brigg Town	32	18	2	12	73	66	38
Louth United	32	12	10	10	99	77	34
Grimsby Town "A"	32	13	7	12	68	60	33
Alford United	32	12	8	12	56	62	32
Lincoln C.S.O.B.	32	12	7	13	76	74	31
Appleby Frodingham Athletic	32	12	5	15	73	69	29
Ashby Institute	32	13	2	17	60	74	28
Holbeach United Reserves	32	10	6	16	61	67	26
Skegness Town Reserves	32	9	7	16	58	74	25
Lysaght's Sports	32	8	6	18	34	72	22
Lincoln Clayton's	32	6	9	17	49	107	21
Spalding United Reserves	32	0	5	27	34	126	5

Gainsborough Trinity Reserves moved to the Yorkshire League and Boston United Reserves also left the league.
Lincoln United joined from the Lincoln League.

1960-61

Barton Town	30	23	3	4	93	35	49
Louth United	30	21	6	3	86	32	48
Brigg Town	30	16	6	8	67	49	38
Grimsby Borough Police	30	16	4	10	78	54	36
Lincoln United	30	14	7	9	79	59	35
Lysaght's Sports	30	14	5	11	42	39	33
Ashby Institute	30	12	8	10	59	37	32
Appleby Frodingham Athletic	30	13	6	11	54	42	32
Lincoln City "A"	30	11	9	10	62	48	31
Lincoln C.S.O.B.	30	13	5	12	58	57	31
Grimsby Town "A"	30	11	3	16	62	76	25
Skegness Town Reserves	30	9	4	17	46	73	22
Lincoln Clayton's	30	8	3	19	49	84	19
Spalding United Reserves	30	7	5	18	47	90	19
Alford United	30	5	6	19	47	105	16
Holbeach United Reserves	30	5	4	21	36	85	14

Grimsby Town "A" left the league.
Ruston Bucyrus joined from the Lincoln League, Gainsborough Trinity Reserves joined from the Yorkshire League while Cleethorpes Town, Boston United Reserves and Bourne Town Reserves also all joined.

A new division was formed to provide additional fixtures for the reserve teams of Lincolnshire's three Football League clubs, plus the county's leading non-League clubs. This was called the Premier Division and was run as a completely separate competition from the Lincolnshire League itself. As Premier Division fixtures were additional to its members' normal programmes, the strength of the teams fielded varied, depending on what other games each club had that might clash with their lower priority Lincolnshire League games. The founder members of the Premier Division were Boston United, Gainsborough Trinity, Spalding United plus the reserves of Grimsby Town, Lincoln City and Scunthorpe United.

1961-62

Grimsby Borough Police	38	27	5	6	104	34	59
Brigg Town	38	26	7	5	146	55	59
Barton Town	38	25	6	7	126	61	56
Ashby Institute	38	22	7	9	97	56	51
Louth United	38	21	6	11	93	47	48
Appleby Frodingham Athletic	38	21	5	12	86	47	47
Skegness Town Reserves	38	16	14	8	75	68	46
Lincoln United	38	19	6	13	106	66	44
Cleethorpes Town	38	19	5	14	90	80	43
Lincoln City "A"	38	16	8	14	80	73	40
Ruston Bucyrus	38	14	12	12	91	84	40
Alford United	38	16	7	15	110	108	39
Lysaght's Sports	38	14	6	18	64	79	34
Boston United Reserves	38	13	5	20	75	103	31
Gainsborough Trinity Reserves	38	12	5	21	87	78	29
Lincoln C.S.O.B.	38	10	7	21	68	87	27
Spalding United Reserves	38	9	5	24	59	107	23
Bourne Town Reserves	38	8	6	24	74	137	22
Lincoln Clayton's	38	6	3	29	51	147	15
Holbeach United Reserves	38	2	3	33	36	201	7

Grantham Reserves joined from the Central Alliance and Holbeach United Reserves left the league.

Premier Division

Scunthorpe United Reserves	10	6	1	3	16	11	13
Boston United	10	6	1	3	20	17	13
Grimsby Town Reserves	10	5	1	4	25	15	11
Lincoln City Reserves	10	5	0	5	18	17	10
Gainsborough Trinity	10	3	2	5	16	23	8
Spalding United	10	2	1	7	14	26	5

Skegness Town joined the Premier Division.

1962-63

Appleby Frodingham Athletic	38	28	4	6	119	52	60
Boston United Reserves	38	24	5	9	120	48	53
Brigg Town	38	24	5	9	129	68	53
Gainsborough Trinity Reserves	38	24	4	10	119	73	52
Ashby Institute	38	22	7	9	93	60	51
Lincoln United	38	20	4	14	110	71	44
Lincoln City "A"	38	18	7	13	101	72	43
Barton Town	38	16	11	11	107	79	43
Louth United	38	18	6	14	92	78	42
Skegness Town Reserves	38	15	7	16	84	94	37
Lincoln C.S.O.B.	38	15	6	17	77	79	36
Ruston Bucyrus	38	13	10	15	77	85	36
Bourne Town Reserves	38	15	6	17	96	110	36
Grimsby Borough Police	38	14	7	17	69	73	35
Cleethorpes Town	38	12	8	18	83	92	32
Lysaght's Sports	38	10	9	19	62	93	29
Grantham Reserves	38	12	3	23	95	132	27
Alford United	38	10	6	22	76	134	26
Spalding United Reserves	38	5	7	26	44	114	17
Lincoln Clayton's	38	2	4	32	30	177	8

Boston United Reserves and Cleethorpes Town both left the league.
Ross Group and Scunthorpe United "A" both joined.

Lincolnshire League (III) 1963-1967

Premier Division

Grimsby Town Reserves	8	5	2	1	19	8	12
Scunthorpe United Reserves	7	2	3	2	15	9	7
Boston United	4	2	2	0	13	6	6
Skegness Town	7	2	2	3	10	16	6
Gainsborough Trinity	5	1	2	2	7	10	4
Lincoln City Reserves	3	1	1	1	4	5	3
Spalding United	4	0	0	4	1	15	0

Because of an exceptionally severe winter, very few games were played anywhere during the first 3 months of 1963. With so many fixtures outstanding, it was decided to abandon the Premier Division season when it stood as above and declare it as void.
Skegness Town left the Premier Division.

1963-64

Lincoln United	38	30	6	2	142	39	66
Brigg Town	38	30	1	7	107	56	61
Lincoln City "A"	38	22	6	10	112	81	50
Ashby Institute	38	22	4	12	86	43	48
Grantham Reserves	38	22	4	12	117	74	48
Louth United	38	17	8	13	82	70	42
Barton Town	38	18	5	15	120	81	41
Skegness Town Reserves	38	18	5	15	91	76	41
Lincoln C.S.O.B.	38	16	8	14	102	92	40
Ruston Bucyrus	38	14	12	12	73	75	40
Ross Group	38	18	3	17	92	85	39
Appleby Frodingham Athletic	38	17	5	16	87	83	39
Scunthorpe United "A"	38	16	6	16	110	83	38
Grimsby Borough Police	38	13	8	17	69	80	34
Bourne Town Reserves	38	12	9	17	100	96	33
Gainsborough Trinity Reserves	38	13	7	18	71	98	33
Lysaght's Sports	38	11	6	21	64	87	28
Spalding United Reserves	38	10	3	25	43	112	23
Alford United	38	3	3	32	64	184	9
Lincoln Clayton's	38	2	3	33	41	178	7

Barton Town moved to the Yorkshire League, Spalding United Reserves moved to the Peterborough League while Grimsby Borough Police, Lincoln City "A" and Scunthorpe United "A" also all left the league.
Boston joined as a newly-formed club.

Premier Division

Scunthorpe United Reserves	10	7	2	1	20	8	16
Lincoln City Reserves	10	6	1	3	21	16	13
Grimsby Town Reserves	10	4	3	3	19	12	11
Boston United	10	2	4	4	12	15	8
Gainsborough Trinity	10	1	4	5	9	20	6
Spalding United	10	1	4	5	7	17	6

Boston United, Gainsborough Trinity and Spalding United all left the league. Boston and Lincoln United both joined.

1964-65

Boston	30	26	2	2	125	34	54
Ashby Institute	30	22	3	5	96	46	47
Brigg Town	30	19	5	6	85	28	43
Lincoln United	30	19	3	8	88	41	41
Ruston Bucyrus	30	17	6	7	85	54	40
Louth United	30	18	1	11	82	57	37
Grantham Reserves	30	14	4	12	75	61	32
Appleby Frodingham Athletic	30	14	3	13	71	62	31
Lysaght's Sports	30	10	8	12	52	62	28
Ross Group	30	12	3	15	67	64	27
Lincoln Clayton's	30	11	5	14	62	68	27
Lincoln C.S.O.B.	30	10	2	18	67	76	22
Bourne Town Reserves	30	9	3	18	68	90	21
Gainsborough Trinity Reserves	30	6	7	17	55	83	19
Skegness Town Reserves	30	2	2	26	30	127	6
Alford United	30	2	1	27	24	179	5

Boston moved to the Central Alliance and were replaced by their reserves.
Bourne Town Reserves and Skegness Town Reserves both left the league.
Winterton Rangers joined from the Scunthorpe & District League.

Premier Division

Scunthorpe United Reserves	8	6	0	2	20	12	12
Lincoln City Reserves	8	4	1	3	19	11	9
Grimsby Town Reserves	8	4	0	4	15	13	8
Lincoln United	8	3	0	5	13	22	6
Boston	8	2	1	5	12	21	5

1965-66

Ashby Institute	28	21	4	3	91	30	46
Brigg Town	28	17	5	6	82	36	39
Lincoln United	28	16	4	8	66	44	36
Louth United	28	15	3	10	71	50	33
Winterton Rangers	28	14	5	9	72	61	33
Gainsborough Trinity Reserves	28	13	7	8	65	58	33
Boston Reserves	28	15	3	10	62	59	33
Ross Group	28	15	2	11	82	62	32
Appleby Frodingham Athletic	28	12	4	12	78	51	28
Lincoln Clayton's	28	9	7	12	55	58	25
Grantham Reserves	28	8	5	15	48	63	21
Lysaght's Sports	28	7	7	14	47	71	21
Ruston Bucyrus	28	6	8	14	47	74	20
Lincoln C.S.O.B.	28	3	6	19	38	90	12
Alford United	28	2	4	22	37	134	8

Boston United Reserves and Lincoln City Reserves both joined the league.
Alford United left the league.

A new division was formed. The existing division became Division One and the new division became Division Two with 17 founder members:
Barton Town Reserves, Lysaght's Sports Reserves, Scotter United and Old Scunthonians all joined from the Scunthorpe & District League.
B.R.S.A. Immingham, Hykeham, Lincoln C.S.O.B. Reserves, Lincoln City Colts, Lincoln Clayton's Reserves, Lincoln United Reserves, Louth United Reserves, Old Lincolnians, Rosemary Old Boys, Ross Group Reserves, Ruston & Hornsby, Ruston Bucyrus Reserves and Saxilby Athletic also all joined.

Premier Division

Lincoln City Reserves	8	5	2	1	15	8	12
Grimsby Town Reserves	8	2	4	2	5	7	8
Lincoln United	8	3	2	3	10	16	8
Boston	8	3	1	4	19	14	7
Scunthorpe United Reserves	8	2	1	5	9	13	5

1966-67

Promoted clubs are shown in bold type, relegated clubs in bold italics.

Division One

Louth United	30	20	5	5	79	29	45
Ashby Institute	30	18	7	5	70	48	43
Grantham Reserves	30	19	4	7	84	53	42
Lincoln United	30	16	9	5	87	37	41
Brigg Town	30	18	5	7	77	44	41
Lincoln Clayton's	30	18	3	9	70	54	39
Appleby Frodingham Athletic	30	14	6	10	68	49	34
Lysaght's Sports	30	13	7	10	62	61	33
Boston United Reserves	30	11	7	12	84	71	29
Ross Group	30	12	4	14	76	73	28
Gainsborough Trinity Reserves	30	10	4	16	54	64	24
Winterton Rangers	30	9	6	15	53	67	24
Ruston Bucyrus	30	7	7	16	58	72	21
Lincoln City Reserves	30	6	3	21	43	93	15
Boston Reserves	30	7	1	22	37	104	15
Lincoln C.S.O.B.	30	2	2	26	35	118	6

Lincoln United moved to the Yorkshire League and Boston Reserves also left the league.

Lincolnshire League (III) 1967-1969

Division Two

Scotter United	32	28	4	0	123	26	60
Lincoln United Reserves	32	23	6	3	104	39	52
Louth United Reserves	32	19	5	8	95	53	43
Old Scunthonians	32	19	5	8	112	64	43
Barton Town Reserves	32	16	6	10	95	63	38
B.R.S.A. Immingham	32	14	7	11	88	75	35
Ruston & Hornsby	32	13	7	12	68	66	33
Rosemary Old Boys	32	16	1	15	83	83	33
Lysaght's Sports Reserves	32	12	8	12	61	63	32
Saxilby Athletic	32	13	6	13	71	75	32
Ruston Bucyrus Reserves	32	13	3	16	56	75	29
Ross Group Reserves	32	12	5	15	76	114	29
Old Lincolnians	32	10	4	18	77	86	24
Lincoln Clayton's Reserves	32	10	4	18	59	83	24
Lincoln City Colts	32	7	3	22	55	113	17
Hykeham	32	5	2	25	47	112	12
Lincoln C.S.O.B. Reserves	32	3	2	27	50	130	8

Barton Town Reserves, Lincoln United Reserves and Lincoln City Colts all left the league. Coningsby, Ermine United, Grimsby Amateurs and Skellingthorpe all joined.

Premier Division

Lincoln City Reserves	8	5	1	2	18	11	11
Grimsby Town Reserves	8	4	2	2	19	10	10
Boston	8	2	3	3	9	13	7
Lincoln United	8	3	0	5	11	12	6
Scunthorpe United Reserves	8	2	2	4	14	25	6

Lincoln United left the league. Louth United joined.

1967-68 Division One

Louth United	30	24	2	4	86	33	50
Appleby Frodingham Athletic	30	23	2	5	82	34	48
Winterton Rangers	30	17	7	6	65	35	41
Grantham Reserves	30	17	5	8	62	36	39
Ross Group	30	13	8	9	66	54	34
Ashby Institute	30	12	9	9	37	35	33
Gainsborough Trinity Reserves	30	11	7	12	67	64	29
Lincoln United Reserves	30	11	5	14	58	58	27
Scotter United	30	12	3	15	53	60	27
Lincoln City Reserves	30	10	6	14	46	47	26
Boston United Reserves	30	10	6	14	51	59	26
Brigg Town	30	10	6	14	65	77	26
Ruston Bucyrus	30	9	7	14	54	73	25
Lysaght's Sports	30	6	10	14	35	58	22
Lincoln Clayton's	30	5	5	20	40	94	15
Lincoln C.S.O.B.	30	4	4	22	43	93	12

Ashby Institute moved to the Midland League while Boston United Reserves, Gainsborough Trinity Reserves and Grantham Reserves also all left. Lincolnshire Constabulary and Skegness Town Reserves both joined.

Division Two

Grimsby Amateurs	32	27	3	2	114	32	57
Coningsby	32	21	5	6	110	54	47
Rosemary Old Boys	32	19	6	7	95	45	44
Louth United Reserves	32	19	1	12	85	62	39
Skellingthorpe	32	16	5	11	84	66	37
B.R.S.A. Immingham	32	15	7	10	80	69	37
Ermine United	32	15	6	11	91	68	36
Saxilby Athletic	32	15	4	13	65	60	34
Lysaght's Sports Reserves	32	15	3	14	72	73	33
Old Scunthonians	32	13	6	13	71	67	32
Ruston & Hornsby	32	13	2	17	67	74	28
Old Lincolnians	32	12	2	18	65	64	26
Ross Group Reserves	32	10	6	16	62	86	26
Lincoln C.S.O.B. Reserves	32	9	5	18	68	102	23
Ruston Bucyrus Reserves	32	8	5	19	51	86	21
Hykeham	32	4	5	23	51	115	13
Lincoln Clayton's Reserves	32	4	3	25	34	142	11

Old Scunthonians moved to the Scunthorpe & District League. Fulbeck United joined from the Grantham & District League and Redbourne Sports joined from the Scunthorpe & District League. Scartho Wanderers and Sleaford Town also joined.

Premier Division

Lincoln City Reserves	8	4	4	0	20	5	12
Scunthorpe United Reserves	8	3	4	1	16	11	10
Grimsby Town Reserves	8	3	2	3	13	14	8
Louth United	8	1	3	4	14	20	5
Boston	8	2	1	5	10	23	5

At the end of this season, the Premier Division was disbanded.

1968-69

Division One

Brigg Town	30	22	4	4	99	38	48
Louth United	30	21	5	4	89	32	47
Winterton Rangers	30	18	8	4	96	49	44
Appleby Frodingham Athletic	30	18	5	7	83	42	41
Ruston Bucyrus	30	14	8	8	52	49	36
Lysaght's Sports	30	13	6	11	69	60	32
Lincoln Clayton's	30	13	5	12	72	70	31
Scotter United	30	13	3	14	70	75	29
Lincoln United Reserves	30	10	7	13	59	58	27
Grimsby Amateurs	30	9	9	12	56	65	27
Lincoln City Reserves	30	11	3	16	56	67	25
Lincolnshire Constabulary	30	9	4	17	54	69	22
Ross Group	30	9	2	19	66	79	20
Lincoln C.S.O.B.	**30**	**7**	**6**	**17**	**37**	**89**	**20**
Coningsby	30	8	3	19	48	87	19
Skegness Town Reserves	30	5	2	23	38	115	12

Division Two

Sleaford Town	34	25	5	4	97	31	55
Scartho Wanderers	34	22	5	7	115	50	49
Fulbeck United	34	21	7	6	88	43	49
Old Lincolnians	34	21	4	9	103	68	46
Ross Group Reserves	34	21	3	10	110	57	45
Louth United Reserves	34	21	3	10	102	58	45
Ermine United	34	17	8	9	80	51	42
B.R.S.A. Immingham	34	16	7	11	84	70	39
Skellingthorpe	34	16	5	13	88	64	37
Ruston Bucyrus Reserves	34	15	6	13	83	71	36
Rosemary Old Boys	34	12	8	14	78	86	32
Lincoln Clayton's Reserves	34	10	7	17	66	91	27
Redbourne Sports	34	10	6	18	70	87	26
Saxilby Athletic	34	12	2	20	78	105	26
Lysaght's Sports Reserves	34	9	6	19	49	85	24
Hykeham	34	5	5	24	49	117	15
Lincoln C.S.O.B. Reserves	34	6	2	26	48	115	14
Ruston & Hornsby	34	0	5	29	19	158	5

Hykeham and Lincoln C.S.O.B. Reserves both left the league. Winterton Rangers Reserves joined from the Scunthorpe & District League. Ruston & Hornsby changed their name to Lincoln Ruston's.

1969-70
Division One

Brigg Town	30	24	3	3	83	32	51
Louth United	30	21	5	4	88	28	47
Winterton Rangers	30	21	4	5	91	39	46
Lincoln City Reserves	30	15	8	7	61	41	38
Scotter United	30	17	2	11	70	54	36
Sleaford Town	30	17	2	11	59	50	36
Ruston Bucyrus	30	14	6	10	69	58	34
Skegness Town Reserves	30	12	5	13	54	69	29
Appleby Frodingham Athletic	30	11	5	14	47	54	27
Lysaght's Sports	30	9	6	15	37	50	24
Grimsby Amateurs	30	8	7	15	58	70	23
Ross Group	30	9	4	17	63	74	22
Lincoln Clayton's	30	9	4	17	44	71	22
Coningsby	30	7	4	19	44	85	18
Lincoln United Reserves	30	6	4	20	44	66	16
Lincolnshire Constabulary	30	4	3	23	37	108	11

Winterton Rangers moved to the Yorkshire League while Coningsby and Lincoln City Reserves also left the league.
Boston United Reserves and Grantham Reserves both joined.

Division Two

Scartho Wanderers	32	25	4	3	95	42	54
Saxilby Athletic	32	24	3	5	82	34	51
Winterton Rangers Reserves	32	22	2	8	97	49	46
Louth United Reserves	32	19	3	10	84	39	41
B.R.S.A. Immingham	32	18	4	10	103	70	40
Old Lincolnians	32	15	8	9	71	51	38
Skellingthorpe	32	16	3	13	69	69	35
Redbourne Sports	32	15	4	13	77	68	34
Fulbeck United	32	14	3	15	83	65	31
Ruston Bucyrus Reserves	32	13	4	15	55	67	30
Ross Group Reserves	32	10	6	16	60	71	26
Lysaght's Sports Reserves	32	11	4	17	58	74	26
Lincoln Ruston's	32	12	2	18	56	87	26
Lincoln Clayton's Reserves	32	10	4	18	56	88	24
Rosemary Old Boys	32	9	3	20	48	78	21
Ermine United	32	7	3	22	60	106	17
Lincoln C.S.O.B.	32	1	2	29	31	127	4

Ermine United, Lincoln C.S.O.B. and Rosemary Old Boys all left the league.
Messingham Trinity joined from the Scunthorpe & District League while Immingham Town, R.A.F. Waddington, Ruskington and Scartho Wanderers Reserves all also joined.

1970-71
Division One

Brigg Town	34	28	3	3	105	29	59
Louth United	34	28	2	4	81	18	58
Ruston Bucyrus	34	26	3	5	87	30	55
Ross Group	34	24	2	8	87	47	50
Grantham Reserves	34	20	4	10	92	42	44
Boston United Reserves	34	18	8	8	72	40	44
Lysaght's Sports	34	15	7	12	61	55	37
Appleby Frodingham Athletic	34	10	12	12	61	58	32
Scotter United	34	13	6	15	48	60	32
Sleaford Town	34	11	7	16	41	56	29
Winterton Rangers Reserves	34	11	6	17	50	61	28
Lincoln United Reserves	34	11	6	17	55	68	28
Grimsby Amateurs	34	10	7	17	33	65	27
Scartho Wanderers	34	7	9	18	50	72	23
Saxilby Athletic	34	9	3	22	44	82	21
Lincoln Clayton's	34	7	4	23	57	88	18
Lincolnshire Constabulary	34	6	5	23	43	112	17
Skegness Town Reserves	34	2	6	26	34	118	10

Lincolnshire Constabulary and Skegness Town Reserves both left the league. Lysaght's Sports changed their name to Normanby Park Works.

Division Two

Messingham Trinity	30	23	5	2	87	22	51
Skellingthorpe	30	23	4	3	88	23	50
Ross Group Reserves	30	18	5	7	88	63	41
Louth United Reserves	30	15	8	7	76	48	38
B.R.S.A. Immingham	30	17	4	9	96	62	38
Immingham Town	30	15	5	10	68	48	35
Redbourne Sports	30	15	5	10	71	74	35
Fulbeck United	30	14	2	14	78	70	30
Old Lincolnians	30	11	6	13	77	77	28
Lincoln Ruston's	30	12	3	15	54	61	27
Ruskington	30	11	3	16	67	92	25
Ruston Bucyrus Reserves	30	10	4	16	45	54	24
Lysaght's Sports Reserves	30	10	1	19	44	67	21
Scartho Wanderers Reserves	30	7	2	21	56	92	16
R.A.F. Waddington	30	4	3	23	41	101	11
Lincoln Clayton's Reserves	30	4	2	24	48	130	10

No Division Two tables have been found between 1971 and 1978, although the division is believed to have continued to operate.

1971-72

Brigg Town	34	24	7	3	88	35	55
Louth United	34	20	6	8	62	34	46
Appleby Frodingham Athletic	34	18	7	9	82	54	43
Grimsby Amateurs	34	19	4	11	78	43	42
Boston United Reserves	34	15	10	9	56	37	40
Ross Group	34	16	8	10	57	40	40
Ruston Bucyrus	34	17	6	11	59	53	40
Skellingthorpe	34	14	10	10	51	43	38
Winterton Rangers Reserves	34	13	10	11	71	58	36
Grantham Reserves	34	12	10	12	71	54	34
Sleaford Town	34	13	6	15	68	74	32
Lincoln United Reserves	34	12	7	15	56	71	31
Scartho Wanderers	34	13	4	17	46	68	30
Messingham Trinity	34	10	9	15	46	61	29
Normanby Park Works	34	10	8	16	49	62	28
Saxilby Athletic	34	6	7	21	42	81	19
Lincoln Clayton's	34	4	8	22	41	90	16
Scotter United	34	4	5	25	38	91	13

Lincoln Clayton's, Lincoln United Reserves, Saxilby Athletic, Scartho Wanderers, Scotter United, Skellingthorpe and Sleaford Town all left the league. Ashby Institute Reserves, Gainsborough United, Lincoln City "A" and Ruston Sports all joined.

1972-73

Louth United	28	21	4	3	83	21	46
Grimsby Amateurs	28	19	4	5	65	32	42
Brigg Town	28	19	3	6	66	20	41
Ross Group	28	16	7	5	70	35	39
Ruston Sports	28	14	5	9	51	34	33
Boston United Reserves	28	13	5	10	45	40	31
Winterton Rangers Reserves	28	11	8	9	52	53	30
Messingham Trinity	28	12	4	12	54	43	28
Lincoln City "A"	28	11	5	12	28	34	27
Gainsborough United	28	9	8	11	54	54	26
Ruston Bucyrus	28	8	8	12	39	47	24
Appleby Frodingham Athletic	28	6	8	14	32	57	20
Grantham Reserves	28	8	2	18	31	65	18
Normanby Park Works	28	2	5	21	23	78	9
Ashby Institute Reserves	28	2	2	24	18	105	6

Boston United disbanded their reserve side while Ashby Institute Reserves, Grantham Reserves and Lincoln City "A" also left the league.
Crowle United, Grantham United, Gunness and Immingham Town all joined. Ross Group changed their name to Ross Sports.

Lincolnshire League (III) 1973-1979

1973-74

Brigg Town	28	23	5	0	77	22	51
Louth United	28	17	9	2	59	20	43
Gainsborough United	28	14	4	10	44	30	32
Ruston Bucyrus	28	12	7	9	47	44	31
Ross Sports	28	12	5	11	53	47	29
Immingham Town	28	12	5	11	49	45	29
Grantham United	28	9	9	10	42	43	27
Messingham Trinity	28	11	5	12	46	48	27
Appleby Frodingham Athletic	28	10	6	12	54	46	26
Gunness	28	10	6	12	40	53	26
Grimsby Amateurs	28	8	9	11	36	40	25
Winterton Rangers Reserves	28	8	6	14	40	47	22
Crowle United	28	9	4	15	44	66	22
Ruston Sports	28	6	9	13	29	44	21
Normanby Park Works	28	3	3	22	20	87	9

Louth United moved to the Midland League while Normanby Park Works and Ruston Sports also left. Lincoln Clayton's and Ruskington both joined.

1974-75

Ruston Bucyrus	26	18	5	3	55	20	41
Brigg Town	26	17	3	6	53	22	37
Grimsby Amateurs	26	13	8	5	41	34	34
Ross Sports	26	15	3	8	59	41	33
Crowle United	26	11	7	8	43	33	29
Gainsborough United	26	11	6	9	49	38	28
Appleby Frodingham Athletic	26	11	5	10	40	32	27
Lincoln Clayton's	26	9	7	10	42	46	25
Gunness	26	9	5	12	39	50	21
Ruskington	26	7	6	13	36	41	20
Grantham United	26	8	4	14	45	54	20
Immingham Town	26	9	1	16	45	65	19
Messingham Trinity	26	7	5	14	27	53	19
Winterton Rangers Reserves	26	4	1	21	20	65	7

Gunness and Winterton Rangers Reserves each had 2 points deducted.
Lincoln United Reserves and Ruston Sports both joined.

1975-76

Brigg Town	30	24	6	0	82	18	54
Gainsborough United	30	17	5	8	62	33	39
Ruston Bucyrus	30	17	4	9	46	31	38
Crowle United	30	16	4	10	67	39	36
Ruston Sports	30	13	9	8	49	41	35
Grimsby Amateurs	30	13	8	9	46	38	34
Appleby Frodingham Athletic	30	12	7	11	54	40	31
Lincoln Clayton's	30	12	7	11	50	49	31
Messingham Trinity	30	13	5	12	48	49	31
Gunness	30	13	3	14	51	47	29
Immingham Town	30	10	6	14	53	64	26
Ross Sports	30	9	7	14	49	58	25
Ruskington	30	8	7	15	45	79	23
Lincoln United Reserves	30	5	10	15	28	54	20
Winterton Rangers Reserves	30	5	7	18	33	59	17
Grantham United	30	2	7	21	25	70	11

Brigg Town moved to the Midland League while Winterton Rangers Reserves and Ruskington also left the league.
Market Rasen Town and Sleaford Town both joined.

1976-77

Appleby Frodingham Athletic	28	22	5	1	98	24	49
Ruston Bucyrus	28	19	4	5	68	31	42
Gainsborough United	28	14	6	8	45	36	34
Messingham Trinity	28	12	8	8	45	30	32
Crowle United	28	14	3	11	69	60	31
Market Rasen Town	28	11	6	11	39	44	28
Gunness	28	11	6	11	44	57	28
Grantham United	28	10	7	11	46	48	27
Immingham Town	28	9	8	11	44	54	26
Grimsby Amateurs	28	10	3	15	51	64	23
Ruston Sports	28	9	4	15	33	41	22
Ross Sports	28	9	4	15	38	53	22
Sleaford Town	28	7	6	15	34	59	20
Lincoln United Reserves	28	6	6	16	25	48	18
Lincoln Clayton's	28	8	2	18	29	57	18

Grantham United, Gunness and Lincoln Clayton's all left the league.
Bottesford Town and Normanby Park Works both joined.

1977-78

Appleby Frodingham Athletic	26	23	1	2	90	22	47
Gainsborough United	26	17	4	5	61	34	38
Crowle United	26	16	4	6	63	37	36
Messingham Trinity	26	14	3	9	56	37	31
Ruston Sports	26	12	5	9	47	34	29
Ross Sports	26	10	7	9	51	51	27
Ruston Bucyrus	26	10	5	11	46	34	25
Grimsby Amateurs	26	10	4	12	33	40	24
Immingham Town	26	10	4	12	38	47	24
Lincoln United Reserves	26	9	4	13	39	59	22
Sleaford Town	26	8	5	13	39	49	21
Normanby Park Works	26	7	5	14	45	59	19
Market Rasen Town	26	6	4	16	29	67	16
Bottesford Town	26	1	3	22	22	89	5

Appleby Frodingham Athletic moved to the Midland League and were replaced by their reserves.
Drewery Sports and Lincoln Clayton's both joined.

1978-79

Premier Division

Drewery Sports	30	21	3	6	79	30	45
Normanby Park Works	30	20	3	7	61	30	43
Ross Sports	30	19	7	4	57	28	41
Appleby Frodingham Athletic Res.	30	18	5	7	62	33	41
Immingham Town	30	16	6	8	55	36	38
Gainsborough United	30	13	10	7	63	42	36
Ruston Sports	30	12	12	6	51	34	34
Ruston Bucyrus	30	12	8	10	49	43	32
Crowle United	30	13	3	14	48	44	29
Messingham Trinity	30	11	6	13	47	47	28
Lincoln Clayton's	30	11	6	13	41	45	28
Sleaford Town	30	10	3	17	37	58	23
Grimsby Amateurs	30	7	3	20	42	75	17
Lincoln United Reserves	30	7	3	20	31	71	17
Bottesford Town	30	3	5	22	32	84	11
Market Rasen Town	30	3	5	22	27	82	11

Ruston Sports had 2 points deducted.
Ross Sports had 4 points deducted.
Louth United joined from the Midland League. Bottesford Town, Lincoln United Reserves and Market Rasen Town all left the league.
Appleby Frodingham Athletic Reserves changed their name to Appleby Frodingham Sports.

Lincolnshire League (III) 1979-1983

Division One

Scunthorpe Desert Rat	30	22	5	3	98	39	49
Mablethorpe Athletic	30	21	3	6	90	39	45
Louth United Reserves	30	21	4	5	76	40	44
Ross Sports Reserves	30	17	6	7	87	57	40
Drewery Sports Reserves	30	16	7	7	69	44	39
Old Humberstonians Athletic	30	14	7	9	74	44	35
Saxilby Athletic	30	14	7	9	46	43	35
B.R.S.A. Immingham	30	12	9	9	61	44	33
Metheringham	30	13	6	11	65	57	32
Messingham Trinity Reserves	30	9	10	11	58	50	28
Immingham Town Reserves	30	10	6	14	63	60	24
Normanby Park Works Reserves	30	9	4	17	57	89	22
Ruston Bucyrus Reserves	30	6	7	17	59	63	19
Grimsby Amateurs Reserves	30	6	5	19	47	96	17
Scotter United	30	3	6	21	35	88	12
Market Rasen Town Reserves	30	1	0	29	27	159	2

Louth United Reserves and Immingham Town Reserves each had 2 points deducted.

1979-80
Premier Division

Gainsborough United	26	17	6	3	64	22	40
Louth United	26	14	7	5	48	30	35
Crowle United	26	14	6	6	43	30	34
Ruston Bucyrus	26	13	5	8	53	35	31
Drewery Sports	26	13	5	8	38	28	31
Ross Sports	26	11	6	9	42	33	28
Normanby Park Works	26	10	8	8	40	34	28
Ruston Sports	26	9	9	8	31	32	27
Messingham Trinity	26	8	8	10	34	32	24
Sleaford Town	26	7	7	12	31	52	21
Immingham Town	26	8	4	14	30	38	20
Lincoln Clayton's	26	8	4	14	42	59	20
Appleby Frodingham Sports	26	7	2	17	33	62	16
Grimsby Amateurs	26	1	7	18	20	62	9

Boston United Reserves and Scunthorpe Desert Rat both joined the league.

The Division One table has not been found for the 1979-80 season.

1980-81
Premier Division

Sleaford Town	30	22	5	3	79	26	49
Ross Sports	30	22	3	5	82	30	47
Ruston Bucyrus	30	21	4	5	75	29	46
Ruston Sports	30	15	8	7	61	39	38
Gainsborough United	30	15	5	10	56	33	35
Immingham Town	30	15	5	10	67	48	35
Scunthorpe Desert Rat	30	15	4	11	55	51	34
Louth United	30	14	5	11	56	37	33
Crowle United	30	13	4	13	49	44	30
Messingham Trinity	30	10	10	10	39	35	30
Appleby Frodingham Sports	30	13	4	13	44	58	30
Drewery Sports	30	8	4	18	41	56	20
Normanby Park Works	30	6	7	17	34	66	19
Lincoln Clayton's	30	8	3	19	36	72	19
Boston United Reserves	30	4	5	21	36	77	13
Grimsby Amateurs	**30**	**0**	**2**	**28**	**16**	**125**	**2**

Normanby Park Works left the league. Grantham Reserves and Hykeham Town both joined.
Barton Town joined Division One from the Yorkshire League.

The Division One table has not been found for the 1980-81 season.

1981-82
Premier Division

Hykeham Town	30	18	3	9	62	33	39
Boston United Reserves	30	15	7	8	61	48	37
Ross Sports	30	15	6	9	66	36	35
Scunthorpe Desert Rat	30	15	5	10	51	35	35
Louth United	30	12	11	7	42	33	35
Ruston Bucyrus	30	14	7	9	52	44	35
Immingham Town	30	12	9	9	46	37	33
Crowle United	30	15	3	12	48	43	33
Sleaford Town	30	14	5	11	49	52	33
Drewery Sports	30	13	5	12	45	38	31
Ruston Sports	30	13	3	14	48	46	29
Grantham Reserves	30	11	4	15	45	62	26
Messingham Trinity	30	9	8	13	42	47	26
Appleby Frodingham Sports	30	9	5	16	36	54	23
Gainsborough United	30	6	7	17	31	58	19
Lincoln Clayton's	30	2	6	22	33	91	10

Ross Sports and Messingham Trinity each had 1 point deducted.
Hykeham Town and Grantham Reserves both left the league.

Division One

Barton Town	**30**	**19**	**8**	**3**	**82**	**24**	**46**
Ruston Bucyrus Reserves	30	17	7	6	60	37	41
Ross Sports Reserves	30	15	7	8	61	33	37
Nettleham United	**30**	**15**	**5**	**10**	**46**	**35**	**35**
Mablethorpe Athletic	30	13	8	9	51	42	34
Market Rasen Town	30	14	5	11	42	46	33
Bottesford Town	30	9	12	9	44	47	30
Grimsby Amateurs	30	12	6	12	41	44	30
Drewery Sports Reserves	30	13	3	14	47	50	29
Lincoln United Reserves	30	11	6	13	50	47	26
Metheringham	30	11	6	13	54	58	26
Messingham Trinity Reserves	30	8	10	12	34	39	26
Immingham Town Reserves	30	8	8	14	31	60	24
Louth United Reserves	30	7	8	15	31	53	22
Saxilby Athletic	30	6	9	15	42	57	21
Scotter United	30	5	6	19	42	86	16

Lincoln United Reserves and Metheringham each had 2 points deducted.

1982-83
Premier Division

Ross Sports	30	17	9	4	65	33	43
Boston United Reserves	30	18	6	6	90	47	42
Drewery Sports	30	18	6	6	73	34	42
Sleaford Town	30	17	6	7	47	29	40
Louth United	30	12	10	8	31	28	34
Immingham Town	30	12	7	11	45	36	31
Barton Town	30	12	7	11	55	48	31
Lincoln Clayton's	30	12	6	12	44	47	30
Crowle United	30	11	8	11	42	53	30
Scunthorpe Desert Rat	30	11	9	10	39	40	29
Ruston Bucyrus	30	9	9	12	42	51	27
Nettleham United	30	10	6	14	37	45	26
Gainsborough United	30	7	8	15	44	60	22
Ruston Sports	30	4	10	16	30	63	18
Appleby Frodingham Sports	30	6	6	18	32	67	18
Messingham Trinity	30	3	9	18	27	62	15

Scunthorpe Desert Rat had 2 points deducted.
Appleby Frodingham Sports and Drewery Sports both left the league.
Skegness Town joined from the Northern Counties (East) League while Gainsborough Town, Grimsby Pelham and Market Rasen Town also all joined.

The Division One table has not been found for the 1982-83 season.

Lincolnshire League (III) 1983-1986

1983-84
Premier Division

Ross Sports	34	21	9	4	94	38	51
Louth United	34	20	10	4	66	30	50
Immingham Town	34	21	6	7	66	32	48
Barton Town	34	21	4	9	80	49	46
Sleaford Town	34	18	10	6	65	39	46
Lincoln Clayton's	34	16	5	13	66	58	37
Gainsborough United	34	14	7	13	49	63	35
Crowle United	34	12	10	12	62	56	34
Ruston Sports	34	13	8	13	50	48	34
Ruston Bucyrus	34	11	11	12	38	50	33
Grimsby Pelham	34	13	6	15	70	63	32
Gainsborough Town	34	11	7	16	52	68	29
Boston United Reserves	34	12	6	16	42	50	28
Nettleham United	34	10	7	17	41	57	27
Skegness Town	34	13	2	19	58	64	25
Market Rasen Town	34	6	9	19	49	85	21
Messingham Trinity	34	7	5	22	42	78	19
Scunthorpe Desert Rat	34	3	6	25	23	85	12

Boston United Reserves had 2 points deducted.
Skegness Town had 3 points deducted.
Scunthorpe Desert Rat disbanded and Boston United Reserves also left.
Cleethorpes Borough joined.

The Division One table has not been found for the 1983-84 season.

1984-85
Premier Division

Skegness Town	32	24	6	2	75	16	54
Louth United	32	22	6	4	98	34	50
Ross Sports	32	22	6	4	84	29	50
Gainsborough Town	32	17	7	8	70	43	39
Cleethorpes Borough	32	12	13	7	62	53	37
Crowle United	32	14	8	10	54	42	36
Grimsby Pelham	32	13	9	10	52	52	35
Immingham Town	32	11	11	10	56	54	33
Barton Town	32	12	8	12	63	60	32
Ruston Bucyrus	32	12	7	13	43	58	31
Ruston Sports	32	11	8	13	54	48	30
Sleaford Town	32	7	12	13	50	56	24
Nettleham United	32	10	4	18	37	59	24
Messingham Trinity	32	8	7	17	49	62	23
Market Rasen Town	32	7	7	18	45	76	21
Lincoln Clayton's	32	6	4	22	42	81	16
Gainsborough United	32	2	1	29	25	136	5

Gainsborough Town and Sleaford Town each had 2 points deducted.
Barton Town and Gainsborough United both left the league.
Grimsby Pelham changed their name to Grimsby S.H.F.S..

Division One

Brigg White Horse	**28**	**21**	**3**	**4**	**72**	**32**	**45**
Mablethorpe Athletic	**28**	**18**	**7**	**3**	**70**	**27**	**43**
Metheringham	28	14	7	7	68	30	35
Bottesford Town	28	15	5	8	58	38	35
Cleethorpes Borough Reserves	28	15	5	8	57	41	35
Grimsby Amateurs	28	13	8	7	61	34	34
Louth United Reserves	28	13	4	11	46	40	30
Grimsby Pelham Reserves	28	11	8	9	53	45	28
Saxilby Athletic	28	10	7	11	47	43	27
Ruston Bucyrus Reserves	28	10	5	13	39	51	25
Nettleham United Reserves	28	8	6	14	31	41	22
Ross Sports Reserves	28	9	5	14	46	80	21
Messingham Trinity Reserves	28	7	2	19	51	71	16
Immingham Town Reserves	28	6	3	19	43	75	15
Market Rasen Town Reserves	28	1	3	24	12	106	5

Grimsby Pelham Reserves and Ross Sports Reserves each had 2 points deducted.

Metheringham left the league. Cleethorpes C.S., Louth Old Boys and Mablethorpe Athletic Reserves all joined.
Grimsby Pelham Reserves changed their name to Grimsby S.H.F.S. Reserves.

1985-86
Premier Division

Louth United	32	26	1	5	102	29	53
Cleethorpes Borough	32	21	6	5	65	24	48
Gainsborough Town	32	20	6	6	70	27	46
Ross Sports	32	15	7	10	61	38	37
Immingham Town	32	14	9	9	48	44	37
Skegness Town	32	13	9	10	56	41	35
Ruston Bucyrus	32	13	8	11	52	44	34
Grimsby S.H.F.S.	32	13	8	11	54	49	34
Nettleham United	32	12	9	11	50	47	33
Crowle United	32	13	5	14	43	48	31
Ruston Sports	32	13	4	15	48	55	30
Sleaford Town	32	10	10	12	34	47	30
Mablethorpe Athletic	32	10	9	13	35	47	29
Messingham Trinity	32	9	1	22	44	91	19
Lincoln Clayton's	32	8	4	20	33	60	16
Market Rasen Town	32	5	5	22	40	89	15
Brigg White Horse	32	4	5	23	37	92	13

Lincoln Clayton's had 4 points deducted.
Gainsborough Town moved to the Central Midlands League and Immingham Town moved to the Northern Counties East League. Brigg White Horse, Grimsby S.H.F.S. and Ruston Bucyrus also left the league.

Division One

Saxilby Athletic	28	20	3	5	77	31	43
Ruston Bucyrus Reserves	28	17	8	3	69	31	42
Louth Old Boys	**28**	**14**	**10**	**4**	**56**	**36**	**38**
Grimsby S.H.F.S. Reserves	28	16	4	8	72	44	36
Grimsby Amateurs	**28**	**16**	**3**	**9**	**46**	**33**	**35**
Bottesford Town	28	13	7	8	57	29	33
Louth United Reserves	28	14	4	10	61	39	32
Cleethorpes Borough Reserves	28	12	4	12	56	35	28
Cleethorpes C.S.	28	11	5	12	53	42	27
Ross Sports Reserves	28	10	4	14	52	44	24
Messingham Trinity Reserves	28	8	5	15	40	76	21
Nettleham United Reserves	28	8	3	17	40	72	19
Immingham Town Reserves	28	8	3	17	34	74	19
Mablethorpe Athletic Reserves	28	4	6	18	36	71	13
Market Rasen Town Reserves	28	3	3	22	23	115	9

Mablethorpe Athletic Reserves had 1 point deducted.

1986-87
Premier Division

Louth United	26	20	5	1	68	18	45
Ross Sports	26	17	7	2	68	24	41
Sleaford Town	26	13	10	3	44	22	33
Ruston Sports	26	15	3	8	59	43	33
Lincoln Clayton's	26	14	4	8	74	41	32
Mablethorpe Athletic	26	12	9	5	39	29	32
Crowle United	26	10	7	9	40	52	27
Cleethorpes Borough	26	8	10	8	38	27	26
Grimsby Amateurs	26	8	7	11	40	38	23
Nettleham United	26	8	6	12	36	37	22
Market Rasen Town	26	4	6	16	44	77	14
Skegness Town	26	4	6	16	34	77	13
Louth Old Boys	26	4	4	18	27	71	12
Messingham Trinity	26	1	4	21	24	79	6

Sleaford Town had 3 points deducted.
Mablethorpe Athletic and Skegness Town each had 1 point deducted.
Louth United and Nettleham United both moved to the Central Midlands League and both were replaced by their reserves. Ross Sports also moved to the Central Midlands League and changed their name to Grimsby Ross. Messingham Trinity moved to the Scunthorpe & District League and Cleethorpes Borough also left. Barton Town joined from the Scunthorpe & District League while Eaton Hall College, Grimsby Athletic, Bottesford Town, Grimsby Park View and Immingham Town Reserves also all joined.

The Division One table has not been found for the 1986-87 season and it may have closed down. There was no Division One the following season.

1987-88

Ruston Sports	32	27	3	2	67	18	57
Lincoln Clayton's	32	26	3	3	104	32	55
Louth United Reserves	32	18	8	6	72	35	43
Bottesford Town	32	18	6	8	77	48	42
Crowle United	32	14	8	10	53	39	36
Barton Town	32	15	6	11	65	67	36
Immingham Town Reserves	32	12	10	10	51	46	34
Market Rasen Town	32	13	4	15	59	64	30
Sleaford Town	32	11	6	15	46	51	28
Eaton Hall College	32	9	8	15	51	59	26
Mablethorpe Athletic	32	11	3	18	52	84	25
Grimsby Amateurs	32	10	4	18	42	50	24
Skegness Town	32	11	2	19	59	69	24
Nettleham United Reserves	32	10	3	19	46	77	23
Grimsby Park View	32	8	7	17	51	84	23
Grimsby Athletic	32	8	5	19	34	74	21
Louth Old Boys	32	6	4	22	27	59	16

Louth United Reserves had 1 point deducted.
Immingham Town Reserves, Lincoln Clayton's and Mablethorpe Athletic all left the league. B.R.S.A. Immingham joined.
Grimsby Park View changed their name to Grimsby Charltons.

1988-89

Ruston Sports	28	21	3	4	75	26	66
Grimsby Charltons	28	20	5	3	65	24	65
Crowle United	28	16	8	4	78	31	56
Louth United Reserves	28	16	5	7	66	45	53
Sleaford Town	28	12	9	7	49	37	45
Skegness Town	28	12	6	10	52	41	42
Grimsby Amateurs	28	12	5	11	48	41	41
Bottesford Town	28	11	4	13	54	54	37
Louth Old Boys	28	8	11	9	39	47	34
Grimsby Athletic	28	9	5	14	57	69	32
B.R.S.A. Immingham	28	8	6	14	35	53	30
Nettleham United Reserves	28	7	6	15	29	65	27
Barton Town	28	7	5	16	50	75	26
Market Rasen Town	28	3	9	16	33	76	18
Eaton Hall College	28	1	7	20	34	80	10

Louth Old Boys had 1 point deducted.

Market Rasen Town, Crowle United and Grimsby Charltons all left the league. Louth United Reserves changed their name to Louth Park Avenue and Nettleham United Reserves changed their name to Nettleham Reserves.

1989-90

Bottesford Town	22	14	4	4	51	19	46
Sleaford Town	22	13	5	4	57	24	44
Skegness Town	22	11	5	6	38	31	38
Ruston Sports	22	10	7	5	46	27	37
Grimsby Amateurs	22	10	5	7	35	25	35
Louth Park Avenue	22	9	6	7	30	26	33
B.R.S.A. Immingham	22	9	5	8	34	38	32
Louth Old Boys	22	7	7	8	31	32	28
Nettleham Reserves	22	6	3	13	34	52	20
Eaton Hall College	22	5	4	13	22	48	19
Grimsby Athletic	22	4	7	11	26	54	19
Barton Town	22	3	4	15	28	56	13

Nettleham Reserves had 1 point deducted.
Grimsby Athletic left the league. Grimsby Amateurs merged with Ross Sports and continued in the league as Grimsby Ross Amateurs. Louth Park Avenue changed their name to Louth United Reserves, B.R.S.A. Immingham changed their name to Immingham Athletic and Nettleham Reserves changed their name to Nettleham Mulsanne. Grimsby Borough joined from the Central Midlands League, Appleby Frodingham Athletic joined from the Scunthorpe & District League while Brigg Town Reserves, Lincoln United Colts, Mablethorpe Athletic and Spilsby Town all also joined.

1990-91

Bottesford Town	32	21	10	1	85	31	73
Grimsby Borough	32	23	4	5	90	38	73
Sleaford Town	32	15	14	3	55	37	59
Barton Town	32	18	5	9	85	55	55
Skegness Town	32	16	8	8	76	58	55
Immingham Athletic	32	14	9	9	63	48	51
Ruston Sports	32	15	5	12	67	51	50
Louth United Reserves	32	14	8	10	51	39	50
Louth Old Boys	32	14	5	13	51	50	47
Appleby Frodingham Athletic	32	13	4	15	66	79	43
Lincoln United Colts	32	11	8	13	67	63	41
Spilsby Town	32	12	3	17	49	64	39
Grimsby Ross Amateurs	32	10	8	14	45	46	38
Nettleham Mulsanne	32	6	8	18	50	76	26
Brigg Town Reserves	32	5	9	18	44	67	24
Eaton Hall College	32	5	6	21	41	91	21
Mablethorpe Athletic	32	1	4	27	24	116	7

Barton Town Old Boys had 4 points deducted.
Skegness Town had 1 point deducted.
Barton Town and Louth Old Boys both left the league.
Hykeham Town, Immingham Town Reserves and Wyberton all joined.

Lincolnshire League (III) 1991-1995

1991-92

Bottesford Town	34	26	1	7	96	37	79
Hykeham Town	34	22	7	5	97	41	73
Brigg Town Reserves	34	22	7	5	76	41	73
Grimsby Borough	34	22	4	8	96	54	70
Grimsby Ross Amateurs	34	19	8	7	73	50	65
Lincoln United Colts	34	18	7	9	72	46	61
Ruston Sports	34	18	6	10	54	35	60
Wyberton	34	17	3	14	67	60	54
Louth United Reserves	34	16	3	15	55	47	51
Appleby Frodingham Athletic	34	13	7	14	76	83	46
Skegness Town	34	13	6	15	69	73	45
Sleaford Town	34	10	7	17	51	88	37
Immingham Town Reserves	34	9	8	17	51	60	35
Mablethorpe Athletic	34	10	1	23	45	89	31
Immingham Athletic	34	8	5	21	30	66	29
Nettleham Mulsanne	34	7	6	21	42	76	27
Spilsby Town	34	6	3	25	25	54	21
Eaton Hall College	34	5	1	28	23	98	16

Brigg Town Reserves and Grimsby Borough both left the league.
Boston Reserves, Humberside United, Lincoln Athletic and Louth Old Boys all joined. Immingham Athletic changed their name to Immingham Blossom Way Sports while Nettleham Mulsanne changed their name to Nettleham Reserves.

1992-93

Humberside United	36	30	4	2	113	28	92
Hykeham Town	36	29	1	6	100	38	88
Appleby Frodingham Athletic	36	22	5	9	103	49	68
+ Immingham Blossom Way Sports	36	17	11	8	79	51	64
Lincoln United Colts	36	19	5	12	82	61	62
Bottesford Town	36	17	8	11	83	62	59
Wyberton	36	17	5	14	88	68	56
Skegness Town	36	15	5	16	84	89	50
Sleaford Town	36	12	9	15	57	57	45
Ruston Sports	36	13	6	17	60	64	45
Louth United Reserves	36	12	9	15	66	77	45
Boston Reserves	36	12	8	16	59	75	44
Spilsby Town	36	12	8	16	56	75	44
++ Grimsby Ross Amateurs	36	12	5	19	64	88	44
Louth Old Boys	36	11	8	17	51	68	41
Nettleham Reserves	36	11	5	20	59	87	38
Lincoln Athletic	36	10	6	20	52	87	36
Mablethorpe Athletic	36	8	6	22	56	101	30
Eaton Hall College	36	3	6	27	36	112	15

Immingham Town Reserves resigned during the season and their record was deleted.
Humberside United had 2 points deducted.
Appleby Frodingham Athletic had 3 points deducted.
+ Immingham Blossom Way Sports had 2 points added.
++ Grimsby Ross Amateurs had 3 points added.
Humberside United and Mablethorpe Athletic both left the league.
Eaton Hall College moved into the ground of Retford Rail, formerly of the Central Midlands League, and changed their name to B.R.S.A. Retford.
Boston United Reserves and Limestone Rangers both joined.
Lincoln Moorlands joined after a year's inactivity following their exit from the Central Midlands League. Grimsby Ross Amateurs changed their name to Grimsby Amateurs, Lincoln Athletic changed their name to Hykeham United and Louth United Reserves changed their name to Louth United Amateurs.

1993-94

Appleby Frodingham Athletic	38	28	3	7	107	39	87
Bottesford Town	38	26	6	6	100	45	81
Wyberton	38	25	6	7	80	40	81
Immingham Blossom Way Sports	38	24	8	6	107	47	80
Hykeham Town	38	24	5	9	118	37	77
Limestone Rangers	38	23	2	13	87	61	71
Lincoln Moorlands	38	21	6	11	89	49	69
Boston United Reserves	38	19	8	11	95	70	65
Sleaford Town	38	19	8	11	86	68	65
Lincoln United Colts	38	20	4	14	84	73	64
Grimsby Amateurs	38	17	5	16	74	68	56
Louth Old Boys	38	12	5	21	54	86	41
Skegness Town	38	13	4	21	67	80	40
Louth United Amateurs	38	11	6	21	62	84	39
B.R.S.A. Retford	38	10	5	23	48	94	35
Ruston Sports	38	9	7	22	57	77	34
Nettleham Reserves	38	10	4	24	62	110	34
Spilsby Town	38	8	7	23	62	90	31
+ Hykeham United	38	5	4	29	42	104	22
+ Boston Reserves	38	2	5	31	29	188	14

Bottesford Town and Skegness Town each had 3 points deducted.
+ Boston Reserves and Hykeham United each had 3 points added.
Boston Reserves and Hykeham United both left the league.
Epworth Town Leisure Centre joined from the Scunthorpe & District League while Grantham Town Reserves also joined.

1994-95

Wyberton	38	28	7	3	116	44	91
Lincoln United Colts	38	27	6	5	102	37	87
Immingham Blossom Way Sports	38	27	6	5	109	48	87
Hykeham Town	38	24	7	7	111	38	79
+ Boston United Reserves	38	21	7	10	109	53	73
Bottesford Town	38	18	10	10	87	58	64
Louth United Amateurs	38	18	5	15	82	74	59
Limestone Rangers	38	17	5	16	101	83	56
Sleaford Town	38	16	7	15	97	93	55
Appleby Frodingham	38	15	8	15	60	62	53
Skegness Town	38	15	4	19	66	84	49
Lincoln Moorlands	38	12	9	17	73	84	45
Epworth Town Leisure Centre	38	11	12	15	79	91	45
Grimsby Amateurs	38	10	13	15	51	69	43
B.R.S.A. Retford	38	11	10	17	68	92	43
Nettleham Reserves	38	9	8	21	60	104	35
Grantham Town Reserves	38	10	7	21	52	89	34
Ruston Sports	38	8	8	22	65	110	32
Louth Old Boys	38	4	6	28	42	125	18
Spilsby Town	38	4	5	29	44	136	17

+ Boston United Reserves had 3 points added.
Grantham Town Reserves had 3 points deducted.
Immingham Blossom Way Sports were expelled as they had been suspended by the county F.A. and owed money to the league.
Barton Town Old Boys joined as a club newly formed by a merger of Barton Old Boys of the Scunthorpe & District League with Barton Town.

Lincolnshire League (III) 1995-2000

1995-96

Lincoln United Colts	36	29	3	4	107	25	87
Boston United Reserves	36	23	7	6	85	38	76
Limestone Rangers	36	23	5	8	89	52	74
Barton Town Old Boys	36	22	6	8	97	47	72
Appleby Frodingham Athletic	36	20	8	8	79	44	68
++ Grimsby Amateurs	36	17	7	12	72	55	61
Sleaford Town	36	17	7	12	74	60	58
Wyberton	36	17	6	13	84	64	56
Hykeham Town	36	17	4	15	77	71	55
Lincoln Moorlands	36	15	5	16	79	71	50
Skegness Town	36	15	4	17	60	72	49
Bottesford Town	36	13	8	15	73	58	47
Epworth Town Leisure Centre	36	14	5	17	62	78	47
Grantham Town Reserves	36	13	5	18	57	81	41
Ruston Sports	36	10	6	20	75	98	36
++ B.R.S.A. Retford	36	8	2	26	56	101	29
+ Louth United Amateurs	36	6	9	21	50	98	29
Louth Old Boys	36	4	8	24	43	109	20
Nettleham Reserves	36	5	3	28	29	126	18

Spilsby Town resigned during the season and their record was deleted.
Lincoln United Colts and Grantham Town Reserves each had 3 points deducted.
Wyberton had 1 point deducted.
++ Grimsby Amateurs and B.R.S.A. Retford each had 3 points added.
+ Louth United Amateurs had 2 points added.
Horncastle Town joined the league. Grimsby Amateurs changed their name to Grimsby & Immingham Amateurs and Lincoln United Colts changed their name to Lincoln United Reserves.

1996-97

Barton Town Old Boys	38	31	3	4	108	32	96
Lincoln United Reserves	38	25	7	6	83	31	82
Appleby Frodingham Athletic	38	24	7	7	71	27	79
Wyberton	38	25	4	9	76	45	79
Limestone Rangers	38	24	4	10	87	47	73
Lincoln Moorlands	38	21	8	9	93	43	71
Boston United Reserves	38	21	5	12	99	62	68
Grimsby & Immingham Amateurs	38	18	10	10	72	46	64
Ruston Sports	38	17	10	11	79	50	61
+ Bottesford Town	38	17	8	13	71	51	61
Sleaford Town	38	16	10	12	88	70	54
Grantham Town Reserves	38	15	6	17	63	66	51
Louth United Amateurs	38	15	5	18	76	68	50
Skegness Town	38	11	7	20	55	86	40
++ Horncastle Town	38	9	7	22	51	80	37
Epworth Town Leisure Centre	38	9	5	24	56	113	32
Hykeham Town	38	8	2	28	43	106	26
++ Louth Old Boys	38	5	6	27	48	124	21
B.R.S.A. Retford	38	4	8	26	42	103	20
Nettleham Reserves	38	1	6	31	30	141	9

Limestone Rangers had 3 points deducted.
Sleaford Town had 4 points deducted.
+ Bottesford Town had 2 points added.
++ Horncastle Town and Louth Old Boys had 3 points added.
Louth Old Boys left the league.
Louth United Amateurs changed their name to Louth United Reserves.

1997-98

Lincoln United Reserves	36	29	4	3	117	29	91
Barton Town Old Boys	36	25	8	3	112	45	83
Grimsby & Immingham Amateurs	36	24	6	6	103	43	78
Sleaford Town	36	23	2	11	77	55	71
Lincoln Moorlands	36	22	6	8	97	39	69
Wyberton	36	19	6	11	84	63	63
Boston United Reserves	36	18	6	12	96	64	60
Bottesford Town	36	17	9	10	66	48	60
+ Limestone Rangers	36	16	7	13	70	71	58
Louth United Reserves	36	17	4	15	88	77	55
Grantham Town Reserves	36	16	6	14	78	77	54
Appleby Frodingham Athletic	36	13	5	18	67	83	44
Ruston Sports	36	13	2	21	67	86	41
Skegness Town	36	11	5	20	63	81	38
Horncastle Town	36	9	9	18	62	78	36
Epworth Town Leisure Centre	36	8	3	25	58	115	27
Hykeham Town	36	5	5	26	31	88	20
B.R.S.A. Retford	36	6	1	29	61	157	19
Nettleham Reserves	36	3	2	31	30	128	11

Lincoln Moorlands had 3 points deducted.
+ Limestone Rangers had 3 points added.
Lincoln Moorlands moved to the Central Midlands League and were replaced by their reserves.
Ruston Sports changed their name to Alstom Sports.

1998-99

Limestone Rangers	36	27	5	4	112	32	86
Barton Town Old Boys	36	24	6	6	124	47	78
Boston United Reserves	36	22	6	8	118	59	72
Grimsby & Immingham Amateurs	36	19	14	3	69	28	71
Lincoln United Reserves	36	22	3	11	80	50	69
Alstom Sports	36	19	4	13	84	68	61
Sleaford Town	36	17	6	13	88	65	57
Epworth Town Leisure Centre	36	17	5	14	60	64	56
Lincoln Moorlands Reserves	36	16	8	12	55	57	56
Grantham Town Reserves	36	16	9	11	73	53	54
Appleby Frodingham Athletic	36	14	8	14	86	71	50
B.R.S.A. Retford	36	13	7	16	55	79	46
+ Skegness Town	36	12	6	18	64	88	45
Louth United Reserves	36	12	6	18	73	81	42
Bottesford Town	36	10	5	21	65	88	35
Wyberton	36	9	5	22	62	97	32
Hykeham Town	36	10	2	24	53	101	32
Horncastle Town	36	7	5	24	42	97	26
Nettleham Reserves	36	0	2	34	28	166	2

Grantham Town Reserves had 3 points deducted.
+ Skegness Town had 3 points added.
Grantham Town Reserves left the league.
Lorne Stewart Barrowby United joined.

1999-2000

Boston United Reserves	34	27	7	0	145	39	88
Limestone Rangers	34	23	8	3	94	48	77
Barton Town Old Boys	34	20	9	5	104	53	69
Grimsby & Immingham Amateurs	34	18	11	5	84	49	65
Lincoln United Reserves	34	16	8	10	64	42	56
Epworth Town Leisure Centre	34	14	8	12	48	45	50
Bottesford Town	34	14	6	14	67	81	48
Lorne Stewart Barrowby United	34	13	7	14	69	74	46
Skegness Town	34	11	10	13	58	62	43
Wyberton	34	12	5	17	53	69	41
Appleby Frodingham Athletic	34	12	5	17	47	63	41
Sleaford Town	34	10	9	15	56	54	39
Alstom Sports	34	9	12	13	52	62	39
Horncastle Town	34	9	6	19	46	86	33
Louth United Reserves	34	8	8	18	47	72	32
Hykeham Town	34	9	4	21	52	82	31
Lincoln Moorlands Reserves	34	7	6	21	48	92	27
B.R.S.A. Retford	34	6	7	21	37	98	25

Lincolnshire League (III) 2000-2006

Nettleham Reserves resigned during the season. Their record was deleted.
Bottesford Town moved to the Central Midlands League, Barton Town Old Boys moved to the Humber Premier League, Wyberton moved to the Boston League and Boston United Reserves also left the league.
Grantham Town Reserves joined.
Lorne Stewart Barrowby United changed their name to Barrowby United.

2000-01

Grantham Town Reserves	28	20	4	4	85	36	64
Grimsby & Immingham Amateurs	28	19	5	4	75	26	62
Skegness Town	28	18	8	2	56	32	62
Lincoln United Reserves	28	15	4	9	48	22	49
Appleby Frodingham Athletic	28	13	9	6	59	30	48
Sleaford Town	28	13	4	11	52	52	43
Hykeham Town	28	10	5	13	47	54	35
Louth United Reserves	28	9	5	14	48	61	32
Alstom Sports	28	9	5	14	51	65	32
Barrowby United	28	9	4	15	40	51	31
Epworth Town Leisure Centre	28	8	6	14	37	64	30
Limestone Rangers	28	8	5	15	40	55	29
Horncastle Town	28	7	6	15	32	44	27
Lincoln Moorlands Reserves	28	6	6	16	38	72	24
B.R.S.A. Retford	28	6	4	18	24	68	22

Epworth Town Leisure Centre left the league. Wyberton joined from the Boston League. B.R.S.A. Retford changed their name to Retford Town.

2001-02

Lincoln United Reserves	26	20	3	3	64	17	63
Grimsby & Immingham Amateurs	26	16	7	3	72	33	55
Wyberton	26	16	5	5	63	33	53
Grantham Town Reserves	26	12	5	9	43	37	41
Sleaford Town	26	11	6	9	58	60	39
Lincoln Moorlands Reserves	26	10	4	12	45	52	34
Skegness Town	26	8	9	9	42	45	33
Alstom Sports	26	9	5	12	52	53	32
Limestone Rangers	26	7	8	11	59	69	29
Louth United Reserves	26	8	6	12	45	57	29
Hykeham Town	26	7	6	13	40	63	27
Horncastle Town	26	5	10	11	28	51	25
Appleby Frodingham Athletic	26	6	5	15	36	54	23
Retford Town	26	5	5	16	33	56	20

Barrowby United resigned from the league during the season and their record was deleted 13 2 2 9 18 41 8
Louth United Reserves had 1 point deducted.
Grantham Town Reserves left the league. Grimsby & Immingham Amateurs changed their name to Grimsby Amateurs.

2002-03

Grimsby Amateurs	24	17	3	4	76	30	54
Sleaford Town	24	17	2	5	68	24	53
Wyberton	24	12	7	5	54	30	43
+ Limestone Rangers	24	11	6	7	58	35	40
Lincoln Moorlands Reserves	24	10	5	9	41	44	35
Alstom Sports	24	10	4	10	43	48	34
Hykeham Town	24	9	6	9	52	54	33
Skegness Town	24	9	5	10	39	43	32
Appleby Frodingham Athletic	24	8	4	12	36	42	28
Lincoln United Reserves	24	6	9	9	39	41	26
Horncastle Town	24	6	7	11	27	41	25
Louth United Reserves	24	4	7	13	30	71	19
Retford Town	24	3	3	18	24	84	12

+ Limestone Rangers had 1 point added.
Lincoln United Reserves had 1 point deducted.
Appleby Frodingham Athletic moved to the Central Midlands League, Retford Town moved to the Notts Alliance while Grimsby Amateurs and Louth United Reserves both disbanded. Grimsby Borough and L.S.S. Lucarlys both joined as newly formed clubs and Harrowby United Reserves also joined. Alstom Sports changed their name to Ruston Sports.

2003-04

Sleaford Town	22	17	4	1	68	24	55
+ Grimsby Borough	22	13	2	7	43	29	43
L.S.S. Lucarlys	22	12	7	3	37	28	43
Wyberton	22	12	4	6	48	28	37
Hykeham Town	22	9	7	6	33	35	34
Lincoln United Reserves	22	9	6	7	45	33	33
+ Harrowby United Reserves	22	7	5	10	36	39	28
Skegness Town	22	7	4	11	26	32	25
Limestone Rangers	22	8	0	14	44	49	24
Horncastle Town	22	5	5	12	21	43	20
++ Lincoln Moorlands Reserves	22	5	1	16	23	59	19
Ruston Sports	22	2	7	13	18	43	13

+ Grimsby Borough and Harrowby United Reserves each had 2 points added.
++ Lincoln Moorlands Reserves had 3 points added.
Wyberton had 3 points deducted.
Sleaford Town moved to the United Counties League and Lincoln United Reserves also left. Grimsby Borough moved to the Central Midlands League, being replaced by their reserves. Louth United joined as a newly re-formed club after leaving the Northern Counties East League in 2003.

2004-05

Wyberton	20	14	4	2	73	23	46
Ruston Sports	20	11	4	5	38	26	37
Louth United	20	9	5	6	39	29	32
L.S.S. Lucarlys	20	10	1	9	43	35	31
Horncastle Town	20	9	4	7	40	34	31
Skegness Town	20	9	2	9	43	46	29
Hykeham Town	20	7	4	9	38	36	25
Grimsby Borough Reserves	20	7	4	9	40	45	25
Harrowby United Reserves	20	6	4	10	29	50	22
Lincoln Moorlands Reserves	20	5	2	13	33	61	17
Limestone Rangers	20	5	2	13	29	60	17

Harrowby United Reserves were disbanded. L.S.S. Lucarlys moved to the Central Midlands League, being replaced by their newly formed reserve side. CGB Humbertherm, Caistor Rovers and Retford Town joined as newly formed clubs and Lincoln United Juniors joined as a newly formed side.

2005-06

Hykeham Town	24	21	0	3	84	19	63
CGB Humbertherm	24	17	3	4	56	23	54
Horncastle Town	24	16	3	5	70	26	51
Wyberton	24	16	3	5	60	33	51
Ruston Sports	24	13	3	8	39	46	42
Louth United	24	12	4	8	54	41	40
Caistor Rovers	24	8	4	12	31	46	28
Skegness Town	24	6	9	9	43	45	27
Lincoln Moorlands Reserves	24	7	4	13	41	49	22
Retford Town	24	5	4	15	28	61	19
Grimsby Borough Reserves	24	4	3	17	31	67	15
Lincoln United Juniors	24	4	2	18	23	61	14
L.S.S. Lucarlys Reserves	24	4	4	16	34	77	13

Limestone Rangers resigned from the league during the season and their record was deleted: 14 0 2 12 7 67 2
They joined the Scunthorpe & District League in 2006-07.
Lincoln Moorlands Reserves and L.S.S. Lucarlys Reserves each had 3 points deducted.
Wyberton moved to the Boston League, Lincoln Moorlands Reserves moved to the Central Midlands League and Retford Town moved to the Doncaster League. Louth United moved to the Central Midlands League and were replaced by their newly formed reserve side. Boston Town Reserves joined from the Boston League having changed their name from Boston Town Colts and Keelby United joined as a newly formed club.
Lincoln United Juniors changed their name to Lincoln United Reserves.

Lincolnshire League (III) 2006-2011

2006-07

Skegness Town	22	17	3	2	55	16	54
Hykeham Town	22	16	3	3	68	21	51
Horncastle Town	22	12	4	6	58	28	40
Ruston Sports	22	12	4	6	42	25	40
CGB Humbertherm	22	12	4	6	42	32	40
Caistor Rovers	22	11	4	7	48	28	37
Lincoln United Reserves	22	8	3	11	43	45	27
Grimsby Borough Reserves	22	8	2	12	42	37	23
Boston Town Reserves	22	6	5	11	21	42	23
Keelby United	22	4	1	17	25	76	13
L.S.S. Lucarlys Reserves	22	4	3	15	24	52	12
Louth United Reserves	22	4	0	18	28	94	12

Grimsby Borough Reserves and L.S.S. Lucarlys Reserves each had 3 points deducted.
Grimsby Borough Reserves left the league. Sleaford Town Reserves joined from the Boston League and Harrowby United joined from the Grantham League. Grimsby Soccer School and Colsterworth United both joined as newly-formed clubs and Grantham Town Reserves joined as a newly-formed team. Lincoln Moorlands Railway Reserves joined as a result of a merger between Lincoln Moorlands of the Northern Counties East League and Moorlands Railway of the Lincoln League. Louth United Reserves changed their name to Louth United (Louth United of the Central Midlands League had changed their name to Louth Town).

2007-08

Skegness Town	30	26	2	2	74	19	77
Ruston Sports	30	20	4	6	87	41	64
Hykeham Town	30	18	9	3	93	34	63
Sleaford Town Reserves	30	16	5	9	57	43	53
Horncastle Town	30	16	4	10	55	44	52
+ Lincoln Moorlands Railway Res.	30	15	3	12	56	43	51
CGB Humbertherm	30	16	1	13	64	55	49
Lincoln United Reserves	30	12	7	11	66	45	43
Louth United	30	12	5	13	64	55	41
Grantham Town Reserves	30	12	1	17	60	79	37
Boston Town Reserves	30	10	6	14	54	65	36
Caistor Rovers	30	11	2	17	57	65	35
Grimsby Soccer School	30	10	5	15	52	76	35
L.S.S. Lucarlys Reserves	30	8	2	20	24	78	26
Colsterworth United	30	6	3	21	48	84	21
Harrowby United	30	1	3	26	25	110	6

Keelby United resigned from the league during the season and their record at the time was deleted: 9 0 1 8 9 44 1
Skegness Town had 3 points deducted.
+ Lincoln Moorlands Railway Reserves had 3 points added.
Harrowby United moved to the Central Midlands League and Colsterworth United moved to the Grantham League. Caistor Rovers and Grimsby Soccer School both disbanded. Grimsby Borough Reserves joined as a newly formed team. L.S.S. Lucarlys Reserves changed their name to Cleethorpes Town Reserves.

2008-09

CGB Humbertherm	22	17	2	3	57	24	53
Ruston Sports	22	15	3	4	54	28	48
Louth United	22	13	3	6	57	30	42
Hykeham Town	22	11	7	4	60	26	40
Skegness Town	22	11	4	7	51	34	37
Horncastle Town	22	10	5	7	42	41	35
Lincoln United Reserves	22	9	5	8	45	39	32
Sleaford Town Reserves	22	8	8	6	35	29	32
Boston Town Reserves	22	7	2	13	39	56	23
Lincoln Moorlands Railway Res.	22	2	7	13	24	42	13
Cleethorpes Town Reserves	22	3	2	17	20	70	11
Grimsby Borough Reserves	22	1	2	19	17	82	5

Grantham Town Reserves resigned from the league during the season and their record was deleted: 11 4 1 6 15 23 13

Heckington United joined from the Lincoln & District League, Harvest joined from the Grimsby & District League having changed their name from Harvest Pet Products, Skellingthorpe PFC joined from the Lincoln & District League having changed their name from Plough Skellingthorpe and Louth Town Reserves joined as a newly formed team.

2009-10

Harvest	28	23	1	4	105	23	70
Hykeham Town	28	20	4	4	95	27	64
Sleaford Town Reserves	28	18	7	3	68	33	61
Ruston Sports	28	18	5	5	63	25	59
Skegness Town	28	14	7	7	56	35	49
Lincoln United Reserves	28	14	5	9	56	40	47
CGB Humbertherm	28	14	4	10	55	42	46
+ Louth Town Reserves	28	11	3	14	58	71	38
Skellingthorpe PFC	28	10	6	12	60	61	36
Heckington United	28	9	6	13	50	71	33
Horncastle Town	28	9	5	14	43	54	32
Lincoln Moorlands Railway Res.	28	5	2	21	44	89	17
Grimsby Borough Reserves	28	4	5	19	31	104	16
Boston Town Reserves	28	3	6	19	27	81	15
Cleethorpes Town (Reserves)	28	3	4	21	28	83	13

Louth United resigned and disbanded during the season and their record at the time was deleted: 23 5 4 14 27 61 19
Cleethorpes Town resigned from the Humber Premier League during the season and took their reserves' place in the Lincolnshire League.
Grimsby Borough Reserves had 1 point deducted.
+ Louth Town Reserves had 2 points added.
Harvest moved to the Grimsby & District League, Lincoln Moorlands Railway Reserves moved to the Central Midlands League as Moorlands Railway and Boston Town Reserves were disbanded. Boston United Reserves joined from youth football and Swineshead Institute joined from the Boston League.

2010-11

Boston United Reserves	26	20	2	4	85	19	62
Lincoln United Reserves	26	15	4	7	75	40	49
Cleethorpes Town	26	14	7	5	70	43	49
Swineshead Institute	26	14	4	8	75	46	46
Skegness Town	26	13	6	7	56	46	45
Horncastle Town	26	13	5	8	74	45	44
Hykeham Town	26	13	5	8	58	36	44
Heckington United	26	13	2	11	52	54	41
CGB Humbertherm	26	12	4	10	64	67	40
Skellingthorpe PFC	26	9	4	13	49	68	31
Louth Town Reserves	26	9	3	14	51	62	30
Ruston Sports	26	5	3	18	27	86	18
Grimsby Borough Reserves	26	2	5	19	29	86	11
Sleaford Town Reserves	26	2	2	22	26	93	8

Skellingthorpe PFC disbanded. Nettleham joined from the Central Midlands League, Market Rasen Town joined from the Lincoln & District League and Skegness United joined as a newly-formed club. Lincoln Moorlands Railway Reserves re-formed and re-joined having resigned in mid-season from the Central Midlands League as Moorlands Railway.

Lincolnshire League (III) 2011-2017

2011-12

Team	P	W	D	L	F	A	Pts
Cleethorpes Town	32	28	3	1	130	18	87
Skegness United	32	26	3	3	111	46	81
Boston United Reserves	32	23	2	7	99	36	71
Grimsby Borough Reserves	32	19	4	9	61	47	61
Hykeham Town	32	17	9	6	66	46	60
Nettleham	32	17	4	11	87	53	55
Heckington United	32	17	3	12	78	65	54
Louth Town Reserves	32	16	4	12	72	73	52
Horncastle Town	32	12	5	15	62	68	41
CGB Humbertherm	32	12	4	16	56	62	40
Lincoln United Reserves	32	10	5	17	40	62	35
Skegness Town	32	10	4	18	55	82	34
Swineshead Institute	32	9	6	17	47	66	33
Market Rasen Town	32	7	4	21	43	87	25
Ruston Sports	32	5	7	20	42	90	22
Lincoln Moorlands Railway Res.	32	5	5	22	44	88	20
Sleaford Town Reserves	32	1	4	27	29	133	7

Cleethorpes Town moved to the Northern Counties East League and were replaced by their newly formed reserve side while Swineshead Institute disbanded. Gainsborough Town joined as a newly formed club and Boston Town Reserves joined as a newly re-formed team.

2012-13

Team	P	W	D	L	F	A	Pts
Skegness United	32	26	4	2	111	33	82
Gainsborough Town	32	22	4	6	101	43	67
Ruston Sports	32	21	4	7	92	54	67
Cleethorpes Town Reserves	32	20	6	6	84	28	66
++ Hykeham Town	32	20	0	12	87	48	63
Boston United Reserves	32	18	4	10	80	46	55
Nettleham	32	17	4	11	70	64	55
Skegness Town	32	17	3	12	78	61	54
Horncastle Town	32	15	3	14	70	63	48
++ Sleaford Town Reserves	32	11	7	14	48	63	43
CGB Humbertherm	32	13	0	19	51	70	39
Louth Town Reserves	32	11	3	18	49	73	36
+ Lincoln United Reserves	32	8	6	18	42	69	32
Grimsby Borough Reserves	32	8	3	21	41	73	27
Market Rasen Town	32	8	0	24	39	99	24
Heckington United	32	7	2	23	38	92	23
Boston Town Reserves	32	2	3	27	25	127	8

Lincoln Moorlands Railway resigned during the season and their record was deleted.
Boston Town Reserves had 1 point deducted.
Gainsborough Town and Boston United Reserves each had 3 points deducted.
+ Lincoln United Reserves had 2 points added.
++ Hykeham Town and Sleaford Town Reserves each had 3 points added.
Boston Town Reserves, Louth Town Reserves and Market Rasen Town all left the league. Grantham Athletic joined.

2013-14

Team	P	W	D	L	F	A	Pts
Skegness Town	24	17	3	4	56	20	54
+ Hykeham Town	24	16	2	6	54	36	53
Gainsborough Town	24	14	5	5	64	33	47
Ruston Sports	24	14	4	6	51	33	46
Boston United Reserves	24	12	6	6	46	29	42
Skegness United	24	10	5	9	47	45	35
CGB Humbertherm	24	9	5	10	41	43	32
Lincoln United Reserves	24	10	2	12	34	43	29
Cleethorpes Town Reserves	24	8	5	11	36	47	29
Horncastle Town	24	7	3	14	26	44	24
Sleaford Town Reserves	24	5	3	16	35	60	18
Nettleham	24	4	5	15	34	58	17
Heckington United	24	4	4	16	22	55	16

Grantham Athletic and Grimsby Borough Reserves both resigned during the season and their records were deleted.
+ Hykeham Town had 3 points added.
Lincoln United Reserves had 3 points deducted.

Boston United Reserves, Gainsborough Town, Heckington United and Lincoln United Reserves all left the league. Wyberton joined from the Boston League while Louth Town Reserves and Market Rasen Town also joined. Cleethorpes Town Reserves changed their name to Cleethorpes Town A.K.P.

2014-15

Team	P	W	D	L	F	A	Pts
Hykeham Town	22	19	2	1	57	9	59
Skegness Town	22	16	4	2	44	18	52
Horncastle Town	22	15	3	4	53	29	48
Wyberton	22	13	1	8	46	36	40
Sleaford Town Reserves	22	12	4	6	37	26	37
Ruston Sports	22	9	5	8	46	35	32
Skegness United	22	7	5	10	39	41	26
Nettleham	22	6	3	13	33	48	21
Cleethorpes Town A.K.P.	22	7	0	15	28	49	21
CGB Humbertherm	22	5	2	15	29	49	17
Market Rasen Town	22	5	2	15	20	60	17
Louth Town Reserves	22	2	1	19	22	54	10

Sleaford Town Reserves had 3 points deducted.
Nettleham and Louth Town Reserves both left the league.
Brigg Town Reserves and Lincoln Railway A.F.C. both joined. Cleethorpes Town A.K.P. changed their name to Cleethorpes Town Development.

2015-16

Team	P	W	D	L	F	A	Pts
Skegness Town	22	17	2	3	78	20	53
Hykeham Town	22	15	2	5	69	27	47
Wyberton	22	14	4	4	56	25	46
Sleaford Town Reserves	22	12	2	8	51	38	38
Brigg Town Reserves	22	11	3	8	40	40	36
Lincoln Railway A.F.C.	22	9	6	7	49	52	33
Cleethorpes Town Development	22	8	8	6	40	35	32
Horncastle Town	22	8	5	9	22	37	29
Skegness United	22	5	5	12	29	46	20
CGB Humbertherm	22	5	3	14	31	55	18
Market Rasen Town	22	4	2	16	25	64	14
Ruston Sports	22	2	2	18	17	68	8

Skegness United moved to the East Lincolnshire League and Lincoln Railway also left the league. Lincoln Moorlands Railway A.F.C. joined after resigning from the Northern Counties East League close to the end of the 2015-16 season and Harrowby United Reserves joined from the Peterborough League. Louth Town and Immingham Town both joined as newly re-formed clubs while Nettleham, Grimsby Borough Reserves and Sleaford Sports also all joined.

2016-17

Team	P	W	D	L	F	A	Pts
Skegness Town	28	23	0	5	114	25	69
Hykeham Town	28	21	3	4	79	36	66
Wyberton	28	18	1	9	75	42	55
Lincoln Moorlands Railway A.F.C.	28	18	1	9	71	44	55
Horncastle Town	28	17	1	10	60	43	52
Immingham Town	28	14	4	10	69	58	46
Sleaford Sports	28	13	3	12	55	56	42
Grimsby Borough Reserves	28	12	5	11	61	48	41
Brigg Town Reserves	28	11	6	11	57	57	39
Louth Town	28	10	5	13	52	67	35
CGB Humbertherm	28	10	4	14	37	73	34
Nettleham	28	9	2	17	40	55	29
Sleaford Town Reserves	28	6	3	19	35	101	21
Market Rasen Town	28	4	2	22	25	84	14
Ruston Sports	28	3	2	23	22	63	11

Harrowby United Reserves and Cleethorpes Town Development both left the league during the season and their records were deleted.
Lincoln Moorlands Railway A.F.C. moved to the Central Midlands League, Hykeham Town disbanded and Sleaford Town Reserves and Market Rasen Town also both left. A.F.C. Boston and Heckington United both joined.

2017-18

+ Ruston Sports	18	12	3	3	60	29	42
Skegness Town	18	13	1	4	54	18	40
Horncastle Town	18	11	4	3	56	25	37
Grimsby Borough Reserves	18	10	2	6	37	27	29
+ Nettleham	18	7	4	7	36	41	28
Wyberton	18	7	6	5	36	27	27
Immingham Town	18	7	3	8	35	43	24
CGB Humbertherm / Louth Town	18	3	3	12	28	57	12
Sleaford Sports	18	4	2	12	33	47	11
Brigg Town Reserves	18	1	2	15	22	83	5

+ Ruston Sports and Nettleham each had 3 points added.
Grimsby Borough Reserves and Sleaford Sports each had 3 points deducted.
Louth Town continued in the league but resigned during the season and their record was deleted. CGB Humbertherm then changed their name to Louth Town.
A.F.C. Boston and Heckington United both resigned during the season and their records were deleted.
Skegness Town moved to the Northern Counties East League and Sleaford Sports also left the league. Spalding United Development joined from the Peterborough League, having changed their name from Spalding United Reserves and Brigg Town joined from the Northern Counties East League, replacing their reserves. Gainsborough Trinity Reserves, Cleethorpes Town Reserves and Lincoln United Development also joined.

2018-19

Lincoln Moorlands Railway	22	17	3	2	87	33	54
Brigg Town	22	15	5	2	49	24	50
Gainsborough Trinity Reserves	22	14	2	6	47	33	44
Nettleham	22	10	2	10	52	47	32
Cleethorpes Town Reserves	22	9	5	8	34	36	32
Wyberton	22	10	1	11	41	41	31
Ruston Sports	22	9	3	10	37	45	30
Lincoln United Development	22	9	2	11	44	41	29
Horncastle Town	22	6	4	12	33	47	22
Immingham Town	22	5	4	13	26	58	19
Grimsby Borough Reserves	22	4	6	12	25	49	18
Louth Town	22	4	3	15	28	49	15

Spalding United Development resigned during the season and their record was deleted.
Brigg Town moved to the Northern Counties East League and Ruston Sports also left the league. Hykeham Town joined as a newly re-formed club while Brigg Town CIC Reserves and Sleaford Town Rangers also joined.

2019-20

The season was terminated on 26th March 2020 due to the effects of the Covid-19 pandemic. The table shown is as it stood on that date.

Hykeham Town	20	15	5	0	60	21	50
Lincoln Moorlands Railway	17	14	0	3	63	20	42
Gainsborough Trinity Reserves	18	13	2	3	46	16	41
Louth Town	20	10	2	8	37	43	32
Horncastle Town	18	9	4	5	40	28	31
Cleethorpes Town Reserves	15	8	0	7	42	33	24
Grimsby Borough Reserves	20	7	3	10	41	40	24
Immingham Town	17	6	4	7	43	41	22
Wyberton	15	6	4	5	21	19	22
Brigg Town CIC Reserves	20	5	2	13	35	57	17
Sleaford Town Rangers	19	4	1	14	12	59	13
Nettleham	16	3	2	11	27	39	11
Lincoln United Development	21	3	1	17	29	80	10

Hykeham Town, Gainsborough Trinity Reserves and Cleethorpes Town Reserves all left the league. Appleby Frodingham joined from the Central Midlands League and Bottesford Town Development, Keelby United, Epworth Town Colts, Grantham Town Academy, Nunsthorpe Tavern and Tetney Rovers also all joined.

2020-21

The season was terminated on 2nd November 2020 due to the continuing Covid-19 pandemic. The table shown is as it stood on that date.

Epworth Town Colts	9	8	1	0	28	6	25
Louth Town	9	7	1	1	28	14	22
Wyberton	12	6	2	4	31	17	20
Immingham Town	8	6	1	1	37	8	19
Grantham Town Academy	7	5	2	0	27	10	17
++ Keelby United	11	4	2	5	15	28	17
+ Tetney Rovers	7	4	2	1	19	11	16
Lincoln Moorlands Railway	10	4	4	2	24	19	15
Grimsby Borough Reserves	11	4	2	5	25	17	14
Lincoln United Development	9	4	0	5	16	16	12
Nunsthorpe Tavern	8	3	2	3	19	23	11
Horncastle Town	7	2	2	3	15	16	8
Nettleham	7	2	0	5	13	23	6
Appleby Frodingham	8	2	0	6	15	28	6
Brigg Town CIC Reserves	11	1	3	7	12	28	6
Bottesford Town Development	10	2	1	7	16	32	4
Sleaford Town Rangers	10	0	1	9	9	53	1

++ Keelby United had 3 points added.
+ Tetney Rovers had 2 points added.
Lincoln Moorlands Railway had 1 point deducted.
Bottesford Town Development had 3 points deducted.
Bottesford Town Development left the league.
Barton Town Reserves joined from the Humber Premier League and Skegness Town Reserves also joined.

NORTHERN COUNTIES (EAST) LEAGUE 1982-2021

The Northern Counties East League was formed in 1982 by a merger of the Midland League with the Yorkshire League. The new competition initially consisted of 5 divisions:

Premier Division – 20 clubs
- 15 clubs who joined from the Midland League, Premier Division:
  Alfreton Town, Appleby Frodingham Athletic, Arnold, Belper Town, Boston, Bridlington Trinity, Eastwood Town, Guisborough Town, Heanor Town, Ilkeston Town, Mexborough Town Athletic, Shepshed Charterhouse, Skegness Town, Spalding United and Sutton Town.
- 5 clubs who joined from the Yorkshire League, Division One:
  Bentley Victoria Welfare, Emley, Guiseley, Thackley and Winterton Rangers.

Division One (North) – 14 clubs
- 7 clubs who joined from the Yorkshire League, Division One:
  Farsley Celtic, Leeds Ashley Road, Liversedge, North Ferriby United, Ossett Albion, Scarborough Reserves and York Railway Institute.
- 7 clubs who joined from the Yorkshire League, Division Two:
  Bradley Rangers, Bridlington Town, Garforth Miners, Hall Road Rangers, Harrogate Town, Hatfield Main and Ossett Town.

Division One (South) – 14 clubs
- 2 clubs who joined from the Midland League, Premier Division:
  Brigg Town and Long Eaton United.
- 3 clubs who joined from the Midland League, Division One:
  Arnold Kingswell, Kimberley Town and Staveley Works.
- 4 clubs who joined from the Yorkshire League, Division One:
  Frecheville Community Association, Hallam, Lincoln United and Sheffield.
- 4 clubs who joined from the Yorkshire League, Division Two:
  B.S.C. Parkgate, Harworth Colliery Institute, Maltby Miners Welfare, Norton Woodseats.
- 1 club who joined from the Yorkshire League, Division Three:
  Denaby United.

Division Two (North) – 14 clubs
- 4 clubs who joined from the Yorkshire League, Division Two:
  Fryston Colliery Welfare, Grimethorpe Miners Welfare, Pilkington Recreation and Yorkshire Amateurs.
- 9 clubs who joined from the Yorkshire League, Division Three:
  Brook Sports, Collingham, Harrogate Railway Athletic, Phoenix Park, Pickering Town, Pontefract Collieries, Selby Town, Tadcaster Albion and Thorne Colliery.
- Rowntree Mackintosh also joined from the York & District League.

Division Two (South) – 14 clubs

- 9 clubs who joined from the Midland League, Division One:
  Blidworth Welfare (having changed their name from Folk House Old Boys), Borrowash Victoria, Creswell Colliery, Graham Street Prims, Long Eaton Grange, Oakham United, Retford Rail, Rolls Royce Welfare and Sutton Trinity.
- 1 club who joined from the Yorkshire League, Division Two: Kiveton Park
- 4 clubs who joined from the Yorkshire League, Division Three:
  Stocksbridge Works, Wombwell Sporting Association, Woolley Miners Welfare and Worsbrough Bridge Miners Welfare.

Promoted clubs are shown in **bold type**, relegated clubs in ***bold italics***.

1982-83

Premier Division

Shepshed Charterhouse	38	24	8	6	109	34	56
Eastwood Town	38	21	11	6	71	41	53
Belper Town	38	21	10	7	75	32	52
Spalding United	38	19	14	5	69	44	52
Guiseley	38	21	9	8	72	35	51
Winterton Rangers	38	20	9	9	55	32	49
Thackley	38	18	11	9	62	42	47
Arnold	38	17	12	9	77	56	46
Heanor Town	38	17	12	9	50	43	46
Emley	38	14	11	13	74	58	39
Appleby Frodingham Athletic	38	15	9	14	59	61	39
Guisborough Town	38	16	6	16	59	59	38
Alfreton Town	38	16	3	19	47	55	35
Sutton Town	38	12	10	16	59	64	34
Ilkeston Town	38	10	11	17	50	73	31
Boston	38	10	11	17	53	91	31
Bridlington Trinity	38	10	3	25	39	89	23
Skegness Town	38	5	8	25	46	82	18
Bentley Victoria Welfare	38	6	2	30	44	107	14
Mexborough Town Athletic	38	2	2	34	32	104	6

Shepshed Charterhouse moved to the Southern League and Skegness Town moved to the Lincolnshire League.

Division One (North)

Scarborough Reserves	26	17	6	3	53	20	40
North Ferriby United	26	14	10	2	48	24	38
Farsley Celtic	26	13	8	5	53	30	34
Harrogate Town	26	12	10	4	42	23	34
Garforth Miners	26	13	6	7	38	30	32
Ossett Town	26	13	5	8	43	30	31
Ossett Albion	26	8	10	8	41	38	26
Liversedge	26	8	9	9	35	35	25
Bradley Rangers	26	8	7	11	41	51	23
Leeds Ashley Road	26	7	6	13	30	44	20
Hatfield Main	26	6	5	15	31	50	17
Bridlington Town	26	3	10	13	28	49	16
York Railway Institute	26	4	6	16	39	64	14
Hall Road Rangers	**26**	**4**	**6**	**16**	**22**	**56**	**14**

Leeds Ashley Road disbanded.

Division One (South)

Lincoln United	26	16	7	3	55	25	39
Staveley Works	26	16	4	6	50	30	36
Sheffield	26	12	8	6	48	34	32
Frecheville Community Association	26	12	7	7	35	28	31
Denaby United	26	11	8	7	54	41	30
Maltby Miners Welfare	26	10	9	7	50	43	29
B.S.C. Parkgate	26	9	6	11	37	37	24
Arnold Kingswell	26	8	8	10	43	46	24
Norton Woodseats	26	10	3	13	32	37	23
Hallam	26	9	5	12	31	44	23
Harworth Colliery Institute	26	5	12	9	34	35	22
Long Eaton United	26	8	6	12	33	40	22
Brigg Town	**26**	**4**	**7**	**15**	**26**	**59**	**15**
Kimberley Town	**26**	**3**	**8**	**15**	**29**	**58**	**14**

Division Two (North)

Rowntree Mackintosh	**26**	**18**	**6**	**2**	**73**	**29**	**42**
Pontefract Collieries	**26**	**18**	**4**	**4**	**63**	**29**	**40**
Tadcaster Albion	26	15	5	6	48	34	35
Yorkshire Amateurs	26	9	9	8	48	38	27
Pilkington Recreation	26	10	7	9	44	44	27
Grimethorpe Miners Welfare	26	8	10	8	36	32	26
Collingham	26	10	6	10	40	43	26
Phoenix Park	26	11	3	12	43	44	25
Fryston Colliery Welfare	26	9	5	12	45	47	23
Thorne Colliery	26	9	5	12	37	57	23
Brook Sports	26	8	6	12	32	47	22
Selby Town	26	8	5	13	38	46	21
Pickering Town	26	7	6	13	26	40	20
Harrogate Railway Athletic	26	2	3	21	19	62	7

Armthorpe Welfare joined from the Doncaster Senior League.

Division Two (South)

Woolley Miners Welfare	**26**	**19**	**4**	**3**	**61**	**13**	**42**
Borrowash Victoria	**26**	**16**	**8**	**2**	**57**	**20**	**40**
Worsbrough Bridge	26	15	3	8	47	40	33
Oakham United	26	14	4	8	51	44	32
Stocksbridge Works	26	12	6	8	41	26	30
Graham Street Prims	26	12	5	9	49	33	29
Kiveton Park	26	11	6	9	52	40	28
Long Eaton Grange	26	9	6	11	40	45	24
Blidworth Welfare	26	10	3	13	40	46	23
Rolls Royce Welfare	26	7	9	10	45	59	23
Creswell Colliery	26	8	3	15	37	60	19
Retford Rail	26	6	4	16	29	57	16
Wombwell Sporting	26	3	8	15	18	44	14
Sutton Trinity	26	3	5	18	19	59	11

Long Eaton Grange and Rolls Royce Welfare (as Rolls Royce (Derby)) both moved to the Central Midlands League and Creswell Colliery moved to the Mansfield League. Retford Town joined from the Derbyshire Premier League and Yorkshire Main Colliery joined from the Sheffield & Hallamshire County Senior League.

Northern Counties (East) League 1983-1984

1983-84 Premier Division

Spalding United	34	20	8	6	76	43	48
Arnold	34	22	3	9	82	37	47
Emley	34	20	7	7	59	32	47
Alfreton Town	34	18	6	10	56	32	42
Eastwood Town	34	17	7	10	75	49	41
Ilkeston Town	34	14	11	9	49	38	39
Guiseley	34	14	11	9	54	48	39
Guisborough Town	34	16	6	12	58	54	38
Thackley	34	14	6	14	61	54	34
Winterton Rangers	34	13	7	14	48	42	33
Belper Town	34	12	8	14	47	46	32
Boston	34	10	12	12	46	57	32
Sutton Town	34	10	7	17	36	63	27
Appleby Frodingham Athletic	34	8	9	17	51	75	25
Mexborough Town Athletic	34	6	12	16	34	68	24
Bridlington Trinity	34	7	9	18	40	60	23
Heanor Town	34	7	9	18	31	68	23
Bentley Victoria Welfare	34	6	6	22	45	82	18

Winterton Rangers disbanded due to financial problems.

Division One (North)

Pontefract Collieries	26	17	5	4	43	24	39
Rowntree Mackintosh	26	16	2	8	59	43	34
Farsley Celtic	26	12	6	8	51	33	30
Bradley Rangers	26	12	6	8	35	36	30
Ossett Albion	26	10	9	7	44	30	29
Garforth Miners	26	10	8	8	45	33	28
Harrogate Town	26	12	4	10	43	31	28
Scarborough Reserves	26	9	7	10	42	43	25
North Ferriby United	26	8	8	10	33	35	24
York Railway Institute	26	9	6	11	35	45	24
Bridlington Town	26	7	9	10	30	50	23
Hatfield Main	26	6	7	13	38	45	19
Liversedge	26	5	7	14	29	53	17
Ossett Town	26	4	6	16	34	60	14

Scarborough Reserves left the league.

Division One (South)

Borrowash Victoria	26	18	3	5	61	24	39
Denaby United	26	16	4	6	58	28	36
Woolley Miners Welfare	26	14	6	6	61	33	34
Sheffield	26	12	6	8	44	38	30
Lincoln United	26	11	7	8	39	30	29
Maltby Miners Welfare	26	11	7	8	36	29	27
B.S.C. Parkgate	26	11	5	10	29	29	27
Staveley Works	26	10	5	11	41	34	25
Hallam	26	8	7	11	28	39	23
Long Eaton United	26	7	8	11	24	38	22
Frecheville Community Association	26	6	10	10	33	48	22
Arnold Kingswell	26	7	7	12	30	44	21
Norton Woodseats	26	5	4	17	23	59	14
Harworth Colliery Institute	26	5	3	18	19	53	13

Maltby Miners Welfare had 2 points deducted.
Norton Woodseats changed their name to Dronfield United.

Division Two (North)

Harrogate Railway Athletic	26	19	6	1	72	23	44
Armthorpe Welfare	26	17	5	4	48	26	39
Yorkshire Amateurs	26	14	7	5	42	21	35
Selby Town	26	12	7	7	48	30	31
Phoenix Park	26	12	7	7	49	36	31
Pickering Town	26	13	2	11	36	34	28
Fryston Colliery Welfare	26	10	6	10	48	41	26
Thorne Colliery	26	10	6	10	43	41	26
Grimethorpe Miners Welfare	26	8	9	9	38	39	25
Hall Road Rangers	26	5	8	13	36	57	18
Collingham	26	5	6	15	26	47	16
Pilkington Recreation	26	4	7	15	33	55	15
Tadcaster Albion	26	3	9	14	23	56	15
Brook Sports	26	5	5	16	27	63	15

Brook Sports moved to the West Riding County Amateur League.

Division Two (South)

Retford Town	24	18	3	3	63	22	39
Kimberley Town	24	16	4	4	39	21	36
Graham Street Prims	24	15	3	6	58	37	33
Brigg Town	24	13	6	5	44	30	32
Oakham United	24	12	3	9	44	28	27
Yorkshire Main Colliery	24	12	3	9	44	37	27
Worsbrough Bridge M.W.	24	12	3	9	51	46	27
Wombwell Sporting Association	24	7	6	11	28	37	20
Blidworth Welfare	24	8	3	13	32	52	19
Kiveton Park	24	7	4	13	31	41	18
Stocksbridge Works S.S.	24	6	5	13	40	44	17
Retford Rail	24	5	4	15	27	53	14
Sutton Trinity	24	0	3	21	21	74	3

Sutton Trinity moved to the Central Midlands League and Retford Rail left senior football for a year but joined the Central Midlands League in 1985.

Divisions One and Two were re-organised into a new Division One with 3 sections – North, Central and South.

Division One (North) consisted of 17 clubs:

- 9 of whom had been members of the division in 1983-84: Bradley Rangers, Bridlington Town, Farsley Celtic, Garforth Miners, Harrogate Town, Liversedge, North Ferriby United, Rowntree Mackintosh and York Railway Institute.
- 8 clubs had been members of Division Two (North) in 1983-84: Collingham, Hall Road Rangers, Harrogate Railway Athletic, Phoenix Park, Pickering Town, Selby Town, Tadcaster Albion and Yorkshire Amateurs.

Division One (Central) consisted of 16 clubs:

- 3 clubs had been members of Division One (North) in 1983-84: Hatfield Main, Ossett Albion and Ossett Town.
- 3 clubs had been members of Division One (South) in 1983-84: B.S.C. Parkgate, Maltby Miners and Woolley Miners Welfare.
- 5 clubs had been members of Division Two (North) in 1983-84: Armthorpe Welfare, Fryston Colliery Welfare, Grimethorpe Miners Welfare, Pilkington Recreation and Thorne Colliery.
- 5 clubs had been members of Division Two (South) in 1983-84: Brigg Town, Stocksbridge Works, Wombwell Sporting Association, Worsbrough Bridge Miners Welfare and Yorkshire Main Colliery.

Division One (South) consisted of 16 clubs:

- 10 of whom had been members of the division in 1983-84: Arnold Kingswell, Borrowash Victoria, Dronfield United, Frecheville Community Association, Hallam, Harworth Colliery Institute, Lincoln United, Long Eaton United, Sheffield and Staveley Works.
- 6 clubs had been members of Division One (South) in 1983-84 Blidworth Welfare, Graham Street Prims, Kimberley Town, Kiveton Park, Oakham United and Retford Town.

Three points were awarded for a win from the next season.

1984-85 Premier Division

Team	P	W	D	L	F	A	Pts
Belper Town	36	25	6	5	74	30	81
Eastwood Town	36	23	3	10	98	59	72
Guiseley	36	21	7	8	78	47	70
Alfreton Town	36	20	6	10	69	39	66
Guisborough Town	36	18	8	10	71	49	62
Denaby United	36	18	8	10	71	51	62
Arnold	36	17	9	10	72	49	60
Emley	36	16	7	13	67	52	55
Bridlington Trinity	36	16	5	15	71	67	53
Thackley	36	15	6	15	55	61	51
Spalding United	36	14	8	14	55	48	50
Sutton Town	36	14	5	17	45	69	47
Ilkeston Town	36	14	4	18	49	54	46
Pontefract Collieries	36	11	10	15	45	54	43
Bentley Victoria Welfare	36	11	6	19	47	67	39
Appleby Frodingham Athletic	36	8	9	19	46	73	33
Boston	36	8	6	22	35	88	30
Heanor Town	36	8	5	23	50	89	29
Mexborough Town Athletic	36	2	8	26	32	84	14

Guisborough Town moved to the Northern League.

Division One (North)

Team	P	W	D	L	F	A	Pts
Farsley Celtic	32	18	10	4	66	28	64
Harrogate Town	32	17	9	6	61	35	60
Bradley Rangers	32	16	11	5	61	35	59
Harrogate Railway Athletic	32	17	7	8	65	41	58
Bridlington Town	32	16	6	10	57	46	54
Rowntree Mackintosh	32	15	8	9	62	37	53
North Ferriby United	32	16	5	11	54	42	53
Liversedge	32	14	6	12	55	50	48
Garforth Miners	32	11	9	12	53	57	42
York Railway Institute	32	11	9	12	51	55	42
Pickering Town	32	11	8	13	37	43	41
Phoenix Park	32	10	8	14	57	59	38
Selby Town	32	10	7	15	43	59	37
Hall Road Rangers	32	9	6	17	45	70	33
Yorkshire Amateurs	32	7	7	18	34	60	28
Collingham	32	5	12	15	42	71	27
Tadcaster Albion	32	3	4	25	23	78	13

Garforth Miners changed their name to Garforth Town and Phoenix Park changed its name to Eccleshill United.

The league was again re-organised at the end of the season with Divisions One, Two and Three replacing the three regional First Divisions.

Harrogate Town, Bradley Rangers, Harrogate Railway Athletic, Bridlington Town, Rowntree Mackintosh and North Ferriby United were placed in Division One.

Liversedge, Garforth Town, York Railway Institute and Pickering Town were placed in Division Two.

Eccleshill United, Selby Town, Hall Road Rangers, Yorkshire Amateurs, Collingham and Tadcaster Albion were placed in Division Three.

Division One (Central)

Team	P	W	D	L	F	A	Pts
Armthorpe Welfare	30	21	5	4	68	26	68
Brigg Town	30	19	7	4	68	36	64
Woolley Miners Welfare	30	19	6	5	67	38	63
Ossett Albion	30	16	7	7	55	28	55
Hatfield Main	30	16	7	7	56	35	55
Pilkington Recreation	30	14	4	12	41	42	46
Thorne Colliery	30	13	6	11	54	45	45
Ossett Town	30	12	6	12	51	37	42
B.S.C. Parkgate	30	12	6	12	52	41	42
Grimethorpe Miners Welfare	30	12	6	12	59	53	42
Maltby Miners Welfare	30	13	3	14	49	46	42
Yorkshire Main Colliery	30	11	8	11	53	56	41
Worsbrough Bridge M.W.	30	8	7	15	48	67	31
Stocksbridge Works	30	6	2	22	31	76	20
Wombwell Sporting Association	30	3	5	22	23	70	14
Fryston Colliery Welfare	30	2	1	27	26	105	7

Brigg Town, Woolley Miners Welfare, Ossett Albion, Hatfield Main and Pilkington Recreation were all placed in the new Division One.

Thorne Colliery, Ossett Town, B.S.C. Parkgate, Grimethorpe Miners Welfare, Maltby Miners Welfare and Yorkshire Main Colliery were all placed in the new Division Two.

Worsbrough Bridge Miners Welfare, Stocksbridge Works, Wombwell Sporting Association and Fryston Colliery Welfare were all placed in the new Division Three.

Division One (South)

Team	P	W	D	L	F	A	Pts
Long Eaton United	30	21	5	4	58	23	68
Borrowash Victoria	30	20	5	5	64	32	65
Dronfield United	30	18	4	8	55	35	58
Retford Town	30	17	5	8	60	36	56
Harworth Colliery Institute	30	14	7	9	42	33	49
Sheffield	30	13	8	9	58	39	47
Staveley Works	30	13	5	12	42	39	44
Arnold Kingswell	30	12	6	12	48	42	42
Hallam	30	10	9	11	46	41	39
Frecheville Community Association	30	10	9	11	47	45	39
Lincoln United	30	10	8	12	37	35	38
Kiveton Park	30	10	5	15	29	49	35
Oakham United	30	8	8	14	30	44	32
Graham Street Prims	30	9	4	17	28	45	31
Blidworth Welfare	30	7	1	22	32	87	22
Kimberley Town	30	2	3	25	21	72	9

Retford Town disbanded.

Borrowash Victoria, Dronfield United, Harworth Colliery Institute and Sheffield were placed in the new Division One.

Staveley Works, Arnold Kingswell, Hallam, Frecheville Community Association, Lincoln United and Kiveton Park were placed in the new Division Two.

Oakham United, Graham Street Prims, Blidworth Welfare and Kimberley Town were placed in the new Division Three.

Glasshoughton Welfare joined the new Division Three from the West Yorkshire League.

1985-86
Premier Division

Team	P	W	D	L	F	A	Pts
Arnold	38	24	8	6	83	36	79
Emley	38	22	11	5	77	47	77
Guiseley	38	22	6	10	81	52	72
Long Eaton United	38	19	11	8	70	39	68
Eastwood Town	38	21	5	12	73	62	67
Alfreton Town	38	21	2	15	66	47	65
Sutton Town	38	18	6	14	69	57	60
Farsley Celtic	38	14	12	12	71	55	54
Belper Town	38	15	9	14	54	45	54
Thackley	38	14	11	13	52	58	53
Denaby United	38	13	14	11	63	56	52
Pontefract Collieries	38	15	7	16	55	54	52
Armthorpe Welfare	38	15	7	16	57	58	52
Bentley Victoria Welfare	38	12	11	15	61	65	47
Heanor Town	38	11	9	18	61	69	41
Spalding United	38	9	12	17	41	62	39
Boston	38	10	6	22	42	79	36
Appleby Frodingham Athletic	38	6	12	20	40	83	30
Bridlington Trinity	38	4	14	20	34	85	26
Ilkeston Town	38	5	7	26	31	72	22

Arnold, Eastwood Town, Denaby United and Heanor Town each had 1 point deducted.

Arnold, Heanor Town and Ilkeston Town moved to the Central Midlands League, Spalding United moved to the United Counties League and Appleby Frodingham Athletic moved to the Scunthorpe & District League.

Northern Counties (East) League 1986-1987

Division One

North Ferriby United	30	18	5	7	54	31	59
Sheffield	30	16	8	6	54	39	56
Harrogate Town	30	16	6	8	65	42	54
Rowntree Mackintosh	30	16	5	9	67	45	53
Ossett Albion	30	13	11	6	54	39	50
Bridlington Town	30	11	13	6	49	41	46
Borrowash Victoria	30	12	10	8	53	48	46
Harworth Colliery Institute	30	12	6	12	51	50	42
Woolley Miners Welfare	30	12	7	11	59	59	42
Bradley Rangers	30	12	4	14	51	51	40
Hatfield Main	30	8	13	9	57	43	37
Brigg Town	30	8	8	14	31	42	32
Mexborough Town Athletic	30	8	7	15	39	68	30
Harrogate Railway Athletic	30	6	6	18	47	70	23
Dronfield United	30	6	6	18	32	61	23
Pilkington Recreation	30	4	9	17	32	66	21

Woolley Miners Welfare, Mexborough Town Athletic, Harrogate Railway Athletic and Dronfield United each had 1 point deducted.
Borrowash Victoria and Harworth Colliery Institute both moved to the Central Midlands League.

Division Two

Lincoln United	30	20	5	5	73	29	65
Garforth Town	30	20	4	6	66	29	64
York Railway Institute	30	17	5	8	58	39	56
Staveley Works	30	17	4	9	52	33	55
Hallam	30	15	2	13	48	42	47
Maltby Miners Welfare	30	12	7	11	44	48	43
Grimethorpe Miners Welfare	30	12	7	11	50	48	40
Kiveton Park	30	11	6	13	42	48	39
B.S.C. Parkgate	30	11	7	12	43	50	39
Liversedge	30	11	5	14	46	56	38
Frecheville Community Association	30	9	8	13	43	61	35
Arnold Kingswell	30	10	4	16	48	57	34
Yorkshire Main Colliery	30	10	5	15	38	53	34
Ossett Town	30	8	7	15	40	53	31
Pickering Town	30	5	10	15	33	52	24
Thorne Colliery	30	7	4	19	31	57	24

B.S.C. Parkgate, Yorkshire Main Colliery, Pickering Town and Thorne Colliery each had 1 point deducted.
Grimethorpe Miners Welfare had 3 points deducted.
Arnold Kingswell and Lincoln United both moved to the Central Midlands League and Thorne Colliery moved to the Doncaster & District League.
Immingham Town joined from the Lincolnshire League and Winterton Rangers as a newly re-formed club.
B.S.C. Parkgate changed their name to Parkgate.

Division Three

Collingham	26	16	7	3	66	23	55
Worsbrough Bridge M.W.	26	14	5	7	60	32	47
Eccleshill United	26	13	6	7	43	34	45
Glasshoughton Welfare	26	12	7	7	42	33	43
Yorkshire Amateurs	26	11	10	5	38	29	42
Hall Road Rangers	26	9	9	8	37	33	36
Oakham United	26	10	6	10	38	35	36
Graham Street Prims	26	10	5	11	43	41	35
Tadcaster Albion	26	9	7	10	44	39	34
Stocksbridge Works	26	9	6	11	42	43	33
Selby Town	26	8	7	11	47	59	31
Fryston Colliery Welfare	26	5	6	15	32	72	21
Wombwell Sporting Association	26	6	5	15	28	49	20
Kimberley Town	26	4	6	16	26	64	18

Yorkshire Amateurs had 1 point deducted.
Wombwell Sporting Association had 3 points deducted.
Blidworth Welfare left the league during the season and their record was expunged. They joined the Central Midlands League in 1986.
At the end of the season, Graham Street Prims, Kimberley Town and Oakham United also moved to the Central Midlands League.
Stocksbridge Works merged with Oxley Park of the Sheffield & Hallamshire County Senior League to form Stocksbridge Park Steels.

All remaining Division Three clubs were promoted to Division Two and Division Three was disbanded, reducing the league to three Divisions, Premier, First and Second.

1986-87

Premier Division

Alfreton Town	36	25	6	5	74	29	81
Farsley Celtic	36	24	6	6	74	41	78
North Ferriby United	36	20	10	6	57	26	70
Emley	36	17	10	9	60	41	61
Sutton Town	36	17	10	9	54	45	61
Denaby United	36	15	10	11	59	43	55
Thackley	36	14	13	9	47	45	55
Pontefract Collieries	36	16	6	14	54	44	54
Harrogate Town	36	14	10	12	48	48	52
Bridlington Town	36	14	10	12	57	49	50
Long Eaton United	36	12	11	13	41	43	47
Armthorpe Welfare	36	13	6	17	55	60	45
Eastwood Town	36	11	9	16	45	57	42
Bentley Victoria Welfare	36	10	9	17	64	77	39
Belper Town	36	8	12	16	49	47	36
Guiseley	36	9	8	19	46	76	35
Bridlington Trinity	36	6	11	19	46	76	29
Brigg Town	36	6	9	21	35	73	27
Boston	36	6	4	26	23	68	22

Alfreton Town, Eastwood Town, Farsley Celtic, Harrogate Town and Sutton Town all moved to the new First Division of the Northern Premier League.
Boston moved to the Central Midlands League and Bentley Victoria Welfare disbanded.

Division One

Ossett Albion	34	22	4	8	65	43	70
Rowntree Mackintosh	34	20	4	10	101	54	64
Hatfield Main	34	19	7	8	69	47	64
Harrogate Railway Athletic	34	19	7	8	65	44	64
Bradley Rangers	34	17	8	9	64	51	59
Hallam	34	16	8	10	49	37	56
Staveley Works	34	14	9	11	51	46	51
York Railway Institute	34	15	5	14	49	56	50
Maltby Miners Welfare	34	13	7	14	53	57	46
Pilkington Recreation	34	13	6	15	51	49	45
Garforth Town	34	11	10	13	44	48	43
Grimethorpe Miners Welfare	34	13	4	17	60	65	43
Woolley Miners Welfare	34	11	9	14	57	61	42
Kiveton Park	34	11	6	17	41	64	39
Parkgate	34	10	8	16	51	57	38
Mexborough Town Athletic	34	8	10	16	38	64	34
Sheffield	34	9	6	19	41	55	33
Dronfield United	34	4	4	26	33	84	16

Division Two

Frecheville Community Assoc.	34	24	7	3	57	27	79
Eccleshill United	34	22	6	6	75	36	72
Immingham Town	34	18	4	12	53	43	58
Hall Road Rangers	34	16	9	9	72	48	57
Collingham	34	14	13	7	67	34	55
Worsbrough Bridge M.W.	34	15	7	12	61	48	52
Stocksbridge Park Steels	34	12	15	7	50	38	51
Selby Town	34	14	8	12	47	42	50
Yorkshire Amateurs	34	12	10	12	47	36	46
Ossett Town	34	12	10	12	42	52	46
Liversedge	34	10	13	11	40	45	43
Glasshoughton Welfare	34	11	9	14	50	52	42
Tadcaster Albion	34	11	7	16	38	46	40
Pickering Town	34	8	15	11	59	57	39
Yorkshire Main Colliery	34	8	13	13	43	60	37
Winterton Rangers	34	7	7	20	30	53	28
Wombwell Sporting Association	34	7	7	20	39	75	28
Fryston Colliery Welfare	34	2	6	26	18	76	12

1987-88

Premier Division

Emley	32	20	8	4	57	21	68
Armthorpe Welfare	32	21	5	6	56	36	68
Denaby United	32	19	4	9	61	46	61
Bridlington Town	32	18	5	9	63	25	59
Thackley	32	16	8	8	50	37	56
North Ferriby United	32	12	11	9	49	41	47
Guiseley	32	14	5	13	52	51	47
Pontefract Collieries	32	11	10	11	42	42	43
Grimethorpe Miners Welfare	32	11	9	12	46	49	42
Hallam	32	11	6	15	48	53	39
Hatfield Main	32	11	6	15	52	59	39
Harrogate Railway Athletic	32	9	9	14	40	56	36
Bridlington Trinity	32	8	9	15	52	68	33
Long Eaton United	32	9	6	17	24	44	33
Brigg Town	32	8	8	16	40	57	32
Belper Town	32	5	12	15	32	52	27
Ossett Albion	32	4	9	19	31	58	21

Division One

York Railway Institute	30	22	2	6	66	29	68
Rowntree Mackintosh	30	20	5	5	74	35	65
Maltby Miners Welfare	30	18	6	6	61	32	60
Parkgate	30	18	4	8	52	34	58
Bradley Rangers	30	15	9	6	64	45	54
Woolley Miners Welfare	30	14	8	8	69	39	50
Eccleshill United	30	13	8	9	49	50	47
Sheffield	30	13	4	13	38	34	43
Immingham Town	30	9	10	11	41	40	37
Frecheville Community Association	30	8	10	12	40	51	34
Kiveton Park	30	10	4	16	29	51	34
Staveley Works	30	9	5	16	42	65	32
Pilkington Recreation	30	6	7	17	30	65	25
Garforth Town	30	6	6	18	29	51	24
Mexborough Town Athletic	30	6	5	19	38	62	23
Dronfield United	**30**	**3**	**7**	**20**	**36**	**75**	**16**

Staveley Works moved to the Central Midlands League.

Division Two

Pickering Town	**28**	**18**	**6**	**4**	**66**	**33**	**60**
Collingham	**28**	**16**	**9**	**3**	**63**	**26**	**57**
Yorkshire Amateurs	28	16	9	3	44	23	57
Ossett Town	28	16	7	5	78	37	55
Worsbrough Bridge M.W.	28	14	4	10	54	43	46
Liversedge	28	13	5	10	51	40	44
Yorkshire Main Colliery	28	11	8	9	53	58	41
Stocksbridge Park Steels	28	11	7	10	50	37	40
Winterton Rangers	28	10	7	11	47	47	37
Selby Town	28	9	4	15	39	48	31
Hall Road Rangers	28	9	4	15	35	63	31
Glasshoughton Welfare	28	6	12	10	29	35	30
Fryston Colliery Welfare	28	6	4	18	30	60	22
Wombwell Sporting Association	28	5	5	18	27	60	20
Tadcaster Albion	28	1	7	20	19	75	10

Wombwell Sporting Association moved to the Central Midlands League.
Brodsworth Miners Welfare joined from the Doncaster Senior League.

1988-89

Premier Division

Emley	32	25	5	2	80	18	80
Hatfield Main	32	21	9	2	67	24	72
Bridlington Town	32	21	5	6	67	26	68
North Ferriby United	32	17	9	6	63	31	60
Guiseley	32	16	10	6	50	27	58
Denaby United	32	13	7	12	52	50	46
Pontefract Collieries	32	10	11	11	37	34	41
Harrogate Railway Athletic	32	10	11	11	41	43	41
Thackley	32	11	6	15	43	59	39
Belper Town	32	9	10	13	45	51	37
Armthorpe Welfare	32	9	9	14	44	60	36
Hallam	32	9	5	18	47	77	32
Long Eaton United	32	8	7	17	32	54	31
Brigg Town	32	8	7	17	43	66	31
Grimethorpe Miners Welfare	32	8	5	19	38	59	29
Bridlington Trinity	32	6	7	19	40	72	25
Ossett Albion	32	5	9	18	33	71	24

Emley moved to the Northern Premier League, changing places with Sutton Town. Long Eaton United moved to the Central Midlands League and North Shields joined from the Northern League.

Division One

Sheffield	**30**	**21**	**5**	**4**	**76**	**25**	**68**
Rowntree Mackintosh	30	18	6	6	68	36	60
Woolley Miners Welfare	30	16	11	3	49	28	59
Maltby Miners Welfare	30	17	5	8	68	38	56
Pickering Town	30	16	4	10	58	54	52
Garforth Town	30	15	5	10	56	34	50
Eccleshill United	30	15	4	11	47	39	49
Collingham	30	14	5	11	38	30	47
Immingham Town	30	12	10	8	39	31	46
Kiveton Park	30	11	1	18	30	44	34
Mexborough Town Athletic	30	8	7	15	28	40	31
Parkgate	30	8	6	16	29	54	30
Frecheville Community Association	30	6	11	13	31	44	29
York Railway Institute	30	6	10	14	25	37	28
Bradley Rangers	**30**	**6**	**3**	**21**	**22**	**62**	**21**
Pilkington Recreation	**30**	**3**	**3**	**24**	**18**	**86**	**12**

Division Two

Ossett Town	**26**	**19**	**3**	**4**	**76**	**17**	**60**
Liversedge	**26**	**16**	**4**	**6**	**52**	**24**	**52**
Selby Town	26	15	5	6	54	35	50
Worsbrough Bridge M.W.	26	14	5	7	64	41	47
Glasshoughton Welfare	26	14	3	9	52	36	45
Dronfield United	26	11	7	8	39	36	40
Hall Road Rangers	26	10	4	12	44	60	34
Yorkshire Main Colliery	26	9	5	12	45	46	32
Stocksbridge Park Steels	26	8	6	12	37	52	30
Tadcaster Albion	26	8	6	12	30	46	30
Winterton Rangers	26	8	6	12	37	63	30
Brodsworth Miners Welfare	26	6	8	12	21	43	26
Yorkshire Amateurs	26	6	3	17	30	55	21
Fryston Colliery Welfare	26	3	5	18	23	50	14

Northern Counties (East) League 1989-1991

1989-90

Premier Division

Bridlington Town	34	22	9	3	72	24	75
North Shields	34	21	6	7	63	31	69
Denaby United	34	19	5	10	55	40	62
Bridlington Trinity	34	18	6	10	82	44	60
Harrogate Railway Athletic	34	17	9	8	59	50	60
North Ferriby United	34	18	5	11	66	43	59
Armthorpe Welfare	34	18	4	12	53	39	58
Sutton Town	34	16	9	9	52	38	57
Sheffield	*34*	*15*	*10*	*9*	*44*	*33*	*55*
Brigg Town	34	13	7	14	57	50	46
Guiseley	34	12	7	15	54	46	43
Belper Town	34	11	6	17	39	50	39
Pontefract Collieries	34	10	7	17	43	67	37
Hallam	*34*	*9*	*8*	*17*	*45*	*64*	*35*
Thackley	34	7	9	18	43	64	30
Ossett Albion	34	6	7	21	27	69	25
Grimethorpe MW	*34*	*7*	*3*	*24*	*40*	*90*	*24*
Hatfield Main	*34*	*6*	*5*	*23*	*27*	*79*	*23*

Sheffield and Hallam were both relegated due to inadequate facilities at their grounds.
Bridlington Town moved to the Northern Premier League and Bridlington Trinity disbanded. Spennymoor United joined from the Northern League.

Division One

Rowntree Mackintosh	*28*	*18*	*7*	*3*	*63*	*23*	*61*
Liversedge	28	17	3	8	57	29	54
Ossett Town	*28*	*15*	*9*	*4*	*49*	*22*	*54*
Woolley Miners Welfare	28	15	5	8	51	33	50
Maltby Miners Welfare	*28*	*12*	*11*	*5*	*51*	*29*	*47*
Garforth Town	28	13	7	8	42	23	46
Eccleshill United	28	11	9	8	50	45	42
Kiveton Park	*28*	*13*	*2*	*13*	*35*	*31*	*41*
Immingham Town	*28*	*10*	*7*	*11*	*28*	*37*	*37*
Collingham	28	10	3	15	29	41	33
Frecheville Community Association	28	8	7	13	41	45	31
Parkgate	28	7	10	11	33	42	31
York Railway Institute	28	9	3	16	34	66	30
Pickering Town	28	6	5	17	39	64	23
Mexborough Town Athletic	28	1	2	25	17	89	5

Rowntree Mackintosh, Kiveton Park and Immingham Town were all relegated due to inadequate facilities at their grounds.
Frecheville Community Association moved to the Sheffield County Senior League while Collingham disbanded and Woolley Miners Welfare also left. Parkgate changed their name to R.E.S. Parkgate.

Division Two

+ Winterton Rangers	26	15	6	5	46	28	51
Selby Town	26	13	8	5	51	29	47
Bradley Rangers	26	12	9	5	48	34	45
Fryston Colliery Welfare	26	12	8	6	39	29	44
Yorkshire Main Colliery	*26*	*13*	*3*	*10*	*41*	*46*	*42*
Glasshoughton Welfare	*26*	*10*	*7*	*9*	*40*	*35*	*37*
Stocksbridge Park Steels	26	9	9	8	36	28	36
Yorkshire Amateurs	26	8	9	9	41	34	33
Brodsworth Miners Welfare	26	7	11	8	35	41	32
Tadcaster Albion	26	8	6	12	31	38	30
Worsbrough Bridge M.W.	26	7	8	11	36	40	29
Hall Road Rangers	26	5	9	12	25	47	24
Dronfield United	26	5	8	13	30	47	23
Pilkington Recreation	26	4	7	15	20	43	19

+ Winterton Rangers were promoted two levels to the Premier Division.

1990-91

Premier Division

Guiseley	30	24	4	2	78	25	76
North Shields	30	23	2	5	75	29	71
Spennymoor United	30	19	4	7	55	29	61
North Ferriby United	30	14	8	8	55	42	50
Brigg Town	30	13	8	9	40	40	47
Maltby Miners Welfare	30	13	7	10	44	46	46
Harrogate Railway Athletic	30	12	9	9	49	40	45
Ossett Town	30	10	10	10	42	38	40
Armthorpe Welfare	30	10	6	14	52	55	36
Winterton Rangers	30	9	9	12	49	65	36
Thackley	30	9	7	14	43	46	34
Sutton Town	30	9	6	15	53	60	33
Belper Town	30	7	10	13	37	52	31
Ossett Albion	30	3	12	15	34	51	21
Denaby United	30	5	6	19	33	81	21
Pontefract Collieries	30	4	4	22	34	74	16

Guiseley moved to the Northern Premier League.

Division One

Sheffield	*24*	*21*	*1*	*2*	*60*	*16*	*64*
Hallam	24	18	1	5	61	27	55
Liversedge	*24*	*15*	*2*	*7*	*61*	*35*	*47*
Pickering Town	24	15	2	7	54	41	47
Eccleshill United	*24*	*14*	*2*	*8*	*58*	*36*	*44*
Garforth Town	24	11	7	6	45	33	40
Selby Town	24	10	3	11	60	41	33
Hatfield Main	24	9	5	10	38	42	32
R.E.S. Parkgate	24	7	6	11	40	49	27
York Railway Institute	24	7	3	14	32	47	24
Glasshoughton Welfare	*24*	*4*	*5*	*15*	*18*	*50*	*17*
Yorkshire Main Colliery	24	2	3	19	16	61	9
Mexborough Town Athletic	24	3	0	21	16	81	9

Grimethorpe Miners Welfare resigned on 20th October 1990 and their record was expunged
| | | 6 | 0 | 0 | 6 | 4 | 23 | 0 |

The club disbanded soon afterwards.
Mexborough Town Athletic moved to the Central Midlands League and Yorkshire Main Colliery moved to the Sheffield & Hallamshire County Senior League. Rossington Main joined from the Central Midlands League.

Division Two

Hall Road Rangers	*24*	*15*	*5*	*4*	*42*	*25*	*50*
Worsbrough Bridge M.W.	*24*	*14*	*5*	*5*	*45*	*22*	*47*
Rowntree Mackintosh	24	12	8	4	46	25	44
Bradley Rangers	*24*	*13*	*5*	*6*	*45*	*32*	*44*
Yorkshire Amateurs	*24*	*13*	*3*	*8*	*47*	*37*	*42*
Tadcaster Albion	*24*	*11*	*3*	*10*	*39*	*34*	*36*
Stocksbridge Park Steels	*24*	*9*	*8*	*7*	*41*	*35*	*35*
Fryston Colliery Welfare	24	9	4	11	44	44	31
Immingham Town	*24*	*7*	*7*	*10*	*29*	*43*	*28*
Kiveton Park	24	7	4	13	30	43	25
Dronfield United	24	5	6	13	29	40	21
Brodsworth Miners Welfare	*24*	*4*	*5*	*15*	*25*	*51*	*17*
Pilkington Recreation	24	3	5	16	25	56	14

Dronfield United changed their name to Norton Woodseats and moved to the Central Midlands League. Fryston Colliery Welfare and Kiveton Park both also moved to the Central Midlands League. Rowntree Mackintosh moved to the Teesside League and Pilkington Recreation disbanded.

Division Two then closed down.

1991-92 Premier Division

North Shields	36	31	3	2	109	14	96
Sutton Town	36	21	9	6	79	41	72
Denaby United	36	22	3	11	78	47	68
North Ferriby United	36	19	8	9	63	45	65
Spennymoor United	36	17	8	11	61	45	59
Sheffield	36	16	9	11	71	48	57
Maltby Miners Welfare	36	16	8	12	61	61	56
Brigg Town	36	15	7	14	44	42	52
Thackley	36	14	9	13	45	45	51
Ossett Albion	36	14	8	14	40	51	50
Belper Town	36	12	11	13	48	50	47
Ossett Town	36	11	12	13	48	57	45
Armthorpe Welfare	36	12	9	15	57	67	45
Liversedge	36	11	8	17	54	72	41
Winterton Rangers	36	10	5	21	53	78	35
Pontefract Collieries	36	9	7	20	36	71	34
Eccleshill United	36	7	10	19	38	83	31
Harrogate Railway Athletic	36	5	8	23	31	60	23
Glasshoughton Welfare	36	5	8	23	35	74	23

Denaby United had 1 point deducted.
North Shields left to join the Northern Premier League but were in administration at the time and unable to give the financial guarantees the league demanded. With new backers, they reformed and joined the Wearside League instead.
Sutton Town changed their name to Ashfield United.

Division One

Stocksbridge Park Steels	30	19	5	6	71	34	62
Pickering Town	30	19	4	7	84	46	61
Bradley Rangers	30	18	7	5	59	26	61
Yorkshire Amateurs	30	18	3	9	56	27	57
Hallam	30	17	6	7	57	36	57
Hall Road Rangers	30	17	5	8	68	36	56
Rossington Main	30	13	5	12	44	48	44
R.E.S. Parkgate	30	12	5	13	41	59	41
Immingham Town	30	12	4	14	48	64	40
Worsbrough Bridge M.W.	30	11	6	13	44	43	39
Garforth Town	30	10	5	15	48	44	35
Tadcaster Albion	30	8	4	18	37	62	28
Selby Town	30	8	4	18	32	67	28
York Railway Institute	30	6	7	17	32	77	25
Brodsworth Miners Welfare	30	6	6	18	45	72	24
Hatfield Main	30	7	2	21	36	71	22

Hatfield Main had 1 point deducted.
York Railway Institute moved to the York & District League. Hucknall Town and Lincoln United joined from the Central Midlands League.

1992-93 Premier Division

Spennymoor United	38	26	7	5	102	33	85
Pickering Town	38	27	4	7	90	48	85
North Ferriby United	38	23	7	8	90	40	76
Maltby Miners Welfare	38	21	11	6	69	40	74
Thackley	38	20	7	11	62	39	67
Brigg Town	38	16	14	8	55	39	62
Denaby United	38	15	11	12	71	63	56
Ossett Albion	38	16	7	15	68	60	55
Eccleshill United	38	16	6	16	65	65	54
Winterton Rangers	38	14	7	17	61	72	49
Ashfield United	38	12	11	15	69	88	47
Ossett Town	38	13	7	18	69	71	46
Belper Town	38	11	12	15	56	62	45
Liversedge	38	12	8	18	56	77	44
Sheffield	38	12	6	20	55	70	42
Stocksbridge Park Steels	38	10	11	17	54	70	41
Pontefract Collieries	38	11	8	19	62	88	41
Glasshoughton Welfare	38	9	9	20	46	77	36
Armthorpe Welfare	38	8	8	22	49	81	32
Harrogate Railway Athletic	38	3	9	26	49	115	18

Spennymoor United moved to the Northern Premier League.

Division One

Lincoln United	26	17	5	4	62	31	56
Hucknall Town	26	15	6	5	54	32	51
Hallam	26	15	5	6	50	23	50
Yorkshire Amateurs	26	14	3	9	42	29	45
R.E.S. Parkgate	26	12	9	5	39	38	45
Tadcaster Albion	26	12	5	9	51	43	41
Rossington Main	26	9	7	10	33	31	34
Hall Road Rangers	26	9	6	11	48	43	33
Garforth Town	26	8	8	10	34	38	32
Worsbrough Bridge M.W.	26	7	8	11	33	48	29
Hatfield Main	26	6	6	14	40	63	24
Immingham Town	26	5	8	13	38	51	23
Brodsworth Miners Welfare	26	6	4	16	41	65	22
Selby Town	26	5	4	17	34	64	19

Bradley Rangers were unable to fulfil their fixtures, were expelled from the league and subsequently disbanded. Their record was expunged.
Arnold Town and Louth United joined from the Central Midlands League.

1993-94 Premier Division

Stocksbridge Park Steels	38	23	5	10	82	39	74
Thackley	38	21	11	6	57	32	74
Lincoln United	38	21	9	8	82	44	72
Sheffield	38	22	5	11	69	49	71
Brigg Town	38	18	8	12	77	54	62
Pickering Town	38	17	10	11	76	61	61
Maltby Miners Welfare	38	18	6	14	77	62	60
Ossett Albion	38	16	12	10	73	59	60
North Ferriby United	38	18	5	15	57	43	59
Armthorpe Welfare	38	14	15	9	55	42	57
Liversedge	38	17	4	17	63	65	55
Glasshoughton Welfare	38	13	11	14	51	58	50
Denaby United	38	13	7	18	66	66	46
Hucknall Town	38	13	5	20	48	65	44
Belper Town	38	12	7	19	57	75	43
Ossett Town	38	10	11	17	43	71	41
Pontefract Collieries	38	10	10	18	52	71	40
Ashfield United	38	9	8	21	50	85	35
Eccleshill United	*38*	*8*	*9*	*21*	*44*	*75*	*33*
Winterton Rangers	*38*	*6*	*4*	*28*	*40*	*103*	*22*

Division One

Arnold Town	28	20	1	7	88	34	61
Hallam	28	18	5	5	64	26	59
Louth United	28	17	4	7	72	38	55
Hatfield Main	28	17	4	7	61	33	55
Yorkshire Amateurs	28	16	4	8	51	25	52
Garforth Town	28	15	6	7	39	28	51
Rossington Main	28	12	4	12	43	47	40
Worsbrough Bridge M.W.	28	11	3	14	49	47	36
Harrogate Railway Athletic	28	10	5	13	47	56	35
Hall Road Rangers	28	9	6	13	57	63	33
Selby Town	28	10	5	13	44	66	29
Tadcaster Albion	28	8	2	18	38	73	26
R.E.S. Parkgate	28	6	5	17	43	69	23
Immingham Town	28	6	5	17	33	76	23
Brodsworth Miners Welfare	28	3	5	20	26	74	14

Selby Town had 6 points deducted.
Blidworth Welfare joined from the Central Midlands League.
R.E.S. Parkgate changed their name to Parkgate.

Northern Counties (East) League 1994-1997

1994-95
Premier Division

Lincoln United	38	29	5	4	116	49	92
Arnold Town	38	25	7	6	98	46	82
Stocksbridge Park Steels	38	21	6	11	74	46	69
Belper Town	38	19	8	11	78	44	65
Ashfield United	38	18	11	9	65	48	65
Pickering Town	38	19	7	12	89	63	64
North Ferriby United	38	18	8	12	68	60	62
Armthorpe Welfare	38	13	18	7	56	41	57
Thackley	38	15	11	12	76	56	56
Ossett Albion	38	15	9	14	48	57	54
Brigg Town	38	14	10	14	49	57	52
Ossett Town	38	12	10	16	50	56	46
Maltby Miners Welfare	38	13	7	18	59	71	46
Denaby United	38	12	9	17	48	77	45
Hucknall Town	38	9	13	16	47	60	40
Glasshoughton Welfare	38	10	9	19	60	68	39
Hallam	38	9	8	21	46	76	35
Sheffield	38	6	12	20	45	87	30
Liversedge	38	7	8	23	48	81	29
Pontefract Collieries	**38**	**3**	**10**	**25**	**30**	**107**	**19**

Lincoln United moved to the Northern Premier League and Goole Town joined from the Northern Premier League.

Division One

Hatfield Main	30	25	2	3	88	32	77
Worsbrough Bridge M.W.	30	19	4	7	66	40	61
Selby Town	30	16	9	5	62	38	57
Immingham Town	30	18	4	8	66	43	56
Yorkshire Amateurs	30	15	8	7	53	29	53
Hall Road Rangers	30	15	7	8	57	44	52
Harrogate Railway Athletic	30	16	4	10	64	52	52
Eccleshill United	30	13	5	12	62	47	44
Garforth Town	30	11	8	11	58	49	41
Louth United	30	9	8	13	39	50	35
Rossington Main	30	9	7	14	48	63	34
Tadcaster Albion	30	6	8	16	36	59	26
Blidworth Welfare	30	7	5	18	39	63	26
Winterton Rangers	30	7	3	20	44	72	24
Parkgate	30	5	5	20	47	84	20
Brodsworth Miners Welfare	30	2	7	21	15	79	13

Immingham Town had 2 points deducted.
Borrowash Victoria joined from the Central Midlands League.

1995-96
Premier Division

Hatfield Main	38	22	9	7	77	45	75
Stocksbridge Park Steels	38	21	10	7	59	36	73
North Ferriby United	38	21	9	8	78	33	72
Belper Town	38	20	10	8	66	39	70
Thackley	38	20	9	9	60	40	69
Denaby United	38	19	5	14	63	56	62
Brigg Town	38	17	8	13	65	50	59
Ashfield United	38	17	5	16	56	50	56
Liversedge	38	16	7	15	52	49	55
Ossett Albion	38	13	12	13	56	55	51
Armthorpe Welfare	38	13	11	14	53	47	50
Pickering Town	38	14	5	19	73	86	47
Goole Town	38	13	8	17	53	74	47
Arnold Town	38	13	7	18	51	57	46
Ossett Town	38	12	9	17	48	61	45
Hucknall Town	38	12	6	20	52	67	42
Hallam	38	11	7	20	41	68	40
Glasshoughton Welfare	38	10	9	19	45	62	39
Maltby Miners Welfare	38	11	5	22	58	83	38
Sheffield	38	6	7	25	46	94	25

Stocksbridge Park Steels moved to the Northern Premier League and Goole Town disbanded. Maltby Miners Welfare changed their name to Maltby Main.

Division One

Selby Town	30	19	6	5	79	34	63
Pontefract Collieries	30	19	6	5	76	33	63
Garforth Town	30	18	7	5	63	27	61
Yorkshire Amateurs	30	18	6	6	51	30	60
Hall Road Rangers	30	17	5	8	65	34	56
Eccleshill United	30	18	1	11	74	53	55
Borrowash Victoria	30	13	5	12	59	46	44
Harrogate Railway Athletic	30	12	5	13	48	52	41
Winterton Rangers	30	11	6	13	44	51	39
Rossington Main	30	10	7	13	43	55	37
Worsbrough Bridge M.W.	30	9	5	16	48	60	32
Louth United	30	8	7	15	54	66	31
Blidworth Welfare	30	9	3	18	47	83	30
Tadcaster Albion	30	6	5	19	25	61	23
Parkgate	30	6	4	20	36	81	22
Brodsworth Miners Welfare	30	2	12	16	23	69	18

Immingham Town disbanded in December 1995 and their record was expunged.
Glapwell joined from the Central Midlands League.

1996-97
Premier Division

Denaby United	38	25	10	3	82	33	85
Belper Town	38	24	7	7	78	41	79
Brigg Town	38	23	8	7	80	43	77
North Ferriby United	38	21	9	8	86	36	72
Ossett Albion	38	21	8	9	73	36	71
Hucknall Town	38	19	8	11	84	48	65
Hallam	38	17	7	14	56	69	58
Ossett Town	38	14	11	13	52	53	53
Arnold Town	38	12	15	11	48	43	51
Glasshoughton Welfare	38	13	12	13	58	58	51
Selby Town	38	14	9	15	63	69	51
Armthorpe Welfare	38	12	9	17	42	48	45
Thackley	38	12	9	17	43	58	45
Maltby Main	38	12	8	18	58	81	44
Pickering Town	38	11	8	19	45	72	41
Pontefract Collieries	38	8	11	19	44	73	35
Hatfield Main	38	8	10	20	40	75	34
Sheffield	38	7	11	20	50	70	32
Ashfield United	38	7	11	20	51	80	32
Liversedge	38	5	9	24	40	87	24

Belper Town moved to the Northern Premier League. Ashfield United temporarily ceased playing until their planned new ground was available. However, this never happened and the club eventually disbanded.
Curzon Ashton joined from the Northern Premier League.

Division One

Eccleshill United	**28**	**21**	**4**	**3**	**81**	**30**	**67**
Garforth Town	28	20	4	4	57	22	64
Harrogate Railway Athletic	28	15	7	6	54	32	52
Yorkshire Amateurs	28	15	4	9	52	52	49
Glapwell	28	14	4	10	52	41	46
Borrowash Victoria	28	12	6	10	47	39	42
Hall Road Rangers	28	12	5	11	48	46	41
Louth United	28	9	9	10	47	37	36
Rossington Main	28	10	6	12	44	46	36
Worsbrough Bridge M.W.	28	9	8	11	41	49	35
Parkgate	28	8	7	13	38	46	31
Winterton Rangers	28	7	9	12	39	51	30
Tadcaster Albion	28	4	10	14	20	51	22
Brodsworth Miners Welfare	28	4	5	19	22	58	17
Blidworth Welfare	28	4	4	20	31	73	16

Staveley Miners Welfare joined from the Central Midlands League.

1997-98 Premier Division

	P	W	D	L	F	A	Pts
Hucknall Town	38	26	8	4	90	34	86
North Ferriby United	38	25	6	7	89	37	81
Ossett Albion	38	21	11	6	59	25	74
Brigg Town	38	20	10	8	76	40	70
Glasshoughton Welfare	38	17	9	12	66	64	60
Maltby Main	38	17	8	13	51	40	59
Ossett Town	38	17	7	14	67	53	58
Eccleshill United	38	16	9	13	64	58	57
Armthorpe Welfare	38	16	8	14	60	44	56
Selby Town	38	15	6	17	60	75	51
Thackley	38	12	12	14	48	55	48
Denaby United	38	14	6	18	55	68	48
Pontefract Collieries	38	13	9	16	60	76	48
Arnold Town	38	10	16	12	55	52	46
Sheffield	38	13	7	18	62	72	46
Pickering Town	38	12	8	18	56	68	44
Hallam	38	10	10	18	52	77	40
Liversedge	38	7	9	22	41	88	30
Curzon Ashton	38	7	8	23	42	75	29
Hatfield Main	**38**	**6**	**5**	**27**	**46**	**98**	**23**

Hucknall Town moved to the Northern Premier League and Curzon Ashton moved to the North-West Counties League.
Buxton joined from the Northern Premier League.

Division One

	P	W	D	L	F	A	Pts
Garforth Town	**28**	**23**	**3**	**2**	**77**	**17**	**72**
Staveley Miners Welfare	**28**	**15**	**9**	**4**	**51**	**30**	**54**
Hall Road Rangers	28	16	4	8	68	34	52
Glapwell	28	14	4	10	59	50	46
Parkgate	28	14	3	11	61	47	45
Louth United	28	14	2	12	73	50	44
Worsbrough Bridge M.W.	28	13	4	11	58	57	43
Borrowash Victoria	28	11	8	9	67	50	41
Rossington Main	28	11	4	13	41	46	37
Winterton Rangers	28	11	3	14	41	55	36
Harrogate Railway Athletic	28	10	4	14	58	52	34
Brodsworth Miners Welfare	28	8	9	11	53	43	33
Tadcaster Albion	28	8	6	14	56	46	30
Yorkshire Amateurs	28	8	5	15	49	57	29
Blidworth Welfare	28	0	0	28	8	186	0

Blidworth Welfare moved to the Central Midlands League.

1998-99 Premier Division

	P	W	D	L	F	A	Pts
Ossett Albion	38	23	5	10	86	50	74
Ossett Town	38	22	7	9	76	44	73
Brigg Town	38	20	12	6	78	43	72
Hallam	38	22	5	11	95	63	71
North Ferriby United	38	19	12	7	92	50	69
Liversedge	38	21	4	13	87	63	67
Arnold Town	38	19	7	12	78	56	64
Denaby United	38	15	12	11	66	60	57
Garforth Town	38	15	9	14	74	70	54
Buxton	38	14	10	14	54	53	52
Selby Town	38	15	7	16	59	61	52
Sheffield	38	15	6	17	55	58	51
Armthorpe Welfare	38	13	11	14	46	50	50
Glasshoughton Welfare	38	13	9	16	58	71	48
Thackley	38	14	5	19	65	77	47
Eccleshill United	38	12	6	20	56	74	42
Staveley Miners Welfare	38	9	11	18	50	84	36
Maltby Main	38	8	6	24	51	87	26
Pontefract Collieries	**38**	**7**	**7**	**24**	**37**	**86**	**26**
Pickering Town	**38**	**5**	**7**	**26**	**44**	**107**	**22**

Staveley Miners Welfare and Pontefract Collieries each had 2 points deducted.
Maltby Main had 4 points deducted.
Ossett Town moved to the Northern Premier League and Alfreton Town joined from the Northern Premier League.

Division One

	P	W	D	L	F	A	Pts
Harrogate Railway Athletic	**24**	**15**	**6**	**3**	**58**	**29**	**51**
Brodsworth Miners Welfare	**24**	**13**	**3**	**8**	**52**	**42**	**42**
Glapwell	24	12	6	6	47	39	42
Parkgate	24	12	5	7	61	32	41
Borrowash Victoria	24	12	5	7	48	38	41
Worsbrough Bridge M.W.	24	9	6	9	49	42	33
Hall Road Rangers	24	9	6	9	44	49	33
Hatfield Main	24	10	3	11	27	47	31
Louth United	24	9	3	12	37	33	30
Yorkshire Amateurs	24	6	7	11	41	49	25
Tadcaster Albion	24	6	6	12	33	51	24
Rossington Main	24	6	4	14	37	51	22
Winterton Rangers	24	3	8	13	22	54	17

Hatfield Main had 2 points deducted.
Goole and Mickleover Sports both joined from the Central Midlands League and Bridlington Town joined from the East Riding County League.

1999-2000
Premier Division

	P	W	D	L	F	A	Pts
North Ferriby United	38	25	10	3	87	31	85
Brigg Town	38	25	6	7	73	38	81
Glasshoughton Welfare	38	20	6	12	68	57	66
Liversedge	38	20	5	13	76	65	65
Alfreton Town	38	17	11	10	73	49	62
Brodsworth Miners Welfare	38	15	10	13	66	69	55
Ossett Albion	38	15	9	14	70	60	54
Arnold Town	38	14	11	13	60	47	53
Selby Town	38	13	14	11	53	49	53
Eccleshill United	38	15	8	15	59	65	53
Armthorpe Welfare	38	14	10	14	45	50	52
Hallam	38	14	9	15	72	67	51
Denaby United	38	13	11	14	46	41	50
Sheffield	38	12	13	13	62	55	49
Garforth Town	38	10	11	17	53	65	41
Harrogate Railway Athletic	38	11	6	21	54	95	39
Maltby Main	**38**	**8**	**12**	**18**	**36**	**58**	**36**
Buxton	38	11	6	21	35	67	36
Staveley Miners Welfare	38	9	8	21	53	83	35
Thackley	38	6	10	22	39	89	28

Buxton had 3 points deducted.
North Ferriby United moved to the Northern Premier League.

Division One

	P	W	D	L	F	A	Pts
Goole	**30**	**22**	**5**	**3**	**66**	**19**	**71**
Glapwell	**30**	**18**	**6**	**6**	**74**	**36**	**60**
Borrowash Victoria	30	14	8	8	48	35	50
Mickleover Sports	30	14	7	9	52	44	49
Bridlington Town	30	15	4	11	43	36	49
Winterton Rangers	30	13	9	8	52	31	48
Yorkshire Amateurs	30	14	5	11	55	37	47
Hall Road Rangers	30	14	5	11	58	49	47
Louth United	30	12	4	14	51	62	40
Worsbrough Bridge M.W.	30	11	6	13	44	46	39
Pickering Town	30	11	5	14	46	36	38
Parkgate	30	11	5	14	58	59	38
Pontefract Collieries	30	8	9	13	34	50	33
Tadcaster Albion	30	7	3	20	33	84	24
Rossington Main	30	5	7	18	27	62	22
Hatfield Main	30	5	4	21	36	91	19

Gedling Town joined from the Central Midlands League.

Northern Counties (East) League 2000-2003

2000-01

Premier Division

	P	W	D	L	F	A	Pts
Brigg Town	38	29	5	4	87	36	92
Ossett Albion	38	25	7	6	84	33	82
Alfreton Town	38	23	4	11	71	44	73
Goole	38	19	9	10	65	46	66
Hallam	38	19	7	12	61	51	64
Arnold Town	38	16	14	8	67	46	62
Sheffield	38	15	15	8	59	38	60
Thackley	38	16	9	13	59	57	57
Selby Town	38	16	7	15	71	71	55
Glapwell	38	13	11	14	62	58	50
Denaby United	38	15	4	19	54	63	49
Buxton	38	12	9	17	38	57	45
Harrogate Railway Athletic	38	11	9	18	59	65	42
Eccleshill United	38	9	13	16	48	58	40
Liversedge	38	9	13	16	50	63	40
Glasshoughton Welfare	38	9	11	18	57	64	38
Garforth Town	38	9	10	19	56	75	37
Brodsworth Miners Welfare	38	11	7	20	41	86	37
Armthorpe Welfare	38	9	7	22	53	81	34
Staveley Miners Welfare	**38**	**6**	**7**	**25**	**42**	**92**	**25**

Brodsworth Miners Welfare had 3 points deducted.
Ossett Albion moved to the Northern Premier League.

Division One

	P	W	D	L	F	A	Pts
Borrowash Victoria	**30**	**22**	**4**	**4**	**74**	**28**	**70**
Pickering Town	**30**	**21**	**6**	**3**	**67**	**24**	**69**
Mickleover Sports	30	18	5	7	65	39	59
Bridlington Town	30	15	7	8	48	41	52
Gedling Town	30	14	7	9	47	37	49
Hall Road Rangers	30	14	6	10	43	37	48
Parkgate	30	13	6	11	60	52	45
Hatfield Main	30	13	4	13	54	49	43
Maltby Main	30	11	6	13	36	48	39
Yorkshire Amateurs	30	9	5	16	33	53	32
Worsbrough Bridge M.W.	30	9	4	17	31	54	31
Louth United	30	8	6	16	48	58	30
Pontefract Collieries	30	6	9	15	37	56	27
Winterton Rangers	30	8	6	16	30	53	27
Rossington Main	30	7	5	18	39	54	26
Tadcaster Albion	30	6	6	18	29	58	24

Winterton Rangers had 3 points deducted.
Lincoln Moorlands joined from the Central Midlands League.

2001-02

Premier Division

	P	W	D	L	F	A	Pts
Alfreton Town	38	27	5	6	94	36	86
Brigg Town	38	25	5	8	90	46	80
Hallam	38	21	6	11	72	62	69
Pickering Town	38	20	8	10	70	38	68
Harrogate Railway Athletic	38	17	10	11	83	61	61
Armthorpe Welfare	38	17	7	14	56	58	58
Selby Town	38	14	12	12	47	47	54
Thackley	38	14	11	13	48	47	53
Sheffield	38	14	10	14	54	62	52
Arnold Town	38	13	10	15	53	55	49
Liversedge	38	14	6	18	59	66	48
Goole	38	13	9	16	43	51	48
Eccleshill United	38	13	9	16	60	72	48
Glapwell	38	12	10	16	66	71	46
Brodsworth Miners Welfare	38	13	9	16	68	74	45
Borrowash Victoria	38	10	13	15	49	67	43
Glasshoughton Welfare	38	10	10	18	49	62	40
Denaby United	38	11	5	22	47	78	38
Buxton	38	8	13	17	43	61	37
Garforth Town	38	8	4	26	46	83	28

Brodsworth Miners Welfare had 3 points deducted.
Alfreton Town moved to the Northern Premier League and Denaby United disbanded. Ossett Albion joined from the Northern Premier League.

Division One

	P	W	D	L	F	A	Pts
Gedling Town	30	21	5	4	75	42	68
Bridlington Town	**30**	**20**	**4**	**6**	**73**	**25**	**64**
Worsbrough Bridge M.W.	30	18	8	4	70	37	62
Lincoln Moorlands	30	15	6	9	52	41	51
Mickleover Sports	30	16	2	12	51	42	50
Maltby Main	30	15	3	12	54	44	48
Winterton Rangers	30	14	6	10	44	36	48
Rossington Main	30	12	7	11	44	46	43
Hall Road Rangers	30	12	7	11	54	57	43
Hatfield Main	30	10	7	13	50	47	37
Louth United	30	10	5	15	36	46	35
Yorkshire Amateurs	30	8	6	16	32	47	30
Tadcaster Albion	30	9	3	18	40	62	30
Parkgate	30	8	3	19	53	80	27
Staveley Miners Welfare	30	4	12	14	32	60	24
Pontefract Collieries	30	4	4	22	23	71	16

Long Eaton United and Shirebrook Town joined from the Central Midlands League.

2002-03

Premier Division

	P	W	D	L	F	A	Pts
Bridlington Town	38	29	5	4	92	33	92
Brigg Town	38	22	6	10	75	42	72
Goole	38	20	11	7	68	36	71
Buxton	38	21	7	10	84	56	70
Ossett Albion	38	21	7	10	70	52	70
Thackley	38	17	11	10	53	39	62
Sheffield	38	17	8	13	74	55	59
Eccleshill United	38	16	7	15	61	57	55
Liversedge	38	16	6	16	59	65	54
Harrogate Railway Athletic	38	15	7	16	87	71	52
Glapwell	38	14	7	17	52	59	49
Glasshoughton Welfare	38	13	9	16	65	74	48
Pickering Town	38	14	5	19	49	51	47
Brodsworth Miners Welfare	38	13	7	18	64	84	46
Arnold Town	38	12	8	18	58	53	44
Selby Town	38	11	7	20	44	73	40
Hallam	38	10	9	19	50	75	39
Armthorpe Welfare	38	10	6	22	53	85	36
Borrowash Victoria	38	9	5	24	41	97	32
Garforth Town	**38**	**9**	**4**	**25**	**47**	**89**	**31**

Bridlington Town moved to the Northern Premier League and Eastwood Town joined from the Northern Premier League.

Division One

	P	W	D	L	F	A	Pts
Mickleover Sports	**32**	**24**	**3**	**5**	**62**	**26**	**75**
Shirebrook Town	32	21	5	6	79	38	68
Long Eaton United	32	17	7	8	66	52	58
Pontefract Collieries	32	16	7	9	68	56	55
Hatfield Main	32	17	4	11	49	42	55
Gedling Town	32	15	8	9	70	48	53
Lincoln Moorlands	32	14	6	12	56	42	48
Parkgate	32	12	10	10	66	52	46
Hall Road Rangers	32	12	8	12	55	67	44
Winterton Rangers	32	10	8	14	48	54	38
Yorkshire Amateurs	32	10	8	14	39	45	38
Rossington Main	32	9	10	13	45	59	37
Louth United	32	10	6	16	48	62	36
Worsbrough Bridge M.W.	32	10	5	17	41	56	35
Maltby Main	32	10	3	19	51	80	33
Tadcaster Albion	32	6	4	22	30	59	22
Staveley Miners Welfare	32	5	6	21	34	69	21

Hatfield Main moved to the Doncaster Senior League. Carlton Town, South Normanton Athletic and Sutton Town (formed in 2000 and known as North Notts until 2002) joined from the Central Midlands League.

2003-04 Premier Division

Team	P	W	D	L	F	A	Pts
Ossett Albion	38	22	10	6	76	37	76
Eastwood Town	38	23	7	8	73	34	76
Brigg Town	38	20	11	7	73	40	71
Sheffield	38	19	12	7	64	40	69
Pickering Town	38	19	10	9	67	44	67
Goole	38	18	10	10	67	44	64
Buxton	38	17	12	9	69	50	63
Selby Town	38	16	11	11	86	57	59
Liversedge	38	17	8	13	72	58	59
Glapwell	38	14	10	14	53	45	52
Thackley	38	14	9	15	61	67	51
Harrogate Railway Athletic	38	12	13	13	63	64	49
Mickleover Sports	38	14	5	19	52	66	47
Armthorpe Welfare	38	14	4	20	48	67	46
Hallam	38	13	5	20	56	76	44
Eccleshill United	38	12	8	18	52	74	44
Glasshoughton Welfare	38	10	7	21	58	83	37
Arnold Town	38	10	6	22	45	67	36
Borrowash Victoria	38	8	7	23	35	84	31
Brodsworth Miners Welfare	38	3	5	30	38	111	14

Ossett Albion, Eastwood Town and Brigg Town all moved to the Northern Premier League.

Division One

Team	P	W	D	L	F	A	Pts
Shirebrook Town	34	22	5	7	59	26	71
Long Eaton United	34	22	2	10	63	40	68
Maltby Main	34	21	7	6	81	49	67
Sutton Town	34	19	8	7	79	37	65
Gedling Town	34	18	9	7	81	49	63
Garforth Town	34	17	7	10	60	47	58
Yorkshire Amateurs	34	15	8	11	57	44	53
Lincoln Moorlands	34	14	10	10	53	40	52
Carlton Town	34	14	7	13	52	51	49
Parkgate	34	12	11	11	52	53	47
Winterton Rangers	34	13	8	13	52	56	47
Rossington Main	34	13	5	16	56	62	44
South Normanton Athletic	34	11	3	20	49	62	36
Hall Road Rangers	34	9	5	20	43	70	32
Worsbrough Bridge M.W.	34	9	2	23	31	75	29
Staveley Miners Welfare	34	7	6	21	41	75	27
Pontefract Collieries	34	5	10	19	30	60	25
Tadcaster Albion	34	6	5	23	32	75	23

Maltby Main had 3 points deducted.
Louth United resigned and disbanded just before the season began. A new Louth United were formed and joined the Lincolnshire League in 2004-05.
Retford United joined from the Central Midlands League.

2004-05 Premier Division

Team	P	W	D	L	F	A	Pts
Goole	38	25	4	9	87	47	79
Selby Town	38	23	8	7	72	43	77
Harrogate Railway Athletic	38	24	4	10	92	54	76
Sheffield	38	22	8	8	78	47	74
Pickering Town	38	18	13	7	62	35	67
Liversedge	38	18	10	10	74	59	64
Mickleover Sports	38	16	10	12	53	45	58
Thackley	38	14	13	11	57	46	55
Buxton	38	14	13	11	59	57	55
Shirebrook Town	38	14	12	12	56	48	54
Glasshoughton Welfare	38	13	13	12	57	55	52
Long Eaton United	38	15	7	16	55	54	52
Glapwell	38	10	15	13	57	57	45
Eccleshill United	38	13	6	19	69	76	45
Arnold Town	38	9	12	17	44	62	39
Hallam	38	10	9	19	45	71	39
Brodsworth Miners Welfare	38	12	4	22	58	85	37
Armthorpe Welfare	38	11	3	24	44	73	36
Maltby Main	38	9	8	21	41	72	33
Borrowash Victoria	38	0	8	30	30	104	8

Brodsworth Miners Welfare had 3 points deducted.
Maltby Main had 2 points deducted.
Goole moved to the Northern Premier Division.

Division One

Team	P	W	D	L	F	A	Pts
Sutton Town	30	22	5	3	94	35	71
Garforth Town	30	21	4	5	65	27	67
Carlton Town	30	21	2	7	64	34	65
Lincoln Moorlands	30	16	7	7	61	39	55
Gedling Town	30	16	7	7	53	39	55
Tadcaster Albion	30	14	8	8	56	38	50
Yorkshire Amateurs	30	10	7	13	57	55	37
Retford United	30	10	7	13	45	58	37
Staveley Miners Welfare	30	11	3	16	50	56	36
Winterton Rangers	30	9	9	12	50	58	36
Hall Road Rangers	30	10	3	17	35	57	33
Parkgate	30	7	8	15	53	80	29
Pontefract Collieries	30	8	6	16	52	67	25
Rossington Main	30	6	9	15	46	64	24
Worsbrough Bridge M.W.	30	5	6	19	36	68	21
South Normanton Athletic	30	6	5	19	37	79	20

Pontefract Collieries had 5 points deducted.
Rossington Main and South Normanton Athletic each had 3 points deducted.
Teversal joined from the Central Midlands League.

2005-06 Premier Division

Team	P	W	D	L	F	A	Pts
Buxton	38	30	5	3	102	27	95
Liversedge	38	25	5	8	106	49	80
Harrogate Railway Athletic	38	22	7	9	92	49	73
Sheffield	38	20	10	8	63	43	70
Arnold Town	38	21	7	10	72	45	67
Pickering Town	38	19	9	10	63	42	66
Sutton Town	38	17	9	12	78	57	60
Selby Town	38	17	5	16	58	60	56
Thackley	38	18	3	17	59	62	54
Garforth Town	38	12	11	15	61	68	47
Armthorpe Welfare	38	13	8	17	65	77	47
Glapwell	38	12	11	15	46	71	47
Mickleover Sports	38	12	8	18	51	73	44
Eccleshill United	38	12	7	19	66	70	43
Shirebrook Town	38	13	4	21	59	85	43
Glasshoughton Welfare	38	11	5	22	52	70	38
Hallam	38	10	8	20	44	73	38
Maltby Main	38	9	11	18	52	70	37
Long Eaton United	38	8	8	22	47	86	29
Brodsworth Miners Welfare	38	6	5	27	47	106	23

Arnold Town, Thackley and Long Eaton United each had 3 points deducted.
Maltby Main had 1 point deducted.
Buxton and Harrogate Railway Athletic both moved to the Northern Premier League. Brodsworth Miners Welfare changed their name to Brodsworth Welfare.

Division One

Team	P	W	D	L	F	A	Pts
Carlton Town	30	23	4	3	68	27	73
Retford United	30	20	5	5	74	28	65
Tadcaster Albion	30	21	1	8	55	35	64
Gedling Town	30	19	5	6	75	34	62
Winterton Rangers	30	18	7	5	71	27	61
Parkgate	30	18	5	7	87	40	59
Lincoln Moorlands	30	16	1	13	56	40	49
Borrowash Victoria	30	15	4	11	50	45	49
Worsbrough Bridge M.W.	30	11	5	14	57	67	38
Staveley Miners Welfare	30	9	4	17	44	57	31
Pontefract Collieries	30	6	7	17	43	64	25
South Normanton Athletic	30	7	4	19	45	86	25
Rossington Main	30	6	5	19	37	67	23
Hall Road Rangers	30	6	5	19	38	82	23
Teversal	30	5	6	19	28	78	21
Yorkshire Amateurs	30	4	4	22	29	80	16

Nostell Miners Welfare and AFC Emley joined from the West Yorkshire League, Nostell from the Premier Division and Emley from Division One. Dinnington Town joined from the Central Midlands League. Worsbrough Bridge Miners Welfare changed their name to Worsbrough Bridge Athletic.

Northern Counties (East) League 2006-2008

2006-07

Premier Division

	P	W	D	L	F	A	Pts
Retford United	38	25	7	6	92	37	82
Sheffield	38	23	8	7	71	39	77
Carlton Town	38	23	4	11	83	41	73
Garforth Town	38	21	7	10	83	44	70
Selby Town	38	21	6	11	75	49	69
Glapwell	38	20	6	12	71	48	66
Mickleover Sports	38	18	9	11	70	62	63
Sutton Town	38	16	11	11	60	42	56
Pickering Town	38	16	8	14	61	54	56
Maltby Main	38	14	10	14	56	58	52
Long Eaton United	38	13	12	13	57	60	51
Liversedge	38	13	10	15	58	60	49
Armthorpe Welfare	38	15	3	20	62	63	48
Hallam	38	14	6	18	57	63	48
Arnold Town	38	12	9	17	66	77	45
Glasshoughton Welfare	38	12	7	19	58	66	43
Eccleshill United	38	10	9	19	63	105	39
Thackley	38	8	8	22	52	89	31
Shirebrook Town	38	7	9	22	44	79	30
Brodsworth Welfare	38	2	5	31	30	133	10

Sutton Town had 3 points deducted.
Thackley and Brodsworth Welfare each had 1 point deducted.
Retford United, Sheffield, Carlton Town and Garforth Town all moved to the Northern Premier League and Sutton Town moved to the Central Midlands League.

Division One

	P	W	D	L	F	A	Pts
Parkgate	32	26	4	2	120	38	82
Winterton Rangers	32	23	2	7	90	38	71
South Normanton Athletic	32	20	5	7	76	34	65
Nostell Miners Welfare	32	20	0	12	66	41	57
Lincoln Moorlands	32	17	5	10	63	42	56
Staveley Miners Welfare	32	16	3	13	57	50	51
Tadcaster Albion	32	14	7	11	60	54	49
Worsbrough Bridge Athletic	32	13	9	10	53	42	48
Dinnington Town	32	12	7	13	52	46	43
Hall Road Rangers	32	12	7	13	48	51	43
Borrowash Victoria	32	10	7	15	38	52	37
Pontefract Collieries	32	10	7	15	35	61	37
AFC Emley	32	10	4	18	48	70	34
Gedling Town	32	9	4	19	45	63	31
Teversal	32	9	4	19	35	69	31
Yorkshire Amateurs	32	7	1	24	33	106	22
Rossington Main	32	4	4	24	27	89	16

Nostell Miners Welfare had 3 points deducted.
Barton Town Old Boys, Bottesford Town and Rainworth Miners Welfare all joined from the Central Midlands League, Leeds Metropolitan Carnegie joined from the West Yorkshire League and Scarborough Athletic joined as a newly formed club. Lincoln Moorlands merged with Moorlands Railway of the Lincoln League to form Lincoln Moorlands Railway.

2007-08

Premier Division

	P	W	D	L	F	A	Pts
Winterton Rangers	38	29	4	5	116	37	91
Glapwell	38	23	9	6	86	38	78
Pickering Town	38	22	7	9	68	42	73
Liversedge	38	20	8	10	73	41	68
Nostell Miners Welfare	38	19	7	12	81	64	64
Hallam	38	19	5	14	82	69	62
Selby Town	38	16	12	10	76	52	60
Parkgate	38	18	4	16	80	54	58
Armthorpe Welfare	38	17	7	14	73	69	58
Arnold Town	38	16	8	14	54	49	56
Eccleshill United	38	15	5	18	57	74	50
Long Eaton United	38	14	7	17	48	63	49
Brodsworth Welfare	38	14	5	19	61	91	45
Mickleover Sports	38	11	10	17	58	78	43
Shirebrook Town	38	11	9	18	38	63	42
Thackley	38	11	7	20	54	75	40
South Normanton Athletic	38	11	9	18	43	64	39
Maltby Main	38	9	9	20	52	72	36
Lincoln Moorlands Railway	38	9	6	23	53	83	33
Glasshoughton Welfare	**38**	**4**	**6**	**28**	**26**	**101**	**18**

Brodsworth Welfare had 2 points deducted.
South Normanton Athletic had 3 points deducted.
Glapwell moved to the Northern Premier League and South Normanton Athletic disbanded. Bridlington Town joined from the Northern Premier League.

Division One

	P	W	D	L	F	A	Pts
Dinnington Town	32	24	6	2	88	40	78
Hall Road Rangers	32	22	1	9	65	42	67
Bottesford Town	32	19	5	8	62	40	62
Rainworth Miners Welfare	32	16	9	7	60	38	57
Scarborough Athletic	32	18	7	7	80	45	55
Gedling Town	32	16	7	9	70	45	55
Leeds Metropolitan Carnegie	32	17	4	11	67	45	55
Staveley Miners Welfare	32	14	4	14	49	53	46
Barton Town Old Boys	32	13	9	10	82	62	45
Teversal	32	10	12	10	58	66	42
AFC Emley	32	10	8	14	59	66	38
Tadcaster Albion	32	9	7	16	48	66	34
Borrowash Victoria	32	8	6	18	49	76	30
Yorkshire Amateurs	32	7	8	17	37	67	29
Worsbrough Bridge Athletic	32	7	6	19	40	67	27
Rossington Main	32	7	3	22	47	87	24
Pontefract Collieries	32	1	6	25	29	85	9

Scarborough Athletic had 6 points deducted.
Barton Town Old Boys had 3 points deducted.
Borrowash Victoria and Gedling Town moved to the newly formed East Midlands Counties League. Appleby Frodingham and Grimsby Borough joined from the Central Midlands League as did Askern Welfare who changed their name to Askern Villa. Hemsworth Miners Welfare and Brighouse Town joined from the West Riding County Amateur League. Leeds Metropolitan Carnegie changed their name to Leeds Carnegie.

2008-09
Premier Division

Mickleover Sports	38	28	4	6	108	47	88
Long Eaton United	38	25	6	7	76	40	81
Selby Town	38	25	5	8	89	40	80
Bridlington Town	38	23	7	8	105	51	76
Winterton Rangers	38	19	7	12	74	49	64
Arnold Town	38	17	13	8	58	46	64
Thackley	38	20	2	16	87	62	62
Dinnington Town	38	19	5	14	73	60	62
Pickering Town	38	17	7	14	81	64	58
Hallam	38	17	5	16	78	69	56
Parkgate	38	15	6	17	67	79	51
Maltby Main	38	15	7	16	63	67	49
Nostell Miners Welfare	38	12	13	13	45	51	49
Liversedge	38	14	7	17	60	64	46
Armthorpe Welfare	38	14	3	21	61	58	45
Hall Road Rangers	38	11	6	21	53	94	39
Shirebrook Town	38	9	4	25	47	85	31
Lincoln Moorlands Railway	38	9	3	26	45	93	30
Brodsworth Welfare	38	5	8	25	46	92	23
Eccleshill United	**38**	**6**	**2**	**30**	**48**	**153**	**20**

Maltby Main and Liversedge each had 3 points deducted.
Mickleover Sports moved to the Northern Premier League.

Division One

Scarborough Athletic	**36**	**29**	**5**	**2**	**121**	**24**	**92**
Rainworth Miners Welfare	**36**	**23**	**9**	**4**	**90**	**42**	**78**
Askern Villa	36	21	9	6	65	34	72
Staveley Miners Welfare	36	20	8	8	77	43	68
Barton Town Old Boys	36	20	7	9	76	53	67
Bottesford Town	36	20	2	14	77	62	62
Leeds Carnegie	36	17	10	9	79	41	61
AFC Emley	36	17	9	10	59	48	60
Pontefract Collieries	36	16	5	15	62	56	53
Hemsworth Miners Welfare	36	13	11	12	57	52	50
Rossington Main	36	12	7	17	53	67	43
Appleby Frodingham	36	11	9	16	58	79	42
Grimsby Borough	36	11	7	18	52	68	40
Teversal	36	12	3	21	59	86	39
Brighouse Town	36	9	8	19	55	73	35
Worsbrough Bridge Athletic	36	9	5	22	45	86	32
Tadcaster Albion	36	9	4	23	47	94	31
Yorkshire Amateurs	36	7	8	21	42	77	29
Glasshoughton Welfare	36	0	6	30	29	118	6

2009-10
Premier Division

Bridlington Town	38	30	4	4	123	36	94
Rainworth Miners Welfare	38	26	5	7	98	46	83
Armthorpe Welfare	38	24	7	7	102	48	79
Thackley	38	25	1	12	113	54	76
Scarborough Athletic	38	22	4	12	100	57	70
Winterton Rangers	38	22	3	13	70	43	69
Pickering Town	38	20	5	13	82	58	65
Arnold Town	38	18	7	13	84	69	61
Liversedge	38	17	5	16	89	83	56
Long Eaton United	38	15	8	15	58	52	53
Hall Road Rangers	38	15	6	17	72	80	51
Dinnington Town	38	14	7	17	62	83	49
Selby Town	38	14	6	18	60	84	48
Parkgate	38	13	6	19	83	87	45
Hallam	38	12	6	20	82	93	42
Maltby Main	38	11	9	18	47	70	42
Lincoln Moorlands Railway	38	10	8	20	57	85	38
Nostell Miners Welfare	38	9	8	21	51	80	35
Shirebrook Town	**38**	**8**	**3**	**27**	**35**	**95**	**27**
Brodsworth Welfare	**38**	**0**	**2**	**36**	**17**	**182**	**2**

Rainworth Miners Welfare moved to the Northern Premier League.

Farsley joined as a club that was newly formed as a replacement for Farsley Celtic who had resigned from the Football Conference and disbanded in March 2010.

Division One

Tadcaster Albion	**34**	**22**	**8**	**4**	**80**	**37**	**74**
Brighouse Town	**34**	**23**	**4**	**7**	**80**	**41**	**73**
Leeds Carnegie	34	23	6	5	101	37	72
Staveley Miners Welfare	34	21	5	8	87	46	68
Pontefract Collieries	34	17	8	9	59	49	59
Barton Town Old Boys	34	18	6	10	59	55	57
Hemsworth Miners Welfare	34	17	4	13	81	68	55
AFC Emley	34	15	8	11	69	50	53
Bottesford Town	34	13	6	15	62	66	45
Rossington Main	34	11	9	14	52	66	42
Teversal	34	12	5	17	56	66	41
Askern Villa	34	14	4	16	63	65	36
Glasshoughton Welfare	34	10	5	19	47	66	35
Yorkshire Amateurs	34	10	4	20	48	70	34
Appleby Frodingham	34	10	4	20	48	75	34
Eccleshill United	34	8	4	22	45	96	28
Grimsby Borough	34	6	7	21	36	70	25
Worsbrough Bridge Athletic	34	5	5	24	36	86	20

Barton Old Boys and Leeds Carnegie each had 3 points deducted.
Askern Villa had 10 points deducted.
Handsworth joined from the Sheffield & Hallamshire County Senior League and Louth Town joined from the Central Midlands League.

2010-11
Premier Division

Farsley	38	27	4	7	108	41	85
Parkgate	38	23	9	6	94	55	78
Bridlington Town	38	20	11	7	94	55	71
Tadcaster Albion	38	20	8	10	90	62	68
Winterton Rangers	38	18	11	9	73	52	65
Lincoln Moorlands Railway	38	17	10	11	90	58	61
Pickering Town	38	18	7	13	81	71	61
Thackley	38	17	9	12	66	50	60
Nostell Miners Welfare	38	16	8	14	60	66	56
Scarborough Athletic	38	15	9	14	69	61	54
Maltby Main	38	15	9	14	59	61	54
Long Eaton United	38	14	12	12	47	59	54
Armthorpe Welfare	38	13	9	16	68	76	48
Hall Road Rangers	38	14	6	18	58	70	48
Selby Town	38	15	3	20	54	75	48
Brighouse Town	38	11	8	19	58	77	41
Liversedge	38	7	12	19	52	76	32
Arnold Town	38	6	12	20	61	95	30
Hallam	**38**	**7**	**6**	**25**	**48**	**96**	**27**
Dinnington Town	**38**	**3**	**5**	**30**	**35**	**109**	**14**

Liversedge had 1 point deducted.
Farsley moved to the Northern Premier League and Retford United joined from the Northern Premier League.

Northern Counties (East) League 2011-2013

Division One

Staveley Miners Welfare	38	26	6	6	95	46	84
Barton Town Old Boys	38	23	8	7	97	45	77
Yorkshire Amateurs	38	23	6	9	81	36	75
Handsworth	38	24	3	11	98	66	75
Pontefract Collieries	38	19	11	8	85	51	68
Louth Town	38	18	8	12	76	59	62
Glasshoughton Welfare	38	19	5	14	65	48	62
AFC Emley	38	18	8	12	63	47	62
Askern Villa	38	17	6	15	66	68	57
Eccleshill United	38	17	5	16	76	62	56
Leeds Carnegie	38	16	7	15	55	56	55
Worsbrough Bridge Athletic	38	16	7	15	58	62	55
Shirebrook Town	38	16	4	18	67	72	52
Rossington Main	38	15	4	19	74	82	49
Grimsby Borough	38	13	8	17	69	69	47
Hemsworth Miners Welfare	38	12	6	20	64	82	42
Bottesford Town	38	10	10	18	56	69	40
Teversal	38	11	5	22	58	78	38
Appleby Frodingham	38	6	3	29	38	116	21
Brodsworth Welfare	38	0	2	36	17	144	2

Brodsworth Welfare disbanded and Adwick Park Rangers of the Doncaster & District Senior League then changed their name to Brodsworth Welfare. Leeds Carnegie also disbanded. Albion Sports joined from the West Riding County Amateur League and Worksop Parramore joined from the Central Midlands League having changed their name from Sheffield Parramore.

Division One

Handsworth	38	27	1	10	89	40	82
Glasshoughton Welfare	38	24	7	7	102	57	79
Worksop Parramore	38	24	5	9	95	52	77
Albion Sports	38	24	4	10	106	70	76
Pontefract Collieries	38	23	3	12	86	49	72
+ Eccleshill United	38	20	4	14	83	57	66
Rossington Main	38	19	7	12	85	57	64
Hemsworth Miners Welfare	38	18	6	14	73	66	60
Dinnington Town	38	18	6	14	68	67	60
AFC Emley	38	17	7	14	83	69	57
Worsbrough Bridge Athletic	38	16	9	13	74	65	57
Louth Town	38	16	7	15	61	64	55
Shirebrook Town	38	14	9	15	75	75	51
Hallam	38	15	6	17	66	74	51
Teversal	38	15	6	17	72	84	51
Bottesford Town	38	9	6	23	52	83	33
Askern Villa	38	10	3	25	54	87	33
Grimsby Borough	38	7	5	26	53	109	26
Yorkshire Amateurs	38	7	7	24	53	112	25
Appleby Frodingham	38	2	2	34	39	132	8

+ Eccleshill United had 2 points added.
AFC Emley had 1 point deducted.
Yorkshire Amateurs had 3 points deducted.
Handsworth moved to the Sheffield & Hallamshire County Senior League. Cleethorpes Town joined from the Lincolnshire League, Knaresborough Town joined from the West Yorkshire League, Athersley Recreation joined from the Sheffield & Hallamshire County Senior League and Clipstone Welfare joined from the Central Midlands League.

2011-12

Premier Division

Retford United	38	25	10	3	97	42	85
Bridlington Town	38	26	6	6	114	54	84
Scarborough Athletic	38	23	5	10	96	50	74
Brighouse Town	38	23	4	11	94	60	73
Staveley Miners Welfare	38	22	5	11	66	52	71
Winterton Rangers	38	21	5	12	71	49	68
Parkgate	38	20	7	11	99	72	67
Tadcaster Albion	38	20	7	11	68	50	67
Arnold Town	38	18	9	11	71	61	63
Thackley	38	18	8	12	71	59	62
Barton Town Old Boys	38	16	5	17	74	77	53
Pickering Town	38	15	6	17	74	75	51
Armthorpe Welfare	38	15	5	18	72	73	50
Liversedge	38	12	5	21	62	80	41
Long Eaton United	38	9	7	22	40	65	34
Hall Road Rangers	38	11	4	23	57	86	34
Nostell Miners Welfare	38	8	8	22	60	98	32
Maltby Main	38	7	8	23	39	82	29
Lincoln Moorlands Railway	38	6	7	25	40	96	25
Selby Town	**38**	**3**	**3**	**32**	**26**	**110**	**12**

Hall Road Rangers had 3 points deducted.
Heanor Town joined from the East Midlands Counties League.

2012-13

Premier Division

Scarborough Athletic	42	30	9	3	129	49	99
Brighouse Town	42	30	7	5	106	46	97
Bridlington Town	42	30	5	7	137	54	95
Retford United	42	24	6	12	78	52	78
Pickering Town	42	24	5	13	89	49	77
Tadcaster Albion	42	23	8	11	84	60	77
Worksop Parramore	42	21	9	12	98	78	72
Barton Town Old Boys	42	19	12	11	81	68	69
Parkgate	42	20	6	16	87	67	66
Thackley	42	17	11	14	77	66	62
Heanor Town	42	18	4	20	84	84	58
Long Eaton United	42	16	9	17	80	84	57
Staveley Miners Welfare	42	15	9	18	71	84	54
Maltby Main	42	14	6	22	60	73	48
Liversedge	42	11	12	19	68	81	45
Glasshoughton Welfare	42	12	10	20	62	84	45
Nostell Miners Welfare	42	10	8	24	51	102	38
Winterton Rangers	42	9	7	26	48	82	34
Arnold Town	42	14	3	25	65	93	32
Armthorpe Welfare	42	8	8	26	68	111	32
Lincoln Moorlands Railway	42	7	7	28	42	136	28
Hall Road Rangers	**42**	**7**	**5**	**30**	**52**	**114**	**26**

Glasshoughton Welfare had 1 point deducted.
Arnold Town had 13 points deducted.
Scarborough Athletic moved to the Northern Premier League and Arnold Town moved to the East Midlands Counties League.
Basford United joined from the East Midlands Counties League and Garforth Town joined from the Northern Premier League.

Division One

Albion Sports	42	28	8	6	121	42	92
Athersley Recreation	42	25	10	7	101	52	85
Louth Town	42	24	8	10	91	62	80
Cleethorpes Town	42	23	10	9	108	63	79
Pontefract Collieries	42	24	6	12	88	50	78
Shirebrook Town	42	24	5	13	91	64	77
AFC Emley	42	23	6	13	111	56	75
Knaresborough Town	42	22	9	11	81	55	75
Worsbrough Bridge Athletic	42	21	9	12	89	61	72
Teversal	42	19	8	15	95	66	65
Clipstone Welfare	42	16	9	17	70	71	57
Hallam	42	15	11	16	76	72	56
Hemsworth Miners Welfare	42	17	5	20	69	81	56
Eccleshill United	42	15	10	17	79	67	55
Bottesford Town	42	14	9	19	77	88	50
Selby Town	42	14	4	24	66	91	46
Grimsby Borough	42	13	6	23	54	74	45
Rossington Main	42	11	6	25	57	105	39
Dinnington Town	42	10	7	25	58	102	37
Appleby Frodingham	42	9	7	26	56	125	34
Yorkshire Amateurs	42	8	5	29	55	120	29
Askern Villa	42	7	2	33	47	173	23

Bottesford Town had 1 point deducted.
Askern Villa changed their name to Askern and moved to the Central Midlands League. Dronfield Town joined from the Central Midlands League and Shaw Lane Aquaforce joined from the Sheffield & Hallamshire County Senior League. Clipstone Welfare changed their name to Clipstone.

Division One

Cleethorpes Town	42	28	7	7	104	50	91
Shaw Lane Aquaforce	42	27	6	9	125	45	87
Bottesford Town	42	24	12	6	101	43	84
Eccleshill United	42	24	9	9	94	51	81
Shirebrook Town	42	22	10	10	90	46	76
Knaresborough Town	42	23	7	12	92	52	76
Clipstone	42	22	10	10	88	63	76
AFC Emley	42	21	11	10	85	65	74
Pontefract Collieries	42	20	13	9	96	58	73
Worsbrough Bridge Athletic	42	20	13	9	94	62	73
Hall Road Rangers	42	17	7	18	94	89	58
Selby Town	42	19	3	20	77	86	57
Rossington Main	42	18	3	21	65	89	57
Dronfield Town	42	13	12	17	71	85	51
Teversal	42	14	8	20	76	91	50
Grimsby Borough	42	15	4	23	73	98	46
Hemsworth Miners Welfare	42	12	9	21	61	79	45
Dinnington Town	42	12	4	26	59	111	40
Yorkshire Amateurs	42	11	5	26	59	99	38
Hallam	42	6	11	25	58	99	29
Louth Town	42	6	2	34	49	136	20
Appleby Frodingham	42	3	4	35	50	164	13

Grimsby Borough and Selby Town each had 3 points deducted.
Dinnington Town and Appleby Frodingham both moved to the Central Midlands League. AFC Mansfield joined from the Central Midlands League and Penistone Church joined from the Sheffield & Hallamshire County Senior League.

2013-14

Premier Division

Brighouse Town	44	32	5	7	138	50	101
Barton Town Old Boys	44	29	6	9	124	52	93
Tadcaster Albion	44	29	10	5	116	48	93
Worksop Parramore	44	29	5	10	105	53	92
Basford United	44	26	6	12	97	57	84
Albion Sports	44	25	5	14	109	77	80
Pickering Town	44	25	4	15	126	78	79
Heanor Town	44	24	5	15	113	81	77
Retford United	44	22	10	12	95	52	76
Athersley Recreation	44	23	7	14	103	73	76
Long Eaton United	44	23	3	18	77	64	72
Bridlington Town	44	21	8	15	100	82	71
Thackley	44	22	4	18	92	83	70
Garforth Town	44	19	7	18	85	70	64
Maltby Main	44	19	3	22	88	87	48
Glasshoughton Welfare	44	14	6	24	59	98	48
Staveley Miners Welfare	44	13	6	25	79	98	44
Armthorpe Welfare	44	11	7	26	59	97	40
Parkgate	44	10	9	25	57	86	39
Liversedge	44	10	6	28	58	115	36
Nostell Miners Welfare	44	6	4	34	64	134	22
Winterton Rangers	**44**	**5**	**6**	**33**	**35**	**139**	**21**
Lincoln Moorlands Railway	**44**	**2**	**2**	**40**	**27**	**214**	**8**

Staveley Miners Welfare had 1 point deducted.
Tadcaster Albion had 4 points deducted.
Maltby Main had 12 points deducted.
Basford United and Long Eaton United both moved to the Midland League and Brighouse Town moved to the Northern Premier League. Worksop Town joined from the Northern Premier League. Worksop Parramore merged with Handsworth of the Sheffield & Hallamshire County Senior League and continued in the Premier Division as Handsworth Parramore.

2014-15

Premier Division

Shaw Lane Aquaforce	40	29	7	4	130	33	94
Worksop Town	40	28	6	6	126	38	90
Tadcaster Albion	40	27	5	8	112	46	86
Cleethorpes Town	40	27	3	10	108	52	84
Barton Town Old Boys	40	24	4	12	94	59	76
Heanor Town	40	23	5	12	92	43	74
Handsworth Parramore	40	22	8	10	90	45	74
Bridlington Town	40	20	11	9	80	54	71
Staveley Miners Welfare	40	20	6	14	68	57	66
Albion Sports	40	19	2	19	93	69	59
Pickering Town	40	17	8	15	79	82	59
Thackley	40	14	7	19	61	80	49
Athersley Recreation	40	13	8	19	52	68	47
Garforth Town	40	11	11	18	59	68	44
Nostell Miners Welfare	40	11	5	24	60	90	38
Parkgate	40	10	8	22	47	80	38
Armthorpe Welfare	40	10	7	23	54	110	37
Liversedge	40	9	7	24	46	93	34
Maltby Main	40	11	3	26	65	119	33
Retford United	40	5	6	29	37	137	21
Glasshoughton Welfare	**40**	**5**	**3**	**32**	**30**	**160**	**18**

Maltby Main had 3 points deducted.
Shaw Lane Aquaforce moved to the Northern Premier League and Heanor Town moved to the Midland League. Brigg Town and Rainworth Miners Welfare both joined from the Northern Premier League.

Northern Counties (East) League 2015-2017

Division One

Clipstone	42	30	3	9	89	34	93
Pontefract Collieries	42	29	4	9	113	43	91
Hemsworth Miners Welfare	42	26	10	6	104	56	88
Shirebrook Town	42	26	6	10	111	54	84
AFC Emley	42	26	6	10	100	46	84
Louth Town	42	26	5	11	113	67	83
AFC Mansfield	42	25	7	10	110	55	82
Bottesford Town	42	22	10	10	78	47	76
Penistone Church	42	20	7	15	79	68	67
Yorkshire Amateurs	42	20	6	16	86	80	66
Selby Town	42	17	10	15	73	74	61
Knaresborough Town	42	16	7	19	72	65	55
Eccleshill United	42	16	5	21	76	67	53
Hallam	42	16	4	22	81	88	52
Rossington Main	42	12	9	21	75	80	45
Worsbrough Bridge Athletic	42	11	11	20	60	84	44
Hall Road Rangers	42	12	7	23	54	97	43
Winterton Rangers	42	9	9	24	48	96	36
Dronfield Town	42	9	8	25	58	96	35
Teversal	42	8	7	27	55	117	31
Lincoln Moorlands Railway	42	7	3	32	61	174	24
Grimsby Borough	42	4	6	32	53	161	18

Louth Town left the league and ceased activity for a season before joining the Lincolnshire League in 2016. Hull United joined from the Humber Premier League and Westella V.I.P. joined from the Central Midlands League.

Division One

Hemsworth Miners Welfare	40	31	5	4	128	49	98
AFC Mansfield	40	26	8	6	98	40	86
Bottesford Town	40	26	4	10	93	49	82
AFC Emley	40	22	11	7	132	50	77
Penistone Church	40	21	12	7	89	49	75
Hallam	40	20	12	8	87	43	72
Shirebrook Town	40	20	9	11	83	53	69
Knaresborough Town	40	19	7	14	82	60	64
Hull United	40	23	7	10	78	47	58
Selby Town	40	16	9	15	73	73	57
Yorkshire Amateurs	40	17	5	18	90	101	56
Westella V.I.P.	40	16	5	19	90	83	53
Eccleshill United	40	13	9	18	86	90	48
Teversal	40	11	12	17	62	90	45
Dronfield Town	40	12	7	21	67	88	43
Glasshoughton Welfare	40	10	7	23	62	101	37
Hall Road Rangers	40	7	11	22	60	106	32
Winterton Rangers	40	8	8	24	58	116	32
Grimsby Borough	40	8	8	24	64	132	32
Rossington Main	40	6	8	26	45	105	26
Worsbrough Bridge Athletic	40	3	6	31	32	134	15

Hull United had 18 points deducted.
Lincoln Moorlands Railway resigned near to the end of the season and their record was deleted: 40 3 1 36 48 173 10
They joined the Lincolnshire League in 2016-17.
Hull United moved to the Humber Premier League. Campion joined from the West Riding County Amateur League and Ollerton Town joined from the Central Midlands League.

2015-16

Premier Division

Tadcaster Albion	42	31	5	6	119	50	98
Handsworth Parramore	42	29	7	6	113	53	94
Cleethorpes Town	42	26	6	10	105	46	84
Worksop Town	42	26	5	11	118	60	83
Bridlington Town	42	25	4	13	83	54	79
Pickering Town	42	24	5	13	94	69	77
Maltby Main	42	20	8	14	85	77	68
Staveley Miners Welfare	42	20	6	16	86	72	66
Rainworth Miners Welfare	42	19	6	17	98	81	63
Barton Town Old Boys	42	18	8	16	75	60	62
Albion Sports	42	17	8	17	80	77	59
Thackley	42	17	8	17	80	84	59
Clipstone	42	15	10	17	85	70	55
Liversedge	42	13	9	20	61	93	48
Retford United	42	12	9	21	66	96	45
Garforth Town	42	12	7	23	64	89	43
Parkgate	42	12	6	24	55	90	42
Athersley Recreation	42	12	6	24	52	93	42
Armthorpe Welfare	42	10	10	22	55	92	40
Pontefract Collieries	**42**	**11**	**6**	**25**	**60**	**110**	**39**
Brigg Town	**42**	**10**	**7**	**25**	**49**	**103**	**37**
Nostell Miners Welfare	**42**	**6**	**8**	**28**	**38**	**102**	**26**

Tadcaster Albion moved to the Northern Premier League.
Harrogate Railway Athletic joined from the Northern Premier League.

2016-17

Premier Division

Cleethorpes Town	42	35	3	4	144	45	108
Pickering Town	42	30	7	5	111	39	97
Bridlington Town	42	28	4	10	112	59	88
Handsworth Parramore	42	26	5	11	127	52	83
Thackley	42	23	9	10	81	46	78
Staveley Miners Welfare	42	20	9	13	96	60	69
AFC Mansfield	42	20	6	16	79	55	66
Albion Sports	42	20	6	16	100	99	66
Hemsworth Miners Welfare	42	19	8	15	92	80	65
Athersley Recreation	42	17	11	14	76	84	62
Liversedge	42	17	8	17	99	73	59
Bottesford Town	42	17	5	20	86	87	56
Worksop Town	42	16	7	19	77	83	55
Maltby Main	42	14	12	16	76	92	54
Garforth Town	42	16	5	21	68	87	53
Clipstone	42	13	10	19	61	83	49
Parkgate	42	11	8	23	56	86	41
Rainworth Miners Welfare	42	11	5	26	71	107	38
Harrogate Railway Athletic	42	11	5	26	60	130	38
Barton Town Old Boys	42	9	7	26	57	132	34
Armthorpe Welfare	**42**	**6**	**6**	**30**	**47**	**115**	**24**
Retford United	**42**	**7**	**6**	**29**	**50**	**132**	**24**

Retford United had 3 points deducted.
Cleethorpes Town moved to the Northern Premier League.
Barton Town Old Boys changed their name to Barton Town.

Promotion Play-offs – Semi-finals

AFC Emley vs Penistone Church	1-3
Grimsby Borough vs Hallam	3-2

Promotion Play-off Final

Grimsby Borough vs Penistone Church	2-4

(Played at Grimsby Borough on 29th April 2017)

Division One

Hall Road Rangers	42	30	6	6	107	45	96
Pontefract Collieries	42	30	5	7	123	48	95
AFC Emley	42	30	5	7	120	48	95
Grimsby Borough	42	27	8	7	102	56	89
Hallam	42	25	7	10	107	48	82
Penistone Church	42	24	10	8	89	51	82
Knaresborough Town	42	19	13	10	80	61	70
Campion	42	20	8	14	98	70	68
Eccleshill United	42	20	6	16	95	80	66
Selby Town	42	16	13	13	61	63	61
Glasshoughton Welfare	42	17	8	17	82	73	59
Winterton Rangers	42	18	5	19	77	69	59
Yorkshire Amateurs	42	15	8	19	80	84	53
Brigg Town	42	15	4	23	60	102	49
Rossington Main	42	12	9	21	57	74	45
Teversal	42	13	6	23	59	86	45
Ollerton Town	42	12	7	23	57	86	43
Shirebrook Town	42	11	6	25	48	95	39
Dronfield Town	42	10	5	27	54	98	35
Worsbrough Bridge Athletic	42	10	5	27	38	113	35
Westella V.I.P.	42	7	6	29	45	104	27
Nostell Miners Welfare	42	3	6	33	47	132	15

Teversal moved to the East Midlands Counties League and Westella V.I.P. moved to the Humber Premier League, changing their name to Westella & Willerby. Swallownest joined from the Sheffield & Hallamshire County Senior League, East Yorkshire Carnegie joined from the Humber Premier League and F.C. Bolsover joined from the Central Midlands League.

Division One

Knaresborough Town	42	31	7	4	91	30	100
Yorkshire Amateurs	42	27	7	8	132	55	88
Grimsby Borough	42	26	7	9	113	56	85
Eccleshill United	42	26	7	9	109	61	85
Shirebrook Town	42	25	6	11	91	60	81
Glasshoughton Welfare	42	23	8	11	85	54	77
Selby Town	42	23	6	13	105	71	75
Hallam	42	21	10	11	100	58	73
Campion	42	22	7	13	95	65	73
Winterton Rangers	42	17	10	15	66	64	61
Swallownest	42	17	7	18	65	76	58
AFC Emley	42	17	6	19	73	78	57
Rossington Main	42	14	11	17	71	85	53
Dronfield Town	42	16	4	22	62	75	52
Ollerton Town	42	13	8	21	66	90	47
Armthorpe Welfare	42	13	7	22	72	97	46
Nostell Miners Welfare	42	12	4	26	61	97	40
East Yorkshire Carnegie	42	10	4	28	64	98	34
Worsbrough Bridge Athletic	42	7	12	23	51	99	33
F.C. Bolsover	42	11	3	28	48	124	30
Brigg Town	42	6	11	25	51	105	29
Retford United	42	6	6	30	42	115	24

F.C. Bolsover had 6 points deducted.
Brigg Town moved to the Lincolnshire League and Retford United moved to the Central Midlands League. Harworth Colliery joined from the Central Midlands League and Skegness Town joined from the Lincolnshire League.

2017-18

Premier Division

Pontefract Collieries	42	33	3	6	134	38	102
Pickering Town	42	29	9	4	127	52	96
AFC Mansfield	42	29	9	4	110	43	96
Handsworth Parramore	42	27	4	11	99	56	85
Maltby Main	42	22	9	11	88	57	75
Hemsworth Miners Welfare	42	22	6	14	104	77	72
Penistone Church	42	20	12	10	93	66	72
Bottesford Town	42	22	3	17	93	84	69
Bridlington Town	42	18	10	14	81	60	64
Rainworth Miners Welfare	42	18	9	15	71	76	63
Liversedge	42	15	12	15	96	93	57
Barton Town	42	17	5	20	64	76	55
Garforth Town	42	14	10	18	72	101	52
Albion Sports	42	14	6	22	76	84	48
Thackley	42	13	8	21	76	85	47
Staveley Miners Welfare	42	13	8	21	52	83	47
Athersley Recreation	42	13	7	22	66	89	46
Worksop Town	42	12	10	20	68	94	46
Hall Road Rangers	42	16	7	19	83	84	43
Harrogate Railway Athletic	42	9	4	29	70	132	31
Parkgate	42	7	5	30	58	116	26
Clipstone	42	0	2	40	37	172	2

Barton Town had 1 point deducted.
Hall Road Rangers had 12 points deducted.
Pontefract Collieries, Pickering Town and AFC Mansfield all moved to the Northern Premier League while Rainworth Miners Welfare and Clipstone both moved to the East Midlands Counties League. Goole joined from the Northern Premier League.

Promotion Play-offs – Semi-finals

Eccleshill United vs Shirebrook Town	4-2
Grimsby Borough vs Glasshoughton Welfare	3-0

Promotion Play-offs – Final

Grimsby Borough vs Eccleshill United	2-3

(Played at Grimsby Borough on 12th May 2018)

2018-19

Premier Division

Worksop Town	38	28	6	4	95	40	90
Penistone Church	38	26	4	8	112	49	82
Bridlington Town	38	24	5	9	98	51	77
Hemsworth Miners Welfare	38	24	3	11	89	51	75
Yorkshire Amateurs	38	23	4	11	83	62	73
Maltby Main	38	19	11	8	66	37	68
Staveley Miners Welfare	38	19	10	9	77	45	67
Handsworth Parramore	38	19	6	13	70	67	63
Knaresborough Town	38	18	6	14	70	57	60
Eccleshill United	38	15	8	15	69	75	53
Barton Town	38	15	7	16	56	53	52
Bottesford Town	38	14	10	14	61	65	52
Liversedge	38	15	3	20	56	80	48
Garforth Town	38	12	6	20	52	60	42
Thackley	38	10	10	18	66	76	40
Albion Sports	38	12	4	22	64	86	40
Athersley Recreation	38	9	4	25	43	88	31
Goole	38	7	2	29	41	102	23
Harrogate Railway Athletic	**38**	**4**	**10**	**24**	**44**	**103**	**22**
Hall Road Rangers	**38**	**5**	**5**	**28**	**50**	**115**	**20**

Worksop Town moved to the Northern Premier League. AFC Mansfield joined from the Northern Premier League and Silsden joined from the North-West Counties League.
Handsworth Parramore changed their name to Handsworth.

Northern Counties (East) League 2019-2021

Division One

	P	W	D	L	F	A	Pts
Grimsby Borough	38	26	6	6	108	44	84
Campion	38	25	7	6	99	50	82
Hallam	38	22	10	6	84	39	76
Winterton Rangers	38	23	6	9	76	38	75
Nostell Miners Welfare	38	22	8	8	78	39	74
Dronfield Town	38	20	7	11	64	47	67
Worsbrough Bridge Athletic	38	19	5	14	76	77	62
Parkgate	38	19	4	15	64	56	61
Selby Town	38	18	3	17	82	76	57
Swallownest	38	15	7	16	57	62	52
Glasshoughton Welfare	38	15	5	18	47	62	50
AFC Emley	38	14	6	18	71	68	48
East Yorkshire Carnegie	38	13	5	20	73	79	44
Rossington Main	38	12	6	20	49	77	42
Skegness Town	38	12	4	22	43	72	40
Ollerton Town	38	10	7	21	48	73	37
Armthorpe Welfare	38	11	4	23	58	89	37
Shirebrook Town	38	9	7	22	55	83	34
F.C. Bolsover	38	9	4	25	49	110	31
Harworth Colliery	38	8	5	25	47	87	29

Harworth Colliery moved to the Central Midlands League, Shirebrook Town moved to the East Midlands Counties League and F.C. Bolsover disbanded. AFC Emley changed their name to Emley and moved to the North-West Counties League. Brigg Town joined from the Lincolnshire League, Retford joined from the Central Midlands League and North Ferriby joined as a newly formed replacement club for North Ferriby United of the Northern Premier League who had disbanded in March 2019.
East Yorkshire Carnegie changed their name to East Hull.

Division One

	P	W	D	L	F	A	Pts
Winterton Rangers	27	19	2	6	48	24	59
Skegness Town	26	18	4	4	58	19	58
Selby Town	25	18	2	5	86	40	56
North Ferriby	26	15	7	4	45	17	52
Campion	24	15	3	6	67	37	48
Retford	28	12	8	8	52	46	44
Glasshoughton Welfare	26	14	1	11	58	47	43
Hallam	23	10	7	6	41	30	37
Swallownest	25	11	4	10	44	43	37
Nostell Miners Welfare	25	11	2	12	55	42	35
Dronfield Town	25	10	5	10	50	43	35
Armthorpe Welfare	28	10	4	14	39	47	34
Parkgate	25	10	4	11	35	51	34
Rossington Main	26	8	7	11	40	46	31
Brigg Town	30	8	6	16	44	63	30
Ollerton Town	26	7	7	12	41	39	28
Hall Road Rangers	24	8	4	12	44	52	28
Worsbrough Bridge Athletic	24	6	5	13	40	50	23
Harrogate Railway Athletic	25	5	1	19	33	68	16
East Hull	26	0	1	25	16	132	1

Ollerton Town moved to the East Midlands Counties League.
Emley joined from the North-West Counties League.

2019-20

The season was terminated on 26th March 2020 due to the effects of the Covid-19 pandemic. The table shown is as it stood on that date.

Premier Division

	P	W	D	L	F	A	Pts
Staveley Miners Welfare	26	17	4	5	59	26	55
Liversedge	24	16	5	3	80	42	53
Yorkshire Amateurs	26	16	5	5	60	27	53
Penistone Church	28	15	8	5	58	32	53
Bridlington Town	25	14	6	5	52	33	48
Hemsworth Miners Welfare	28	13	6	9	53	42	45
Maltby Main	28	13	4	11	44	46	43
Garforth Town	28	12	5	11	54	58	41
Grimsby Borough	26	13	1	12	59	53	40
Silsden	28	10	7	11	46	51	37
Barton Town	27	11	3	13	51	51	36
Eccleshill United	25	11	2	12	47	45	35
Knaresborough Town	25	9	5	11	42	39	32
Thackley	26	9	5	12	48	53	32
Handsworth	23	8	6	9	39	55	30
AFC Mansfield	26	7	7	12	33	43	28
Goole	28	7	4	17	40	61	25
Bottesford Town	27	7	2	18	43	71	23
Albion Sports	25	6	4	15	39	55	22
Athersley Recreation	27	3	3	21	29	93	12

There were no changes to membership of the Premier Division at the end of the 2019-20 season.

2020-21

The season was terminated on 2nd November 2020 due to the continuing Covid-19 pandemic. The table shown is as it stood on that date.

Premier Division

	P	W	D	L	F	A	Pts
Yorkshire Amateurs	11	9	2	0	36	9	29
Bridlington Town	9	7	0	2	39	15	21
Liversedge	7	7	0	0	25	3	21
Garforth Town	9	7	0	2	22	12	21
Maltby Main	10	5	3	2	23	17	18
AFC Mansfield	9	5	2	2	26	9	17
Handsworth	12	5	2	5	28	31	17
Grimsby Borough	10	5	1	4	28	22	16
Barton Town	11	4	2	5	16	25	14
Albion Sports	9	4	1	4	14	14	13
Eccleshill United	11	4	1	6	14	18	13
Penistone Church	7	4	0	3	17	11	12
Hemsworth Miners Welfare	7	4	0	3	8	5	12
Goole	11	3	2	6	13	34	11
Silsden	10	3	1	6	16	22	10
Thackley	11	2	2	7	13	24	8
Staveley Miners Welfare	6	2	1	3	9	10	7
Knaresborough Town	9	2	1	6	9	18	7
Bottesford Town	11	1	1	9	15	39	4
Athersley Recreation	10	1	0	9	9	42	3

Bridlington Town, Liversedge and Yorkshire Amateurs all moved to the Northern Premier League. Sherwood Colliery joined from the East Midlands Counties League.

Division One

Emley	10	8	2	0	27	9	26
Campion	11	8	0	3	36	19	24
Winterton Rangers	9	7	1	1	34	11	22
North Ferriby	10	7	1	2	20	9	22
Retford	13	6	3	4	29	23	21
Brigg Town	11	6	2	3	32	19	20
Rossington Main	12	5	3	4	29	24	18
Skegness Town	8	5	1	2	17	12	16
Parkgate	10	5	1	4	26	28	16
Hall Road Rangers	10	4	2	4	17	20	14
Hallam	8	4	1	3	21	17	13
Nostell Miners Welfare	12	4	0	8	20	28	12
Glasshoughton Welfare	12	3	2	7	22	21	11
Armthorpe Welfare	12	3	2	7	21	35	11
Swallownest	8	3	1	4	16	17	10
Dronfield Town	11	3	1	7	17	28	10
Harrogate Railway Athletic	8	2	3	3	16	25	9
East Hull	10	2	1	7	10	33	7
Worsbrough Bridge Athletic	13	1	3	9	14	35	6
Selby Town	6	1	0	5	9	20	3

Campion moved to the North-West Counties League and Skegness Town moved to the United Counties League. Clipstone, Ollerton Town, Rainworth Miners Welfare, Shirebrook Town and Teversal all joined from the East Midlands Counties League.

East Hull changed their name to F.C. Humber United.

SHEFFIELD & HALLAMSHIRE COUNTY SENIOR LEAGUE 1983-2021

In 1960, the Sheffield Association League changed its name to become the Sheffield & Hallamshire County Senior League. It merged with the Hatchard League in 1983 to form the present competition but continued with the same title.

(Promoted clubs are shown in bold type, relegated clubs in ***bold italics***)

1983-84
Premier Division

Windsor	26	13	9	4	64	36	35
Swinton Athletic	26	13	8	5	59	31	34
Rotherham Club	26	15	2	9	53	43	32
Oughtbridge War Memorial S.C.	26	10	11	5	48	33	31
Ecclesfield Red Rose	26	9	13	4	41	30	31
B.S.C. Parkgate Reserves	26	11	8	7	52	37	30
Mexborough Main Street	26	10	9	7	45	33	29
Maltby Miners Welfare Reserves	26	12	4	10	53	59	28
Stocksbridge Works Reserves	26	11	5	10	46	49	27
Centralians	26	7	7	12	53	51	21
Frecheville Community Assoc. Res	26	9	3	14	38	41	21
Treeton Welfare	26	8	5	13	43	59	21
Old Edwardians	26	6	8	12	35	42	20
Penistone Church	26	0	4	22	26	112	4

Stocksbridge Works Reserves left the league.

Division One

Crookes W.M.C.	26	24	0	2	109	20	48
Ash House (G C)	26	20	3	3	65	28	43
Pilkington Recreation Reserves	26	14	3	9	60	53	31
Jubilee Sports	26	12	6	8	62	61	30
East Dene Social Club	26	12	4	10	67	42	28
Davy McKee Sports & Social Club	26	12	4	10	46	47	28
Hallam Reserves	26	12	3	11	58	48	27
Sheffield Reserves	26	10	6	10	45	48	26
Forgemasters Sports & Social Club	26	9	5	12	39	69	23
Oughtbridge W.M.S.C. Reserves	26	6	8	12	36	58	20
Phoenix	26	5	8	13	35	47	18
Norton Woodseats Reserves	26	5	8	13	40	58	18
Kiveton Park Reserves	26	5	6	15	38	69	16
Worsbrough Bridge M.W. Res.	26	2	4	20	37	89	8

Jubilee Sports left the league. Norton Woodseats Reserves changed their name to Dronfield United Reserves.

Division Two

Champions: Woodsetts Welfare (promoted)
Also promoted: Arthur Lee S.C. and Firparnians

The Division Two table has not been found for the 1983-84 season.

Division Three

Champions: Stella

The Division Three table has not been found for the 1983-84 season.

1984-85
Premier Division

Ecclesfield Red Rose	26	19	4	3	67	23	42
Ash House (G C)	26	16	5	5	52	27	37
B.S.C. Parkgate Reserves	26	16	3	7	61	34	35
Oughtbridge War Memorial S.C.	26	13	5	8	56	42	31
Windsor	26	14	3	9	47	33	31
Mexborough Main Street	26	11	8	7	54	44	30
Crookes W.M.C.	26	12	5	9	59	36	29
Swinton Athletic	26	10	6	10	40	39	26
Frecheville Community Assoc. Res.	26	9	5	12	43	60	23
Centralians	26	10	2	14	32	38	22
Treeton Welfare	26	6	9	11	38	58	21
Maltby Miners Welfare Reserves	26	8	3	15	42	55	19
Rotherham Club	26	3	5	18	25	73	11
Pilkington Recreation Reserves	26	3	1	22	26	80	7

Crookes W.M.C. changed their name to Crookes.

Division One

Firparnians	26	16	5	5	73	42	37
Davy McKee Sports & Social Club	26	15	6	5	66	41	36
Arthur Lee S.C.	26	14	7	5	45	28	35
Hallam Reserves	26	12	6	8	62	48	30
Woodsetts Welfare	26	11	8	7	48	39	30
Old Edwardians	26	11	7	8	41	39	29
Sheffield Reserves	26	11	5	10	53	56	27
Kiveton Park Reserves	26	9	5	12	33	49	23
Dronfield United Reserves	26	8	6	12	49	51	22
East Dene Social Club	26	9	4	13	46	50	22
Forgemasters Sports & Social Club	26	7	5	14	43	59	19
Phoenix	26	6	7	13	38	58	19
Penistone Church	26	7	4	15	37	51	18
Oughtbridge W.M.S.C. Reserves	26	5	7	14	31	54	17

Sheffield & Hallamshire County Senior League 1985-1988

Division Two

Champions: Brunsmeer Athletic (promoted).
Also promoted: Bankers and Oxley Park

The Division Two table has not been found for the 1984-85 season.

Division Three

Champions: Staveley Works Reserves

The Division Three table has not been found for the 1984-85 season.

1985-86

Premier Division

B.S.C. Parkgate Reserves	26	17	7	2	69	28	41
Windsor	26	18	3	5	59	37	39
Crookes	26	15	6	5	54	29	36
Mexborough Main Street	26	12	4	10	47	38	28
Ash House (G C)	26	10	8	8	35	28	28
Swinton Athletic	26	10	7	9	42	40	27
Centralians	26	10	6	10	43	41	26
Treeton Welfare	26	10	6	10	38	42	26
Firparnians	26	8	6	12	42	58	22
Frecheville Community Assoc. Res.	26	7	6	13	37	55	20
Arthur Lee S.C.	26	6	7	13	41	63	19
Davy McKee Sports & Social Club	26	4	10	12	41	49	18
Ecclesfield Red Rose	*26*	*7*	*4*	*15*	*46*	*55*	*18*
Oughtibridge War Memorial S.C.	*26*	*4*	*8*	*14*	*39*	*70*	*16*

Crookes moved to the Central Midlands League.
Firparnians changed their name to Metalloy and Centralians changed their name to Sheffield Centralians.

Division One

Oxley Park	**26**	**18**	**5**	**3**	**72**	**26**	**41**
Sheffield Reserves	**26**	**18**	**5**	**3**	**59**	**30**	**41**
Old Edwardians	**26**	**17**	**5**	**4**	**50**	**14**	**39**
Brunsmeer Athletic	26	17	5	4	73	38	39
Dronfield United Reserves	26	13	3	10	52	42	29
Pilkington Recreation Reserves	26	11	6	9	40	36	28
Bankers	26	11	3	12	56	48	25
Hallam Reserves	26	9	5	12	44	44	23
Maltby Miners Welfare Reserves	26	8	7	11	49	59	23
Woodsetts Welfare	26	8	3	15	47	43	19
East Dene Social Club	26	7	4	15	35	70	18
Kiveton Park Reserves	26	8	1	17	47	59	17
Forgemasters Sports & Social Club	*26*	*6*	*3*	*17*	*35*	*80*	*15*
Rotherham Club	26	2	3	21	26	96	7

Rotherham Club left the league. Oxley Park merged with Stocksbridge Works of the Northern Counties East League to form Stocksbridge Park Steels and were promoted to the Premier Division as Stocksbridge Park Steels Reserves. Bankers changed their name to Sheffield Bankers.

Division Two

Champions: Worsbrough Bridge Miners Welfare Reserves.
Also promoted: Aurora United and Staveley Works Reserves

The Division Two table has not been found for the 1985-86 season.

Division Three

Champions: Bradley

The Division Three table has not been found for the 1985-86 season.

1986-87

Premier Division

Mexborough Main Street	26	18	6	2	74	25	42
Ash House (G C)	26	18	4	4	61	27	40
Windsor	26	16	4	6	74	37	36
B.S.C. Parkgate Reserves	26	16	4	6	59	27	36
Davy McKee Sports & Social Club	26	11	6	9	61	49	28
Old Edwardians	26	11	5	10	40	42	27
Treeton Welfare	26	9	8	9	46	52	26
Frecheville Community Assoc. Res.	26	9	7	10	43	45	25
Arthur Lee S.C.	26	9	6	11	40	53	24
Swinton Athletic	26	8	6	12	33	50	22
Metalloy	26	8	4	14	44	48	20
Sheffield Centralians	*26*	*6*	*7*	*13*	*32*	*58*	*19*
Sheffield Reserves	*26*	*5*	*2*	*19*	*29*	*77*	*12*
Stocksbridge Park Steels Reserves	*26*	*1*	*5*	*20*	*25*	*71*	*7*

Arthur Lee S.C. left the league.

Division One

Maltby Miners Welfare Reserves	**26**	**18**	**7**	**1**	**61**	**23**	**43**
Aurora United	**26**	**17**	**4**	**5**	**79**	**37**	**38**
Oughtibridge War Memorial S.C.	**26**	**17**	**4**	**5**	**62**	**36**	**38**
Hallam Reserves	26	14	4	8	61	38	32
Ecclesfield Red Rose	26	11	6	9	51	48	28
Brunsmeer Athletic	26	9	10	7	43	42	28
Staveley Works Reserves	26	11	3	12	50	47	25
Sheffield Bankers	26	11	3	12	42	46	25
Woodsetts Welfare	26	7	8	11	45	51	22
Worsbrough Bridge M.W. Res.	26	9	2	15	49	60	20
Pilkington Recreation Reserves	26	7	6	13	38	54	20
East Dene Social Club	26	4	10	12	41	64	18
Kiveton Park Reserves	*26*	*7*	*3*	*16*	*32*	*62*	*17*
Dronfield United Reserves	*26*	*3*	*4*	*19*	*28*	*74*	*10*

East Dene Social Club left the league.

Division Two

Champions: Parramore Sports
Also promoted: Sheffield Gas, Stella

The Division Two table has not been found for the 1986-87 season.

Division Three

Champions: Denaby & Cadeby Miners Welfare (promoted)

The Division Three table has not been found for the 1986-87 season.

1987-88

Premier Division

Ash House (G C)	24	16	5	3	70	27	37
Davy McKee Sports & Social Club	24	13	5	6	52	27	31
Windsor	24	13	4	7	35	31	30
Mexborough Main Street	24	12	5	7	43	32	29
Swinton Athletic	24	11	5	8	44	37	27
Maltby Miners Welfare Reserves	24	10	6	8	42	42	26
Metalloy	24	11	4	9	45	48	26
Aurora United	24	8	6	10	44	49	22
B.S.C. Parkgate Reserves	24	7	8	9	36	45	22
Oughtibridge War Memorial S.C.	24	8	5	11	42	50	21
Frecheville Community Assoc. Res.	24	5	7	12	29	45	17
Treeton Welfare	*24*	*4*	*7*	*13*	*38*	*53*	*15*
Old Edwardians	*24*	*3*	*3*	*18*	*22*	*56*	*9*

Metalloy changed their name to East Pennine.

Division One

	P	W	D	L	F	A	Pts
Ecclesfield Red Rose	26	16	6	4	52	20	38
Worsbrough Bridge M.W. Res.	26	16	5	5	40	28	37
Hallam Reserves	26	15	5	6	65	29	35
Woodsetts Welfare	26	15	4	7	62	47	34
Stella	26	10	7	9	62	50	27
Brunsmeer Athletic	26	10	5	11	41	39	25
Parramore Sports	26	11	3	12	35	40	25
Sheffield Centralians	26	11	2	13	38	40	24
Sheffield Reserves	26	9	4	13	35	53	22
Stocksbridge Park Steels Reserves	26	8	5	13	39	42	21
Pilkington Recreation Reserves	26	7	7	12	40	53	21
Staveley Works Reserves	26	8	5	13	37	50	21
Sheffield Gas	*26*	*8*	*3*	*15*	*35*	*64*	*19*
Sheffield Bankers	*26*	*5*	*5*	*16*	*35*	*61*	*15*

Stella left the league.

Division Two

Champions: Denaby & Cadeby Miners Welfare
Runners-up: Bethesda
Also promoted: Elsecar Main and Woodhouse Stag ABM.

The Division Two table has not been found for the 1987-88 season.

Division Three

Champions: Caribbean Sports
Runners-up: Goldthorpe Colliery (also promoted)

The Division Three table has not been found for the 1987-88 season.

1988-89
Premier Division

	P	W	D	L	F	A	Pts
Ash House (G C)	26	18	4	4	74	29	40
Aurora United	26	17	4	5	69	35	38
Mexborough Main Street	26	16	4	6	66	35	36
Davy McKee Sports & Social Club	26	12	9	5	57	35	33
Ecclesfield Red Rose	26	14	4	8	55	30	32
Windsor	26	11	6	9	44	38	28
Swinton Athletic	26	10	5	11	44	45	25
Hallam Reserves	26	10	5	11	43	58	25
Oughtibridge War Memorial S.C.	26	10	4	12	42	41	24
Frecheville Community Assoc. Res.	26	8	6	12	58	54	22
Worsbrough Bridge M.W. Res.	26	9	3	14	37	57	21
East Pennine	*26*	*7*	*4*	*15*	*32*	*59*	*18*
B.S.C. Parkgate Reserves	*26*	*6*	*4*	*16*	*32*	*67*	*16*
Maltby Miners Welfare Reserves	*26*	*3*	*0*	*23*	*29*	*99*	*6*

Division One

	P	W	D	L	F	A	Pts
Denaby & Cadeby Miners Welfare	26	19	2	5	62	32	40
Woodhouse Stag ABM	26	14	6	6	53	39	34
Parramore Sports	26	13	6	7	52	33	32
Woodsetts Welfare	26	12	6	8	47	42	30
Staveley Works Reserves	26	11	8	7	51	48	30
Pilkington Recreation Reserves	26	10	8	8	47	29	28
Sheffield Reserves	26	10	7	9	50	43	27
Bethesda	26	10	6	10	42	39	26
Brunsmeer Athletic	26	10	1	15	41	51	21
Old Edwardians	26	9	3	14	41	59	21
Elsecar Main	26	7	6	13	35	50	20
Treeton Welfare	26	9	2	15	49	69	20
Sheffield Centralians	*26*	*7*	*5*	*14*	*40*	*54*	*19*
Stocksbridge Park Steels Reserves	*26*	*5*	*6*	*15*	*29*	*51*	*16*

Staveley Works disbanded.

Division Two

Champions: Goldthorpe Colliery
Runners-up: Caribbean Sports (also promoted)
Third: Dronfield United Reserves (also promoted)

The Division Two table has not been found for the 1988-89 season.

Division Three

Champions: Wath St. James
Runners-up: St. Patrick's (also promoted)
Third: Wath Saracens Athletic (also promoted)

The Division Three table has not been found for the 1988-89 season.

1989-90
Premier Division

	P	W	D	L	F	A	Pts
Ash House (G C)	26	19	4	3	70	22	42
Aurora United	26	15	6	5	57	29	36
Mexborough Main Street	26	11	8	7	53	42	30
Denaby & Cadeby Miners Welfare	26	12	6	8	50	40	30
Hallam Reserves	26	12	5	9	51	38	29
Oughtibridge War Memorial S.C.	26	12	3	11	49	40	27
Parramore Sports	26	11	5	10	38	40	27
Windsor	26	12	3	11	36	43	27
Swinton Athletic	26	10	6	10	46	45	26
Ecclesfield Red Rose	26	10	6	10	39	44	26
Woodhouse Stag ABM	26	9	6	11	42	43	24
Frecheville Community Ass. Res.	*26*	*7*	*4*	*15*	*36*	*61*	*18*
Davy McKee Sports & Social Club	*26*	*5*	*4*	*17*	*30*	*53*	*14*
Worsbrough Bridge M.W. Res.	*26*	*3*	*2*	*21*	*18*	*75*	*8*

Division One

	P	W	D	L	F	A	Pts
Caribbean Sports	**26**	**17**	**7**	**2**	**60**	**21**	**41**
East Pennine	**26**	**18**	**2**	**6**	**73**	**27**	**38**
Goldthorpe Colliery	**26**	**14**	**7**	**5**	**55**	**37**	**35**
Sheffield Reserves	26	13	7	6	51	31	33
B.S.C. Parkgate Reserves	26	14	4	8	62	44	32
Brunsmeer Athletic	26	12	4	10	52	47	28
Treeton Welfare	26	10	6	10	47	46	26
Maltby Miners Welfare Reserves	26	11	3	12	47	50	25
Dronfield United Reserves	26	9	3	14	45	56	21
Woodsetts Welfare	26	7	7	12	49	73	21
Elsecar Main	26	7	5	14	36	47	19
Bethesda	26	5	6	15	41	62	16
Old Edwardians	*26*	*6*	*3*	*17*	*34*	*67*	*15*
Pilkington Recreation Reserves	*26*	*5*	*4*	*17*	*21*	*65*	*14*

Bethesda and Maltby Miners Welfare Reserves both left the league. Frecheville Community Association joined from the Northern Counties East League, replacing their reserves, who had been relegated from the Premier Division. B.S.C. Parkgate Reserves changed their name to R.E.S. Parkgate Reserves.

Division Two

Champions: Wath St. James (promoted)
Runners-up: Phoenix (promoted)
Third: Wath Saracens Athletic (promoted)

The Division Two table has not been found for the 1989-90 season.

Division Three

Champions: Treble (promoted)
Runners-up: Rawmarsh Star (promoted)
Third: Mexborough Northgate (promoted)

The Division Three table has not been found for the 1989-90 season.

Sheffield & Hallamshire County Senior League 1990-1992

1990-91
Premier Division

Team	P	W	D	L	F	A	Pts
Ash House (G C)	26	19	3	4	62	22	60
Denaby & Cadeby Miners Welfare	26	16	6	4	56	31	54
Parramore Sports	26	13	7	6	54	43	46
Mexborough Main Street	26	12	9	5	55	24	45
East Pennine	26	9	10	7	48	39	37
Goldthorpe Colliery	26	10	6	10	40	32	36
Caribbean Sports	26	10	6	10	41	36	36
Hallam Reserves	26	9	8	9	41	43	35
Oughtibridge War Memorial S.C.	26	7	10	9	35	34	31
Woodhouse Stag ABM	26	10	1	15	41	60	31
Ecclesfield Red Rose	26	7	8	11	41	62	29
Windsor	26	7	6	13	36	48	27
Aurora United	26	8	4	14	37	60	27
Swinton Athletic	*26*	*1*	*4*	*21*	*23*	*76*	*7*

Aurora United had 1 point deducted.
Aurora United and Windsor both left the league.
East Pennine changed their name to White Rose Throstles and Woodhouse Stag ABM changed their name to A.B.M..

Division One

Team	P	W	D	L	F	A	Pts
Wath Saracens Athletic	24	14	6	4	49	27	48
Wath St. James	24	14	6	4	52	31	48
Phoenix	24	13	6	5	44	22	45
R.E.S. Parkgate Reserves	24	13	5	6	52	28	44
Elsecar Main	24	8	8	8	39	41	32
Brunsmeer Athletic	24	7	9	8	41	44	30
Frecheville Community Association	24	7	8	9	30	27	29
Worsbrough Bridge M.W. Res.	24	6	10	8	28	35	28
Woodsetts Welfare	24	9	1	14	42	61	28
Sheffield Reserves	24	6	8	10	35	45	26
Treeton Welfare	24	6	6	12	46	57	24
Davy McKee Sports & Social Club	*24*	*6*	*6*	*12*	*29*	*46*	*24*
Dronfield United Reserves	24	5	5	14	39	62	20

Dronfield United Reserves moved to the Central Midlands League – Reserve Division, changing their name to Norton Woodseats Reserves while Elsecar Main and Sheffield Reserves also both left the league.
Yorkshire Main joined from the Northern Counties East League.

Division Two

Team	P	W	D	L	F	A	Pts
Thurcroft Ivanhoe	**26**	**18**	**3**	**5**	**63**	**37**	**57**
Loxley College	**26**	**15**	**6**	**5**	**46**	**31**	**51**
St. Patrick's	**26**	**16**	**2**	**8**	**70**	**42**	**50**
Stocksbridge Park Steels Reserves	26	13	8	5	60	44	47
Rawmarsh Star	26	11	6	9	51	42	39
Rotherham United "A"	26	10	8	8	53	40	38
Dawlish United	26	11	3	12	49	71	36
Sheffield Centralians	26	10	5	11	48	46	35
Sheffield Bankers	26	9	8	9	45	43	35
Penistone Church	26	10	4	12	47	51	34
Sheffield Oakhouse	26	7	6	13	39	44	27
Old Edwardians	*26*	*7*	*4*	*15*	*39*	*57*	*25*
Oughtibridge W.M.S.C. Reserves	26	6	5	15	41	61	23
Pilkington Recreation Reserves	26	3	4	19	25	67	13

Pilkington Recreation disbanded while Dawlish United, Oughtibridge W.M.S.C. Reserves and Rotherham United "A" also all left the league.

Division Three

Team	P	W	D	L	F	A	Pts
High Green Villa	**22**	**19**	**3**	**0**	**98**	**15**	**60**
British Gas S.C.	**22**	**16**	**3**	**3**	**71**	**22**	**51**
Industry	**22**	**16**	**3**	**3**	**68**	**24**	**51**
Sheffield Post Office	22	15	2	5	70	29	47
Sheffield Gas	22	12	1	9	51	49	37
Tinsley Wire	22	11	2	9	45	43	35
British Steel Tinsley	22	6	4	12	38	43	22
Forgemasters Sports & Social Club	22	6	2	14	39	77	20
Abbeydale	22	5	2	15	27	69	17
Clifton Rovers	22	4	4	14	26	69	16
Penistone Church Reserves	22	3	4	15	28	76	13
Kiveton Park Reserves	22	3	2	17	23	68	11

Forgemasters Sports & Social Club left the league.
Staveley Miners Welfare joined from the Chesterfield & District Amateur League and Throstles Ridgeway also joined.
British Steel Tinsley changed their name to British Steel Stainless.

1991-92
Premier Division

Team	P	W	D	L	F	A	Pts
Phoenix	26	20	3	3	50	18	63
Ash House (G C)	26	17	6	3	67	30	57
Mexborough Main Street	26	13	7	6	63	32	46
Goldthorpe Colliery	26	11	7	8	34	32	40
Oughtibridge War Memorial S.C.	26	10	7	9	46	37	37
A.B.M.	26	11	3	12	39	47	36
Hallam Reserves	26	10	5	11	51	43	35
Denaby & Cadeby Miners Welfare	26	8	11	7	51	43	35
Wath Saracens Athletic	26	9	6	11	44	45	33
Parramore Sports	26	9	4	13	41	56	31
White Rose Throstles	26	8	6	12	41	43	30
Wath St. James	*26*	*7*	*7*	*12*	*32*	*48*	*28*
Ecclesfield Red Rose	*26*	*7*	*3*	*16*	*36*	*53*	*24*
Caribbean Sports	*26*	*3*	*3*	*20*	*18*	*86*	*12*

Division One

Team	P	W	D	L	F	A	Pts
Frecheville Community Assoc.	**20**	**14**	**6**	**0**	**54**	**13**	**48**
Worsbrough Bridge M.W. Res.	**20**	**13**	**5**	**2**	**42**	**23**	**44**
R.E.S. Parkgate Reserves	**20**	**9**	**8**	**3**	**39**	**21**	**35**
Yorkshire Main	20	9	3	8	34	39	30
Treeton Welfare	20	7	5	8	39	38	26
St. Patrick's	20	7	5	8	30	37	26
Thurcroft Ivanhoe	20	6	7	7	30	34	25
Swinton Athletic	20	7	2	11	38	50	23
Brunsmeer Athletic	20	5	7	8	38	38	22
Loxley College	20	2	6	12	28	48	12
Woodsetts Welfare	20	2	4	14	28	59	10

Loxley College and St. Patrick's both left the league.

Division Two

Team	P	W	D	L	F	A	Pts
High Green Villa	**18**	**15**	**1**	**2**	**51**	**23**	**46**
Rawmarsh Star	**18**	**12**	**3**	**3**	**46**	**22**	**39**
Davy McKee Sports & Social Club	18	10	3	5	41	30	33
British Gas S.C.	**18**	**9**	**2**	**7**	**42**	**44**	**29**
Penistone Church	**18**	**7**	**4**	**7**	**44**	**32**	**25**
Industry	**18**	**7**	**1**	**10**	**35**	**42**	**22**
Sheffield Oakhouse	18	5	5	8	32	52	20
Stocksbridge Park Steel Reserves	18	4	4	10	32	39	16
Sheffield Centralians	18	3	4	11	23	44	13
Sheffield Bankers	18	2	5	11	23	41	11

Davy McKee Sports & Social Club left the league.
Rawmarsh Star changed their name and were promoted as Rawmarsh & Ryecroft W.M.C.. Rossington Main Reserves joined.

Division Three

Team	P	W	D	L	F	A	Pts
Staveley Miners Welfare	20	17	2	1	71	15	53
Clifton Rovers	20	13	2	5	54	27	41
Throstles Ridgeway	20	12	4	4	54	24	40
Sheffield Post Office	20	11	1	8	45	33	34
Sheffield Gas	20	10	3	7	48	31	33
Kiveton Park Reserves	20	8	7	5	43	33	31
Tinsley Wire	20	9	5	6	40	30	31
Penistone Church Reserves	20	4	5	11	35	53	17
Old Edwardians	20	4	4	12	33	49	16
Abbeydale	20	1	6	13	21	58	8
British Steel Stainless	20	0	3	17	14	105	2

Abbeydale, British Steel Stainless and Tinsley Wire each had 1 point deducted.
Tinsley Wire left the league.

The remaining clubs moved up into Division Two and Division Three closed down.

1992-93

Premier Division

Frecheville Community Association	26	18	4	4	66	23	58
Ash House (G C)	26	17	3	6	54	23	54
Mexborough Main Street	26	16	5	5	52	32	53
Goldthorpe Colliery	26	16	2	8	68	40	50
White Rose Throstles	26	15	3	8	64	38	48
Parramore Sports	26	10	8	8	36	31	38
Hallam Reserves	26	10	7	9	48	45	37
Phoenix	26	10	5	11	31	46	35
Denaby & Cadeby Miners Welfare	26	9	6	11	57	50	33
Worsbrough Bridge M.W. Res.	26	8	4	14	34	48	28
Wath Saracens Athletic	26	8	3	15	36	51	27
R.E.S. Parkgate Reserves	26	8	3	15	33	64	27
A.B.M.	26	5	5	16	42	73	20
Oughtibridge War Memorial S.C.	**26**	**1**	**4**	**21**	**26**	**83**	**7**

A.B.M. and White Rose Throstles both left the league.

Division One

High Green Villa	**26**	**22**	**3**	**1**	**83**	**13**	**69**
Brunsmeer Athletic	**26**	**18**	**6**	**2**	**59**	**19**	**60**
Treeton Welfare	**26**	**17**	**4**	**5**	**91**	**46**	**55**
Penistone Church	26	16	3	7	90	56	51
British Gas S.C.	26	12	7	7	68	48	42
Thurcroft Ivanhoe	26	11	5	10	67	45	37
Caribbean Sports	26	10	5	11	44	54	35
Yorkshire Main	26	9	4	13	51	74	31
Wath St. James	26	8	6	12	44	60	30
Woodsetts Welfare	26	8	2	16	50	80	26
Rawmarsh & Ryecroft W.M.C.	26	7	4	15	43	55	25
Industry	26	8	1	17	38	83	25
Swinton Athletic	26	4	4	18	29	70	16
Ecclesfield Red Rose	26	3	4	19	25	79	13

British Gas S.C. and Thurcroft Ivanhoe each had 1 point deducted.
Industry and Thurcroft Ivanhoe both left the league.
Wombwell Town joined from the Central Midlands League.
Woodsetts Welfare changed their name to Woodsetts Sports.

Division Two

Staveley Miners Welfare	28	23	4	1	106	22	73
Throstles Ridgeway	**28**	**20**	**5**	**3**	**66**	**26**	**65**
Stocksbridge Park Steel Reserves	**28**	**17**	**6**	**5**	**75**	**43**	**57**
Sheffield Gas	28	14	4	10	56	35	46
Sheffield Oakhouse	28	14	4	10	68	56	46
Clifton Rovers	28	11	9	8	58	54	42
Sheffield Centralians	28	10	10	8	35	33	40
Kiveton Park Reserves	28	11	4	13	41	42	37
Sheffield Bankers	28	9	5	14	53	58	31
Penistone Church Reserves	28	8	5	15	43	59	29
Rossington Main Reserves	28	6	11	11	40	60	29
Sheffield Post Office	28	7	5	16	46	72	26
British Steel Stainless	28	7	3	18	53	72	24
Old Edwardians	28	6	6	16	35	63	24
Abbeydale	28	6	1	21	38	118	19

Sheffield Bankers had 1 point deducted.
Staveley Miners Welfare moved to the Central Midlands League.
Sheffield Gas and Sheffield Post Office both left. Grimethorpe Miners Welfare, Davy, Pinegrove and Grapes Northern General all joined.
British Steel Stainless changed their name to Avesta Sheffield.

1993-94

Premier Division

Mexborough Main Street	26	18	5	3	56	27	59
High Green Villa	26	16	7	3	51	28	55
Ash House (G C)	26	15	4	7	65	33	49
Frecheville Community Association	26	14	3	9	69	42	45
Parramore Sports	26	12	6	8	51	44	42
Denaby & Cadeby Miners Welfare	26	12	4	10	48	54	40
Brunsmeer Athletic	26	11	6	9	54	41	39
Phoenix	26	8	8	10	53	42	32
Hallam Reserves	26	10	2	14	46	63	32
Wath Saracens Athletic	26	8	7	11	36	40	31
Worsbrough Bridge M.W. Res.	26	8	3	15	35	53	27
Goldthorpe Colliery	**26**	**7**	**4**	**15**	**40**	**77**	**25**
Treeton Welfare	**26**	**4**	**6**	**16**	**49**	**68**	**18**
R.E.S. Parkgate Reserves	**26**	**4**	**5**	**17**	**35**	**76**	**17**

Goldthorpe Colliery changed their name to Dearne Colliery Miners Welfare, Brunsmeer Athletic changed their name to A.B.M. and R.E.S. Parkgate Reserves changed their name to Parkgate Reserves.

Division One

Penistone Church	24	15	3	6	74	35	48
Stocksbridge Park Steel Reserves	**24**	**14**	**4**	**6**	**65**	**36**	**46**
Throstles Ridgeway	**24**	**13**	**6**	**5**	**56**	**28**	**45**
Oughtibridge War Memorial S.C.	24	12	3	9	45	42	39
Wath St. James	24	12	3	9	43	41	39
Ecclesfield Red Rose	24	11	5	8	45	26	38
Yorkshire Main	24	11	3	10	47	50	36
Caribbean Sports	24	8	9	7	47	34	33
British Gas S.C.	24	9	6	9	45	52	33
Wombwell Town	24	10	2	12	42	45	32
Woodsetts Sports	24	8	6	10	38	47	30
Swinton Athletic	**24**	**1**	**6**	**17**	**26**	**74**	**9**
Rawmarsh & Ryecroft W.M.C.	24	1	6	17	21	84	9

Rawmarsh & Ryecroft W.M.C. left the league.
Wath St. James changed their name to Thurcroft Double Barrel.

Division Two

Grimethorpe Miners Welfare	**26**	**23**	**2**	**1**	**93**	**20**	**71**
Pinegrove	**26**	**23**	**1**	**2**	**97**	**25**	**70**
Grapes Northern General	**26**	**16**	**5**	**5**	**80**	**37**	**53**
Davy	26	12	8	6	46	32	43
Sheffield Centralians	26	11	5	10	42	39	38
Sheffield Bankers	26	10	7	9	54	44	37
Sheffield Oakhouse	26	9	7	10	51	55	34
Avesta Sheffield	26	9	7	10	49	59	34
Kiveton Park Reserves	26	10	2	14	42	57	32
Clifton Rovers	26	7	5	14	45	87	26
Rossington Main Reserves	26	6	5	15	33	57	23
Penistone Church Reserves	26	5	6	15	36	61	21
Abbeydale	26	5	6	15	36	67	21
Old Edwardians	26	2	2	22	20	84	8

Davy had 1 point deducted.
Sheffield Oakhouse left the league. Worksop Town Reserves joined from the Doncaster & District League and Wickersley Old Boys also joined.

Sheffield & Hallamshire County Senior League 1994-1996

1994-95

Premier Division

Team	P	W	D	L	F	A	Pts
Frecheville Community Association	26	21	3	2	64	22	66
Mexborough Main Street	26	18	4	4	77	42	58
High Green Villa	26	15	6	5	46	27	51
A.B.M.	25	14	4	7	61	39	46
Denaby & Cadeby Miners Welfare	26	14	4	8	51	32	46
Stocksbridge Park Steel Reserves	26	11	9	6	59	47	42
Ash House (G C)	25	12	1	12	56	49	37
Throstles Ridgeway	26	10	2	14	48	58	32
Penistone Church	26	9	4	13	51	65	31
Parramore Sports	26	7	9	10	51	59	30
Worsbrough Bridge M.W. Res.	26	5	9	12	34	42	24
Wath Saracens Athletic	**26**	**5**	**4**	**17**	**31**	**63**	**19**
Phoenix	26	4	3	19	31	87	15
Hallam Reserves	**26**	**3**	**4**	**19**	**36**	**64**	**12**

Hallam Reserves had 1 point deducted.
Ash House (G C) vs A.B.M. was not played.
Ash House (G C) merged with Phoenix and continued playing in the Premier Division as Ash House Phoenix.
Wath Saracens Athletic changed their name to Wath Saracens.

Division One

Team	P	W	D	L	F	A	Pts
Grimethorpe Miners Welfare	**26**	**17**	**7**	**2**	**73**	**28**	**58**
Oughtibridge War Memorial S.C.	**26**	**15**	**8**	**3**	**59**	**29**	**53**
Caribbean Sports	**26**	**16**	**5**	**5**	**50**	**22**	**53**
Thurcroft Double Barrel	25	14	4	7	52	30	46
Pinegrove	26	13	5	8	54	35	41
Grapes Northern General	26	11	7	8	65	53	40
Wombwell Town	25	11	7	7	48	44	39
Dearne Colliery Miners Welfare	26	9	5	12	55	54	32
British Gas S.C.	26	9	4	13	64	66	31
Treeton Welfare	26	9	3	14	51	61	30
Ecclesfield Red Rose	26	8	5	13	45	57	29
Parkgate Reserves	26	7	2	17	52	66	20
Yorkshire Main	26	5	5	16	25	65	20
Woodsetts Sports	26	2	3	21	31	114	9

Wombwell Town had 1 point deducted.
Pinegrove and Parkgate Reserves each had 3 points deducted.
Thurcroft Double Barrel vs Wombwell Town was not played.
British Gas S.C., Pinegrove and Dearne Colliery Miners Welfare all left.

Division Two

Team	P	W	D	L	F	A	Pts
Davy	**24**	**17**	**4**	**3**	**64**	**24**	**55**
Swinton Athletic	**24**	**15**	**7**	**2**	**54**	**20**	**52**
Sheffield Bankers	**24**	**15**	**6**	**3**	**74**	**28**	**51**
Worksop Town Reserves	24	14	5	5	58	27	47
Wickersley Old Boys	24	14	4	6	69	31	46
Avesta Sheffield	24	11	4	9	64	57	37
Clifton Rovers	24	10	5	9	53	47	35
Sheffield Centralians	24	9	6	9	29	32	33
Penistone Church Reserves	24	9	3	12	47	49	30
Rossington Main Reserves	24	7	2	15	32	71	23
Abbeydale	24	5	2	17	40	74	17
Old Edwardians	24	2	2	20	18	91	8
Kiveton Park Reserves	24	1	4	19	31	82	7

Elsecar Market Hotel, Harworth Colliery Institute Reserves, N.C.B. Maltby Miners Welfare and The Wetherby all joined.

1995-96

Premier Division

Team	P	W	D	L	F	A	Pts
High Green Villa	26	21	3	2	74	20	66
Ash House Phoenix	26	17	4	5	63	21	55
Grimethorpe Miners Welfare	26	15	4	7	54	36	49
A.B.M.	26	14	5	7	57	45	47
Denaby & Cadeby Miners Welfare	26	12	6	8	58	39	42
Frecheville Community Association	26	11	5	10	64	50	38
Parramore Sports	26	12	2	12	46	46	38
Worsbrough Bridge Miners Welfare Reserves							
Oughtibridge War Memorial S.C.	26	9	7	10	38	41	34
Mexborough Main Street	26	7	9	10	46	46	30
Stocksbridge Park Steel Reserves	26	8	5	13	44	46	23
Caribbean Sports	26	6	4	16	40	79	22
Penistone Church	**26**	**6**	**1**	**19**	**37**	**62**	**19**
Throstles Ridgeway	**26**	**3**	**1**	**22**	**23**	**106**	**10**

Stocksbridge Park Steel Reserves had 6 points deducted.
Worsbrough Bridge Miners Welfare Reserves are shown in the correct position in the table but their playing record has not been found.
Grimethorpe Miners Welfare moved to the Central Midlands League.

Division One

Team	P	W	D	L	F	A	Pts
Ecclesfield Red Rose	**24**	**19**	**5**	**0**	**76**	**22**	**62**
Parkgate Reserves	**24**	**15**	**3**	**6**	**67**	**42**	**48**
Wombwell Town	**24**	**13**	**5**	**6**	**47**	**26**	**44**
Thurcroft Double Barrel	24	12	4	8	68	42	40
Swinton Athletic	24	11	5	8	42	31	38
Grapes Northern General	24	12	4	8	64	64	38
Treeton Welfare	24	8	7	9	48	58	31
Davy	24	9	3	12	48	56	30
Sheffield Bankers	24	6	11	7	40	45	29
Wath Saracens	24	7	7	10	30	37	28
Hallam Reserves	24	7	3	14	34	49	24
Woodsetts Sports	24	3	5	16	31	77	14
Yorkshire Main	**24**	**2**	**2**	**20**	**24**	**70**	**8**

Grapes Northern General had 2 points deducted.
Woodsetts Sports left the league.

Division Two

Team	P	W	D	L	F	A	Pts
Wickersley Old Boys	**26**	**18**	**7**	**1**	**83**	**32**	**61**
The Wetherby	**26**	**19**	**3**	**4**	**81**	**18**	**60**
Worksop Town Reserves	**26**	**18**	**4**	**4**	**71**	**27**	**58**
N.C.B. Maltby Miners Welfare	26	17	3	6	71	33	54
Clifton Rovers	26	16	4	6	68	32	52
Elsecar Market Hotel	26	14	2	10	65	50	44
Avesta Sheffield	26	14	1	11	76	64	43
Rossington Main Reserves	26	11	5	10	47	57	38
Sheffield Centralians	26	7	5	14	29	52	26
Penistone Church Reserves	26	6	6	14	37	59	24
Abbeydale	26	5	3	18	41	81	18
Harworth Colliery Institute Reserves	26	5	3	18	33	80	18
Kiveton Park Reserves	26	4	1	21	36	106	13
Old Edwardians	26	3	3	20	30	97	12

Abbeydale and Kiveton Park Reserves both left the league.
Wombwell Main joined from the Barnsley Association League, Norton Woodseats joined as a newly re-formed club while Sheffield Reserves, Sheffield Lane Top, and Queens Hotel also all joined.

1996-97

Premier Division

Team	P	W	D	L	F	A	Pts
Denaby & Cadeby Miners Welfare	26	18	4	4	60	19	58
A.B.M.	26	16	4	6	62	33	52
Frecheville Community Association	26	15	6	5	60	37	51
Ash House Phoenix	26	12	9	5	57	36	45
High Green Villa	26	13	3	10	37	29	42
Ecclesfield Red Rose	26	11	8	7	39	37	41
Stocksbridge Park Steel Reserves	26	10	6	10	49	48	36
Mexborough Main Street	26	10	5	11	38	37	35
Caribbean Sports	26	10	6	10	50	52	33
Wombwell Town	26	8	6	12	40	51	30
Parkgate Reserves	26	8	5	13	43	54	29
Parramore Sports	*26*	*8*	*4*	*14*	*41*	*67*	*28*
Oughtibridge War Memorial S.C.	*26*	*3*	*5*	*18*	*21*	*50*	*14*
Worsbrough Bridge M.W. Res.	26	2	5	19	29	76	11

Caribbean Sports had 3 points deducted.
Worsbrough Bridge Miners Welfare Reserves left the league.
Ash House Phoenix changed their name to Phoenix Sports & Social while Denaby & Cadeby Miners Welfare became Denaby United Reserves.

Division One

Team	P	W	D	L	F	A	Pts
Swinton Athletic	**24**	**15**	**6**	**3**	**59**	**23**	**51**
Worksop Town Reserves	**24**	**15**	**3**	**6**	**67**	**42**	**48**
Penistone Church	**24**	**14**	**3**	**7**	**59**	**30**	**45**
Wath Saracens	24	13	6	5	65	40	45
Wickersley Old Boys	24	11	5	8	67	38	38
Hallam Reserves	24	12	4	8	51	41	37
Sheffield Bankers	24	11	4	9	44	46	37
Treeton Welfare	24	10	5	9	53	49	35
The Wetherby	24	9	6	9	60	44	33
Thurcroft Double Barrel	24	8	3	13	42	64	27
Grapes Northern General	24	6	5	13	64	68	23
Davy	24	4	4	16	38	67	16
Throstles Ridgeway	24	1	0	23	22	139	3

Hallam Reserves had 3 points deducted.
Thurcroft Double Barrel and Throstles Ridgeway both left the league.
Grapes Northern General changed their name to Grapes Roy Hancock.

Division Two

Team	P	W	D	L	F	A	Pts
Wombwell Main	**28**	**25**	**2**	**1**	**110**	**22**	**77**
Avesta Sheffield	**28**	**21**	**4**	**3**	**67**	**33**	**67**
N.C.B. Maltby Miners Welfare	**28**	**18**	**6**	**4**	**79**	**31**	**60**
Sheffield Lane Top	**28**	**17**	**7**	**4**	**101**	**25**	**58**
Sheffield Centralians	28	17	6	5	59	31	57
Norton Woodseats	28	15	4	9	63	44	49
Queens Hotel	28	12	4	12	71	71	40
Elsecar Market Hotel	28	10	7	11	50	41	37
Yorkshire Main	28	11	3	14	51	47	36
Rossington Main Reserves	28	6	6	16	37	61	24
Clifton Rovers	28	7	3	18	43	83	24
Old Edwardians	28	7	1	20	41	85	22
Sheffield Reserves	28	4	9	15	41	78	21
Penistone Church Reserves	28	4	3	21	27	79	15
Harworth Colliery Institute Res.	28	3	2	23	25	134	9

Clifton Rovers left the league. Athersley Recreation joined from the Barnsley Association League while Brinsworth Athletic, Hare & Hounds, Thorpe Hesley and Woodhouse West End also all joined.

1997-98

Premier Division

Team	P	W	D	L	F	A	Pts
Phoenix Sports & Social	26	18	1	7	67	42	55
Frecheville Community Association	26	17	3	6	53	24	54
Ecclesfield Red Rose	26	16	3	7	59	36	51
Worksop Town Reserves	26	14	4	8	53	32	46
Mexborough Main Street	26	13	7	6	54	39	46
Caribbean Sports	26	11	3	12	59	56	36
Stocksbridge Park Steel Reserves	26	9	7	10	37	41	34
Parkgate Reserves	26	9	6	11	61	60	33
Denaby United Reserves	26	8	8	10	45	45	32
Penistone Church	26	8	5	13	37	59	29
Wombwell Town	26	8	4	14	51	64	28
High Green Villa	*26*	*7*	*6*	*13*	*27*	*44*	*27*
A.B.M.	26	6	5	15	37	75	23
Swinton Athletic	*26*	*4*	*6*	*16*	*26*	*49*	*18*

A.B.M. left the league.

Division One

Team	P	W	D	L	F	A	Pts
The Wetherby	**24**	**17**	**4**	**3**	**76**	**30**	**55**
Wombwell Main	**24**	**14**	**5**	**5**	**55**	**31**	**47**
Sheffield Lane Top	**24**	**14**	**4**	**6**	**62**	**45**	**46**
Hallam Reserves	24	14	3	7	48	39	45
Oughtibridge War Memorial S.C.	24	11	5	8	50	38	38
Parramore Sports	24	10	4	10	38	48	34
Treeton Welfare	24	9	4	11	54	54	31
N.C.B. Maltby Miners Welfare	24	8	5	11	43	45	29
Avesta Sheffield	24	9	1	14	41	61	28
Wickersley Old Boys	24	6	7	11	47	53	25
Sheffield Bankers	24	6	7	11	41	47	25
Grapes Roy Hancock	24	5	5	14	64	89	20
Davy	*24*	*3*	*6*	*15*	*24*	*63*	*15*

Wath Saracens resigned during the season and their record was deleted.

Division Two

Team	P	W	D	L	F	A	Pts
Athersley Recreation	**28**	**25**	**2**	**1**	**116**	**23**	**77**
Hare & Hounds	**28**	**22**	**4**	**2**	**103**	**28**	**70**
Sheffield Reserves	**28**	**19**	**5**	**4**	**75**	**36**	**62**
Norton Woodseats	28	16	6	6	82	36	54
Woodhouse West End	28	17	4	7	67	42	52
Sheffield Centralians	28	15	3	10	48	36	48
Yorkshire Main	28	13	3	12	57	51	42
Thorpe Hesley	28	12	4	12	56	51	40
Elsecar Market Hotel	28	8	6	14	59	67	30
Brinsworth Athletic	28	9	6	13	54	64	30
Queens Hotel	28	9	2	17	48	89	29
Penistone Church Reserves	28	5	4	19	38	61	19
Rossington Main Reserves	28	5	2	21	38	119	17
Old Edwardians	28	3	4	21	31	96	13
Harworth Colliery Institute Res.	28	3	3	22	32	105	12

Woodhouse West End and Brinsworth Athletic each had 3 points deducted.
Yorkshire Main moved to the Central Midlands League.
South Kirkby Colliery joined from the Doncaster & District League and A.B.S. Kilnhurst also joined.

Sheffield & Hallamshire County Senior League 1998-2001

1998-99

Premier Division

Wombwell Main	26	16	2	8	56	38	50
Phoenix Sports & Social	26	13	8	5	78	40	47
Parkgate Reserves	26	15	1	10	59	39	46
Frecheville Community Association	26	12	6	8	54	37	42
Ecclesfield Red Rose	26	12	5	9	52	39	41
Denaby United Reserves	26	11	8	7	47	48	41
The Wetherby	26	11	6	9	45	39	39
Wombwell Town	26	10	7	9	37	53	37
Mexborough Main Street	26	9	9	8	39	35	36
Sheffield Lane Top	26	10	5	11	55	50	35
Worksop Town Reserves	26	10	1	15	56	53	31
Penistone Church	**26**	**9**	**4**	**13**	**45**	**61**	**31**
Stocksbridge Park Steel Reserves	**26**	**6**	**3**	**17**	**37**	**64**	**21**
Caribbean Sports	**26**	**3**	**5**	**18**	**32**	**96**	**14**

Division One

Hare & Hounds	26	20	4	2	62	17	64
Athersley Recreation	26	20	1	5	79	35	61
Hallam Reserves	26	18	3	5	61	27	57
N.C.B. Maltby Miners Welfare	26	11	5	10	50	56	38
High Green Villa	26	11	4	11	45	47	37
Treeton Welfare	26	10	5	11	48	62	35
Parramore Sports	26	10	3	13	59	58	33
Wickersley Old Boys	26	9	4	13	52	52	31
Sheffield Reserves	26	9	4	13	51	56	31
Swinton Athletic	26	8	7	11	47	60	31
Oughtibridge War Memorial S.C.	26	9	3	14	45	62	30
Avesta Sheffield	26	8	3	15	53	64	27
Grapes Roy Hancock	**26**	**8**	**2**	**16**	**55**	**89**	**26**
Sheffield Bankers	**26**	**6**	**2**	**18**	**43**	**65**	**20**

Division Two

Norton Woodseats	22	16	3	3	59	25	51
Woodhouse West End	**22**	**16**	**2**	**4**	**63**	**32**	**50**
Thorpe Hesley	**22**	**15**	**3**	**4**	**65**	**32**	**48**
Davy	22	13	2	7	63	43	41
Sheffield Centralians	22	10	5	7	43	27	35
South Kirkby Colliery	22	9	4	9	52	62	31
A.B.S. Kilnhurst	22	8	5	9	48	43	29
Rossington Main Reserves	22	8	1	13	52	54	25
Queens Hotel	22	6	7	9	43	46	25
Old Edwardians	22	5	3	14	45	73	18
Penistone Church Reserves	22	5	1	16	33	60	16
Harworth Colliery Institute Res.	22	2	2	18	25	94	8

Brinsworth Athletic and Elsecar Market Hotel both resigned during the season and their records were deleted.
Norton Woodseats disbanded and Harworth Colliery Institute Reserves and Rossington Main Reserves also both left the league. Groves Social joined.

1999-2000

Premier Division

Athersley Recreation	26	16	7	3	59	23	55
Phoenix Sports & Social	26	14	4	8	49	33	46
Wombwell Town	26	14	4	8	46	38	46
Parkgate Reserves	26	14	4	8	53	47	46
Wombwell Main	26	11	7	8	43	24	40
Mexborough Main Street	26	10	6	10	40	50	36
Worksop Town Reserves	26	8	10	8	43	29	34
Frecheville Community Association	26	10	4	12	37	49	34
The Wetherby	26	9	5	12	36	42	32
Ecclesfield Red Rose	26	8	7	11	43	55	31
Hare & Hounds	26	8	6	12	34	48	30
Hallam Reserves	26	6	8	12	39	50	26
Sheffield Lane Top	**26**	**7**	**5**	**14**	**37**	**54**	**26**
Denaby United Reserves	**26**	**5**	**7**	**14**	**40**	**57**	**22**

Hare & Hounds vs Phoenix Sports & Social was not played.
Wombwell Town disbanded.

Division One

Wickersley Old Boys	26	17	4	5	74	40	55
Thorpe Hesley	26	15	7	4	55	28	52
Parramore Sports	26	16	2	8	54	41	50
High Green Villa	26	14	6	6	55	33	48
Avesta Sheffield	26	12	6	8	53	56	42
Sheffield Reserves	26	12	5	9	59	34	41
Stocksbridge Park Steel Reserves	26	12	2	12	59	45	38
Penistone Church	26	11	5	10	45	38	38
Oughtibridge War Memorial S.C.	26	11	4	11	37	46	37
Woodhouse West End	26	10	2	14	46	52	32
Swinton Athletic	26	6	7	13	51	58	25
Treeton Welfare	26	7	4	15	50	70	25
Caribbean Sports	26	6	2	18	45	67	20
N.C.B. Maltby Miners Welfare	**26**	**4**	**2**	**20**	**26**	**101**	**14**

Woodhouse West End, Sheffield Reserves and N.C.B. Maltby Miners Welfare all left the league.

Division Two – Clubs played each other 3 times.

Grapes Roy Hancock	27	20	3	4	115	45	63
Sheffield Bankers	27	20	2	5	63	38	62
Groves Social	27	17	1	9	67	47	52
South Kirkby Colliery	27	16	3	8	55	28	51
A.B.S. Kilnhurst	27	12	4	11	55	50	40
Sheffield Centralians	27	10	4	13	46	44	34
Penistone Church Reserves	27	7	3	17	39	64	24
Queens Hotel	27	7	3	17	36	84	24
Old Edwardians	27	7	2	18	54	91	23
Davy	27	4	5	18	40	79	17

Queens Hotel and A.B.S. Kilnhurst both left the league.
The Forum joined from the South Yorkshire Amateur League and Dinnington Town Reserves also joined.

2000-01

Premier Division

The Wetherby	26	17	4	5	59	30	55
Frecheville Community Association	26	15	5	6	60	43	50
Wombwell Main	26	12	8	6	45	36	44
Worksop Town Reserves	26	12	6	8	56	48	42
Hare & Hounds	25	13	3	9	51	43	42
Phoenix Sports & Social	25	11	6	8	55	43	39
Mexborough Main Street	26	10	6	10	50	45	36
Athersley Recreation	26	10	5	11	33	32	35
Hallam Reserves	26	10	5	11	58	60	35
Ecclesfield Red Rose	26	10	5	11	48	56	35
Parkgate Reserves	26	7	6	13	49	61	27
Thorpe Hesley	26	6	6	14	37	58	24
Parramore Sports	**26**	**5**	**6**	**15**	**36**	**70**	**21**
Wickersley Old Boys	**26**	**4**	**7**	**15**	**41**	**53**	**19**

Worksop Town Reserves left the league.

Division One

Penistone Church	**24**	**17**	**4**	**3**	**63**	**27**	**55**
Swinton Athletic	**24**	**14**	**6**	**4**	**53**	**30**	**48**
Groves Social	**24**	**14**	**4**	**6**	**64**	**38**	**46**
Stocksbridge Park Steel Reserves	24	13	3	8	62	36	42
Sheffield Lane Top	24	12	2	10	56	41	38
Oughtibridge War Memorial S.C.	24	10	6	8	45	43	36
Grapes Roy Hancock	24	10	4	10	53	45	34
Caribbean Sports	24	10	4	10	59	64	34
Sheffield Bankers	24	9	3	12	54	54	30
Avesta Sheffield	24	7	6	11	40	61	27
High Green Villa	24	6	4	14	40	75	22
Denaby United Reserves	24	4	5	15	36	68	17
Treeton Welfare	**24**	**2**	**5**	**17**	**34**	**77**	**11**

Sheffield Bankers changed their name to Georgia Pacific and Avesta Sheffield changed their name to Avesta Polarit.

Division Two – Clubs played each other 4 times.

South Kirkby Colliery	28	24	3	1	76	22	75
Davy	28	16	3	9	71	38	51
The Forum	28	14	5	9	56	46	47
Dinnington Town Reserves	28	12	5	11	43	37	41
Sheffield Centralians	28	11	2	15	41	47	35
N.C.B. Maltby Miners Welfare	28	9	6	13	39	53	33
Penistone Church Reserves	28	6	6	16	51	69	24
Old Edwardians	28	4	2	22	35	100	14

Old Edwardians left. Hollinsend Amateurs joined from the South Yorkshire Amateur League while Elm Tree, HSBC Sheffield and Renishaw Juniors also all joined.

2001-02

Premier Division

Wombwell Main	26	20	4	2	87	32	64
Athersley Recreation	26	20	0	6	66	26	60
Phoenix Sports & Social	26	14	5	7	56	42	47
Mexborough Main Street	26	12	5	9	61	50	41
Hallam Reserves	26	12	4	10	56	36	40
Swinton Athletic	26	12	3	11	37	49	39
Penistone Church	26	10	8	8	41	33	38
Parkgate Reserves	26	9	7	10	49	40	34
Hare & Hounds	26	8	6	12	32	55	30
Thorpe Hesley	26	9	1	16	34	63	28
Groves Social	26	8	3	15	40	54	27
Ecclesfield Red Rose	**26**	**7**	**6**	**13**	**39**	**53**	**27**
The Wetherby	**26**	**7**	**5**	**14**	**35**	**57**	**26**
Frecheville Community Assoc.	**26**	**4**	**3**	**19**	**18**	**61**	**15**

Division One

Wickersley Old Boys	**26**	**21**	**1**	**4**	**85**	**30**	**64**
South Kirkby Colliery	**26**	**18**	**8**	**0**	**89**	**39**	**62**
Grapes Roy Hancock	**26**	**19**	**1**	**6**	**76**	**48**	**58**
Stocksbridge Park Steel Reserves	26	15	4	7	79	29	49
Georgia Pacific	26	14	6	6	81	59	48
Oughtibridge War Memorial S.C.	26	12	3	11	46	43	39
Parramore Sports	26	11	4	11	59	54	37
Sheffield Lane Top	26	11	3	12	52	60	36
Avesta Polarit	26	9	4	13	56	73	31
Caribbean Sports	26	8	6	12	63	56	30
The Forum	26	9	2	15	58	87	29
High Green Villa	**26**	**4**	**6**	**16**	**43**	**88**	**18**
Davy	**26**	**2**	**4**	**20**	**42**	**89**	**10**
Denaby United Reserves	26	2	2	22	38	112	8

Denaby United Reserves left the league.
The Forum changed their name to Rising Sun.

Division Two – Clubs played each other 4 times.

Elm Tree	28	19	2	7	68	29	59
Hollinsend Amateurs	28	17	5	6	68	33	56
HSBC Sheffield	28	17	4	7	74	37	55
Renishaw Juniors	28	14	4	10	54	52	46
N.C.B. Maltby Miners Welfare	28	12	3	13	48	54	39
Sheffield Centralians	28	7	7	14	34	50	28
Dinnington Town Reserves	28	7	3	18	33	74	24
Penistone Church Reserves	28	2	6	20	26	76	12

Treeton Welfare resigned during the season and their record was deleted. They returned to the league for the 2002-03 season.
Edlington W.M.C., Gate 13, Psalter Vigo, Harworth Colliery Institute Colts, Grimethorpe Miners Welfare, Manvers Park and Wath Athletic all joined.

2002-03

Premier Division

Wombwell Main	24	17	5	2	57	17	56
Penistone Church	24	15	4	5	43	22	49
Mexborough Main Street	24	15	2	7	70	39	47
Athersley Recreation	24	15	1	8	47	25	46
Hallam Reserves	24	13	4	7	69	32	43
South Kirkby Colliery	24	13	4	7	55	41	43
Parkgate Reserves	24	11	3	10	56	55	36
Groves Social	24	9	5	10	46	46	32
Wickersley Old Boys	24	9	5	10	46	56	32
Grapes Roy Hancock	24	9	0	15	43	47	27
Thorpe Hesley	24	7	4	13	29	45	25
Swinton Athletic	24	3	1	20	26	71	10
Phoenix Sports & Social	24	0	2	22	16	107	2

Hare & Hounds resigned during the season and their record was deleted.
Hallam Reserves and Parkgate Reserves both left the league.
Grapes Roy Hancock changed their name to Sportsman Roy Hancock.

Division One

Elm Tree	**26**	**18**	**3**	**5**	**64**	**33**	**57**
HSBC Sheffield	**26**	**15**	**7**	**4**	**70**	**35**	**52**
Sheffield Lane Top	**26**	**15**	**4**	**7**	**66**	**42**	**49**
Oughtibridge War Memorial S.C.	26	14	3	9	51	40	45
Hollinsend Amateurs	26	13	5	8	57	40	44
Parramore Sports	26	11	4	11	55	48	37
Rising Sun	26	11	4	11	60	61	37
Stocksbridge Park Steel Reserves	26	11	2	13	50	37	35
The Wetherby	26	10	5	11	45	42	35
Frecheville Community Association	26	9	6	11	42	50	33
Georgia Pacific	26	10	3	13	46	60	33
Ecclesfield Red Rose	26	7	8	11	36	47	29
Avesta Polarit	26	6	6	14	45	74	24
Caribbean Sports	26	1	2	23	20	98	5

Rising Sun left the league.

Division Two

Edlington W.M.C.	**26**	**22**	**3**	**1**	**66**	**23**	**69**
High Green Villa	**26**	**17**	**3**	**6**	**63**	**32**	**54**
Renishaw Juniors	26	17	1	8	83	39	52
Treeton Welfare	**26**	**13**	**7**	**6**	**65**	**39**	**46**
Wath Athletic	26	12	8	6	60	38	44
Sheffield Centralians	26	13	5	8	50	44	44
Grimethorpe Miners Welfare	26	11	8	7	56	48	41
Gate 13	26	10	7	9	49	54	37
Penistone Church Reserves	26	8	5	13	40	60	29
Dinnington Town Reserves	26	9	1	16	56	61	28
Davy	26	7	6	13	50	58	27
Manvers Park	26	6	6	14	49	56	24
Psalter Vigo	26	6	1	19	38	66	19
Harworth Colliery Institute Colts	26	0	1	25	19	126	1

N.C.B. Maltby Miners Welfare resigned during the season and their record was deleted.
Grimethorpe Miners Welfare disbanded and Psalter Vigo and Renishaw Juniors also both left the league. Silkstone United joined from the South Yorkshire Amateur League while AFC Barnsley, Houghton Main, Dodworth Miners Welfare, Silverwood Colliery Miners Welfare, Handsworth and De La Salle Old Boys also all joined.

2003-04

Premier Division

Athersley Recreation	26	23	1	2	95	21	70
Mexborough Main Street	26	19	2	5	72	20	59
HSBC Sheffield	26	19	2	5	74	27	59
Wombwell Main	26	16	3	7	58	27	51
Penistone Church	26	12	9	5	62	32	45
Groves Social	26	13	3	10	61	59	42
Thorpe Hesley	26	11	2	13	41	55	35
South Kirkby Colliery	26	8	8	10	44	33	32
Elm Tree	26	9	2	15	37	52	29
Wickersley Old Boys	26	7	6	13	28	46	27
Sportsman Roy Hancock	26	7	1	18	42	74	22
Swinton Athletic	***26***	***6***	***2***	***18***	***42***	***95***	***20***
Sheffield Lane Top	***26***	***6***	***2***	***18***	***31***	***87***	***20***
Phoenix Sports & Social	***26***	***4***	***1***	***21***	***23***	***82***	***13***

Division One

Hollinsend Amateurs	***24***	***20***	***2***	***2***	***55***	***12***	***62***
Stocksbridge Park Steel Reserves	***24***	***16***	***2***	***6***	***58***	***34***	***50***
Oughtibridge War Memorial S.C.	***24***	***14***	***4***	***6***	***39***	***29***	***46***
The Wetherby	24	14	1	9	44	30	43
Georgia Pacific	24	12	3	9	47	36	39
Frecheville Community Association	24	10	4	10	37	38	34
Ecclesfield Red Rose	24	10	3	11	44	39	33
High Green Villa	24	7	7	10	32	42	28
Edlington W.M.C.	24	8	3	13	32	36	27
Treeton Welfare	24	7	5	12	41	54	26
Parramore Sports	24	6	5	13	37	44	23
Avesta Polarit	24	6	4	14	35	54	22
Caribbean Sports	***24***	***3***	***3***	***18***	***23***	***76***	***12***

Treeton Welfare left the league and AFC Cutlers joined.
Avesta Polarit changed their name to Outo Kumpu S. & S.C..

Division Two

AFC Barnsley	28	24	2	2	106	27	74
Silkstone United	***28***	***20***	***5***	***3***	***85***	***29***	***65***
Houghton Main	***28***	***19***	***4***	***5***	***90***	***32***	***61***
Dinnington Town Reserves	28	17	3	8	71	40	54
Dodworth Miners Welfare	28	14	9	5	61	39	51
Davy	28	11	7	10	66	53	40
Wath Athletic	28	12	3	13	51	55	39
Silverwood Colliery M.W.	28	11	4	13	48	76	37
Handsworth	28	10	5	13	47	58	35
Penistone Church Reserves	28	9	6	13	48	64	33
Manvers Park	28	7	6	15	54	79	27
Gate 13	28	5	11	12	37	68	26
Sheffield Centralians	28	6	4	18	28	67	22
De La Salle Old Boys	28	5	4	19	45	84	19
Harworth Colliery Institute Colts	28	2	3	23	24	90	9

AFC Barnsley moved to the Central Midlands League. Manvers Park, Wath Athletic and Silverwood Colliery Miners Welfare all left the league.
Everest and Worsbrough Bridge Athletic Reserves both joined.
Harworth Colliery Institute Colts changed their name to Harworth Colliery Institute Reserves.

2004-05

Premier Division

Athersley Recreation	26	23	3	0	78	22	72
Oughtibridge War Memorial S.C.	26	16	7	3	64	34	55
HSBC Sheffield	26	13	4	9	80	50	43
Stocksbridge Park Steel Reserves	26	12	7	7	50	34	43
Hollinsend Amateurs	26	11	10	5	41	30	43
Sportsman Roy Hancock	26	10	7	9	58	57	37
Mexborough Main Street	26	10	6	10	53	41	33
South Kirkby Colliery	26	10	3	13	39	49	33
Penistone Church	26	8	7	11	33	38	31
Thorpe Hesley	26	8	6	12	49	59	30
Wombwell Main	26	7	9	10	34	52	30
Elm Tree	***26***	***6***	***8***	***12***	***45***	***60***	***26***
Wickersley Old Boys	***26***	***5***	***5***	***16***	***42***	***57***	***19***
Groves Social	26	1	2	23	32	115	5

Mexborough Main Street had 3 points deducted.
Wickersley Old Boys had 1 point deducted.
Groves Social left the league.
Sportsman Roy Hancock changed their name to Roy Hancock Old Crown.

Division One

Edlington W.M.C.	***26***	***21***	***1***	***4***	***75***	***32***	***64***
Houghton Main	***26***	***17***	***4***	***5***	***70***	***24***	***55***
Silkstone United	***26***	***16***	***6***	***4***	***71***	***29***	***54***
The Wetherby	26	15	4	7	67	41	49
Georgia Pacific	26	12	6	8	55	46	42
Ecclesfield Red Rose	26	11	5	10	44	40	38
Outo Kumpu S. & S.C.	26	10	3	13	55	67	33
High Green Villa	26	9	5	12	43	52	32
Swinton Athletic	26	10	2	14	40	57	32
Frecheville Community Association	26	7	9	10	30	38	30
Sheffield Lane Top	26	8	5	13	56	76	29
Parramore Sports	26	7	7	12	41	53	28
Phoenix Sports & Social	***26***	***5***	***3***	***18***	***42***	***83***	***18***
AFC Cutlers	***26***	***3***	***2***	***21***	***24***	***75***	***11***

The Wetherby left the league.
Swinton Athletic changed their name to Dearne/Swinton.

Division Two

Dodworth Miners Welfare	***22***	***17***	***4***	***1***	***62***	***22***	***55***
Dinnington Town Reserves	***22***	***16***	***4***	***2***	***57***	***20***	***52***
Handsworth	***22***	***15***	***4***	***3***	***71***	***25***	***49***
Davy	22	14	5	3	52	21	47
Worsbrough Bridge Athletic Res.	22	13	2	7	66	38	41
Everest	22	9	2	11	51	40	29
Sheffield Centralians	22	8	2	12	34	54	26
De La Salle Old Boys	22	6	5	11	46	54	23
Caribbean Sports	22	7	1	14	46	56	22
Penistone Church Reserves	22	5	3	14	24	47	18
Gate 13	22	3	3	16	35	66	12
Harworth Colliery Institute Res.	22	1	1	20	15	116	4

Gate 13 left the league. Sheffield Bankers joined from the South Yorkshire Amateur League while Parkgate Reserves, Worsbrough Common and Armthorpe Welfare Reserves also joined.
Davy changed their name to Half Moon.

2005-06

Premier Division

Mexborough Main Street	26	19	4	3	76	28	61
Athersley Recreation	26	16	7	3	53	16	55
Stocksbridge Park Steel Reserves	26	12	10	4	58	34	46
Roy Hancock Old Crown	26	11	8	7	54	42	41
HSBC Sheffield	26	11	6	9	47	38	39
Hollinsend Amateurs	26	10	8	8	36	30	38
Houghton Main	26	10	7	9	33	36	37
Wombwell Main	26	9	8	9	42	35	35
Penistone Church	26	8	7	11	37	55	31
Edlington W.M.C.	26	7	9	10	34	52	30
Thorpe Hesley	26	7	8	11	38	45	29
Oughtibridge War Memorial S.C.	26	9	2	15	35	52	29
South Kirkby Colliery	**26**	**5**	**5**	**16**	**24**	**54**	**20**
Silkstone United	**26**	**1**	**5**	**20**	**28**	**78**	**8**

Roy Hancock Old Crown left the league.

Division One

Sheffield Lane Top	**24**	**15**	**4**	**5**	**78**	**36**	**49**
Outo Kumpu S. & S.C.	24	14	4	6	71	45	46
Dinnington Town Reserves	24	12	6	6	41	30	42
Handsworth	24	10	8	6	61	50	38
Wickersley Old Boys	24	9	7	8	33	27	34
Parramore Sports	24	9	7	8	44	46	34
Georgia Pacific	24	9	6	9	42	48	33
Dearne/Swinton	24	8	7	9	66	52	31
Elm Tree	24	9	4	11	46	57	31
Ecclesfield Red Rose	24	9	4	11	45	62	31
Frecheville Community Association	24	7	5	12	40	49	26
Dodworth Miners Welfare	24	7	4	13	45	59	25
High Green Villa	**24**	**1**	**8**	**15**	**21**	**72**	**11**

Dearne/Swinton changed their name to Dearne Colliery Miners Welfare and Georgia Pacific changed their name to A.D.S. Precision.

Division Two

Parkgate Reserves	**26**	**22**	**2**	**2**	**110**	**26**	**68**
Half Moon	**26**	**18**	**6**	**2**	**62**	**18**	**56**
Worsbrough Common	**26**	**14**	**7**	**5**	**58**	**24**	**49**
Sheffield Bankers	26	14	5	7	56	31	47
Caribbean Sports	26	13	7	6	64	42	46
AFC Cutlers	26	12	6	8	62	53	42
Worsbrough Bridge Athletic Res.	26	11	7	8	52	42	37
Phoenix Sports & Social	26	9	4	13	47	63	31
Sheffield Centralians	26	9	4	13	45	63	31
Everest	26	7	5	14	51	71	26
De La Salle Old Boys	26	6	7	13	44	66	25
Armthorpe Welfare Reserves	26	5	5	16	41	64	20
Penistone Church Reserves	26	4	7	15	45	87	19
Harworth Colliery Institute Res.	26	1	2	23	13	100	5

Half Moon had 4 points deducted.
Worsbrough Bridge Athletic Reserves had 3 points deducted.
Armthorpe Welfare Reserves moved to the Doncaster & District League, Harworth Colliery Institute Reserves moved to the Gainsborough & District League and AFC Cutlers also left the league. Thorncliffe joined from the South Yorkshire Amateur League while Sheffield Athletic, Millmoor Juniors, Bramley Sunnyside Juniors and Frickley Athletic Reserves also all joined.
Half Moon changed their name to Springwood Davy.

2006-07

Premier Division

Athersley Recreation	26	21	3	2	74	21	66
Stocksbridge Park Steel Reserves	26	17	4	5	72	25	55
Wombwell Main	26	15	6	5	73	34	51
Mexborough Main Street	26	14	3	9	61	39	45
Hollinsend Amateurs	26	10	6	10	36	45	36
HSBC Sheffield	26	10	4	12	58	67	34
Outo Kumpu S. & S.C.	26	9	6	11	56	76	33
Sheffield Lane Top	26	9	5	12	56	45	32
Oughtibridge War Memorial S.C.	26	9	5	12	50	59	32
Thorpe Hesley	26	11	2	13	46	58	32
Dinnington Town Reserves	26	9	4	13	47	50	31
Houghton Main	**26**	**7**	**5**	**14**	**29**	**51**	**26**
Penistone Church	**26**	**6**	**4**	**16**	**33**	**65**	**22**
Edlington W.M.C.	26	5	3	18	27	83	18

* Thorpe Hesley had 3 points deducted.
Edlington W.M.C. left the league.

Division One

Springwood Davy	**26**	**19**	**4**	**3**	**65**	**29**	**61**
Dearne Colliery M.W.	**26**	**21**	**2**	**3**	**84**	**31**	**59**
Parkgate Reserves	**26**	**15**	**4**	**7**	**73**	**33**	**49**
Worsbrough Common	26	14	3	9	58	45	45
Frecheville Community Association	26	11	6	9	64	44	39
Handsworth	26	14	3	9	57	44	39
A.D.S. Precision	26	12	3	11	49	46	39
Dodworth Miners Welfare	26	11	2	13	53	55	31
Silkstone United	26	8	6	12	41	55	30
Ecclesfield Red Rose	26	8	5	13	40	46	29
South Kirkby Colliery	26	7	7	12	32	42	28
Wickersley Old Boys	26	6	4	16	33	57	22
Parramore Sports	26	6	3	17	37	76	21
Elm Tree	26	2	4	20	26	109	10

Dodworth Miners Welfare had 4 points deducted.
Dearne Colliery M.W. and Handsworth each had 6 points deducted.
Dodworth Miners Welfare moved to the Wakefield & District League while A.D.S. Precision and Elm Tree also both left the league.

Division Two

Worsbrough Bridge Athletic Res.	**24**	**16**	**3**	**5**	**64**	**37**	**51**
Everest	**24**	**14**	**4**	**6**	**47**	**28**	**46**
Sheffield Athletic	**24**	**12**	**7**	**5**	**67**	**44**	**43**
Sheffield Bankers	24	13	3	8	49	39	42
Sheffield Centralians	24	12	4	8	42	38	40
Caribbean Sports	24	14	2	8	60	45	38
Millmoor Juniors	24	10	4	10	62	55	34
Thorncliffe	24	9	4	11	42	53	31
Bramley Sunnyside Juniors	24	8	6	10	57	52	30
De La Salle Old Boys	24	7	8	9	47	57	29
Frickley Athletic Reserves	24	4	6	14	35	57	18
Penistone Church Reserves	24	3	5	16	29	66	14
High Green Villa	24	4	4	16	25	55	13

Caribbean Sports had 6 points deducted.
High Green Villa had 3 points deducted.
Phoenix Sports & Social resigned during the season and their record was deleted. They joined the Central Midlands League in 2007-08.
Frickley Athletic Reserves and Sheffield Centralians both left the league.
Sheffield Reserves, Shafton & District, Blackburn Railway and Phoenix Sports & Social Reserves all joined.

Sheffield & Hallamshire County Senior League 2007-2009

2007-08

Premier Division

Wombwell Main	24	18	4	2	64	28	58
Athersley Recreation	24	18	3	3	67	23	57
Hollinsend Amateurs	24	12	5	7	52	40	41
Dinnington Town Reserves	24	10	5	9	51	39	35
Mexborough Main Street	24	11	5	8	47	41	35
Stocksbridge Park Steel Reserves	24	10	2	12	39	50	32
HSBC Sheffield	24	8	4	12	55	58	28
Oughtibridge War Memorial S.C.	24	8	3	13	51	62	27
Thorpe Hesley	24	8	3	13	43	64	27
Springwood Davy	24	10	2	12	43	56	26
Dearne Colliery Miners Welfare	24	7	5	12	41	55	26
Outo Kumpu S. & S.C.	**24**	**8**	**1**	**15**	**48**	**63**	**22**
Sheffield Lane Top	**24**	**5**	**4**	**15**	**37**	**59**	**19**

Mexborough Main Street and Outo Kumpu S&SC had 3 points deducted.
Springwood Davy had 6 points deducted.
Parkgate Reserves resigned from the league during the season and their record was deleted: 12   2   2   8   17   32   8

Division One

Handsworth	**24**	**19**	**1**	**4**	**67**	**25**	**58**
Penistone Church	**24**	**16**	**1**	**7**	**49**	**35**	**49**
Houghton Main	**24**	**14**	**2**	**8**	**60**	**41**	**44**
Everest	24	13	4	7	59	37	43
Parramore Sports	24	12	6	6	48	41	39
Silkstone United	24	11	3	10	48	52	36
Worsbrough Common	24	12	1	11	49	38	34
Worsbrough Bridge Athletic Res.	24	11	1	12	47	47	34
Frecheville Community Association	24	8	2	14	46	56	26
Ecclesfield Red Rose	24	7	4	13	34	52	25
Sheffield Athletic	24	7	2	15	62	76	23
South Kirkby Colliery	24	6	4	14	39	59	22
Wickersley Old Boys	24	2	5	17	20	69	11

Parramore Sports and Worsbrough Common had 3 points deducted.
Parramore Sports moved to the Central Midlands League.

Division Two

Millmoor Juniors	**22**	**17**	**4**	**1**	**63**	**19**	**55**
Sheffield Reserves	**22**	**15**	**4**	**3**	**62**	**22**	**49**
Caribbean Sports	**22**	**13**	**3**	**6**	**45**	**29**	**42**
Shafton & District	22	11	1	8	46	32	40
Bramley Sunnyside Juniors	22	9	6	7	47	35	33
High Green Villa	22	9	6	7	47	36	33
Sheffield Bankers	22	6	5	11	35	51	23
Penistone Church Reserves	22	6	5	11	35	55	23
Thorncliffe	22	3	10	9	33	57	19
Blackburn Railway	22	3	8	11	32	48	16
De La Salle Old Boys	22	3	7	12	38	72	16
Phoenix Sports & Social Reserves	22	3	5	14	30	57	14

Blackburn Railway had 1 point deducted.
Blackburn Railway and Shafton & District both left the league.
Athersley Recreation Reserves and Aston both joined from the South Yorkshire Amateur League while Parramore Sports Reserves, Handsworth Reserves and Hallam Reserves also all joined.

2008-09

Premier Division

Athersley Recreation	24	20	1	3	58	18	61
Wombwell Main	24	15	5	4	50	27	50
Stocksbridge Park Steel Reserves	24	12	6	6	46	31	42
Dearne Colliery Miners Welfare	24	11	6	7	59	40	39
Handsworth	24	12	1	11	62	54	37
Oughtibridge War Memorial S.C.	24	11	4	9	51	56	37
Dinnington Town Reserves	24	8	10	6	43	32	34
Springwood Davy	24	11	3	10	51	43	33
Mexborough Main Street	24	8	4	12	46	61	28
Penistone Church	24	8	2	14	32	49	26
Houghton Main	24	5	4	15	44	63	19
HSBC Sheffield	24	4	4	16	40	67	16
Thorpe Hesley	**24**	**3**	**6**	**15**	**44**	**85**	**15**

Springwood Davy had 3 points deducted.
Hollinsend Amateurs resigned during the season and their record was deleted.
Houghton Main left the league.
Springwood Davy changed their name to Davy Parramores.

Division One

Sheffield Reserves	**26**	**19**	**7**	**0**	**92**	**29**	**64**
Millmoor Juniors	**26**	**19**	**3**	**4**	**90**	**30**	**60**
Caribbean Sports	**26**	**17**	**4**	**5**	**60**	**39**	**55**
Worsbrough Common	26	15	5	6	68	40	47
Sheffield Athletic	26	13	3	10	73	56	39
Outo Kumpu S. & S.C.	26	11	5	10	53	56	38
Everest	26	10	6	10	51	45	36
Silkstone United	26	8	6	12	40	55	30
Wickersley Old Boys	26	7	8	11	42	50	29
Ecclesfield Red Rose	26	8	4	14	49	52	28
South Kirkby Colliery	26	9	2	15	50	63	26
Worsbrough Bridge Athletic Res.	26	7	5	14	42	78	26
Frecheville Community Assoc.	**26**	**7**	**4**	**15**	**54**	**68**	**25**
Sheffield Lane Top	**26**	**0**	**2**	**24**	**28**	**131**	**2**

Worsbrough Common, Sheffield Athletic and South Kirkby Colliery each had 3 points deducted.
Wickersley Old Boys changed their name to Wickersley and Outo Kumpu S. & S.C. changed their name to Brinsworth Whitehill.

Division Two

Aston	**22**	**13**	**5**	**4**	**56**	**32**	**44**
Hallam Reserves	**22**	**13**	**4**	**5**	**51**	**21**	**43**
High Green Villa	**22**	**12**	**6**	**4**	**42**	**16**	**42**
Bramley Sunnyside Juniors	22	10	8	4	66	33	38
Handsworth Reserves	22	11	3	8	67	44	36
Penistone Church Reserves	22	11	3	8	42	48	36
Parramore Sports Reserves	22	9	8	5	56	32	35
Athersley Recreation Reserves	22	9	4	9	42	33	31
Thorncliffe	22	6	3	13	40	51	21
De La Salle Old Boys	22	5	4	13	36	43	19
Sheffield Bankers	22	4	7	11	38	46	14
Phoenix Sports & Social Reserves	22	1	1	20	16	153	4

Sheffield Bankers had 5 points deducted.
Parramore Sports Reserves left the league. South Elmsall United Services, Upton & Harewood Social and Sheffield City all joined.

2009-10
Premier Division

Team	P	W	D	L	F	A	Pts
Sheffield Reserves	22	12	7	3	55	26	42
Athersley Recreation	22	14	3	5	48	24	42
Handsworth	22	12	4	6	46	28	40
Millmoor Juniors	22	9	7	6	35	36	34
Stocksbridge Park Steel Reserves	22	10	3	9	35	27	33
Wombwell Main	22	9	5	8	44	39	32
Penistone Church	22	9	2	11	31	35	29
Oughtibridge War Memorial S.C.	22	7	6	9	41	44	27
Caribbean Sports	22	8	3	11	33	57	27
HSBC Sheffield	22	7	1	14	41	54	21
Dinnington Town Reserves	22	5	6	11	29	35	18
Davy Parramores	22	4	5	13	26	59	17

Sheffield Reserves and HSBC Sheffield each had 1 point deducted.
Athersley Recreation and Dinnington Town Reserves each had 3 points deducted.
Dearne Colliery Miners Welfare and Mexborough Main Street both resigned during the season and their records were deleted.
Dearne C.M.W. record was: 22 7 2 13 33 56 23
Mexborough Main Street record: 19 5 3 11 28 38 18
Handsworth moved to the Northern Counties East League and HSBC Sheffield also left the league.
Davy Parramores changed their name to Davy.

Division One

Team	P	W	D	L	F	A	Pts
Ecclesfield Red Rose	24	17	4	3	88	36	55
Aston	24	16	4	4	77	42	52
South Kirkby Colliery	24	16	3	5	64	35	51
High Green Villa	24	15	5	4	62	31	50
Hallam Reserves	24	14	4	6	55	38	46
Everest	24	11	4	9	64	47	37
Wickersley	24	10	6	8	45	40	36
Worsbrough Common	24	10	1	13	56	55	24
Worsbrough Bridge Athletic Res.	24	8	2	14	42	76	23
Sheffield Athletic	24	5	2	17	40	82	17
Thorpe Hesley	24	4	4	16	41	68	16
Brinsworth Whitehill	24	5	4	15	42	76	16
Silkstone United	24	2	3	19	24	74	9

Worsbrough Bridge Athletic Reserves and Brinsworth Whitehill both had 3 points deducted.
Worsbrough Common had 7 points deducted.
Brinsworth Whitehill left the league.
Aston changed their name to Swallownest Miners Welfare.

Division Two

Team	P	W	D	L	F	A	Pts
Frecheville Community Assoc.	22	15	3	4	61	32	48
South Elmsall United Services	22	14	4	4	65	30	46
Upton & Harewood Social	22	16	0	6	64	25	45
Handsworth Reserves	22	14	1	7	58	40	43
Penistone Church Reserves	22	12	3	7	37	25	39
Bramley Sunnyside Juniors	22	8	4	10	44	53	28
Thorncliffe	22	8	4	10	45	64	28
Athersley Recreation Reserves	22	6	6	10	39	46	24
Sheffield City	22	7	3	12	39	53	23
Sheffield Bankers	22	6	5	11	34	50	23
De La Salle Old Boys	22	3	5	14	28	60	14
Sheffield Lane Top	22	3	2	17	32	68	11

Upton & Harewood Social had 3 points deducted.
Sheffield City had 1 point deducted.
Phoenix Sports & Social Reserves resigned during the season and their record was deleted.
Upton & Harewood Social left the league. Boynton Sports, Millmoor Juniors Reserves and New Bohemians all joined from the South Yorkshire Amateur League, Clowne Wanderers joined from the Chesterfield & District League, Swinton Station Athletic joined from the Doncaster Senior League while Sheffield Parramore Reserves, Clowne Villa and Houghton Main also all joined. South Elmsall United Services changed their name to Frickley Colliery and Sheffield City changed their name to Sheffield City Frecheville.

2010-11
Premier Division

Team	P	W	D	L	F	A	Pts
Swallownest Miners Welfare	26	19	7	0	69	30	64
Athersley Recreation	26	18	5	3	84	28	56
Penistone Church	26	13	6	7	43	30	45
Millmoor Juniors	26	15	0	11	62	60	45
Stocksbridge Park Steel Reserves	26	13	4	9	44	39	43
South Kirkby Colliery	26	12	5	9	60	34	41
High Green Villa	26	11	5	10	44	42	38
Sheffield Reserves	26	9	7	10	56	58	34
Ecclesfield Red Rose	26	9	5	12	44	54	32
Davy	26	6	10	10	38	51	28
Wombwell Main	26	6	8	12	49	53	26
Oughtibridge War Memorial S.C.	26	6	5	15	35	51	23
Dinnington Town Reserves	26	6	4	16	28	47	19
Caribbean Sports	26	1	5	20	24	103	7

Athersley Recreation and Dinnington Town Reserves each had 3 points deducted.
Caribbean Sports had 1 point deducted.
Dinnington Town Reserves left the league.

Division One

Team	P	W	D	L	F	A	Pts
Handsworth Reserves	24	21	2	1	89	35	62
Penistone Church Reserves	24	16	3	5	54	34	51
Everest	24	14	6	4	55	28	48
Hallam Reserves	24	15	4	5	55	30	46
Sheffield Athletic	24	13	1	10	54	48	40
Frickley Colliery	24	11	2	11	47	51	35
Frecheville Community Association	24	10	4	10	55	61	34
Wickersley	24	8	4	12	44	53	28
Worsbrough Common	24	7	5	12	42	49	26
Bramley Sunnyside Juniors	24	6	4	14	40	43	22
Worsbrough Bridge Athletic Res.	24	7	1	16	56	82	22
Thorpe Hesley	24	6	2	16	29	53	20
Silkstone United	24	2	2	20	21	74	8

Handsworth Reserves and Hallam Reserves each had 3 points deducted.
Frickley Colliery left the league.
Worsbrough Common changed their name to Aqua Force Barnsley.

Division Two

Team	P	W	D	L	F	A	Pts
Houghton Main	26	20	2	4	111	27	62
Swinton Station Athletic	26	17	5	4	84	31	56
Sheffield Parramore Reserves	26	17	5	4	96	46	55
Clowne Villa	26	18	2	6	65	37	53
Athersley Recreation Reserves	26	13	8	5	72	25	44
Millmoor Juniors Reserves	26	13	2	11	49	41	41
De La Salle Old Boys	26	11	4	11	50	53	37
Sheffield Lane Top	26	10	6	10	50	45	36
Thorncliffe	26	10	4	12	41	59	34
Boynton Sports	26	8	5	13	49	59	29
Sheffield Bankers	26	7	3	16	40	68	24
Clowne Wanderers	26	4	2	20	28	131	14
New Bohemians	26	3	6	17	28	81	12
Sheffield City Frecheville	26	4	0	22	28	88	12

Sheffield Parramore Reserves had 1 point deducted.
Clowne Villa, Athersley Recreation Reserves and New Bohemians each had 3 points deducted.
Clowne Wanderers and Sheffield City Frecheville both left the league.
Gleadless joined from the South Yorkshire Amateur League and Frecheville Community Association also joined. Sheffield Parramore Reserves changed their name to Worksop Parramore Reserves.

Sheffield & Hallamshire County Senior League 2011-2013

2011-12

Premier Division

Athersley Recreation	26	20	2	4	67	19	62
Stocksbridge Park Steel Reserves	26	16	8	2	41	16	56
Swallownest Miners Welfare	26	16	4	6	60	29	52
Penistone Church	26	14	9	3	66	29	51
High Green Villa	26	9	10	7	42	39	37
Millmoor Juniors	26	9	8	9	41	47	35
Wombwell Main	26	10	4	12	42	44	34
Everest	26	8	9	9	33	37	33
Handsworth Reserves	26	7	7	12	35	44	28
South Kirkby Colliery	26	6	7	13	38	49	25
Davy	25	6	6	13	35	59	24
Ecclesfield Red Rose	26	7	3	16	29	55	24
Hallam Reserves	**25**	**4**	**8**	**13**	**43**	**80**	**20**
Sheffield Reserves	26	5	3	18	32	57	17

Sheffield Reserves had 1 point deducted.
Hallam Reserves vs Davy was not played.
Athersley Recreation moved to the Northern Counties East League and Sheffield Reserves also left the league. Handsworth joined from the Northern Counties East League and replaced their reserves.
Kinsley Boys joined from the Central Midlands League.

Division One

Houghton Main	**26**	**19**	**6**	**1**	**91**	**20**	**63**
Aqua Force Barnsley	25	16	4	5	67	35	52
Frecheville Community Assoc.	26	16	4	6	64	46	52
Penistone Church Reserves	26	13	4	9	54	45	43
Thorpe Hesley	26	12	6	8	60	38	41
Worksop Parramore Reserves	25	12	3	10	49	53	39
Swinton Station Athletic	26	10	8	8	66	46	38
Oughtibridge War Memorial S.C.	26	11	4	11	45	48	37
Silkstone United	26	9	9	8	50	48	36
Worsbrough Bridge Athletic Res.	26	8	5	13	43	67	29
Bramley Sunnyside Juniors	26	9	5	12	51	80	29
Wickersley	26	6	4	16	34	51	22
Sheffield Athletic	26	4	3	19	54	92	15
Caribbean Sports	26	2	3	21	35	94	9

Thorpe Hesley had 1 point deducted.
Bramley Sunnyside Juniors had 3 points deducted.
Aqua Force Barnsley vs Worksop Parramore Reserves not played.
Worksop Parramore Reserves left the league.
Aqua Force Barnsley changed their name to Shaw Lane Aqua Force and Swinton Station Athletic changed their name to Swinton Athletic.

Division Two

Athersley Recreation Reserves	**20**	**17**	**1**	**2**	**53**	**15**	**52**
Gleadless	20	16	1	3	71	21	49
Thorncliffe	**20**	**11**	**2**	**7**	**44**	**33**	**35**
Sheffield Bankers	**20**	**9**	**4**	**7**	**42**	**43**	**31**
Millmoor Juniors Reserves	20	8	3	9	37	32	27
Clowne Villa	20	8	3	9	40	38	27
Boynton Sports	20	7	5	8	40	37	26
Frecheville C.A. Res.	20	7	2	11	35	52	23
De La Salle Old Boys	20	5	3	12	24	47	18
New Bohemians	20	5	3	12	25	50	18
Sheffield Lane Top	20	2	3	15	20	63	9

De La Salle Old Boys, Gleadless and Clowne Villa all left the league.
AFC Dronfield Woodhouse joined from the Hope Valley Amateur League, Jubilee Sports joined from the South Yorkshire Amateur League while Hare & Hounds, Kiveton Park Reserves and Kingstone United all also joined.

2012-13

Premier Division

Shaw Lane Aquaforce	28	22	5	1	76	28	71
Millmoor Juniors	28	19	5	4	76	39	62
Penistone Church	28	17	8	3	61	28	59
Handsworth	28	17	5	6	80	34	56
Houghton Main	28	16	6	6	56	35	54
Swallownest Miners Welfare	28	13	8	7	63	50	47
Stocksbridge Park Steel Reserves	28	9	6	13	46	57	33
Everest	28	9	5	14	54	57	32
Wombwell Main	28	6	10	12	35	54	28
High Green Villa	28	6	9	13	38	57	27
Ecclesfield Red Rose	28	7	5	16	42	52	26
Kinsley Boys	28	8	3	17	57	74	24
Frecheville Community Association	28	6	6	16	44	75	24
Davy	**28**	**6**	**3**	**19**	**49**	**96**	**21**
South Kirkby Colliery	**28**	**5**	**4**	**19**	**35**	**76**	**19**

Kinsley Boys had 3 points deducted.
Shaw Lane Aquaforce moved to the Northern Counties East League and Kinsley Boys moved to the Central Midlands League.

Division One

Oughtibridge War Memorial S.C.	26	21	1	4	98	28	64
Athersley Recreation Reserves	26	19	6	1	83	25	63
Swinton Athletic	26	15	6	5	73	41	51
Penistone Church Reserves	26	12	6	8	58	50	42
Thorpe Hesley	26	12	5	9	48	51	41
Hallam Reserves	26	12	4	10	64	64	40
Silkstone United	26	11	7	8	51	55	40
Bramley Sunnyside Juniors	26	10	6	10	53	46	36
Sheffield Athletic	26	10	6	10	57	58	36
Sheffield Bankers	26	9	4	13	46	69	31
Wickersley	26	6	5	15	40	60	23
Thorncliffe	26	3	8	15	38	73	17
Worsbrough Bridge Athletic Res.	**26**	**4**	**4**	**18**	**32**	**65**	**16**
Caribbean Sports	**26**	**3**	**2**	**21**	**26**	**82**	**10**

Caribbean Sports had 1 point deducted.
Bramley Sunnyside Juniors changed their name to Joker.

Division Two

Jubilee Sports	**18**	**15**	**2**	**1**	**77**	**18**	**47**
Millmoor Juniors Reserves	**18**	**11**	**3**	**4**	**41**	**23**	**36**
Hare & Hounds	**18**	**11**	**3**	**4**	**42**	**30**	**36**
AFC Dronfield Woodhouse	18	10	2	6	39	30	32
Sheffield Lane Top	18	9	2	7	39	40	29
New Bohemians	18	6	4	8	36	38	22
Kiveton Park Reserves	18	6	2	10	32	46	20
Kingstone United	18	5	1	12	30	46	16
Boynton Sports	18	4	2	12	36	54	14
Frecheville C.A. Res.	18	2	1	15	29	76	7

Bawtry Town and Bramley Sunnyside both joined from the Doncaster & District League, North Gawber Colliery joined from the South Yorkshire Amateur League and Kiveton Park joined from the Central Midlands League, replacing their reserves. Maltby Main Reserves and Sheffield Reserves also joined. Hare & Hounds changed their name to Rotherham Town and AFC Dronfield Woodhouse changed their name to AFC Dronfield.

2013-14

Premier Division

Handsworth	26	21	1	4	70	24	64
Oughtibridge War Memorial S.C.	26	18	4	4	56	30	58
Houghton Main	26	16	3	7	57	40	51
Penistone Church	26	15	3	8	59	35	48
Swallownest Miners Welfare	26	12	4	10	49	40	40
Athersley Recreation Reserves	26	11	4	11	51	50	37
Millmoor Juniors	26	11	4	11	46	53	37
Stocksbridge Park Steel Reserves	26	10	6	10	59	45	36
Swinton Athletic	26	10	0	16	43	42	30
Wombwell Main	26	8	4	14	42	70	28
Frecheville Community Association	26	6	8	12	36	55	26
Everest	26	7	3	16	37	52	24
Ecclesfield Red Rose	**26**	**6**	**5**	**15**	**34**	**59**	**23**
High Green Villa	**26**	**4**	**5**	**17**	**29**	**73**	**17**

Penistone Church moved to the Northern Counties East League (NCEL). Handsworth merged with Worksop Parramore of the NCEL to form Handsworth Parramore whose reserves replaced Handsworth in the Sheffield & Hallamshire County Senior League – Premier Division.

Division One

Jubilee Sports	26	16	5	5	66	35	53
Joker	26	16	4	6	67	44	52
Wickersley	**26**	**15**	**6**	**5**	**62**	**41**	**51**
Millmoor Juniors Reserves	26	14	2	10	74	72	44
Rotherham Town	26	13	4	9	72	50	43
Penistone Church Reserves	26	13	4	9	71	49	43
Silkstone United	26	12	7	7	61	48	43
Thorncliffe	26	10	5	11	64	61	35
Sheffield Athletic	26	11	1	14	58	62	34
Hallam Reserves	26	9	5	12	61	73	32
South Kirkby Colliery	26	8	4	14	52	61	28
Thorpe Hesley	26	7	5	14	43	62	26
Sheffield Bankers	26	6	2	18	50	72	20
Davy	26	4	2	20	47	118	14

Hallam Reserves left the league.

Division Two

North Gawber Colliery	**26**	**20**	**5**	**1**	**93**	**23**	**65**
Kingstone United	**26**	**17**	**3**	**6**	**81**	**43**	**54**
AFC Dronfield	**26**	**14**	**4**	**8**	**71**	**54**	**46**
Sheffield Lane Top	26	12	7	7	54	46	43
Bawtry Town	26	10	9	7	69	62	39
Caribbean Sports	26	11	4	11	48	52	37
Maltby Main Reserves	26	11	3	12	65	81	36
Sheffield Reserves	26	10	5	11	54	45	35
Worsbrough Bridge Athletic Res.	26	9	5	12	49	54	32
Bramley Sunnyside	26	10	2	14	57	72	32
Boynton Sports	26	9	2	15	58	77	28
New Bohemians	26	6	7	13	53	65	25
Kiveton Park	26	5	8	13	32	53	23
Frecheville C.A. Reserves	26	5	2	19	32	89	17

Boynton Sports had 1 point deducted.
Boynton Sports, Bramley Sunnyside and Sheffield Reserves all left the league. Denaby Main and Denaby United both joined from the Doncaster & District League, Byron House joined from the South Yorkshire Amateur League, Shaw Lane Aqua Force Reserves and Treeton Terriers both joined from the U-21 Division and Parkgate Reserves also joined.

2014-15

Premier Division

Swinton Athletic	24	16	3	5	62	42	51
Houghton Main	24	14	6	4	43	25	48
Swallownest Miners Welfare	24	14	2	8	52	35	44
Handsworth Parramore Reserves	24	11	4	9	50	44	37
Jubilee Sports	24	10	6	8	49	41	36
Stocksbridge Park Steel Reserves	24	9	7	8	40	32	34
Oughtibridge War Memorial S.C.	24	9	6	9	42	40	33
Athersley Recreation Reserves	24	8	8	8	37	37	32
Joker	24	8	3	13	36	56	27
Millmoor Juniors	24	7	4	13	60	65	25
Wombwell Main	**24**	**6**	**7**	**11**	**41**	**54**	**25**
Wickersley	24	7	4	13	43	64	25
Frecheville Community Association	24	6	2	16	35	55	20

Everest resigned during the season and their record was deleted.
Joker left the league.
Swallownest Miners Welfare changed their name to Swallownest.

Division One

North Gawber Colliery	**22**	**16**	**3**	**3**	**57**	**21**	**51**
Penistone Church Reserves	**22**	**15**	**5**	**2**	**66**	**18**	**50**
Thorpe Hesley	**22**	**13**	**4**	**5**	**52**	**36**	**43**
Ecclesfield Red Rose	22	12	3	7	51	35	39
Silkstone United	22	12	3	7	49	39	39
Kingstone United	22	10	4	8	39	33	34
High Green Villa	22	9	5	8	42	30	32
South Kirkby Colliery	22	8	3	11	43	56	27
AFC Dronfield	22	6	2	14	45	76	20
Sheffield Bankers	22	5	2	15	35	63	17
Davy	22	4	3	15	27	60	15
Millmoor Juniors Reserves	22	3	1	18	22	61	10

Rotherham Town, Sheffield Athletic and Thorncliffe all resigned during the season and their records were deleted.
Penistone Church Reserves changed their name to AFC Penistone Church and Ecclesfield Red Rose changed their name to Ecclesfield Red Rose 1915.

Division Two

Denaby Main	**24**	**17**	**3**	**4**	**77**	**32**	**54**
Caribbean Sports	**24**	**16**	**5**	**3**	**71**	**28**	**53**
Denaby United	**24**	**15**	**4**	**5**	**65**	**33**	**49**
Byron House	**24**	**15**	**2**	**7**	**69**	**39**	**47**
Worsbrough Bridge Athletic Res.	24	12	2	10	41	35	38
Parkgate Reserves	24	10	3	11	49	57	33
Maltby Main Reserves	24	10	3	11	41	69	33
Frecheville C.A. Reserves	24	9	5	10	49	47	32
Shaw Lane Aqua Force Reserves	24	8	4	12	44	62	28
Kiveton Park	24	7	3	14	30	46	24
New Bohemians	24	6	5	13	44	50	23
Sheffield Lane Top	24	5	1	18	24	62	16
Bawtry Town	24	3	6	15	39	83	15

Treeton Terriers resigned during the season and their record was deleted.
Frecheville C.A. Reserves, Parkgate Reserves and Shaw Lane Aqua Force Reserves all left. Grimethorpe Sports and Brinsworth Whitehill both joined from the South Yorkshire Amateur League, Hemsworth Miners Welfare Reserves joined from the Doncaster & District League while North Gawber Colliery Reserves, Houghton Main Reserves and Swallownest Reserves all joined.

Sheffield & Hallamshire County Senior League 2015-2017

2015-16

Premier Division

Frecheville Community Association	26	19	3	4	69	38	60
Swinton Athletic	26	16	4	6	60	31	52
Houghton Main	26	15	4	7	54	31	49
AFC Penistone Church	26	12	7	7	51	41	43
Stocksbridge Park Steel Reserves	26	12	7	7	44	35	43
North Gawber Colliery	26	11	5	10	52	51	38
Swallownest	26	10	3	13	47	49	33
Millmoor Juniors	26	9	5	12	61	67	32
Athersley Recreation Reserves	26	9	4	13	34	45	31
Jubilee Sports	26	8	6	12	40	54	30
Handsworth Parramore Reserves	26	7	7	12	46	54	28
Oughtibridge War Memorial S.C.	26	9	1	16	33	64	28
Wickersley	26	7	4	15	53	63	25
Thorpe Hesley	26	5	6	15	38	59	21

Thorpe Hesley left the league.

Division One

Denaby United	24	16	5	3	76	36	53
Wombwell Main	24	16	2	6	81	45	50
Denaby Main	24	14	7	3	54	29	49
Caribbean Sports	24	15	2	7	64	43	47
Silkstone United	24	14	1	9	73	55	43
Ecclesfield Red Rose 1915	24	12	4	8	62	47	40
South Kirkby Colliery	24	11	2	11	54	50	35
Sheffield Bankers	24	9	6	9	43	49	33
AFC Dronfield	24	9	4	11	65	60	31
Davy	24	7	3	14	45	65	24
Byron House	24	5	4	15	48	71	19
High Green Villa	24	3	4	17	35	83	13
Millmoor Juniors Reserves	24	2	2	20	30	97	8

Kingstone United left during the season and their record was deleted.
Byron House left the league at the end of the season.

Division Two

Hemsworth Miners Welfare Res.	20	16	2	2	75	21	50
Grimethorpe Sports	20	15	2	3	80	26	47
Brinsworth Whitehill	20	12	3	5	63	35	39
North Gawber Colliery Reserves	20	10	5	5	40	41	35
Houghton Main Reserves	20	10	3	7	46	41	33
Swallownest Reserves	20	10	1	9	58	39	31
New Bohemians	20	9	4	7	48	37	31
Kiveton Park	20	8	2	10	37	37	26
Worsbrough Bridge Athletic Res.	20	3	4	13	22	61	13
Bawtry Town	20	1	3	16	28	102	6
Sheffield Lane Top	20	1	1	18	26	83	4

Maltby Main Reserves left during the season and their record was deleted. They joined Division Two South (see below) in 2016-17.
North Gawber Colliery Reserves and Swallownest Reserves both left the league.

2016-17

Premier Division

Swallownest	26	22	1	3	77	20	67
Swinton Athletic	26	17	3	6	74	40	54
Frecheville Community Association	26	15	6	5	62	37	51
Stocksbridge Park Steel Reserves	26	15	6	5	52	32	50
AFC Penistone Church	26	15	3	8	76	39	48
Handsworth Parramore Reserves	26	14	5	7	49	31	47
Jubilee Sports	26	13	5	8	65	64	44
Houghton Main	26	11	7	8	52	37	40
North Gawber Colliery	26	10	3	13	56	51	33
Wombwell Main	26	8	4	14	42	64	28
Athersley Recreation Reserves	26	6	6	14	51	58	24
Millmoor Juniors	26	5	1	20	35	101	16
Denaby United	26	3	3	20	40	82	12
Denaby Main	26	1	2	23	22	97	5

Swallownest moved to the Northern Counties East League and Athersley Recreation Reserves were merged into Grimethorpe Sports.

Division One

Grimethorpe Sports	26	18	1	7	110	62	55
South Kirkby Colliery	26	17	2	7	60	34	53
Oughtibridge War Memorial S.C.	26	16	4	6	69	29	52
Ecclesfield Red Rose 1915	26	16	3	7	66	41	51
Wickersley	26	13	4	9	68	40	43
Caribbean Sports	26	13	4	9	60	55	43
Brinsworth Whitehill	26	13	4	9	56	53	43
High Green Villa	26	12	4	10	63	64	40
Sheffield Bankers	26	11	6	9	58	44	39
AFC Dronfield	26	11	4	11	62	51	37
Silkstone United	26	9	5	12	53	64	32
Davy	26	5	4	17	42	91	19
Hemsworth Miners Welfare Res.	26	3	2	21	37	109	11
Millmoor Juniors Reserves	26	1	1	24	23	90	4

Millmoor Juniors Reserves disbanded and Davy also left the league.

Division Two was expanded and split into North and South sections.

The North section consisted of 11 clubs, 3 of whom had been members of Division Two in 2015-16: Bawtry Town, Houghton Main Reserves and Worsbrough Bridge Athletic Reserves (who became Worsbrough Bridge Athletic Development). The 8 new clubs were Euroglaze and Working Wonders (both from the South Yorkshire Amateur League), FC Gracehome (from the Doncaster & District League), Hepworth United (from the Huddersfield & District League), Dodworth Miners Welfare (a newly re-formed club), South Kirkby Colliery Reserves, Stocksbridge Park Steels Development and Wombwell Main Development.

The South section consisted of 12 clubs, 4 of whom had been members of Division Two in 2015-16: Kiveton Park, Maltby Main Reserves, New Bohemians and Sheffield Lane Top. The 8 new clubs were Davy Reserves, Sheffield Bankers Reserves, Sheffield Medics and Swinton Athletic Reserves (all from the South Yorkshire Amateur League), AFC Dronfield Reserves (from the Hope Valley Amateur League), Caribbean Sports Reserves, Millmoor Juniors Development and Renishaw Rangers.

Division Two (North)

Dodworth Miners Welfare	20	15	3	2	80	20	48
Hepworth United	20	15	2	3	83	15	47
Stocksbridge Park Steels Dev.	20	15	2	3	67	20	47
Euroglaze	20	13	2	5	55	28	41
FC Gracehome	20	11	1	8	57	27	34
Houghton Main Reserves	20	10	1	9	38	42	31
South Kirkby Colliery Reserves	20	6	3	11	29	67	21
Bawtry Town	20	5	3	12	31	61	18
Wombwell Main Development	20	5	1	14	41	72	16
Worsbrough Bridge Athletic Res.	20	3	3	14	23	78	12
Working Wonders	20	1	1	18	18	92	4

Bawtry Town, Euroglaze, FC Gracehome and Houghton Main Reserves all disbanded. Worsbrough Bridge Athletic Reserves changed their name to Worsbrough Bridge Athletic Development.

Division Two (South)

Sheffield Medics	22	15	2	5	79	29	47
Caribbean Sports Reserves	22	13	4	5	65	33	43
Kiveton Park	22	13	4	5	58	36	43
Swinton Athletic Reserves	22	13	1	8	56	32	40
Davy Reserves	22	13	0	9	61	52	39
New Bohemians	22	10	4	8	40	48	34
AFC Dronfield Reserves	22	7	4	11	43	48	25
Maltby Main Reserves	22	7	4	11	44	65	25
Sheffield Lane Top	22	7	2	13	37	62	23
Sheffield Bankers Reserves	22	6	4	12	38	53	22
Millmoor Juniors Development	22	6	4	12	38	60	22
Renishaw Rangers	22	5	1	16	33	74	16

Davy Reserves, Sheffield Lane Top and Millmoor Juniors Development all disbanded and Renishaw Rangers moved to the Central Midlands League. The two sections of Division Two combined to form a single division. Burngreave, Boynton Sports, Manor Hotel and Thurcroft Miners Institute all joined as newly formed clubs while North Gawber Colliery Reserves also joined.

2017-18

Premier Division

Swinton Athletic	28	21	2	5	83	33	65
Stocksbridge Park Steel Reserves	28	21	1	6	88	36	64
AFC Penistone Church	28	17	6	5	86	25	57
North Gawber Colliery	28	16	7	5	77	48	55
++ Frecheville Community Assoc.	28	15	6	7	71	39	53
Grimethorpe Sports	28	15	7	6	85	37	51
Jubilee Sports	28	15	4	9	96	53	49
+ Oughtibridge War Memorial S.C.	28	10	6	12	60	34	37
South Kirkby Colliery	28	10	6	12	37	52	35
Wombwell Main	28	9	7	12	43	49	34
Handsworth Parramore Reserves	28	8	8	12	40	41	32
Denaby United	28	5	10	13	55	88	25
++ **Denaby Main**	**28**	**3**	**4**	**21**	**30**	**116**	**15**
Houghton Main	**28**	**4**	**2**	**22**	**25**	**78**	**14**
Millmoor Juniors	**28**	**2**	**2**	**24**	**18**	**165**	**8**

++ Frecheville Community Association and Denaby Main each had 2 points added.
+ Oughtibridge War Memorial S.C. had 1 point added.
Grimethorpe Sports and South Kirkby Colliery had 1 point deducted.
AFC Penistone Church changed their name to Penistone Church Reserves and Frecheville Community Association changed their name to Frecheville.

Division One

Dodworth Miners Welfare	**22**	**19**	**2**	**1**	**70**	**22**	**59**
High Green Villa	**22**	**14**	**2**	**6**	**54**	**41**	**44**
Hepworth United	**22**	**13**	**4**	**5**	**48**	**32**	**43**
Kiveton Park	22	10	3	9	63	56	33
Ecclesfield Red Rose 1915	22	9	3	10	41	45	30
Sheffield Medics	22	8	4	10	35	46	28
AFC Dronfield	22	8	3	11	58	56	27
Hemsworth Miners Welfare Res.	22	7	5	10	45	56	26
Caribbean Sports	22	7	4	11	34	39	25
Brinsworth Whitehill	22	7	3	12	36	49	24
Stocksbridge Park Steels Dev.	**22**	**4**	**6**	**12**	**28**	**52**	**18**
Silkstone United	22	4	5	13	36	54	17

Wickersley and Sheffield Bankers both resigned during the season and their records were deleted. Sheffield Bankers rejoined in 2018-19.
Silkstone United left the league.

Division Two

++ **Burngreave**	**26**	**20**	**2**	**4**	**119**	**48**	**65**
Wombwell Main Development	**26**	**17**	**2**	**7**	**80**	**53**	**50**
Boynton Sports	**26**	**14**	**6**	**6**	**95**	**48**	**48**
Manor Hotel	26	15	3	8	88	63	48
Sheffield Bankers Reserves	26	15	2	9	74	68	47
+ Swinton Athletic Reserves	26	13	4	9	62	48	45
Caribbean Sports Reserves	26	12	5	9	94	61	41
New Bohemians	26	13	2	11	61	55	41
Worsbrough Bridge Athletic Dev.	26	10	3	13	71	82	33
Maltby Main Reserves	26	9	6	11	39	50	33
Working Wonders	26	8	6	12	71	63	30
North Gawber Colliery Reserves	26	3	7	16	24	91	16
AFC Dronfield Reserves	26	3	6	17	38	88	14
Thurcroft Miners Institute	26	1	4	21	25	123	7

++ Burngreave had 3 points added.
+ Swinton Athletic Reserves had 2 points added.
AFC Dronfield Reserves had 1 point deducted.
Wombwell Main Development had 3 points deducted.
South Kirkby Colliery Reserves resigned during the season and their record was deleted.
Working Wonders moved to the Yorkshire Christian League while Manor Hotel, Caribbean Sports Reserves, Sheffield Bankers Reserves, Maltby Main Reserves and North Gawber Colliery Reserves also all left the league. United Worksop joined from the Midland Amateur Alliance, Sheffield Union joined from the Sheffield & District Fair Play League, Wombwell Town joined as a newly formed club while Ardsley Athletico Junior and Dodworth Miners Welfare Reserves also both joined. Wombwell Main Development changed their name to Wombwell Main Reserves.

2018-19

Premier Division

North Gawber Colliery	28	21	5	2	80	31	68
Dodworth Miners Welfare	28	20	4	4	69	26	64
Swinton Athletic	28	17	5	6	79	39	56
Penistone Church Reserves	28	16	5	7	69	29	53
Stocksbridge Park Steel Reserves	28	14	6	8	53	48	48
Frecheville	28	13	4	11	68	57	43
Wombwell Main	28	14	0	14	69	43	42
Grimethorpe Sports	28	13	2	13	65	73	41
Hepworth United	28	11	6	11	39	40	39
High Green Villa	28	9	7	12	58	54	34
Jubilee Sports	28	8	7	13	44	49	31
Oughtibridge War Memorial S.C.	28	7	6	15	38	52	27
Handsworth Parramore Reserves	**28**	**4**	**6**	**18**	**34**	**62**	**18**
Denaby United	28	5	3	20	33	105	18
South Kirkby Colliery	**28**	**4**	**2**	**22**	**20**	**110**	**14**

Denaby United moved to the Doncaster & District League replaced by Wakefield, a newly formed club. Grimethorpe Sports changed their name to Grimethorpe LLUK, Handsworth Parramore Reserves changed their name to Handsworth Reserves and Frecheville changed their name to Frecheville Davys.

Division One

Burngreave	**24**	**20**	**2**	**2**	**89**	**39**	**62**
Ecclesfield Red Rose 1915	**24**	**20**	**0**	**4**	**78**	**29**	**60**
Houghton Main	**24**	**17**	**3**	**4**	**61**	**33**	**54**
AFC Dronfield	24	17	2	5	77	36	53
Denaby Main	24	15	1	8	97	31	46
Kiveton Park	24	10	5	9	50	43	35
Hemsworth Miners Welfare Res.	24	9	3	12	47	48	27
Wombwell Main Reserves	24	7	4	13	48	69	25
Caribbean Sports	24	7	3	14	50	58	24
Sheffield Medics	24	6	6	12	53	62	24
+ Boynton Sports	24	4	5	15	36	71	20
Sheffield Bankers	24	5	4	15	49	93	19
Millmoor Juniors	24	0	0	24	22	145	0

Hemsworth Miners Welfare Reserves had 3 points deducted.
+ Boynton Sports had 3 points added.
Brinsworth Whitehill left during the season and their record was deleted.
Boynton Sports moved to the Central Midlands League while Sheffield Bankers, Millmoor Juniors, Hemsworth Miners Welfare Reserves and Caribbean Sports also all left the league. Wombwell Main Reserves changed their name to Wombwell Main Development.

Division Two

Wombwell Town	**20**	**17**	**2**	**1**	**63**	**16**	**53**
Stocksbridge Park Steels Dev.	20	15	4	1	74	27	49
Sheffield Union	**20**	**11**	**5**	**4**	**58**	**30**	**38**
New Bohemians	**20**	**10**	**1**	**9**	**48**	**51**	**31**
Ardsley Athletico Junior	**20**	**9**	**3**	**8**	**43**	**28**	**30**
Dodworth Miners Welfare Reserves	20	8	3	9	42	27	27
Swinton Athletic Reserves	20	7	3	10	38	47	24
United Worksop	**20**	**6**	**5**	**9**	**35**	**37**	**23**
AFC Dronfield Reserves	20	7	0	13	37	48	21
Thurcroft Miners Institute	20	4	5	11	31	77	17
Worsbrough Bridge Athletic Dev.	20	0	1	19	14	95	1

AFC Dronfield Reserves, Dodworth Miners Welfare Reserves, Stocksbridge Park Steels Development and Worsbrough Bridge Athletic Development all left the league. Kinsley Boys joined from the Doncaster & District League, Frecheville Community Association joined as a newly formed club while Athersley Recreation Reserves, Bank End, Burngreave Reserves, Houghton Main Reserves, Jubilee Sports Development, Sheffield Reserves, Silkstone United and South Elmsall United Services also all joined.

Sheffield & Hallamshire County Senior League 2019-2021

2019-20

The season was terminated on 26th March 2020 due to the effects of the Covid-19 pandemic. The table shown is as it stood on that date.

Premier Division

Swinton Athletic	18	17	1	0	86	14	52
Dodworth Miners Welfare	18	10	4	4	34	28	34
Ecclesfield Red Rose 1915	21	10	4	7	37	32	34
Penistone Church Reserves	18	10	3	5	38	19	33
North Gawber Colliery	15	9	4	2	31	16	31
Grimethorpe LLUK	15	9	1	5	42	34	28
Stocksbridge Park Steel Reserves	19	8	4	7	39	33	28
Wombwell Main	16	8	4	4	39	33	28
Wakefield	22	8	4	10	38	45	28
High Green Villa	18	7	6	5	35	34	27
Oughtibridge War Memorial S.C.	20	7	4	9	29	31	25
Hepworth United	20	4	8	8	28	28	20
Houghton Main	17	6	1	10	33	48	19
Burngreave	25	6	0	19	50	80	18
Jubilee Sports	18	5	0	13	24	41	15
Frecheville Davys	18	1	0	17	19	86	3

Grimethorpe LLUK disbanded.
Burngreave changed their name to Sheffield Town.

Division One

Wombwell Town	17	14	1	2	48	21	43
Handsworth Reserves	17	12	0	5	62	26	36
AFC Dronfield	17	11	1	5	39	27	34
Kiveton Park	14	8	1	5	32	24	25
South Kirkby Colliery	14	7	1	6	27	25	22
Sheffield Medics	15	7	0	8	36	32	21
Denaby Main	13	6	1	6	23	20	19
Wombwell Main Development	13	5	0	8	25	34	15
Sheffield Union	17	5	1	11	27	41	15
New Bohemians	13	3	0	10	11	36	9
United Worksop	14	0	2	12	20	64	2

Sheffield Union had 1 point deducted.
Ardsley Athletico Juniors resigned during the season and their record was deleted.
United Worksop left the league.

Division Two

South Elmsall United Services	15	12	1	2	63	22	37
Swinton Athletic Reserves	19	12	1	6	56	32	37
Sheffield Reserves	16	11	1	4	51	34	34
Kinsley Boys	15	11	0	4	56	27	33
Frecheville Community Association	14	8	3	3	54	30	27
Athersley Recreation Reserves	13	8	3	2	44	22	27
Houghton Main Reserves	15	6	1	8	30	33	19
Bank End	19	6	0	13	44	76	18
Burngreave Reserves	19	5	1	13	40	80	16
Jubilee Sports Development	13	4	2	7	31	37	14
Thurcroft Miners Institute	16	3	1	12	30	62	10
Silkstone United	16	2	0	14	24	68	6

Frecheville Community Association disbanded while Burngreave Reserves, Jubilee Sports Development and Sheffield Reserves also left the league. Stocksbridge Park Steels Development, Caribbean Sports, Millmoor Juniors, Sheffield Lane Top, Kiveton Park Reserves, Wakefield EFP and Parkgate Reserves all joined. Houghton Main Reserves changed their name to Houghton Main Development and Thurcroft Miners Institute changed their name to Thurcroft.

2020-21

The season was terminated on 2nd November 2020 due to the continuing Covid-19 pandemic. The table shown is as it stood on that date.

Premier Division

Dodworth Miners Welfare	9	7	1	1	29	5	22
Swinton Athletic	7	7	0	0	24	4	21
North Gawber Colliery	9	4	2	3	26	15	14
Ecclesfield Red Rose 1915	9	4	2	3	21	12	14
Oughtibridge War Memorial S.C.	8	4	1	3	15	19	13
Wakefield	6	4	0	2	14	8	12
Penistone Church Reserves	7	4	0	3	14	12	12
Hepworth United	8	4	0	4	12	15	12
Wombwell Main	5	3	0	2	13	12	9
Jubilee Sports	5	2	0	3	6	13	6
Stocksbridge Park Steel Reserves	9	2	0	7	13	26	6
Sheffield Town	5	1	0	4	8	11	3
Houghton Main	6	1	0	5	13	25	3
High Green Villa	6	1	0	5	12	24	3
Frecheville Davys	5	1	0	4	2	21	3

Frecheville Davys left the league.

Division One

Handsworth Reserves	6	5	1	0	24	6	16
Denaby Main	7	4	3	0	15	6	15
Kiveton Park	6	4	0	2	19	9	12
Wombwell Town	5	3	1	1	13	6	10
South Kirkby Colliery	6	3	1	2	10	13	10
South Elmsall United Services	6	3	0	3	14	13	9
AFC Dronfield	4	2	1	1	6	6	7
Athersley Recreation Reserves	8	2	1	5	13	17	7
Sheffield Union	4	2	0	2	8	9	6
Sheffield Medics	5	1	1	3	7	8	4
Kinsley Boys	3	1	0	2	3	7	3
New Bohemians	5	1	0	4	5	22	3
Main Wombwell Development	7	0	1	6	8	23	1

Wombwell Main Development changed their name to Wombwell Main Reserves and Athersley Recreation Reserves changed their name to Athersley Recreation Development.

Division Two

Caribbean Sports	8	8	0	0	32	8	24
Swinton Athletic Reserves	8	6	1	1	33	13	19
Millmoor Juniors	8	5	3	0	32	10	18
Silkstone United	7	6	0	1	20	10	18
Houghton Main Development	7	2	2	3	14	20	8
Sheffield Lane Top	8	2	2	4	13	20	8
Kiveton Park Reserves	6	2	0	4	16	17	6
Stocksbridge Park Steels Dev.	6	2	0	4	20	23	6
Wakefield EFP	4	1	1	2	6	14	4
Bank End	6	1	1	4	6	17	4
Parkgate Reserves	8	1	0	7	12	21	3
Thurcroft	6	0	0	6	5	36	0

Stocksbridge Park Steels Development, Houghton Main Development, Bank End and Wakefield EFP all left the league. Wakefield U-23, Boynton Sports, Hepworth United Development, North of England Football Academy, Sheffield City, Pontefract Collieries Reserves, Worsbrough Common Athletic and Mexborough Athletic all joined.

HUMBER PREMIER LEAGUE 2000-2021

The Humber Premier League was formed in 2000 to cater for clubs close to the Humber estuary, from both the East Riding of Yorkshire and also from north Lincolnshire. There were 16 founder members.

2000-01

Reckitts	30	26	3	1	108	29	81
Chisholms	30	19	6	5	72	25	63
Barton Town Old Boys	30	19	5	6	68	40	62
Sculcoates Amateurs	30	19	3	8	97	37	60
Hall Road Rangers Reserves	30	16	6	8	71	49	54
Driffield	30	15	5	10	58	57	50
North Cave	30	14	2	14	60	68	44
North Ferriby United Reserves	30	14	2	14	64	78	44
Beverley Town	30	13	4	13	79	56	43
Hider Foods	30	13	2	15	72	82	41
Easington United	30	11	6	13	68	63	39
Westella & Willerby	30	11	4	15	57	67	37
Hedon United	30	10	6	14	52	65	36
Hutton Cranswick United	30	4	2	24	31	102	14
Walkington Wanderers	30	3	3	24	27	101	12
Bridlington Town Reserves	30	2	3	25	35	100	9

Barton Town Old Boys moved to the Central Midlands League, Walkington Wanderers moved to the East Riding County Amateur League and North Cave also left the league. Bridlington Sports Club joined.

2001-02

Reckitts	24	22	1	1	83	18	67
Sculcoates Amateurs	24	15	5	4	69	36	50
Westella & Willerby	24	12	6	6	60	40	42
Beverley Town	24	12	5	7	60	41	41
North Ferriby United Reserves	24	12	4	8	61	35	40
Hutton Cranswick United	24	11	5	8	53	46	38
Easington United	24	11	4	9	60	39	37
Hider Foods	24	9	4	11	40	50	31
Hall Road Rangers Reserves	24	9	2	13	44	45	29
Driffield	24	8	4	12	35	46	28
Bridlington Town Reserves	24	4	3	17	24	74	15
Hedon United	24	3	4	17	44	94	13
Bridlington Sports Club	24	3	3	18	25	94	12

Chisholms resigned from the league during the season and their record at the time was deleted: 14 7 0 7 33 33 21
Hall Road Rangers Reserves left the league. Pocklington Town joined from the Driffield & District League, St. Andrews Sutton joined from the Hull Sunday League, Withernsea joined from the East Riding County Amateur League and Keyingham also joined.

2002-03

Reckitts	30	26	3	1	96	29	81
Hutton Cranswick United	30	19	6	5	76	36	63
North Ferriby United Reserves	30	18	5	7	89	52	59
Hider Foods	30	16	6	8	66	41	54
Easington United	30	15	7	8	65	53	52
Sculcoates Amateurs	30	15	6	9	68	52	51
Westella & Willerby	30	14	7	9	71	50	49
Beverley Town	30	13	7	10	57	44	46
Driffield	30	12	6	12	60	53	39
St. Andrews Sutton	30	12	2	16	53	66	38
Withernsea	30	8	5	17	36	73	29
Keyingham	30	8	2	20	48	95	26
Bridlington Town Reserves	30	6	7	17	44	65	25
Bridlington Sports Club	30	7	4	19	56	88	25
Pocklington Town	30	6	5	19	38	75	23
Hedon United	30	3	6	21	29	80	15

Driffield had 3 points deducted.

North Ferriby United Reserves left the league.
East Hull Amateurs joined from the East Riding County Amateur League.

2003-04

Hutton Cranswick United	30	21	5	4	65	25	68
Easington United	30	20	3	7	85	44	63
Reckitts	30	19	5	6	95	40	62
Sculcoates Amateurs	30	18	5	7	64	38	59
Hider Foods	30	18	3	9	62	38	57
Westella & Willerby	30	17	5	8	74	45	56
Bridlington Town Reserves	30	16	6	8	62	35	54
Beverley Town	30	13	6	11	64	58	45
Withernsea	30	12	4	14	62	75	40
Keyingham	30	10	2	18	55	73	32
Hedon United	30	8	6	16	35	53	30
St. Andrews Sutton	30	9	2	19	52	78	29
East Hull Amateurs	30	7	4	19	35	74	25
Driffield	30	6	6	18	41	76	24
Bridlington Sports Club	30	6	5	19	45	87	23
Pocklington Town	30	5	3	22	22	79	18

Bridlington Sports Club left the league and Hornsea Town joined.
St. Andrews Sutton changed their name to Sutton Rangers.

2004-05

Reckitts	30	23	4	3	78	23	73
Sculcoates Amateurs	30	20	9	1	83	27	69
Easington United	30	15	9	6	66	37	54
Beverley Town	30	16	5	9	68	43	53
Westella & Willerby	30	15	5	10	74	47	50
Hider Foods	30	14	7	9	66	44	49
Pocklington Town	30	13	9	8	58	36	48
Hutton Cranswick United	30	13	6	11	50	34	45
Hornsea Town	30	10	10	10	63	59	40
Sutton Rangers	30	10	6	14	33	52	36
Bridlington Town Reserves	30	12	4	14	43	59	28
Keyingham	30	6	8	16	50	64	26
Hedon United	30	7	3	20	29	78	24
East Hull Amateurs	30	5	8	17	31	69	23
Driffield	30	7	5	18	35	79	23
Withernsea	30	3	4	23	28	104	13

Bridlington Town Reserves had 12 points deducted.
Driffield had 3 points deducted.
Sutton Rangers changed their name to St. Andrews Sutton, Keyingham changed their name to Hedon Rangers and Hider Foods changed their name to Hessle Rangers.

An additional division was added. All clubs in the existing division became members of the new Premier Division with the exception of East Hull Amateurs who joined the new Division One.

There were 10 further clubs who became founder members of Division One: Barton Town Old Boys Reserves joined from the Scunthorpe & District League; AFC Charleston, Pinefleet Wolfreton and St. Andrews Police Club all joined from the East Riding Amateur League; Anlaby United, Brandesburton, Bransholme Athletic and North Ferriby United Reserves all joined from the East Riding County League while Discount Carpets and Malet Lambert Youth Club also joined.

Humber Premier League 2005-2008

2005-06
Premier Division

Reckitts	26	20	4	2	78	20	64
Sculcoates Amateurs	26	17	5	4	75	32	56
Hutton Cranswick United	26	16	4	6	65	31	52
Hessle Rangers	26	14	4	8	51	34	46
Westella & Willerby	26	13	6	7	50	35	45
Easington United	26	12	8	6	48	47	44
Pocklington Town	26	13	4	9	45	23	43
Beverley Town	26	11	6	9	51	40	39
Hornsea Town	26	8	6	12	29	46	30
Bridlington Town Reserves	26	7	4	15	31	54	25
Driffield	26	5	7	14	35	62	22
Hedon Rangers	26	5	3	18	43	75	18
Withernsea	26	4	3	19	36	102	15
Hedon United	26	3	4	19	30	66	13

St. Andrews Sutton resigned after losing their first game 5-0 and their record was deleted.
Driffield left the league.

Division One

North Ferriby United Reserves	**20**	**12**	**4**	**4**	**55**	**25**	**40**
Barton Town Old Boys Reserves	**20**	**14**	**4**	**4**	**51**	**29**	**40**
Anlaby United	20	12	3	5	40	26	39
Discount Carpets	20	11	3	6	44	37	36
Pinefleet Wolfreton	20	9	7	4	42	32	34
Malet Lambert Youth Club	20	6	8	6	32	38	26
AFC Charleston	20	7	6	7	38	47	24
Brandesburton	20	5	3	12	39	52	18
Bransholme Athletic	20	4	5	11	34	50	17
St. Andrews Police Club	20	4	4	12	28	48	16
East Hull Amateurs	20	3	3	14	24	43	12

AFC Charleston had 3 points deducted.
AFC Charleston left the league just before the start of the 2006-07 season.
Hall Road Rangers Reserves, Long Riston and North Cave all joined from the East Riding County Amateur League, Smith & Nephew joined from the Hull Sunday League and LSS Lucarlys joined from the Central Midlands League.

2006-07
Premier Division

Sculcoates Amateurs	26	20	6	0	81	19	66
Westella & Willerby	26	15	6	5	62	32	51
Hutton Cranswick United	26	16	1	9	70	34	49
Reckitts	26	13	9	4	69	30	48
North Ferriby United Reserves	26	13	6	7	55	42	45
Hornsea Town	26	14	2	10	61	45	44
Easington United	26	13	5	8	57	41	44
Beverley Town	26	10	5	11	50	47	35
Pocklington Town	26	10	4	12	36	35	34
Barton Town Old Boys Reserves	26	9	6	11	52	58	27
Hedon Rangers	26	5	5	16	36	71	20
Hessle Rangers	26	5	2	19	29	70	17
Hedon United	26	5	2	19	41	108	17
Withernsea	26	4	1	21	31	98	13

Bridlington Town Reserves resigned during the season and their record at the time was deleted: 14 4 2 8 27 59 14
Barton Town Old Boys Reserves had 6 points deducted.
Hedon United moved to the East Riding County League.

Division One

Smith & Nephew	22	21	0	1	79	12	63
Malet Lambert Youth Club	22	16	1	5	61	23	49
LSS Lucarlys	22	14	2	6	62	33	44
North Cave	22	11	4	7	38	44	37
Brandesburton	22	8	8	6	36	43	32
Pinefleet Wolfreton	22	8	5	9	46	45	29
St. Andrews Police Club	22	6	7	9	45	46	25
Hall Road Rangers Reserves	22	6	7	9	37	58	25
Discount Carpets	22	5	6	11	51	59	21
Long Riston	22	4	8	10	24	42	20
Bransholme Athletic	22	5	3	14	26	55	18
East Hull Amateurs	22	2	1	19	26	71	7

Anlaby United resigned from the league during the season and their record at the time was deleted: 9 2 1 6 13 21 7
East Hull Amateurs left the league.
Hessle Sporting Club and Kinnersley both joined from the East Riding Amateur League, Mill Lane United joined from Sunday football and Selby Town Reserves joined as a newly formed team.

2007-08
Premier Division

Sculcoates Amateurs	30	21	4	5	71	30	67
Smith & Nephew	30	19	4	7	82	33	61
Reckitts	30	17	8	5	65	32	59
Beverley Town	30	16	7	7	61	32	55
Hutton Cranswick United	30	14	7	9	74	52	49
North Ferriby United Reserves	30	13	8	9	62	48	47
Pocklington Town	30	13	7	10	52	44	46
Westella & Willerby	30	13	6	11	56	40	45
Hedon Rangers	30	12	7	11	73	67	43
LSS Lucarlys	30	14	1	15	56	65	43
Easington United	30	11	7	12	52	47	40
Malet Lambert Youth Club	30	9	8	13	43	62	35
Hornsea Town	30	8	9	13	43	48	33
Barton Town Old Boys Reserves	30	5	5	20	46	74	20
Hessle Rangers	30	5	3	22	34	92	18
Withernsea	**30**	**4**	**1**	**25**	**25**	**129**	**13**

Hutton Cranswick United and Westella & Willerby both moved to the Central Midlands League and were replaced by their reserves who both joined from the East Riding County League. LSS Lucarlys changed their name to Cleethorpes Town and Smith & Nephew changed their name to Chalk Lane.

Division One

St. Andrews Police Club	**18**	**12**	**2**	**4**	**49**	**28**	**38**
Kinnersley	18	9	4	5	47	32	31
North Cave	18	9	3	6	41	26	30
Hall Road Rangers Reserves	18	9	5	4	40	37	29
Selby Town Reserves	18	9	1	8	46	43	28
Pinefleet Wolfreton	18	8	2	8	45	37	26
Bransholme Athletic	18	6	4	8	36	43	22
Hessle Sporting Club	18	7	1	10	45	55	22
Brandesburton	18	5	2	11	35	48	17
Long Riston	18	3	2	13	24	59	11

Hall Road Rangers Reserves had 3 points deducted.
Discount Carpets resigned from the league during the season and their record was deleted: 11 2 2 7 11 30 8
Mill Lane United resigned from the league during the season and their record was deleted: 6 2 2 2 14 15 8
Pinefleet Wolfreton moved to the East Riding Amateur League and Selby Town Reserves also left the league. Kingburn Athletic and Inter Charter both joined from the East Riding Amateur League, North Ferriby Athletic joined from the East Riding County League, Bridlington Sports Club joined from the Driffield & District League and Scarborough Athletic Reserves joined as a newly-formed team.

2008-09
Premier Division

	P	W	D	L	F	A	Pts
Chalk Lane	28	22	3	3	107	25	69
Reckitts	28	21	3	4	80	31	66
Sculcoates Amateurs	28	19	1	8	73	46	58
Easington United	28	15	6	7	71	55	51
St. Andrews Police Club	28	15	4	9	66	64	49
Beverley Town	28	15	3	10	45	33	48
Hedon Rangers	28	12	3	13	53	52	39
Pocklington Town	28	10	6	12	39	47	36
Cleethorpes Town	28	11	5	12	46	61	35
Hornsea Town	28	8	5	15	48	64	29
North Ferriby United Reserves	28	7	6	15	36	53	27
Westella & Willerby Reserves	28	8	3	17	35	63	27
Malet Lambert Youth Club	28	5	7	16	33	66	22
Barton Town Old Boys Reserves	28	6	2	20	27	59	20
Hessle Rangers	28	5	5	18	36	76	20

Cleethorpes Town had 3 points deducted.
Hutton Cranswick United Reserves resigned during the season and their record was deleted.
Easington United moved to the Central Midlands League and Barton Town Old Boys Reserves also left the league.
St. Andrews Police Club changed their name to St. Andrews.

Division One

	P	W	D	L	F	A	Pts
Hall Road Rangers Reserves	22	17	1	4	74	22	52
Hessle Sporting Club	22	16	2	4	61	33	50
Bransholme Athletic	22	14	3	5	69	43	45
North Cave	22	13	1	8	59	37	40
North Ferriby Athletic	22	12	3	7	56	31	39
Scarborough Athletic Reserves	22	9	3	10	61	51	30
Brandesburton	22	9	2	11	50	59	29
Kingburn Athletic	22	7	4	11	45	62	25
Bridlington Sports Club	22	8	1	13	46	56	25
Withernsea	22	6	2	14	48	77	20
Inter Charter	22	4	7	11	36	55	19
Long Riston	22	2	1	19	23	102	7

Kinnersley resigned from the league during the season and their record at the time was deleted: 20 10 2 8 62 53 32
Crown joined from the East Riding Amateur League and East Riding Rangers joined from youth football.

2009-10
Premier Division

	P	W	D	L	F	A	Pts
Reckitts	26	18	4	4	75	29	58
Hornsea Town	26	15	4	7	57	40	49
Sculcoates Amateurs	26	14	6	6	64	38	48
Hessle Rangers	26	13	5	8	52	41	44
Beverley Town	26	12	6	8	48	37	42
Hall Road Rangers Reserves	26	14	1	11	71	63	40
Chalk Lane	26	10	9	7	49	33	39
Hedon Rangers	26	12	3	11	65	51	39
Hessle Sporting Club	26	10	5	11	57	53	35
North Ferriby United Reserves	26	10	3	13	54	58	33
Malet Lambert Youth Club	26	6	7	13	44	74	25
St. Andrews	26	7	3	16	46	78	24
Pocklington Town	26	6	4	16	32	50	22
Westella & Willerby Reserves	26	3	4	19	25	94	13

Hall Road Rangers Reserves had 3 points deducted.
Cleethorpes Town resigned during the season and their record was deleted. They immediately moved to the Lincolnshire League and took over their reserves' fixtures.

Division One

	P	W	D	L	F	A	Pts
Crown	22	15	4	3	69	35	49
Bridlington Sports Club	22	15	2	5	91	41	47
North Cave	22	14	4	4	76	25	46
North Ferriby Athletic	22	13	3	6	69	42	42
Bransholme Athletic	22	11	4	7	49	44	37
Kingburn Athletic	22	8	5	9	36	35	29
Scarborough Athletic Reserves	22	9	2	11	48	70	29
Brandesburton	22	7	3	12	32	52	24
East Riding Rangers	22	6	3	13	34	58	21
Withernsea	22	5	6	11	33	61	21
Long Riston	22	5	2	15	39	69	17
Inter Charter	22	4	2	16	31	75	14

Hodgsons and Howden Amateurs both joined from the East Riding County League, Howden Amateurs changing their name to Howden.

2010-11
Premier Division

	P	W	D	L	F	A	Pts
Sculcoates Amateurs	30	23	3	4	97	33	72
Reckitts	30	20	4	6	81	32	64
Chalk Lane	30	14	7	9	58	35	49
North Ferriby United Reserves	30	15	4	11	67	53	49
Beverley Town	30	13	7	10	56	48	46
Crown	30	12	9	9	45	45	45
Pocklington Town	30	10	11	9	47	53	41
Hessle Rangers	30	12	5	13	51	64	41
Hall Road Rangers Reserves	30	12	4	14	56	55	40
Bridlington Sports Club	30	13	1	16	64	71	40
Hornsea Town	30	11	5	14	57	66	38
St. Andrews	30	11	1	18	44	70	34
Hedon Rangers	30	9	5	16	45	75	32
Westella & Willerby Reserves	30	9	4	17	49	77	31
Malet Lambert Youth Club	**30**	**7**	**9**	**14**	**56**	**74**	**30**
Hessle Sporting Club	**30**	**7**	**5**	**18**	**40**	**62**	**26**

Division One

	P	W	D	L	F	A	Pts
Hodgsons	22	19	2	1	94	33	59
North Cave	22	18	2	2	79	22	56
Brandesburton	22	14	1	7	68	44	43
North Ferriby Athletic	22	10	4	8	70	65	34
Bransholme Athletic	22	9	5	8	61	64	32
Scarborough Athletic Reserves	22	9	4	9	66	45	31
Howden	22	7	5	10	69	75	26
Kingburn Athletic	22	7	5	10	33	39	26
Withernsea	22	8	1	13	50	79	25
East Riding Rangers	22	5	4	13	37	50	19
Long Riston	22	5	2	15	37	81	17
Inter Charter	22	3	1	18	34	101	10

Kingburn Athletic and Inter Charter both moved to the East Riding Amateur League. Driffield Evening Institute joined from the East Riding County League, Driffield Junior joined from the Driffield & District League and Hessle United also joined. Scarborough Town joined after leaving the Wearside League in 2010 to join the Northern Counties (East) League for which they needed floodlights. However planning permission was not granted in time and so they had been inactive in 2010-11.

Humber Premier League 2011-2014

2011-12

Premier Division

Reckitts	30	24	2	4	68	29	74
Sculcoates Amateurs	30	22	3	5	83	19	69
Chalk Lane	30	18	5	7	86	35	59
North Cave	30	16	6	8	66	39	54
Hornsea Town	30	15	7	8	69	59	52
Beverley Town	30	13	7	10	49	54	46
Hessle Rangers	30	13	5	12	48	52	44
Crown	30	13	4	13	66	58	43
Hall Road Rangers Reserves	30	13	2	15	92	68	38
Pocklington Town	30	11	4	15	46	61	37
Westella & Willerby Reserves	30	9	9	12	48	68	36
North Ferriby United Reserves	30	10	4	16	62	70	34
Bridlington Sports Club	30	8	4	18	52	90	28
Hodgsons	30	8	4	18	50	95	28
St. Andrews	30	6	7	17	39	60	25
Hedon Rangers	**30**	**4**	**1**	**25**	**33**	**100**	**13**

Hall Road Rangers Reserves had 3 points deducted.
Hall Road Rangers Reserves moved to the East Riding Amateur League.
Westella & Willerby Reserves changed their name to Westella & Willerby as the first team in the Central Midlands League changed their name to Westella Hanson.

Division One

Scarborough Town	**26**	**21**	**1**	**4**	**118**	**37**	**64**
Bransholme Athletic	**26**	**20**	**2**	**4**	**97**	**48**	**62**
East Riding Rangers	26	15	7	4	74	46	52
Hessle Sporting Club	26	15	5	6	69	47	50
Brandesburton	26	13	5	8	59	63	44
Scarborough Athletic Reserves	26	10	7	9	62	49	37
North Ferriby Athletic	26	10	6	10	73	68	36
Withernsea	26	10	5	11	69	81	35
Malet Lambert Youth Club	26	9	5	12	56	67	32
Driffield Evening Institute	26	9	3	14	55	60	30
Hessle United	26	9	4	13	64	64	28
Driffield Junior	26	6	4	16	55	88	22
Long Riston	26	3	3	20	32	83	12
Howden	26	2	3	21	49	131	9

Hessle United had 3 points deducted.
Pinefleet Wolfreton joined from the East Riding Amateur League, Little Weighton joined from the East Riding County League and Goole United also joined.

2012-13

Premier Division

Beverley Town	24	18	5	1	57	24	59
North Ferriby United Reserves	24	15	6	3	58	27	51
Sculcoates Amateurs	24	14	5	5	66	34	47
Crown	24	13	5	6	47	34	44
Reckitts	24	12	7	5	48	31	43
Hornsea Town	24	10	3	11	43	50	33
North Cave	24	10	2	12	55	50	32
Pocklington Town	24	10	1	13	50	36	31
Hessle Rangers	24	8	5	11	37	43	29
Chalk Lane	24	7	3	14	40	57	24
St. Andrews	24	6	3	15	39	58	21
Bridlington Sports Club	24	5	3	16	39	80	18
Westella & Willerby	24	3	2	19	22	77	11

Scarborough Town resigned and disbanded during the season and their record was deleted. Bransholme Athletic and Hodgsons also both resigned during the season and their records were deleted. Hodgsons joined the East Riding County League in 2013-14. North Ferriby United Reserves left the league.

Division One

Goole United	**30**	**23**	**5**	**2**	**124**	**38**	**74**
Scarborough Athletic Reserves	**30**	**22**	**4**	**4**	**93**	**39**	**70**
Hedon Rangers	**30**	**20**	**6**	**4**	**88**	**42**	**66**
Little Weighton	30	16	4	10	83	50	52
Hessle Sporting Club	30	13	8	9	68	55	47
North Ferriby Athletic	30	13	5	12	82	78	44
Driffield Evening Institute	30	14	2	14	74	82	44
Malet Lambert Youth Club	30	13	3	14	64	69	42
Brandesburton	30	13	3	14	73	82	42
Hessle United	30	13	3	14	55	75	42
East Riding Rangers	30	11	6	13	71	62	39
Long Riston	30	12	1	17	54	92	37
Driffield Junior	30	11	1	18	65	80	34
Pinefleet Wolfreton	30	7	4	19	68	87	25
Howden	30	5	3	22	50	112	18
Withernsea	30	5	0	25	44	113	15

Wawne United and South Cave both joined from the East Riding County League and Rapid Solicitors joined from the East Riding Amateur League.

2013-14

Premier Division

Beverley Town	28	25	2	1	90	18	77
Reckitts	28	22	2	4	78	26	68
Sculcoates Amateurs	28	17	6	5	89	42	57
Chalk Lane	28	17	3	8	70	41	54
Crown	28	15	4	9	75	47	49
Goole United	28	13	7	8	77	55	46
Hessle Rangers	28	12	4	12	80	72	40
North Cave	28	10	9	9	50	52	39
Pocklington Town	28	11	1	16	52	65	34
Scarborough Athletic Reserves	28	10	3	15	50	76	33
Hornsea Town	28	8	5	15	36	61	26
Bridlington Sports Club	28	6	4	18	43	94	22
St. Andrews	28	7	1	20	51	103	22
Hedon Rangers	28	6	3	19	36	64	21
Westella & Willerby	28	4	0	24	34	95	12

Hornsea Town had 3 points deducted.
North Cave and Westella & Willerby both left the league.
St. Andrews changed their name to Hull United.

Division One

Wawne United	**26**	**19**	**3**	**4**	**111**	**47**	**60**
East Riding Rangers	**26**	**14**	**7**	**5**	**54**	**40**	**49**
Brandesburton	26	15	3	8	82	57	48
Rapid Solicitors	26	14	5	7	86	56	47
Driffield Evening Institute	26	13	6	7	75	57	45
South Cave	26	12	6	8	70	57	42
Hessle United	26	9	7	10	69	72	34
Little Weighton	26	10	4	12	61	64	34
North Ferriby Athletic	26	10	5	11	58	65	32
Howden	26	9	3	14	52	62	30
Pinefleet Wolfreton	26	6	6	14	52	88	24
Driffield Junior	26	6	5	15	51	80	23
Long Riston	26	6	4	16	53	93	22
Hessle Sporting Club	26	6	2	18	45	81	20

North Ferriby Athletic had 3 points deducted.
Malet Lambert Youth Club and Withernsea both resigned during the season and their records were deleted. Withernsea joined the East Riding County League in 2014-15. Pinefleet Wolfreton left the league while AFC Rovers joined from the East Riding County League.

2014-15
Premier Division

Sculcoates Amateurs	26	21	3	2	89	18	66
Hull United	26	18	3	5	78	23	57
Crown	26	18	1	7	63	37	55
Reckitts	26	14	5	7	69	39	47
East Riding Rangers	26	14	4	8	64	45	46
Pocklington Town	26	11	6	9	44	45	39
Beverley Town	26	10	6	10	39	46	36
Chalk Lane	26	9	6	11	43	44	33
Hessle Rangers	26	9	3	14	49	72	30
Goole United	26	9	1	16	48	59	28
Hedon Rangers	26	8	4	14	42	59	28
Wawne United	26	7	4	15	52	66	25
Bridlington Sports Club	26	7	2	17	29	85	23
Hornsea Town	26	2	2	22	33	104	5

Hornsea Town had 3 points deducted.
Hull United moved to the Northern Counties East League.

Division One

AFC Rovers	**22**	**16**	**2**	**4**	**66**	**33**	**50**
Driffield Evening Institute	**22**	**12**	**6**	**4**	**52**	**37**	**42**
North Ferriby Athletic	22	13	2	7	56	35	41
South Cave	**22**	**12**	**5**	**5**	**60**	**41**	**41**
Hessle United	22	11	3	8	51	41	36
Howden	22	9	6	7	55	40	33
Long Riston	22	10	2	10	54	44	32
Driffield Junior	22	8	5	9	59	52	29
Little Weighton	22	8	3	11	47	62	27
Brandesburton	22	6	2	14	38	66	20
Rapid Solicitors	22	6	1	15	46	73	19
Hessle Sporting Club	22	2	1	19	30	90	7

Hessle Sporting Club left the league. AFC Northfield, Hull United Reserves, Park Athletic and Walkington all joined from the East Riding County League and Westella & Willerby and Hall Road Rangers Reserves also both joined. Rapid Solicitors changed their name to Hunters.

2015-16
Premier Division

Wawne United	30	22	2	6	101	55	68
Crown	30	20	3	7	75	40	63
Pocklington Town	30	16	8	6	65	39	56
Sculcoates Amateurs	30	16	7	7	75	37	55
Reckitts	30	15	7	8	77	50	52
East Riding Rangers	30	14	10	6	60	39	52
Chalk Lane	30	15	7	8	52	40	52
Goole United	30	12	4	14	67	67	40
Hessle Rangers	30	11	4	15	55	77	37
Beverley Town	30	10	6	14	58	57	36
South Cave	30	10	5	15	55	71	35
Bridlington Sports Club	30	9	5	16	64	76	32
Hedon Rangers	30	8	2	20	46	87	26
AFC Rovers	30	8	2	20	42	90	26
Driffield Evening Institute	**30**	**6**	**7**	**17**	**58**	**73**	**25**
Hornsea Town	**30**	**7**	**3**	**20**	**53**	**105**	**24**

Wawne United moved to the East Riding County League and Bridlington Sports Club also left the league.
Easington United joined from the Central Midlands League.
AFC Rovers changed their name to East Yorkshire Carnegie.

Division One

North Ferriby Athletic	22	18	0	4	70	22	54
Hunters	22	15	3	4	91	47	48
Walkington	22	13	6	3	67	36	45
Long Riston	22	10	3	9	37	44	33
Park Athletic	22	10	1	11	52	54	31
Hessle United	22	9	4	9	50	54	31
Hull United Reserves	22	8	5	9	33	44	29
AFC Northfield	22	6	7	9	52	59	25
Westella & Willerby	22	6	5	11	33	56	23
Brandesburton	22	6	3	13	49	73	21
Howden	22	6	1	15	46	64	19
Hall Road Rangers Reserves	22	5	2	15	32	59	17

Driffield Junior and Little Weighton both left during the season and their records were deleted.
Long Riston moved to the East Riding County League, Park Athletic disbanded and both AFC Northfield and Hull United Reserves also left the league. Hull United joined from the Northern Counties East League, Bridlington Town Reserves joined from the East Riding County League and LIV Supplies joined as a newly formed club. Hunters changed their name to Hanson Jewellers and Hessle United changed their name to Hessle Sporting United.

2016-17
Premier Division

Crown	28	21	3	4	79	33	66
Sculcoates Amateurs	28	18	5	5	86	33	59
Chalk Lane	28	17	2	9	57	41	53
Pocklington Town	28	15	5	8	86	49	50
East Yorkshire Carnegie	28	15	4	9	65	51	49
Hessle Rangers	28	13	9	6	73	63	48
Reckitts	28	14	3	11	66	57	45
East Riding Rangers	28	13	5	10	54	47	44
Beverley Town	28	12	6	10	56	41	42
South Cave	28	9	4	15	58	63	31
Goole United	28	9	3	16	54	88	30
North Ferriby Athletic	28	6	7	15	32	47	25
Hedon Rangers	28	6	7	15	51	90	25
Hanson Jewellers	28	5	4	19	42	101	19
Easington United	**28**	**2**	**3**	**23**	**45**	**100**	**9**

East Yorkshire Carnegie moved to the Northern Counties East League. South Cave changed their name to South Cave United. Westella VIP joined from the Northern Counties East League, changing their name to Westella & Willerby. Goole United and Hanson Jewellers both left the league.

Division One

Hornsea Town	**20**	**16**	**1**	**3**	**69**	**29**	**49**
Walkington	**20**	**15**	**2**	**3**	**62**	**23**	**47**
Bridlington Town Reserves	20	9	4	7	40	34	31
Driffield Evening Institute	20	8	2	10	44	50	26
LIV Supplies	20	7	4	9	38	38	25
Hall Road Rangers Reserves	20	7	4	9	33	55	25
Howden	20	6	5	9	33	48	23
Brandesburton	20	5	7	8	46	54	22
Westella & Willerby	20	6	4	10	36	45	22
Hull United	20	6	3	11	39	51	21
Hessle Sporting United	20	6	2	12	39	52	20

North Ferriby United Academy joined from the East Riding County League becoming North Ferriby United Reserves. Driffield Junior and Barton Town Reserves also joined. Walkington changed their name to AFC Walkington and Westella & Willerby changed their name to Blackburn Athletic.

Humber Premier League 2017-2020

2017-18

Premier Division

Chalk Lane	26	19	1	6	61	20	58
Pocklington Town	26	15	5	6	73	27	50
Beverley Town	26	14	4	8	60	34	46
Sculcoates Amateurs	26	14	4	8	58	48	46
Reckitts	26	11	7	8	45	41	40
AFC Walkington	26	12	4	10	59	56	40
Hedon Rangers	26	12	1	13	51	60	37
Hessle Rangers	26	9	6	11	40	56	33
Crown	26	10	3	13	37	54	33
Westella & Willerby	26	8	8	10	51	55	32
South Cave United	26	7	9	10	60	64	30
East Riding Rangers	26	6	7	13	43	71	25
Hornsea Town	26	6	5	15	50	77	23
North Ferriby Athletic	26	4	6	16	38	63	18

Crown left the league. AFC Walkington changed their name to Walkington.

Division One

Beverley Town Reserves	24	18	4	2	93	48	58
Driffield Junior	24	16	5	3	80	33	53
Barton Town Reserves	24	16	1	7	77	36	49
Bridlington Town Reserves	24	15	1	8	67	40	46
Howden	24	13	5	6	71	59	44
Brandesburton	24	11	4	9	61	53	37
Goole United	24	11	1	12	44	55	34
Easington United	24	10	3	11	51	60	33
Driffield Evening Institute	24	10	2	12	63	52	32
North Cave	24	8	4	12	50	55	25
Blackburn Athletic	24	7	4	13	47	51	22
Hessle Sporting United	24	0	5	19	38	102	5
Hall Road Rangers Reserves	24	1	1	22	30	128	4

North Cave and Blackburn Athletic each had 3 points deducted.
North Cave left the league. Kingfields and Reckitts Reserves both joined from the East Riding County League and St. Marys also joined.
Hessle Sporting United changed their name to Hessle Sporting Club.

2018-19

Division One

LIV Supplies	24	20	3	1	88	38	63
Hull United	24	19	2	3	76	30	59
North Ferriby United Reserves	24	15	1	8	90	57	46
Bridlington Town Reserves	24	15	1	8	65	37	46
Brandesburton	24	13	4	7	67	53	43
Easington United	24	8	8	8	51	46	32
Blackburn Athletic	24	7	6	11	46	60	27
Driffield Evening Institute	24	8	3	13	38	55	27
Howden	24	8	2	14	60	78	26
Driffield Junior	24	6	2	16	38	57	20
Hall Road Rangers Reserves	24	6	6	12	50	66	18
Barton Town Reserves	24	6	2	16	54	79	17
Hessle Sporting United	24	4	2	18	45	112	14

Hall Road Rangers Reserves had 6 points deducted.
Barton Town Reserves had 3 points deducted.
North Ferriby United Reserves left the league.
Beverley Town Reserves and North Cave both joined from the East Riding County League and Goole United also joined.

Premier Division

Chalk Lane	28	23	4	1	101	31	73
Pocklington Town	28	22	2	4	78	29	68
Beverley Town	28	17	3	8	84	43	54
Reckitts	28	14	3	11	70	54	45
Hull United	28	12	7	9	58	54	43
Hornsea Town	28	13	4	11	72	78	43
Sculcoates Amateurs	28	10	10	8	61	59	40
LIV Supplies	28	11	5	12	70	77	38
North Ferriby Athletic	28	11	2	15	56	85	35
Westella & Willerby	28	9	7	12	52	54	34
Hessle Rangers	28	10	3	15	42	60	33
South Cave United	28	8	5	15	49	62	29
Walkington	28	6	5	17	52	75	23
Hedon Rangers	28	4	8	16	47	88	20
East Riding Rangers	**28**	**5**	**2**	**21**	**44**	**87**	**17**

A new club called North Ferriby was formed as a replacement for North Ferriby United of the Northern Premier League who had disbanded.
The new club joined the Northern Counties East League and North Ferriby Athletic continued playing in the Humber Premier League as the new club's reserve side.

2019-20

The season was terminated on 26th March 2020 due to the effects of the Covid-19 pandemic. The table shown is as it stood on that date.

Premier Division

South Cave United	24	18	4	2	57	20	58
Chalk Lane	24	18	1	5	72	22	55
Westella & Willerby	24	17	3	4	57	39	54
Beverley Town	26	15	3	8	63	28	48
Pocklington Town	25	14	3	8	54	39	45
Walkington	22	13	3	6	49	30	42
Hessle Rangers	21	10	3	8	49	46	33
Hull United	23	9	4	10	41	55	31
LIV Supplies	21	8	5	8	53	50	29
Hedon Rangers	28	8	3	17	46	75	27
Sculcoates Amateurs	21	7	5	9	33	33	26
Driffield Junior	22	7	3	12	31	53	24
Hornsea Town	20	6	1	13	42	50	19
Reckitts	25	4	5	16	27	49	17
Barton Town Reserves	22	4	2	16	24	55	14
North Ferriby Reserves	26	3	4	19	29	83	13

Division One

Hessle Sporting Club	21	11	4	6	55	51	37
East Riding Rangers	19	10	6	3	39	24	36
Reckitts Reserves	18	11	2	5	57	42	35
Kingfields	19	10	3	6	56	40	33
Brandesburton	16	8	3	5	40	26	27
Driffield Evening Institute	17	8	3	6	43	34	27
Easington United	16	6	5	5	37	30	23
Bridlington Town Reserves	19	6	4	9	41	39	22
St. Marys	18	5	7	6	43	52	22
Goole United	16	6	3	7	29	38	21
Blackburn Athletic	18	5	2	11	25	39	17
Beverley Town Reserves	19	4	4	11	30	43	16
Howden	16	2	2	12	23	60	8

Hall Road Rangers Reserves resigned during the season and their record was deleted. They joined the East Riding County League in 2020-21 as Hall Road Rangers Development.
Cherry Burton joined from the East Riding County League and Sproatley Juniors joined from youth football. Howden moved to the York League and Kingfields also left the league.

2020-21

The clubs played each other just once due to the effects of the ongoing Covid-19 pandemic.

Premier Division

Beverley Town	15	14	0	1	51	15	42
LIV Supplies	15	9	4	2	44	22	31
Westella & Willerby	15	8	4	3	39	26	28
Hull United	15	9	1	5	38	27	28
South Cave United	15	8	4	3	26	15	28
Hedon Rangers	15	8	1	6	30	28	25
Pocklington Town	15	6	4	5	38	22	22
Barton Town Reserves	15	6	2	7	28	29	20
Driffield Junior	15	6	2	7	31	43	20
Sculcoates Amateurs	15	5	4	6	28	27	19
Reckitts	15	4	4	7	25	31	16
Chalk Lane	15	5	1	9	29	39	16
Hornsea Town	15	5	1	9	30	53	16
Hessle Rangers	15	4	3	8	26	39	15
Walkington	15	3	5	7	22	35	14
North Ferriby Reserves	15	0	0	15	17	51	0

Barton Town Reserves moved to the Lincolnshire League.
Walkington and North Ferriby Reserves also both left the league.

Division One

It did not prove possible for even the fixturs to be completed so final positions were decided on a Points per Game basis.

Cherry Burton	11	8	1	2	43	18	25	2.27
East Riding Rangers	12	8	2	2	30	22	26	2.17
St. Marys	12	6	3	3	42	22	21	1.75
Brandesburton	11	6	1	4	36	25	19	1.73
Easington United	11	5	3	3	25	23	18	1.64
Hessle Sporting Club	11	5	3	3	28	18	18	1.64
Blackburn Athletic	9	4	2	3	24	14	14	1.56
Goole United	11	4	3	4	21	23	15	1.36
Bridlington Town Reserves	12	5	1	6	24	32	16	1.33
Driffield Evening Institute	8	2	1	5	12	17	7	0.88
Reckitts Reserves	12	2	4	6	12	36	10	0.83
Beverley Town Reserves	12	2	2	8	21	34	8	0.67
Sproatley Juniors	12	1	2	9	21	55	5	0.42

Sproatley Juniors left. Chaos United and Hutton Cranswick SRA both joined from the East Riding County League. Bridlington Town Reserves changed their name to Bridlington Town Rovers.

NOTTS ALLIANCE – UPDATED INFORMATION

When we published Notts Alliance tables in 2020 as part of the Non-League Tables of the East Midlands, we stated that research was ongoing and not all final tables had yet been found. In the 12 months since then, we have managed to find additional tables from a number of different sources, the principal of which was Richard Laurence who was kind enough to grant us access to his own private records. Furthermore, we have been able to update some tables with additional or corrected information. All additional and updated tables are shown below.

Research is still ongoing and we hope to publish further updates in future.

1899-1900

Nottingham St. Alban's	18	17	0	1	73	4	34
Boots Athletic	18	15	0	3	64	20	30
Radcliffe-on-Trent	16	12	0	4	55	16	24
Lawrence's Athletic	18	9	2	7	45	34	20
Southwell St. Mary's	14	6	2	6	42	27	14
Ruddington	14	5	0	9	25	65	10
Nottingham St. Mary's	14	5	1	8	20	35	9
Thos. Adams Ltd.	17	4	1	12	22	41	9
Midland Railway	14	1	1	12	16	48	3
Bingham & District	15	1	1	13	11	83	3

Ruddington were suspended for non-compliance with rules.
Nottingham St. Mary's had 2 points deducted.

1900-01

Radcliffe-on-Trent	19	17	1	1	43	13	35
Nottingham St. Alban's	18	15	1	2	53	9	31
Nottingham St. Andrew's	17	10	4	3	41	19	24
Newark Avenue	19	10	3	6	47	12	23
Beeston Rangers	18	8	1	9	36	33	17
Lawrence's Athletic	20	6	5	9	29	38	17
Southwell St. Mary's	17	7	2	8	28	27	16
Boots Athletic	17	7	2	8	28	30	16
Wilford	20	6	0	14	22	42	10
Nottingham St. Mary's	17	2	1	14	10	72	5
Keyworth/Belvoir Rangers	15	1	1	13	11	83	3

Wilford had 2 points deducted.
Belvoir Rangers withdrew during the season and Keyworth completed their fixtures.

1901-02

Kimberley St. John's	22	18	3	1	56	19	39
Nottingham St. Andrew's	22	15	5	2	47	19	35
Newark Avenue	21	10	5	6	44	19	25
Lawrence's Athletic	22	10	5	7	44	19	25
Southwell St. Mary's	22	8	5	9	40	40	21
Beeston Rangers	22	9	2	11	34	41	20
Radcliffe-on-Trent	22	6	7	9	33	38	19
Notts Jardine's	22	8	3	11	31	44	19
Wilford	22	9	0	13	30	51	18
Raleigh Athletic	22	5	6	11	35	47	16
Radford Church	21	6	2	13	21	48	14
Nottingham St. Mary's	22	5	1	16	24	54	11

Nottingham St. Mary's had 2 points deducted.

Notts Alliance Update 1902-1929

1902-03

	P	W	D	L	F	A	Pts
Notts Jardine's	18	13	2	3	41	23	28
Raleigh Athletic	18	12	3	3	46	17	27
Lawrence's Athletic	18	12	1	5	31	18	25
Wilford	17	7	3	7	24	28	17
Mansfield Mechanics Institute	17	6	4	7	38	36	16
Newark Avenue	18	6	3	9	37	41	15
Southwell St. Mary's	18	5	5	8	15	29	13
Nottingham St. Andrew's	18	5	2	11	25	39	12
Kimberley St. John's	18	5	5	8	19	29	11
Radcliffe-on-Trent	18	3	2	13	22	38	6

Southwell St. Mary's and Radcliffe-on-Trent each had 2 points deducted.
Kimberley St. John's had 4 points deducted.

1907-08

	P	W	D	L	F	A	Pts
Sneinton	24	20	3	1	91	13	43
Netherfield Rangers	24	18	1	5	84	30	37
Basford United	24	18	1	5	57	25	35
Jardine's Athletic	24	15	1	8	50	34	31
Notts Olympic Reserves	24	13	3	8	43	25	27
Swain's Athletic	24	12	1	11	58	46	25
Keyworth	24	11	3	10	50	51	25
Radcliffe-on-Trent	24	9	2	13	38	51	20
Boots Athletic	24	4	7	13	19	52	15
Albany United	24	7	0	17	29	56	14
Nottingham St. Andrew's	24	5	4	15	26	75	12
Ruddington	24	5	3	16	23	61	11
Jacoby's	24	4	1	19	18	70	9

Ruddington had 2 points deducted.

1910-11

	P	W	D	L	F	A	Pts
Netherfield Rangers (champions)	21	15	3	3	55	26	33
Sneinton	21	15	3	3	65	21	33
Arnold St. Mary's	22	14	3	5	52	19	31
Basford United	22	13	4	5	71	25	30
Player's Athletic	22	13	2	7	43	28	28
Notts Jardine's	22	12	3	7	54	31	27
Notts Rangers	22	11	1	10	35	26	23
Mapperley	22	6	7	9	25	39	19
Keyworth	21	4	5	12	27	73	13
Notts Olympic	22	4	4	14	24	54	12
Radcliffe-on-Trent	22	1	3	18	14	76	5
Sherwood Institute	21	1	4	16	12	54	3

Sherwood Institute had 2 points deducted.

1914-15

	P	W	D	L	F	A	Pts
Netherfield Rangers	17	17	0	0	83	10	34
Arnold St. Mary's	18	13	2	3	61	20	28
Sneinton	18	11	3	4	55	34	25
Basford United	18	9	3	6	45	29	21
Notts Olympic	17	6	4	7	27	37	16
Mapperley	18	5	5	8	35	50	15
Boots Athletic	18	3	7	8	29	46	13
Ericssons Athletic	18	4	4	10	31	45	12
Colwick St. John's	18	1	5	12	13	60	7
Notts Rangers	18	2	3	13	12	60	7

1915-16

Champions: Smith Bros.

1916-19

The competition was suspended between 1916 and 1919.

1919-20

Basford United (champions), Arnold St. Mary's, Bestwood Colliery, Boots Athletic, Burton Joyce, Clifton Colliery, Comrades, Ericssons Athletic, Gedling, Netherfield Rangers, North Street, Nottingham Discharged Soldiers & Sailors, Players Athletic, Rufford Colliery and Sneinton.

1920-21

Also: Lenton resigned during the season and their record was deleted.

1921-22

	P	W	D	L	F	A	Pts
Player's Athletic	22	18	3	1	80	13	39
Boots Athletic	22	17	4	1	63	14	38
Clifton Colliery	17	11	4	2	27	14	26
Gedling	22	10	4	8	38	41	24
Lenton	20	8	5	7	40	26	21
Newark Athletic	21	7	7	7	37	38	21
Eastwood Town	22	5	8	9	18	30	18
Sneinton	19	6	3	10	34	50	15
Ericssons Athletic	20	5	5	10	25	43	15
Basford United	20	4	5	11	36	40	13
Arnold St. Mary's	19	5	3	11	25	61	13
Netherfield Rangers	21	0	3	18	18	76	3

Rufford Colliery resigned during the season and their record was deleted.

1923-24

	P	W	D	L	F	A	Pts
Player's Athletic	18	16	2	0	91	17	34
Boots Athletic	18	14	2	2	56	12	30
Lenton	18	13	2	3	53	17	28
Ransome & Marles	18	9	4	5	50	32	22
Gedling Colliery Welfare	18	8	3	7	42	30	19
Stapleford Brookhill	18	7	3	8	46	42	17
Sneinton	18	8	0	10	33	37	16
Basford United	18	3	2	13	25	42	8
Colwick Junction	18	3	0	15	17	88	6
Netherfield Rangers	18	0	0	18	9	104	0

1926-27

	P	W	D	L	F	A	Pts
Player's Athletic	20	16	2	2	65	32	34
Lenton	20	16	1	3	78	39	33
Sutton Junction	20	13	3	4	70	45	29
Clifton Colliery	20	12	0	8	49	37	24
Boots Athletic	20	9	4	7	59	46	22
Sneinton	20	9	0	11	47	51	18
Gedling Colliery Welfare	20	8	2	10	57	68	18
Basford United	20	5	5	10	46	59	15
Ransome & Marles	20	5	4	11	48	64	14
Arnold Town	20	2	3	15	27	76	7
Hucknall Byron	20	1	4	15	26	55	6

1927-28

Division One

Also: Clifton Colliery resigned during the season and their record was deleted.

Division Two

Also: Verdonis Athletic had 2 points deducted. Their points total should be 27 rather than 29.

1928-29

Division One

Also: Hucknall Byron resigned during the season and their record was deleted.

1929-30

Division One
Ransome & Marles	22	18	1	3	88	24	37
Boots Athletic	22	14	3	5	93	30	31
Player's Athletic	22	11	2	9	51	46	24
Sneinton Church Institute	22	10	5	7	50	47	25
Basford United	22	9	5	8	47	46	23
Lenton	22	10	3	9	41	44	23
Sneinton	22	8	6	8	50	55	22
Sutton Junction	22	10	1	11	50	51	21
Newark Castle Rovers	22	7	7	8	54	68	21
Bilsthorpe Colliery	22	8	4	10	46	63	20
Raleigh Athletic	22	3	3	16	38	86	9
Gedling Colliery Welfare	22	2	4	16	17	65	8

Division Two
Basford Town	32	27	1	4	155	53	55
Radcliffe Olympic	32	26	2	4	134	33	54
West Bridgford	32	22	5	5	111	52	49
Basford Olympic	32	22	1	9	112	56	45
Kimberley Amateurs	31	19	5	7	122	52	43
Whitemoor Baptists	32	20	2	10	102	55	42
Carlton Rangers	32	14	4	14	72	71	32
Hyson Green Rangers	32	14	2	16	89	103	30
Hucknall British Legion	32	13	3	16	65	91	29
Arnold United	31	10	4	17	56	98	24
Hucknall Holy Cross	32	8	6	18	58	110	22
Electricity Dept.	32	8	4	20	59	96	20
Hockley Prims.	32	8	4	20	45	102	20
Nottingham L.M.S.	32	9	1	22	77	114	19
Cropwell Bishop	32	9	3	20	61	112	19
Linby Colliery	32	7	5	20	59	123	19
Moore's Athletic	32	6	6	20	56	116	18

Cropwell Bishop had 2 points deducted.

1930-31

Division One
Ransome & Marles	26	22	0	4	119	46	44
Bilsthorpe Colliery	26	19	4	3	101	61	42
Boots Athletic	26	19	2	5	99	46	40
Lenton	26	14	4	8	80	72	32
Sneinton	26	13	2	11	72	52	28
Rufford Colliery	26	11	5	10	87	73	27
Sneinton Church Institute	26	11	4	11	68	68	26
Player's Athletic	26	11	3	12	93	76	25
St. Jude's	26	10	2	14	50	89	22
Newark Castle Rovers	26	10	4	12	65	79	20
Sutton Junction	26	7	6	13	64	92	20
Basford United	26	4	7	15	44	86	15
Arnold St. Mary's	26	4	3	19	63	111	11
Raleigh Athletic	26	1	6	19	65	129	8

Newark Castle Rovers had 4 points deducted.

Division Two
West Bridgford	16	15	0	1	98	16	30
Home Brewery	16	10	3	3	60	28	23
Radcliffe Olympic	15	10	1	4	74	28	21
Nottingham L.M.S.	16	8	3	5	67	34	19
Boots Athletic Reserves	16	8	0	8	53	51	16
Electricity Dept.	16	5	2	9	57	67	12
L.N.E.R.	15	5	1	9	28	68	11
St. Jude's Reserves	16	2	1	13	24	97	5
Gresham Athletic	16	1	1	14	16	88	3

1931-32

Division One
Boots Athletic	28	21	4	3	97	46	46
Welbeck Colliery	28	19	4	5	111	56	42
Rufford Colliery	28	17	4	7	102	69	38
Ransome & Marles	28	18	1	9	90	53	37
Bilsthorpe Colliery	28	21	2	5	128	42	36
Basford United	28	14	4	10	71	72	32
Stapleford Brookhill	28	12	5	11	77	60	29
Sneinton Church Institute	28	12	5	11	75	79	29
Lenton	28	11	3	14	69	70	25
Newark Castle Rovers	28	9	6	13	71	80	24
Player's Athletic	28	9	3	16	89	92	21
Sneinton	28	8	5	15	48	74	21
St. Jude's	**28**	**7**	**3**	**18**	**64**	**129**	**17**
Raleigh Athletic	28	4	1	23	47	122	9
Arnold St. Mary's	**28**	**1**	**2**	**25**	**38**	**132**	**4**

Bilsthorpe Colliery had 8 points deducted.
Gedling Colliery resigned during the season and their record was deleted.

Division Two
Also: L.N.E.R. and Raleigh Athletic Reserves both resigned during the season and their records were deleted.

1932-33

Division One
Ransome & Marles	26	19	6	1	96	35	44
Johnson & Barnes	26	16	4	6	90	47	36
Rufford Colliery	26	14	2	10	87	75	30
Welbeck Colliery	26	13	3	10	75	52	29
Sandiacre Excelsior	26	10	9	7	74	60	29
Raleigh Athletic	26	13	2	11	79	69	28
Lenton	26	10	7	9	43	43	27
Player's Athletic	26	10	6	10	68	65	26
Boots Athletic	26	12	2	12	55	58	26
Bilsthorpe Colliery	26	10	6	10	76	66	26
Basford United	26	9	5	12	53	73	23
Stapleford Brookhill	26	9	5	12	55	66	23
Newark Castle Rovers	26	5	0	21	43	104	10
Sneinton Church Institute	26	3	1	22	50	131	7

Division Two
Kimberley Amateurs	26	19	3	4	117	42	41
Electricity Dept.	26	20	1	5	97	44	41
Netherfield Albion	26	18	1	7	88	38	37
Lenton Gregory	26	16	3	7	100	45	35
Boots Athletic Reserves	26	14	6	6	64	45	34
Bramcote Methodists	26	13	4	9	79	62	30
Alfred Street United Meth. Church	26	12	4	10	60	61	28
West Bridgford	26	12	3	11	77	63	27
Radcliffe Olympic	26	12	3	11	81	71	27
Bulwell Wesleyan Mission	26	9	1	16	69	107	19
Arnold St. Mary's	26	8	1	17	82	102	17
St. Jude's	26	6	2	18	55	83	14
Player's Athletic Reserves	26	6	1	19	58	105	13
Nottingham L.M.S.	26	0	1	25	23	180	1

Notts Alliance Update 1933-1939

1933-34

Division Two

Netherfield Albion	22	18	3	1	105	23	39
Carlton Athletic	22	19	1	2	93	25	39
Beeston St. John's	22	12	6	4	62	33	30
Bramcote Methodists	22	13	1	8	55	44	27
Lenton Gregory	22	10	4	8	54	44	24
Raleigh Athletic Reserves	22	11	2	9	59	55	24
Radcliffe Olympic	**22**	**9**	**0**	**13**	**50**	**69**	**18**
West Bridgford	22	7	4	11	42	65	18
Mapperley	22	5	4	13	38	62	14
Boots Athletic Reserves	22	5	4	13	43	79	14
Arnold St. Mary's	22	2	6	14	46	95	10
Player's Athletic Reserves	22	3	1	18	38	96	7

Championship decider

Netherfield Albion vs Carlton Athletic   2-0
(Played at Lawrence's Athletic Ground, Colwick on 14th September 1934)

1934-35

Division One

Also: Lenton and Sneinton Church Institute both resigned during the season and their records were deleted.

Division Two

Carlton Athletic	26	20	3	3	98	25	43
Netherfield Albion	**26**	**20**	**2**	**4**	**104**	**27**	**42**
West Bridgford	26	19	1	6	109	32	39
Beeston St. John's	26	17	4	5	81	38	38
Quarry Road Old Boys	26	16	3	7	77	44	35
Raleigh Athletic Reserves	26	13	4	9	71	48	30
Bramcote	26	13	1	12	75	74	27
Cleansing Department	26	12	1	13	63	96	25
Player's Athletic Reserves	26	10	2	14	79	80	22
Butler's Hill W.S.	26	8	1	17	48	82	17
Hucknall Social Centre	26	5	7	14	41	87	17
Mapperley	26	5	3	18	35	86	13
Boots Athletic Reserves	26	2	5	19	33	119	9
Gas Sports	26	3	1	22	33	109	7

1935-36

Division One

Also: Radcliffe Olympic resigned during the season and their record was deleted.

Division Two

Also: Hucknall Portland and Radcliffe Olympic Reserves both resigned during the season and their records were deleted.

1937-38

Division One

Ransome & Marles	24	20	4	0	86	22	44
Netherfield Albion	24	16	3	5	69	56	35
Raleigh Athletic	24	16	1	7	81	57	33
Bilsthorpe Colliery	24	13	5	6	61	40	31
Rufford Colliery	24	9	6	9	83	73	24
Player's Athletic	24	8	8	8	72	57	24
Stanton Ironworks	24	8	7	9	56	58	23
Boots Athletic	24	8	5	11	56	60	21
Basford United	24	8	5	11	49	54	21
Bestwood Colliery	24	7	5	12	60	69	19
Beeston St. John's	24	6	6	12	59	68	18
Teversal Colliery	24	6	2	16	45	87	14
Sandiacre Excelsior	24	2	1	21	39	135	5

Division Two

Berridge Institute	24	20	2	2	92	22	42
Estates Department	24	20	2	2	122	29	40
Bestwood Colliery Reserves	24	14	1	9	67	64	29
City Treasurers	24	12	4	8	61	57	28
Cranfleet	24	10	6	8	69	44	26
West Bridgford	24	12	2	10	56	69	26
Raleigh Athletic Reserves	24	11	2	11	86	60	24
Player's Athletic Reserves	24	9	4	11	62	69	22
Boots Athletic Reserves	24	9	3	12	65	69	21
Dunkirk Y.M.C.	24	9	2	13	54	76	20
Lenton United	24	7	2	15	35	71	16
Christ Church	24	3	5	16	34	92	11
Aspley Social Centre	24	2	1	21	26	107	5

Estates Department had 2 points deducted.

1938-39

Division One

Ransome & Marles	26	22	0	4	117	38	44
Stanton Ironworks	26	20	1	5	114	46	41
Player's Athletic	26	17	3	6	103	52	37
Bilsthorpe Colliery	26	18	1	7	93	52	37
Netherfield Albion	26	13	4	9	73	61	30
Boots Athletic	26	14	1	11	75	63	29
Bestwood Colliery	26	12	3	11	67	68	27
Sutton Town	26	9	8	9	74	74	26
Basford United	26	9	3	14	60	57	21
Teversal Colliery	26	7	7	12	46	72	21
Rufford Colliery	26	8	1	17	78	92	17
Beeston St. John's	26	8	1	17	43	90	17
Raleigh Athletic	26	7	1	18	43	75	15
Sandiacre Excelsior	26	1	0	25	30	176	2

Division Two

Estates Department	22	19	1	2	122	22	39
Boots Athletic Reserves	22	18	0	4	86	52	36
Raleigh Athletic Reserves	22	14	2	6	68	47	30
Carlton Athletic	22	14	1	7	63	54	29
Ericsson's Athletic	22	13	0	9	64	44	26
Bestwood Colliery Reserves	21	10	1	10	43	60	21
Royal Ordnance	21	8	0	13	47	70	16
Player's Athletic Reserves	22	7	1	14	67	84	15
Cranfleet	22	6	2	14	51	65	14
Christ Church	22	5	4	13	40	63	14
West Bridgford	22	5	1	16	49	88	11
City Treasurers	22	5	1	16	37	88	11

Berridge Institute resigned during the season and their record was deleted.

1947-48

Division One

Linby Colliery	26	20	4	2	105	27	44
Gedling Colliery Welfare	26	20	2	4	90	39	42
Huthwaite C.W.S.	26	17	6	3	96	35	40
Player's Athletic	26	12	9	5	68	44	33
Bestwood Colliery	26	12	5	9	52	50	29
Basford United	26	12	4	10	61	51	28
Rufford Colliery	26	12	3	11	74	67	27
Boots Athletic	26	12	3	11	60	64	27
Netherfield Albion	26	11	4	11	69	68	26
Raleigh Athletic	26	9	5	12	60	55	23
Bilsthorpe Colliery	26	5	3	18	51	92	13
Ericsson Athletic	26	6	3	17	41	99	13
Cinderhill Colliery	26	4	1	21	40	112	9
Parliament Street Methodists	26	3	2	21	40	104	8

Ericsson Athletic had 2 points deducted.

Division Two

Kirkby L.M.S.	26	23	1	2	138	44	47
Mapperley	26	22	1	3	125	27	45
Christ Church	26	17	1	8	91	63	35
Player's Athletic Reserves	26	15	3	8	79	53	33
Mapperley Villa	26	15	3	8	79	62	33
Stanton Ironworks	26	14	4	8	74	73	32
Raleigh Athletic Reserves	26	16	1	9	81	56	31
Carlton Athletic	26	12	4	10	69	61	28
Cranfleet	26	8	1	17	88	98	17
Electricity Dept.	26	8	1	17	63	80	17
Chilwell Ordnance	26	6	3	17	33	94	15
Boots Athletic Reserves	26	6	0	20	41	99	12
Parliament Street Methodists Res.	26	4	0	22	28	117	8
Bestwood Colliery Reserves	26	4	1	21	34	96	7

Raleigh Athletic Reserves and Bestwood Colliery Reserves each had 2 points deducted.

NOTTS ALLIANCE 1950-1957

Between 1950 and 1957, final tables are still to be found so those shown below are the latest available with a handful of games still to be played.

1950-51

Division One

Gedling Colliery Welfare	23	23	0	0	124	16	46
Huthwaite C.W.S.	26	18	4	4	78	42	40
Raleigh Athletic	25	17	2	6	78	43	36
Player's Athletic	25	16	3	6	97	49	35
Rufford Colliery	26	12	7	7	76	62	31
Cinderhill Colliery	24	9	6	9	67	67	24
Basford United	26	11	2	13	60	65	24
Bilsthorpe Colliery	26	12	1	13	52	72	23
Boots Athletic	24	8	6	10	49	51	22
Worthington-Simpson	26	9	3	14	53	65	21
Parliament Street Methodists	24	6	2	16	39	58	14
Netherfield Albion	25	5	4	16	48	72	14
Bestwood Colliery	25	4	6	15	30	77	14
Stanton Ironworks	25	1	2	22	15	131	4

Bilsthorpe Colliery had 2 points deducted.

Division Two

Carlton Athletic	22	15	3	4	70	31	33
Christ Church	22	14	4	4	73	34	32
Mapperley Villa	22	13	3	6	55	33	29
Kirkby L.M.S.	22	11	4	7	52	47	26
Parliament Street Methodists Res.	22	10	4	8	59	48	24
Cranfleet	22	10	3	9	51	40	23
Boots Athletic Reserves	22	9	3	10	47	60	21
Raleigh Athletic Reserves	21	8	4	9	52	45	20
Player's Athletic Reserves	21	8	3	10	39	50	19
Wilford	21	4	3	14	39	76	11
Gedling Colliery Welfare Reserves	22	5	1	16	36	72	11
Mapperley	21	3	5	13	29	66	11

Bestwood Colliery Reserves and Ericsson Athletic both resigned during the season and their records were deleted.

1951-52

Division One

Gedling Colliery Welfare	24	22	1	1	106	25	45
Blackwell Miners Welfare	26	19	3	4	109	48	41
Raleigh Athletic	26	14	5	7	56	49	33
Basford United	25	14	4	7	58	41	32
Worthington-Simpson	25	14	2	9	68	57	30
Netherfield Albion	25	12	5	8	51	45	29
Parliament Street Methodists	26	8	7	11	61	74	23
Player's Athletic	24	6	10	8	52	52	22
Boots Athletic	26	9	4	13	67	72	22
Rufford Colliery	26	7	7	12	46	73	21
Huthwaite C.W.S.	26	8	4	14	47	67	20
Cinderhill Colliery	26	6	3	17	39	71	15
Bilsthorpe Colliery	26	5	5	16	49	90	15
Bestwood Colliery	25	2	4	19	42	89	8

Division Two

Lenton Gregory	28	22	3	3	105	23	47
Kirkby L.M.S.	30	21	3	6	100	48	45
Newstead Welfare	29	20	3	6	117	52	43
Parliament Street Methodists Res.	29	17	4	8	79	55	38
Raleigh Athletic Reserves	29	14	7	8	71	55	35
Stapleford Villa	29	15	4	10	126	89	34
Gedling Colliery Welfare Reserves	30	16	4	10	86	63	36
Carlton Athletic	30	15	3	12	61	69	33
Mapperley Villa	28	14	3	11	57	61	31
Christ Church	30	13	4	13	77	81	30
Cranfleet	29	8	4	17	64	91	20
Bilsthorpe Colliery Reserves	28	7	4	17	53	94	18
Player's Athletic Reserves	27	5	6	16	41	76	16
Wilford	30	5	6	19	58	119	16
Boots Athletic Reserves	29	4	5	20	49	93	13
Mapperley	29	3	3	23	41	113	9

1952-53

Division One

Worthington-Simpson	25	23	1	1	110	41	47
Gedling Colliery Welfare	25	22	0	3	119	29	44
Blackwell Miners Welfare	25	15	1	9	85	63	31
Raleigh Athletic	25	14	3	8	70	53	31
Parliament Street Methodists	25	11	6	8	71	51	28
Boots Athletic	25	12	3	10	69	77	27
Heanor Town	25	11	3	11	60	57	25
Player's Athletic	24	11	3	10	71	68	25
Bestwood Colliery	25	7	7	11	41	56	21
Rufford Colliery	26	6	7	13	58	81	19
Cinderhill Colliery	26	7	3	16	48	85	17
Basford United	25	4	5	16	48	82	13
Netherfield Albion	25	4	5	16	40	86	13
Bilsthorpe Colliery	26	4	3	19	46	107	11

Notts Alliance Update 1953-1957

Division Two

Lenton Gregory	27	23	0	4	121	40	46
Stapleford Villa	28	21	2	5	119	66	44
Kirkby L.M.S.	27	21	1	5	107	40	43
Parliament Street Methodists Res.	27	19	4	4	87	40	42
Gedling Colliery Welfare Reserves	28	12	5	11	73	65	29
Player's Athletic Reserves	28	11	5	12	63	63	27
Mapperley	28	12	1	15	80	98	25
Cranfleet	28	9	6	13	71	81	24
Wilford	28	11	2	15	85	99	24
Christ Church	28	9	5	14	54	89	23
Mapperley Villa	28	7	8	13	60	79	22
Carlton Athletic	28	11	0	17	60	81	22
Raleigh Athletic Reserves	27	7	4	16	50	85	18
Boots Athletic Reserves	28	8	1	19	48	97	17
Bilsthorpe Colliery Reserves	28	3	4	21	44	99	10

Newstead Welfare resigned during the season and their record was deleted.

1953-54

Division One

Gedling Colliery Welfare	25	21	2	2	118	23	44
Eastwood Town	25	19	2	4	97	52	40
Blackwell Miners Welfare	23	18	1	4	92	43	37
Player's Athletic	26	16	3	7	96	59	35
Worthington-Simpson	25	13	3	9	74	57	29
Cinderhill Colliery	26	14	1	11	62	57	29
Raleigh Athletic	25	11	2	12	66	68	24
Bilsthorpe Colliery	26	8	6	12	65	87	22
Boots Athletic	26	8	4	14	44	83	20
Netherfield Albion	25	8	3	14	43	72	19
Parliament Street Methodists	24	8	2	14	53	85	18
Rufford Colliery	26	7	2	17	56	84	16
Bestwood Colliery	25	3	6	16	44	83	12
Basford United	25	2	3	20	24	82	7

Division Two

Kirkby L.M.S.	26	23	2	1	108	24	48
Stapleford Villa	26	20	1	5	111	58	41
Gedling Colliery Welfare Reserves	26	17	5	4	64	34	39
Lenton Gregory	26	17	4	5	128	46	38
Parliament Street Methodists Res.	26	15	4	7	89	54	34
Wilford	26	13	2	11	66	83	28
Player's Athletic Reserves	26	13	1	12	56	59	27
Cranfleet	26	11	3	12	77	57	25
Mapperley Villa	26	10	5	11	75	60	25
Raleigh Athletic Reserves	25	8	2	15	74	91	18
Carlton Athletic	25	7	2	16	44	76	16
Christ Church	26	4	1	21	35	96	9
Boots Athletic Reserves	25	2	3	20	36	116	7
Mapperley	25	2	1	22	31	141	5

1954-55

Division One

Blackwell Miners Welfare	24	21	1	2	104	38	43
Gedling Colliery Welfare	26	18	1	7	99	38	37
Eastwood Town	25	16	4	5	120	55	36
Boots Athletic	24	16	3	5	98	62	35
Raleigh Athletic	25	13	6	6	78	41	32
Player's Athletic	25	14	4	7	70	63	32
Bilsthorpe Colliery	25	12	2	11	78	65	26
Parliament Street Methodists	26	10	4	12	62	75	24
Basford United	26	8	5	13	44	83	21
Worthington-Simpson	26	8	0	18	65	95	16
Bestwood Colliery	23	6	3	14	36	76	15
Cinderhill Colliery	26	6	2	18	52	89	14
Netherfield Albion	24	5	3	16	49	66	13
Rufford Colliery	26	2	4	20	20	119	8

Division Two

Lenton Gregory	27	24	1	2	150	25	49
Kirkby L.M.S.	27	22	3	2	90	38	47
Carlton Athletic	28	18	4	6	124	59	40
Stapleford Villa	26	16	1	9	102	62	33
Gedling Colliery Welfare Reserves	28	14	5	9	75	65	33
Cranfleet	27	13	3	11	92	53	29
Wilford	28	12	5	11	83	66	29
Eastwood Town Reserves	27	12	1	14	61	63	25
Player's Athletic Reserves	28	9	6	13	61	72	24
Parliament Street Methodists Res.	28	10	3	15	63	88	23
Ericsson's Athletic	27	7	8	12	41	62	22
Raleigh Athletic Reserves	28	8	6	14	53	100	22
Boots Athletic Reserves	28	7	4	17	54	104	18
Christ Church	28	4	4	20	46	130	12
Mapperley	27	1	4	22	30	138	6

1955-56

Division One

Gedling Colliery Welfare	26	21	2	3	115	22	44
Eastwood Town	24	18	2	4	87	27	38
Bilsthorpe Colliery	25	17	1	7	92	58	35
Boots Athletic	24	15	4	5	98	35	34
Raleigh Athletic	25	14	5	6	78	43	33
Bestwood Colliery	25	14	3	8	75	46	31
Player's Athletic	25	11	6	8	76	64	28
Blackwell Miners Welfare	22	12	1	9	72	47	25
Parliament Street Methodists	25	9	1	15	50	54	19
Worthington-Simpson	25	6	4	15	51	75	16
Basford United	25	6	4	15	51	81	16
Rufford Colliery	24	5	2	17	37	107	12
Netherfield Albion	24	3	6	15	36	102	12
Cinderhill Colliery	26	1	1	24	27	190	3

Division Two

Lenton Gregory	28	22	5	1	135	43	49
Ericsson's Athletic	29	22	4	3	86	35	48
Gedling Colliery Welfare Reserves	28	21	2	5	120	32	44
Eastwood Town Reserves	27	19	3	5	124	37	41
Stapleford Villa	28	17	5	6	121	46	39
Cranfleet	29	18	2	9	89	51	38
Radford & Wollaton	29	14	4	11	72	63	32
Carlton Athletic	29	13	5	11	89	77	31
Christ Church	30	10	4	16	60	95	24
Raleigh Athletic Reserves	30	10	4	16	62	105	24
Wilford	29	9	5	15	66	93	23
Boots Athletic Reserves	27	6	5	16	42	80	17
Kirkby L.M.S.	29	5	5	19	51	117	15
Mapperley	28	5	2	21	45	117	12
Parliament Street Methodists Res.	29	2	7	20	43	121	11
Player's Athletic Reserves	29	3	4	22	38	134	10

1956-57

Division One

Eastwood Town	26	22	2	2	129	43	46
Gedling Colliery Welfare	24	22	0	2	124	20	44
Raleigh Athletic	25	21	2	2	115	31	44
Bestwood Colliery	25	12	6	7	49	51	30
Lenton Gregory	25	12	3	10	58	76	27
Parliament Street Methodists	26	11	5	10	75	60	27
Player's Athletic	25	11	4	10	74	68	26
Netherfield Albion	26	10	4	12	59	82	24
Bilsthorpe Colliery	25	8	4	13	54	78	20
Worthington-Simpson	26	8	3	15	68	89	19
Boots Athletic	26	5	7	14	61	90	17
Basford United	26	5	7	14	61	90	17
Blackwell Miners Welfare	24	3	3	18	41	110	9
Rufford Colliery	25	2	4	19	41	111	8

Division Two

Ericsson's Athletic	29	27	1	1	167	22	55
Eastwood Town Reserves	30	24	2	4	116	40	50
Cranfleet	27	19	3	5	97	36	41
Gedling Colliery Welfare Reserves	27	19	3	5	99	40	41
Radford & Wollaton	28	17	3	8	79	60	37
Stapleford Villa	29	16	3	10	144	76	35
Carlton Athletic	30	13	5	12	78	74	31
Kirkby L.M.S.	30	12	5	13	90	90	29
Grove Celtic	30	10	5	15	92	95	25
Christ Church	29	10	4	15	59	94	24
Mapperley	28	8	4	16	70	101	20
Raleigh Athletic Reserves	30	8	4	18	75	121	20
Wilford	29	8	3	18	68	122	19
Parliament Street Methodists Res.	28	4	7	17	36	92	15
Player's Athletic Reserves	29	6	2	21	49	138	14
Boots Athletic Reserves	29	3	0	26	44	162	6

1957-58

The latest tables found had too many games outstanding to be meaningful and so the clubs who competed are shown below in likely finishing order.

Division One

Gedling Colliery Welfare (champions), Eastwood Town, Ericsson's Athletic, Raleigh Athletic, Boots Athletic, Rufford Colliery, Parliament Street Methodists, Lenton Gregory, Bilsthorpe Colliery, Worthington-Simpson, Netherfield Albion, Player's Athletic, Basford United and Bestwood Colliery.

Division Two

Eastwood Town Reserves (champions), Gedling Colliery Welfare Reserves, Carlton Athletic, Cranfleet, Ericsson's Athletic Reserves, Grove Celtic, Stapleford Villa, Christ Church, Parliament Street Methodists Reserves, Kirkby L.M.S., Wilford, Mapperley, Raleigh Athletic Reserves, Boots Athletic Reserves, Radford & Wollaton and Player's Athletic Reserves.

NOTTS ALLIANCE 1958-1983

Additional Senior Division tables found are shown below.

1978-79

Rainworth Miners Welfare	30	22	7	1	75	18	51
Hucknall Colliery Welfare	30	20	5	5	69	41	45
Clipstone Miners Welfare	30	14	9	7	43	32	37
Gedling Colliery Welfare	30	13	9	8	55	36	35
Meadows Albion	30	13	8	9	57	45	34
Nottingham Academicals	30	13	8	9	57	45	34
Boots Athletic	30	11	10	9	45	43	32
Thoresby Colliery Welfare	30	12	7	11	49	32	31
Keyworth United	30	11	6	13	50	54	28
Worthington-Simpson	30	7	11	12	34	46	25
Plessey	30	9	7	14	47	61	25
City & Sherwood Hospital	30	6	11	13	37	53	23
Carlton Athletic	30	8	6	16	41	65	22
Player's Athletic	30	8	6	16	37	66	22
Basford United	30	6	7	17	31	58	19
Nottinghamshire Police	30	5	7	18	29	64	17

Additional Division One tables found are shown below

1977-78

Keyworth United	28	23	2	3	91	30	48
Carlton Athletic Reserves	28	18	5	5	66	44	41
Hucknall Colliery Welfare Reserves	28	15	6	7	50	28	36
Dunkirk	28	12	10	6	50	35	34
Rainworth Miners Welfare Res.	28	13	5	10	53	49	31
Hyson Green Old Boys	28	12	5	11	66	52	29
Clipstone Miners Welfare Res.	28	11	7	10	38	37	29
Thoresby Colliery Welfare Res.	28	11	4	13	53	59	26
Slack & Parr	28	9	6	13	42	48	24
Stapleford Villa	28	9	5	14	37	50	23
Player's Athletic Reserves	28	10	3	15	54	72	23
Boots Athletic Reserves	28	8	6	14	51	59	22
Royal Ordnance Factory	28	9	3	16	51	57	21
Parliament Street Methodists	28	8	3	17	38	75	19
Greenwood Rovers	**28**	**6**	**2**	**20**	**44**	**89**	**14**

1981-82

Southwell City	30	20	6	4	74	23	46
Clipstone Miners Welfare Res.	30	18	6	6	76	36	42
John Player Reserves	30	18	6	6	68	38	42
Hucknall Colliery Welfare Res.	30	13	6	11	62	38	32
Rainworth Miners Welfare Res.	30	12	7	11	49	50	31
Clifton All Whites	30	11	8	11	57	40	30
Dunkirk	30	12	6	12	63	54	30
Bulwell Forest Villa	30	13	4	13	54	62	30
Radcliffe Olympic	30	9	10	11	51	61	28
Parliament Street Methodists	30	10	6	14	59	56	26
Worthington-Simpson Reserves	30	9	8	13	49	48	26
Meadows Albion Reserves	30	11	4	15	63	65	26
Keyworth United Reserves	30	12	2	16	44	62	26
Royal Ordnance Factory	30	7	9	14	34	48	23
Boots Athletic Reserves	30	8	5	17	47	71	21
Thoresby Colliery Welfare Res.	30	10	1	19	43	65	21